Breaking up the British State: Scotland, Independence & Socialism

Breaking up the British State: Scotland, Independence & Socialism

Edited by
Bob Fotheringham
Dave Sherry
& Colm Bryce

Breaking up the British State:
Scotland, Independence and Socialism
Edited by Bob Fotheringham, Dave Sherry & Colm Bryce

First edition published by Bookmarks in 2021
© Bookmarks Publications Ltd
c/o 1 Bloomsbury Street, London WC1B 3QE
bookmarksbookshop.co.uk

ISBN 978-1-912926-68-8 paperback
ISBN 978-1-912926-69-5 Kindle
ISBN 978-1-912926-70-1 epub
ISBN 978-1-912926-71-8 pdf

Typeset by Colm Bryce & Simon Guy
for Bookmarks Publications
Cover design by Ben Windsor
Printed by Halstan & Co, Amersham, England

Contents

Acknowledgments

Many people have helped in the production of this book. In particular the editors would like to thank Carol Williams and Sandra Shepherd who did the proofreading. Thanks also to Simon Guy for help with the layout and to Ben Windsor for his striking cover design. Various earlier drafts of the book were read by Héctor Sierra, Raymie Kiernan, Charlie Kimber, Julie Sherry, Camilla Royle and Donny Gluckstein, all of whom offered valuable comments and advice.

About the authors

The authors are all members of the Socialist Workers Party in Scotland.

Preface

The essays in this collection are as pertinent as they are timely. The structure of the British state is under threat in a way that it hasn't been since 1919, when working class revolt and the struggle for Irish self-determination were reaching their climax. Today, with polls now favouring a united Ireland and Scottish independence, even the name, 'United Kingdom', has become a joke. The essays explain the events that shaped the modern British state and Scotland's changing relationship to it. Written from an avowedly Marxist perspective, this new collection is intended as a guide to action and not mere commentary; thus it concludes with concrete suggestions for what needs to be done.

There are two pitfalls for the left when approaching the national question. One is to demonise and dismiss all national movements out of hand; the other is to romanticise and capitulate to them. The Marxist method, as developed by the Russian revolutionary Vladimir Lenin, acknowledges this and presents a more concrete, nuanced approach by showing how class and nation interact under capitalism. But as Lenin insisted, there is a tension in this interplay: "the demand for a 'yes' or 'no' reply to the question of secession of every nation may seem a very practical one. In reality it is absurd. The bourgeoisie always places its national demands at the forefront, and does so in a categorical fashion. With the proletariat, however, these demands are subordinated to the interests of the class struggle."[1] For Lenin the truth was always concrete.

The Introduction by Keir McKechnie and Angela McCormick

looks at the current state of the independence movement in Scotland and addresses important debates taking place within it and with those on the left in Scotland who are opposed to Scottish independence. It also sets out the global context in which the Scottish movement for independence has grown. It argues that British imperialism is the main enemy of the working class and why the left should welcome its demise by striving to shape the independence campaign, with class politics and socialist ideas. Highlighting the pernicious influence of British nationalism on the working class, mediated through the Labour Party and the trade union leaders over the last hundred years, the chapter argues for the labour movement and the wider working class to break from toxic British nationalism.

The next two chapters set the scene for the essays that follow. Chapter 1 looks at the Marxist understanding of the national question and how it applies to Scotland, emphasising the need to view the question of independence from the point of view of the global struggle of the working class for socialism, rather than confining it to the limited viewpoint of the local capitalist class. Chapter 2 'The Formation of Scotland' explores the tensions and contradictions that shaped how the British capitalist state emerged out of the crisis of feudalism in 17th century England. It also investigates Scotland's transition from feudalism to being a major partner in the British capitalist state. Donny Gluckstein draws on a Marxist understanding of the "bourgeois revolutions" to unlock this complex process, with reference to events like the Darien Scheme, the rise of the Covenanters, the Act of Union of 1707 and the defeat of the Jacobite Rebellion of 1745-46.

In Chapter 3 'The Formation of the Scottish Working Class', Charlie McKinnon looks at how this new capitalist state enforced its brutal class rule on the new and rapidly expanding working class. He also catalogues the violent process of the Clearances, whereby the new state moved to repress any threat to its class rule. McKinnon brings to life the rich history of workers' struggles from below; from the Calton Weavers' Strike to the 1820 radical uprising in west central Scotland and the Chartist movement, all of which raise a central argument of this book, that the working class is the only social class with both the objective interest and the collective power to overthrow capitalism and break up the British state.

The book moves beyond a mere timeline of historical events by examining in detail the various responses of the British state to maintain the hegemony of capital and its Union. This includes the role of the Labour Party and the British trade union leaders in propping up the British state at critical moments in the 20th century. Chapter 4 'Red Clydeside' lays bare the catastrophic results for the international working class of their so called socialist leadership's failure to oppose, let alone halt, the First World War. With the exception of the Russian Bolsheviks and the small Bulgarian and Serbian socialist organisations, all the main socialist parties across Europe belonging to the Second International capitulated to their own ruling class and abandoned internationalism. Scottish revolutionary socialist John Maclean insisted that the war served only the interests of the competing imperialist powers. Resistance to the global carnage led to revolts in the colonies and mutinies and revolution in Russia and Germany, which ended the war. Dave Sherry's chapter highlights the collaboration between the Labour and trade union leaders and the British state, which undermined the great revolts between 1915 and 1920, with Red Clydeside in the vanguard. In Chapter 5 'The Decline of the Scottish Labour Party', Dave Sherry and Julie Sherry examine the relationship between class struggle and the decline of the Labour Party, from its electoral high point of the 1960s to its disastrous slump in the new millennium.

In Chapter 6 'Racism and Anti-racism in Scotland', Charlotte Ahmed and Henry Maitles add valuable insight into Scotland's role in the transatlantic slave trade and how the Scottish ruling class were central in shaping the architecture of the British empire. It covers the little known resistance movement to slavery in Scotland and the importance of abolitionists like Frederick Douglass and his successful speaking tour to bolster the anti-slavery forces in 1846, one of the highlights being a packed meeting of over 2,000 people at the Music Hall in Edinburgh. There is a fresh examination of the different waves of migration to Scotland and an inspiring account of migrant and anti-racist struggles that have helped to shape modern Scotland. The chapter highlights the toxic racism that plagues the British state, the institutional racism that persists in Scotland, and the role of migrant communities in the struggles against racism and exploitation.

The second half of the book challenges the ideas underpinning the nationalist project of the Scottish National Party (SNP). In Chapter 7 'The History of the Independence Movement', Bob Fotheringham charts its trajectory from a marginal force throughout the last century to replacing Labour as the dominant force in Scottish politics. In Chapter 8 'Neoliberalism with a Heart? The Reality of Life Under the SNP', Iain Ferguson and Gerry Mooney look at the record of the SNP in office and concludes that whilst some mild, though important, reforms have been implemented, the SNP leadership's vision for an independent Scotland is not a radical one that offers any break with neoliberal capitalism.

The final chapter 'Scottish Independence: Beyond the Limitations of Nationalism' starts with an assessment of the important theoretical contributions on nationalism made by left-wing thinkers such as Tom Nairn, Stephen Maxwell and, more recently, George Kerevan. It then develops the Marxist critique of nationalism in general and signals the dangers of adopting a nationalist all class alliance approach to independence that limits itself to establishing a new Scottish capitalism trapped by the same pressures and powerful interests that control the British state. The book ends on a positive note, arguing that the only practical alternative is for the working class to take the leading role in the struggle for independence, with a more far reaching and revolutionary vision of social change. This means charting a different road as well as a different destination from that of the SNP within the wider movement for independence.

Introduction

Keir McKechnie & Angela McCormick

The Scottish independence referendum of September 2014 posed a serious threat to the unity of the British state—a chilling experience the British ruling class has no wish to revisit. A Yes victory in the 2014 referendum would have shaken them to their core, significantly weakening the economic, military and ideological coherence of one of the oldest imperialist powers. It would also have weakened Britain's role on the international stage and been a snub for US imperialism, Britain's closest ally. Fear of 'losing Scotland' is again alarming the establishment and concentrating the minds of the Tory party. The *Financial Times* in July 2020 speculated that Boris Johnson's place in history "first looked like Brexit; more recently he seemed to be the pandemic premier, a new fear is that he might be known as the leader who lost the union".[1]

British capitalism has been facing the consequences of Brexit and its extrication from the European Union, its largest trading partner. The fear of losing a key component part of the 'United Kingdom' at this critical juncture is again palpable. Far from the 2014 referendum killing off Scottish independence, an editorial in the Tory *Sunday Telegraph* lamented that support for independence has been in the majority during most of 2020, with every opinion poll showing more in favour of leaving the UK than remaining.[2]

A poll for the think tank Progress Scotland in October 2020 illustrates a shift in political mood showing that a third of those who voted No in 2014 had changed their minds. Some 13 percent of former No voters back independence while a further 19 percent of them now say they do not know. Almost twice as many No voters have moved to Yes than have moved in the opposite direction. The key reasons cited for this shift in voting intentions are the NHS, the state of the economy and Brexit.[3]

The continuation of the independence movement today stems from the fact that at its height in 2014 it was a radical mass movement, energised by the prospect of breaking from the British state. For ordinary working class people, it was the chance of living in a society without poverty, inequality, racism and nuclear weapons. These concerns drove up support for independence. Had the official Yes campaign and the SNP leadership under Alex Salmond put class issues to the fore of the campaign from the very start, the prospects of winning would have risen. The determined mood following the defeat in 2014 found political expression in the spectacular increase in SNP membership to over 125,000 members, making it, per head of population, the biggest political party in Europe.[4] Importantly, the social forces that fuelled this dramatic growth took to the streets in an unprecedented wave of huge demonstrations organised by the grassroots pro independence organisation All Under One Banner. In January 2020, weeks after Johnson's election victory, 80,000 people—overwhelmingly working class—marched in a torrential downpour through Glasgow in an impressive show of support for independence and of opposition to Tory austerity, racism and British nationalism.

There are different and competing ideas circulating inside the independence movement, of which Scottish nationalist ideas are unsurprisingly the dominant current. Yet it is clear from the demonstrations, public meetings, local Yes group events and the large online assemblies organised by All Under One Banner during 2020 that there is a large and growing audience who support refugees and oppose racism, austerity, war, nuclear weapons and environmental destruction. Whilst the working class is clearly not the only social class supporting independence, it is the largest social force taking to the streets and campaigning for it. There is also a growing current in the movement that does not see independence as an end in itself. Hence delegates who took part in two large All Under One Banner assemblies in the autumn of 2020 opposed the view put forward by some nationalists that discussing the reasons for and benefits of independence must be avoided. The notion that "we should only discuss independence and nothing else until after independence" for fear of offending and losing the support of the middle classes and sections of big business is still a powerful argument. Yet, it is increasingly being challenged as thousands of activists openly identify the independence project as an historic opportunity for transformative and radical change in Scotland.

Another welcome development is the desire amongst sections of the independence movement to engage with and learn from other social movements such as Black Lives Matter, the climate justice movement and the trade union movement. For example, the mission statement of Now Scotland, the new grassroots, membership led organisation launched in February 2021, states "we seek an independent nation built on foundations of human equality, internationalism, social and economic justice; and which mobilises against climate change".[5]

While the base of the movement becomes more impatient and combative, the leadership of the SNP and the Scottish government continue with their timid, lacklustre approach to winning independence. Prior to the Covid-19 pandemic, SNP leader Nicola Sturgeon had insisted that the vote against Brexit in Scotland, 62 percent to 38 percent, represented a "material change in circumstances".[6] She argued that the Brexit result gave her government a fresh mandate to ask Westminster for a new order under section 30 of the Scotland Act to hold a second referendum on independence before the end of 2020. Sturgeon promptly jettisoned this idea in March 2020, ruling out any possibility of another referendum "for as long as it takes" to cope with the Covid-19 pandemic and the ensuing economic catastrophe.[7] This untenable position collapsed under the pressure of events and the resurgent independence movement. The fallout from the pandemic and the ensuing economic crisis has supercharged support in Scotland for ending the Union. So Sturgeon has conceded that the Holyrood election in May 2021 *will* be a vote on independence and give any new SNP government a mandate to apply for a new section 30 order and to call an advisory referendum if the Tory government continues to refuse to grant a second referendum.[8]

But growing numbers of SNP members and supporters are not convinced its leadership is serious about taking the essential next steps to win independence. Two examples illustrate this growing criticism of Sturgeon and the SNP leadership. First, Robin McAlpine, former director of left-wing think tank Common Weal, launched an attack claiming that independence will not happen in the next five years if Sturgeon is still in power. He accuses her of hiding behind her "self-image" for three years, Brexit for another three years and hiding behind Covid-19 for the next five years.[9]

Secondly, George Kerevan, former SNP MP for East Lothian and leading member of Now Scotland summed up the mood in a series of articles. He describes the SNP as "now controlled by a tiny group headed by Sturgeon and her husband Peter Murell, the party's full-time Chief Executive, and...the party's elected representatives are drawn from an increasingly narrow band of professionals. The result is that the SNP in office has become bureaucratised, pursuing its own electoral interests rather than those of the wider independence movement." This process has, according to Kerevan, "culminated in the SNP... moving sharply to the right, as they sought to win support from local and foreign capital. All this imperils the success of the independence struggle."[10] A group of SNP MPs, MSPs and councillors are increasingly bitter in their criticisms of the leadership's refusal to countenance a Plan B given the complete intransigence of the Tories over a second referendum. In response to this, and with growing pressure from activists in the movement, Sturgeon said that if there is an independence majority in the Scottish Parliament after the May election in 2021, she will bring forward a bill in Holyrood to hold a second referendum. As her expectation is that this will be tested and likely rejected in the British courts this is unlikely to be any more successful than Plan A.

This failure is aggravating the crisis of leadership inside the SNP and serious splits and factional tensions have appeared, with thousands of SNP members having left the party. The splits at the top of the party reflect tensions rooted in the lack of a coherent strategy to shift the Tory government or to come up with a real alternative strategy as Westminster continues to refuse indyref2. This paralysis of leadership shows the SNP's fear of unleashing a radical and militant mass movement willing to pursue the kind of direct action that can defeat the real power of the British state.

Arguably the SNP has been the most successful centrist party in Europe throughout the last decade, praised for its unity, its self-discipline in government and its continuing popularity. Much as the SNP leadership would like this to continue, Scotland is not immune to the volatility and political polarisation that has wreaked havoc in so many other countries. Recently the SNP monolith has begun to crack with Alex Salmond setting up the new Alba party and attracting many defectors from the SNP.

Some sections of the radical left say they believe the SNP "in its present state is unreformable". While this is undoubtedly true, instead of striking out on their own and presenting a radical, socialist alternative in the movement, many have opted for membership of the Alba party to "seek to build a left, progressive wing of the independence movement elsewhere".

Those on the left who make this move are making a big mistake if they think Alba can be the vehicle to overcome the shortcomings of the SNP—especially if this signals a turn away from strengthening the mass movement from below, a project that has recently seen important progress and will be absolutely central if the professional politicians are to be held to account or forced aside if necessary.

Beneath the superficial differences, both Salmond and Sturgeon offer the same set of neo-liberal policies and lack of strategy. It is crucial that the grassroots movement looks outwards to new forces and looks to mass action from below. Street protests, mass demonstrations and civil disobedience and the building of workers' action matters much more than elections and SNP manoeuvres in parliament. This is the key to forcing the Tories to concede indyref2 and in delivering an independence that brings about real change.

The 'Democratic Deficit' & the Brexit power grab

The Tory government is digging in hard against a second referendum. Former Tory Chancellor George Osborne's rant in the London *Evening Standard* that Johnson should continue to deny Scotland a second referendum and jail the leaders of the independence movement should they go for a Catalan-style referendum, is instructive.[11] It demonstrates the utter contempt the British state has for any democracy in Scotland when it threatens their class power. The Tories are pursuing a post-Brexit 'power grab', taking back many of the powers devolved to the Holyrood parliament and insisting the Union Jack is flown in perpetuity above every public building in Scotland.

Such moves are fuelling support for a clean break from Britain. The Scottish Parliament responded to this 'power grab' by voting by 90 to 28 to reject the British government's Internal Market Bill in October 2020, arguing that the legislation "constrains the competence of the Scottish parliament and breaches international law".[12] A Scottish Trade Union Congress (STUC) statement prior to the vote marks a decisive shift in favour of a second referendum: "The STUC is strongly opposed to the Internal Market Bill, which would limit the ability of the Scottish Parliament to influence public policy and represents an attack on devolution. The STUC's concern mainly relates to state aid, the market access commitment and intergovernmental relations. Should the British government proceed against the wishes of the Scottish Parliament it makes the case for a second independence referendum unanswerable".[13]

British Labour Party leader Keir Starmer's intervention into the independence debate has resulted in the Labour Party becoming increasingly irrelevant in Scotland, standing in third place behind the Tories in some opinion polls. Starmer has wrapped himself in the Union Jack and continues to promote Labour's patriotic Unionist credentials. The witch hunt against former leader Jeremy Corbyn and the replacement of Scottish Labour leader Richard Leonard, a Corbyn supporter, is a declaration of a future Labour government's unquestioning commitment to British and US imperialism. Both the British and Scottish Labour Party are not only opposed to independence in Scotland, they even deny the democratic right of Scottish people to decide the issue for themselves. It is an act of political suicide.

The triple crisis of capitalism

There are important global factors reshaping the political landscape and sharpening the tensions between Scotland and the British state—most notably intensifying economic rivalry between Britain and Europe and the US and China. As Joseph Choonara has pointed out, there is "a more general sense of crisis eroding the stability of capitalism. We are experiencing a 'triple crisis' for the system; the contours of which are likely to shape anti-systemic movements in the period ahead."[14] This 'triple crisis' alludes to (1) the Covid-19 pandemic, (2) the economic crisis which predates but has been accelerated by the pandemic and (3) the accelerating global ecological crisis. These interlocking crises are the backdrop to all of the different struggles taking place globally and are shaping political events in Scotland.

The Covid-19 pandemic has magnified the deep class and racial inequalities both internationally and across Britain, including in Scotland. The disproportionate level of deaths amongst poor working class people and those from black and minority ethnic communities has exposed the systemic inequalities woven into the fabric of the capitalist system. The criminal handling of the pandemic by the Tories has propelled more support towards independence. Johnson's incoherent and fatal response in comparison to Sturgeon's more cautious and media savvy approach has strengthened the idea that Scotland would do much better on its own. Yet, the Covid-19 pandemic has also exposed the SNP's inability to break with the neoliberal agenda set by the Tories and big business. The large number of deaths of older people in Scottish care homes and the infamous SNP U-turn to fully reopen secondary schools in August 2020 highlight the real limitations of the SNP government. The economic catastrophe arising from the pandemic will shape economic and political struggles for a long time to come. Independent or not, there will have to be a struggle in Scotland to fight the powerful economic pressures exerted by the British state, the big banks and the finance houses in London and Edinburgh to make sure that working people are not made to pay for the crisis of the system.

The lack of democracy at the heart of the British state is being increasingly exposed. Its oldest institutions face a deep crisis of popular legitimacy, with support for the monarchy and the House of Lords in steep decline. There is also a growing sense in Scotland that Westminster, the so called 'mother of all parliaments', is nothing but a sham. The Thatcher years and the de-industrialisation of the 1980s hammered Scotland, South Wales, the North of England, Yorkshire as well as other parts of Britain. Huge swathes of Scotland have been Tory free zones ever since. But the fact that Scotland still gets Tory governments despite voting against them consistently since 1959—in 17 general elections in a row—has convinced the majority to conclude that the British state is both fraudulent and corrupt. An independent Scotland that seeks to be transformative and democratic in nature has to end support for the monarchy and the Bank of England and its unelected governors; it has to create genuinely democratic forums of mass participation, and bodies that are both representative of and accountable to the mass of the population. That can only happen if the struggle for independence is fought on a class basis. Without that, the lack of democracy that characterises Westminster would simply be reproduced on a smaller territory.

Polarisation and the threat of the far right

Across Europe politics are polarising to the right as well as the left. The far right have developed their own strategy to try and fill the vacuum left by the collapse of the social democratic parties on the back of their failure to deliver real change that benefits the great majority.

We need to understand the lessons from the rise of far right movements like the Vox party in Spain if we are to avoid making the same mistakes in Scotland and elsewhere. The financial crash of 2008 saw Spain's conservative People's Party (PP) and the Labour type Socialist Party (PSOE) implement brutal austerity policies. The hopes of millions were further dashed when, at the end of 2019, the supposedly radical Podemos party joined a coalition with the PSOE, the authors of the original austerity package that had wreaked havoc on the living standards of millions of working class people. Vox tried to exploit the disillusionment created by the failures of the PSOE and Podemos, by mobilising against Muslims, immigrants, women's rights and the left. In two elections held in 2019, Vox went from having no seats in Spain's national parliament to having 52 and becoming the official opposition.[15] Vox has also made gains in many regional parliaments throughout Spain, including Andalusia, Valencia and Madrid. Even in Catalonia, which has seen massive radical mobilisations for independence in recent years and a surge in support for pro independence parties, Vox, who are hostile to secession, won almost 8 percent of the votes and 11 seats in the Catalan parliament in early 2021, overtaking its rival conservative parties.[16]

In Greece, a similar polarisation has played out in recent

years. The Greek social democratic party, PASOK, like the Labour Party in Britain, continued the austerity and the neoliberal policies of their Tory predecessors. PASOK paid the price when Greek workers rejected their government, leading to a spectacular collapse in support from 2012.[17] This situation opened the door to the radical left Syriza party, which went from being a relatively small left party to winning the general election in 2015 on a promise to resist austerity. Tragically, Syriza failed to use the stunning result of the 2015 referendum—61 percent voting 'Oxi' or 'No'—to reject the austerity plan imposed by the EU. Syriza's capitulation played straight into the hands of the openly fascist Golden Dawn, which blamed immigrants for Greece's problems and launched violent attacks on migrants, socialists and trade unionists. It took a combative, grassroots street movement to drive the fascists back. This involved building a united front that adopted a twin track approach of mobilising the youth, migrant organisations, the trade union movement and the left to confront Golden Dawn on the streets, workplaces and student campuses, whilst simultaneously exposing them as a fascist movement. The anti-fascist movement has broken Golden Dawn and its leaders are in jail. Greece offers us both hope and a stark warning of the dangers of failure at the same time.[18]

Deteriorating social conditions that can lead to polarisation and the growth of the far right are present in Scotland too. The brutal killing of Sheku Bayoh in Kirkcaldy in 2015 and the tragic death of 34 year old Ugandan Mercy Baguma—a refugee seeking asylum found dead in a Glasgow flat with her hungry child lying next to her—are shocking reminders of a 'hostile environment' and institutional racism, despite official pronouncements. The Tories will continue to deploy racist scapegoating as a key prop of their divide and rule strategy to divert attention away from the economic catastrophe and to save their Union.

Avoiding the disillusionment and demoralisation seen in other parts of Europe requires an entirely different strategy from what is on offer from the SNP. Their Sustainable Growth

Commission shows how committed they are to implementing further austerity and acquiescing with the neoliberal structures and regulations of the EU. The SNP are effectively signing up to a decade of austerity in order to meet the criteria for rejoining the EU. To avoid this means preparing a far more radical assault on wealth and power than the SNP is willing to countenance.

Ecological crisis

The Intergovernmental Panel on Climate Change estimates that by 2035 planet earth will have passed a tipping point and saving the ecosystem will not be possible. The burning of the Amazon rain forests, the flooding of cities like Jakarta, raging fires in Australia and the US are just some of the devastating consequences of climate change. The rise of radical movements such as Extinction Rebellion challenges fossil fuel, carbon-based economies.

Scotland has to end its relationship with North Sea oil and gas and keep the oil in the soil. Far from being the basis for an independent Scottish economy, fossil fuel capitalism is destroying the planet. Slashing carbon emissions now and building a new green economy, with hundreds of thousands of green jobs, is the most urgent task.[19] This means breaking with the SNP's neoliberal Growth Commission and confronting the power of the multinational oil and gas corporations like BP, Shell and Ineos rather than seducing them with tax breaks and grants. In 2016 the Scottish government awarded Ineos, the fracking giant, an £8 million free handout on top of the £250 million given to Ineos by the British government to import shale gas from America.[20]

The Growth Commission would lock a future independent Scotland into a neoliberal straitjacket, at the mercy of finance capital and the Bank of England, especially if it retains the pound as its currency. Scotland would not be able to tax the super rich or redirect investments into environmental recovery. Instead, international markets will impose their will and restrict borrowing. The essential investments in public housing, transport and a green industrial strategy can only happen if an independent Scotland breaks free from a banking and finance system that blocks redistribution of wealth and the renationalisation of utilities like gas, electricity and transport. The SNP leadership want an independent Scotland, but only in order to find its own place in the neoliberal world order by rejoining the EU. The SNP's economic plan commits an independent Scotland to cutting the fiscal deficit, i.e. public spending, in order to meet the EU criteria. Failure to move beyond their neoliberal approach will mean warm words and empty rhetoric on the environment, while the big multinational corporations continue to plunder natural resources and accelerate the process of environmental degradation. The COP26 conference in Glasgow in November 2021 provides a unique opportunity for the independence and climate justice movements to come together to campaign for radical action against fossil-fuel capitalism.

British nationalism and the working class

A key task for the left today is to weaken and defeat the pernicious influence of British nationalism inside the working class movement across Britain. Socialists as internationalists and should welcome the opportunity to weaken imperialism. While Scotland, unlike Ireland, never was an oppressed nation, Socialists support for Scottish independence is driven by the desire to weaken Britain as a major imperialist power, to undermine its ability to launch imperialist wars against countries like Iraq and Afghanistan or to aid and abet the proxy wars of states like Saudi Arabia through arms sales. Britain's role as a key ally of US imperialism rests to a significant degree on its commitment to host and upgrade Trident nuclear missiles on the Clyde. Britain remains a major player in the NATO military alliance and in the United Nations Security Council. These alone provide reason enough for socialists to actively campaign in support of independence and to see Britain's influence undermined as a consequence of the break up of the British state. It would be a grave mistake to underestimate the importance of weakening British imperialism and the benefits it would accrue to the working class across Britain and further afield.

British imperialism is still the main enemy confronting the English, Scottish, Welsh and Irish working class. We cannot ignore its savage history and its toxic legacy. Britain ruled one third of humanity at the height of Empire. In 1851, in response to the boast that the British Empire was a place where the sun never set, Chartist leader Ernest Jones replied "and where the blood never dries".[21] The horror it unleashed is unprecedented and unsurpassed in human history: the plundering of Ireland, North America, the Caribbean, the Indian Subcontinent, China, Australasia, the African continent and the Middle East. Author Mike Davis, in his book *Late Victorian Holocausts*, summed up the age of Empire as "the new dark age of colonial war, indentured labour, concentration camps, genocide, forced migration, famine and disease".[22]

The legacy of Empire and unionism in Scotland is still very real, even if weakened by the growing independence movement and other important social changes over the last half century. Its sectarian bile is paraded on our streets every time the loyalists of the Orange Order march to celebrate their hatred of Catholics. That the Tories in Scotland still call themselves the Conservative and Unionist Party shows that they still rely on this backward loyalist support and will no doubt seek to utilise these forces to block independence. Breaking up the British state would further weaken the influence of such racist and reactionary ideas. Additionally, a defeat for the British state in Scotland can help accelerate the momentum for a united Ireland. It would be a small but important victory for the international working class and those fighting oppression across the world.

There is a long history of resistance to British imperialism. The 1916 Easter Rising in Ireland is one of the great revolts against empire and war. Russian revolutionary Lenin supported the Dublin Rising, taking issue with those on the left who condemned it as an adventurist putsch. Lenin was right to argue that any revolt that struck a blow against the British Empire and the First World War should be welcomed.

Lenin was able to distinguish between the nationalism of an oppressor nation and that of an oppressed nation, concluding that socialists should support the rights of oppressed nations to self-determination, even if they were led by petty bourgeois nationalist forces with all sorts of backward prejudices and ideas that were hostile to the interests of the working class.

But Lenin was absolutely clear that while socialists should support nationalist movements, "they must not amalgamate with it" and "must unconditionally maintain the independence of the workers' movement", by making a conscious effort not to paint nationalism in "communist colours".[23] This remains an important consideration in the struggle for independence.

Socialist support for Scottish independence is not predicated on grounds that Scotland has suffered national oppression by the British state in any way resembling the experiences of Ireland or India. The historical evidence on this is overwhelming. From the Act of Union in 1707 onwards the Scottish nobility and Scotland's rising merchant class played a full and bloody part in enforcing the rule of British imperialism. The new Union cemented Scotland's role as key partner in the British state. Scotland's new capitalist class then reaped the huge economic rewards from helping to expand the British Empire and Scottish regiments were deployed routinely as its shock troops.

The Irish general election of 1918 is a powerful example of how the British state ruthlessly deployed military force to crush the democratic will of the Irish people. As Clydeside socialist John Maclean observed in his 1920 pamphlet *Ireland's Tragedy: Scotland's Disgrace:* "The vote shows that by four to one the people of Ireland wish to look after their own affairs." He condemned the fact "that Scots regiments are pouring into Ireland and others are held in readiness. It seems the Scots are being used to crush the Irish. Let Labour effectively reply." Maclean called for a general strike of trade unionists across

Britain to demand the withdrawal of troops from Ireland.[24]

There is no history of resistance to British imperialism from the Scottish ruling class, precisely because they became partners in Empire and shared in its profits.

Scotland and the Union—from Riches to Ruin

Scottish nationalism slowly emerged in reaction to Scottish capitalism's relative decline within the British economy in the inter-war years. From the late 19th century British imperialism was overtaken by its major economic rivals—Germany and the US. Britain's dominance was reduced further during the inter-war years as it experienced what Trotsky called the 'law of uneven and combined development' at work in reverse. Scotland's former position as a major beneficiary of the Union diminished considerably as Scottish capitalists became increasingly side-lined and marginalised.

Tom Devine argues that this reversal of fortunes was beginning to assert itself even before 1914. After the First World War Scotland was unable to take advantage of the third industrial revolution.

> The strategic weaknesses of the extraordinarily successful Scottish heavy industry economy were now revealed in stark detail. The achievement had been built on low wages and the interlocking critical mass of shipbuilding, engineering, coal, iron and steel, which fixed the economy into the past rather than creating fresh opportunities for the future. Despite some attempts, the 'new' consumer-based manufactures (household goods, electrical products, motor cars and cycles), which were expanding south of the border, did not take off in Scotland because of the levels of relative poverty among the mass of the population and the small size of the domestic market. The nation, therefore, missed out on the next big stage of economic development.[25]

This turnaround paved the way for the emergence of Scottish nationalism from its tiny beginnings in the late 1920s, ushering in a new renaissance of cultural and political nationalism. However, the resilience of the British state was sustained by the efforts of the Labour Government of 1945 to 1951. Major reforms such as the National Health Service (NHS), the welfare state and a wave of nationalisations to improve workers' living standards at the end of the Second World War, combined with the long post-war economic boom and Labour's ideological attachment to state intervention throughout the 1960s, ensured that unionism held sway in Scotland. At least for as long as the economy was booming and reforms kept coming.

The end of the long boom in the late 1960s, the ensuing world economic crisis in the mid-1970s, and the devastating impact of Thatcherism in the 1980s, strengthened the appeal of Scottish nationalism among wider sections of Scottish society. The failure of Blair to offer any kind of alternative to the Tories, allied to his warmongering, paved the way for the SNP at key stages to present itself in 'Old Labour', social democratic clothing and ultimately defeat Labour—first in Holyrood, then at Westminster—to win political hegemony in Scotland.

British and Scottish nationalism—twin evils?

Some on the left make the mistake of equating Scottish nationalism with British nationalism. Former left-wing MP George Galloway, for instance, sees Scottish nationalism as a more divisive and dangerous force than the chauvinism of the British state. Tragically, this has led a former anti-imperialist into an unholy alliance with rich unionist landowners and Scottish Tory Michael Gove![26]

More seriously, many good trade union activists, under the influence of labourism, confuse the unity of the working class with the unity of the British state and see support for independence as the slippery slope to bourgeois nationalism. This mistake, at least for some, stems from a desire to defend the long tradition of united struggle—from the Chartists, the Suffragettes, the General Strike of 1926, the Great Miners' Strike of 1984-5, the battle against Thatcher's hated poll tax and so on. Yet, workers' solidarity has nothing to do with being part of the British state. Real unity and class solidarity, across borders, is not inevitably compromised by breaking up the capitalist imperialist state into its component parts and opposing the interests it serves. Consequently, those on the left who fail to grasp this, dismiss and thereby cut themselves off from the best activists and the large base of working class supporters of independence. The independence movement can only benefit from socialist and labour movement participation. The working class is the only force capable of winning a genuine transformation of social and economic power in an independent Scotland.

Commitment to the 'national interest' has tied some Labour and trade union leaders to the idea that workers' interests are bound up with those of British capitalism. This was the case during the First World War, the Second World War, and with Blair and Brown's wars against Afghanistan and Iraq. Today it continues with Keir Starmer wrapping himself in the Union Jack and with union leaders who look to partnership and collaboration with the bosses.

There is an ongoing argument in the British labour movement that workers in other countries are stealing 'our' jobs. The racist and divisive slogan 'British jobs for British workers', coined by former Labour prime minister Gordon Brown and supported by some union leaders, is a warning of how such backward nationalist ideas still infect the working class movement.

Trotsky's writings on Britain in the 1920s warned of the conservative nature of the leaders of the British Labour Party and trade union movement, explaining how British capitalism could rely on them in a crisis: "The left is the useful, appropriate, necessary, succouring ballast without which the ship of British imperialism would long ago have gone down." Trotsky was referring to the betrayals by the so called left leaders of the Trade Union Congress (TUC) that sold out the General Strike in 1926.[27] It should be noted that belief in capitalism as the only viable system extends to the SNP, though a Scottish version is what they favour.

The left needs to oppose the patriotic and unionist approach adopted by Keir Starmer and the Scottish Labour Party. Firstly, the left should champion the democratic right of the Scottish people to determine their own future in a referendum—as the STUC have now done. This is the key starting point for being on the right side of the argument. Secondly, the left and the wider labour movement should campaign for the position that Scottish independence and the breakup of the British state would be a positive development for the British working class, a significant blow to British capitalism at home and to its imperialist interests abroad. Thirdly, it is essential to remain committed to the principles of internationalism and to consciously confront British nationalism as well as the real dangers of 'Scottish capitalism' being touted by the SNP leadership.

Combining the radical forces of the independence movement with the collective power of the trade union movement could see off the attacks that are sure to come in a separate Scottish state, in an attempt to subordinate the interests of the working class to the interests of local and foreign capital. It means rejecting alliances with Scottish business leaders like Jim McColl and union busters like Stagecoach boss Brian Souter. Scottish business covets a separate Scottish state only in so far as it assists in securing and expanding their profits. They look to the potential advantages of a low wage economy with low corporation taxes and oppose anything that challenges their wealth and power.

Conclusion

For socialists, the national question is best approached by assessing the concrete political and economic circumstances that currently prevail. The majority of Scotland's population find themselves more and more pitted against the British state for the reasons cited above. There has been a long tradition of working class solidarity with people struggling against oppression by British imperialism abroad. From the CND marches against US Polaris nuclear submarines imposed on the banks of Holy Loch in the 1960s to the huge Anti-Apartheid movement across Scotland in solidarity with the people of South Africa, there exists a strong tradition of progressive internationalism in Scotland. It is no accident that the first international city Nelson Mandela visited on his release from Robben Island prison was Glasgow. The huge anti-war movement across Scotland opposing the wars on Afghanistan and Iraq bore witness to the currents of internationalism that characterise past and present struggles against the British state.

Swathes of the new independence movement are influenced by these struggles against injustice and are imbued with an urge to right the wrongs of the past, but that can only happen if socialist demands are fundamental to the struggle for independence.

The great battles north and south of the border against Thatcher's hated poll tax, the Great Miners' Strike of 1984 and more recently the Tory government's bedroom tax, show why the independence movement must continue to build solidarity with working people struggling against British capitalism north and south of the border and with those battling against imperialism abroad.

The fractures in the British state are widening. The Tories' refusal to heed the democratic will of the people of Scotland by refusing them a second referendum, the impact of Brexit and the post-Brexit 'power grab', and the catastrophic economic consequences of the pandemic are combining to turbo-charge support for a break from the British state. The majority of the working class now support Scottish independence as a way out of the deepening economic and social crises. Putting the interests of the working class at the heart of the struggle to win independence is critical if we are to defeat the British state and win. That means confronting it with something much more powerful than constitutional or legal arguments. It will require a persistent and united effort to build a mass social movement, deploying tactics of civil disobedience, demonstrations and strikes—in other words a movement that can make Scotland ungovernable for the British state. Building grassroots organisations such as All Under One Banner and Now Scotland is essential if we are to fully mobilise the collective social power of the working class, the only force capable of confronting state power and moving beyond the timidity of the parliamentary wing of the independence movement.

The left has an opportunity to promote an alternative radical vision of an independent Scotland and a different road map to victory. The SNP's neoliberal economic model should be rejected. We are not fighting to simply replace the British capitalist state with a new capitalist state in Scotland, constrained by membership of the EU, where the institutions of capitalist rule and exploitation dominate. We are fighting to ensure that working class interests are not abandoned to accommodate the powerful forces that are mustering against change—be it those based in Westminster, the City of London or the finance houses of Edinburgh.

The challenges we face are enormous. The prize of striking a blow against British imperialism and starting down the road to a new society, with a genuine transformation of wealth and power, is worth fighting for. Independence is only the first step in a much longer journey to building a better world and a socialist future. Socialists are internationalists not nationalists. An independent Scotland would be isolated and defeated by its enemies unless it forms part of a much wider international struggle to liberate humanity from global capitalism. The need for socialist transformation, which puts people before profit and confronts the reality of inequality, poverty, climate change, racism and the drive to war inherent in the current system, has never been greater. Let's seize the time.

Chapter 1

Scotland, the National Question and Marxism

Donny Gluckstein & Bob Fotheringham

The modern nation state is a product of capitalism. National identity and nationalism, on the other hand, are a much more complex set of ideas which, for those involved, can shift and move over time with a different meaning in different periods. In the case of Scotland, for example, support for Scotland existing as a fully independent country is a fairly recent phenomenon. Despite the fact that Scotland has been part of a political union with England since 1707, it was only in June 2020 that an unbroken string of opinion polls showed a majority in favour of independence, for example.

While there is plenty of evidence of conflict with England prior to the Act of Union and subsequent examples of anti-English sentiment leading some to support Scottish independence, there is little evidence that this was even remotely the majority position for the bulk of the time Scotland has been part of Britain. Certainly, during the 20th century, the first in which there existed universal adult suffrage, the vast majority of Scottish people chose to vote for parties loyal to the Union and displayed little interest in anything describing itself as Scottish Nationalist.

Nevertheless, stories, myths and romantic history have

played a role in keeping the idea of Scotland alive, at least for the core of its nationalist supporters. Robert the Bruce, Wallace, Culloden and the Declaration of Arbroath are examples of historical figures and history discussed and lauded by those at the core of the nationalist movement determined to fight for what they understand to be 'Scottish Freedom' and to achieve a Scotland liberated from the yoke of English domination.

Marxists on the other hand must take a different route. The why and wherefore of Scottish independence must be understood in historically accurate terms and support for it dependent on whether it advances the interests of working class communities in all their diversity. It also has to be placed in its context. Scotland is not alone in providing an example of a movement for national independence that was previously in a minority gaining widespread popular support. Catalonia is another example. Both Scotland and Catalonia are generally, though not universally, considered on the left to be examples worth supporting, while other more reactionary examples, such as the Northern League in Italy, are much more problematic.

Marx and the national question

Marx and Engels's initial position on the national question was to support revolutionary struggles in countries such as Germany, Poland, Hungary and Italy in 1848/89 as a means of removing the last remnants of feudalism in Europe. These struggles were national movements to unite each individual country and create revolutionary democratic republics based on the French example of 1789. Marx and Engels started out as extreme democrats but very quickly moved to the position that only working class revolution could fulfill the promise of democracy. So, for them, support for national movements was dependent upon their capacity to advance the interest of the workers' movement and remove the last vestiges of absolutism. They opposed all attempts by the bourgeoisie to compromise with the old order.

While Marx and Engels railed against capitalism, its exploitation of workers and its destructive impact, they did nonetheless consider the defeat of feudalism historically progressive for two reasons. The first is that it created a world market and productive capacity that made another form of society possible, free from exploitation and oppression. Second, it created a class in society, the working class, capable of putting an end to the destructive aspect of capitalism, which for Marx was at the very heart of the system.

> But not only has the bourgeoisie forged the weapons that bring death to itself; it has also called into existence the men who are to wield those weapons—the modern working class—the proletarians.[1]

The state under capitalism plays a particular role. As trade and commerce spread across the world and the first fruits of industry and manufacturing began to grow, initially in Holland and England, it was necessary for the emerging capitalist class to develop an administrative apparatus capable of advancing its interests and an army to protect its markets and trade routes as well as opening new parts of the world to exploitation and plunder. As capitalism began to expand in other countries, they found that states advanced in the process had a monopoly on trade and so they too had to follow suit. Of course, this was not a linear process. It could involve compromise with the existing feudal order. It led to war, revolution, bitter rivalry and to alliances between different countries as the emerging capitalist order developed across Europe and North America. However, the direction of travel was clear—the global spread of the capitalist system. The function of the state in the process is not one of benign neutrality. It is to support and nurture the class it represents. As Marx puts it: "The executive of the modern state is but a committee for managing the common affairs of the whole bourgeoisie."[2]

As the consequences of increased competition and imperialist rivalry became apparent, Marx and Engels' views began to shift on the national question, with particular regard to British repression in Ireland. It was in the process of doing so that they began to see that workers, by supporting the repression and exploitation of Ireland by Britain, ensured that they tied themselves politically and ideologically to their own rulers.

> The English working class...will never be able to do anything decisive here in England before they separate their attitude towards Ireland definitively from that of the ruling classes, and not only make common cause with the Irish, but even take the initiative in dissolving the Union established in 1801. And this must be done not out of sympathy with the Irish, but as a demand on the interests of the English proletariat. If not the English proletariat will forever remain bound to the leading strings of the ruling classes, because they will be forced to make a common front with them against Ireland.[3]

Lenin and the national question

For most socialists who identify with the tradition of Marx, Lenin and Trotsky, any understanding of the national question and nationalism in reality begins with Lenin's writings on the issue. His development of how Marxists should respond to the demand for the "right of nations to self-determination" took place in vastly different circumstances to those encountered by Marx and Engels. By that time, any idea that there was a "progressive" aspect of capitalism was well and truly superseded by imperialism; the competitive carving of the world into areas for exploitation by the major capitalist countries, and the brutal military competition and economic rivalry which led to the carnage of the First World War.

Lenin took issue with the arguments put forward by another great revolutionary, Rosa Luxemburg. Her argument was that the economic development of capitalism had created a world market which made the idea of "self-determination" and the independent existence of small nations an illusion.

Can one speak with any seriousness of the "self-determination" of peoples which are formally independent, such as the Montenegrins, Bulgarians, Romanians, the Serbs, the Greeks...? From this point of view, the idea of insuring all the nations the possibility of self-determination is the equivalent of reverting from great capitalist development to the small medieval states, far earlier than the 15th and 16th centuries.[4]

Lenin on the other hand framed the issue of self-determination around the question of political struggle and democracy. Revolutionaries could not take an abstentionist position on the national question but instead should fight to ensure that the working class take a leading role and place its own interest at the centre of the struggle. It has to be stressed here that when Lenin talks of "democracy", he is not referring to this in the limited sense used by bourgeois politicians but one in which society in all aspects is brought under the control of the mass of the population, that is, the working class. True democracy for Lenin could only be realised in the socialist revolution. Nevertheless, it was essential that working class organisation should participate in "national movements" as part of the battle for democracy. However, Lenin was also clear that insofar as socialists fought alongside the bourgeoisie of oppressed nations, "they always only give the bourgeoisie *conditional* support".[5]

The issue of self-determination was also of great importance to those socialists fighting to overthrow their government in Russia, an oppressor country. They should support the demand in colonies such as Poland for self-determination. To do otherwise would mean that socialists in Russia would in fact be assisting the nationalists of their own country. Working class unity was not an abstract principal but one that had to be fought for. In the case of Russia and Poland this required Russian socialists supporting the right of Poland to secede from Russian control. It should also be pointed out that Lenin maintained this position after the socialist revolution took place. While he believed that as a socialist society developed the state would wither away and national antagonisms and frontiers would disappear, in the interim there would be a "workers' state" which would bring about the full democratic control of society. Such a society would have to continue to recognise the rights of countries to form their own state. The idea that smaller countries would be forcibly incorporated into much bigger federations was completely alien to Lenin.[6] In this regard Lenin was a much more consistent internationalist than those who simply ignored national divisions.

Lenin made a number of qualifications on his position on the national question. While socialists should support the right of small nations to self-determination, it did not always follow that they should advocate this in all circumstances. There were conditions when nationalist arguments became entwined with German imperialism, for example in Poland during the First World War. He was also clear that support for self-determination did not mean automatic support for any independence movement, no matter how it was constituted.

> There is not one of these (democratic) demands which could not serve and has not served, under certain circumstances, as an instrument in the hands of the bourgeoisie for deceiving the workers ... In practice the proletariat can retain its independence only by subordinating its struggle for all democratic demands to the revolutionary struggle for the overthrow of the bourgeoisie... On the other hand, Marx ... put the fundamental principle of internationalism and socialism in the foreground—no nation can be free if it oppresses other nations.[7]

Lenin was also opposed to the issue of national self-determination leading to splits or sectional and national interests leading to divisions in the workers' movement itself. His whole approach was to create an organisation capable of uniting the working class in the struggle against capitalism.

There is a contradiction at the heart of the demand for national independence. On the one hand the struggle for national liberation can lead to a revolutionary struggle against imperialism which has the potential to destabilise great powers—the American defeat in Vietnam being a classic example. On the other hand, the motivation of those who lead such movements is to create a capitalist state within the system which ultimately leads them to accept the logic of capitalism.

Lenin, like Marx before him, commented on the struggle for Irish liberation from British domination. In the wake of the Easter Rising in 1916, which involved the seizure of the Post Office and other strategic buildings in central Dublin by a combination of nationalist forces and workers led by James Connolly, some in the socialist movement criticised the events as a putsch without social backing. To this Lenin replied:

> To imagine that social revolution is conceivable without revolts by small nations in the colonies and in Europe, without revolutionary outbursts by sections of the petty bourgeoisie with all its prejudices, without a movement of the politically non-conscious proletarian and semi-proletarian masses against oppression by the landowners, the church and the monarchy, against national oppression, etc.—to imagine all this is to repudiate social revolution.[8]

The Irish rebellion of 1916 was suppressed and its leaders, including James Connolly, were executed by the British state. But the movement for independence re-emerged with even greater force as the First World War drew to a close and led to a revolutionary war against British imperialism. This was given support by the mass of the population, including Irish workers, and involved general strikes against conscription and in support of political prisoners, and even short lived workers' "soviets" in towns like Limerick, as well as open military conflict.

Significantly, the beginning of the War of Independence coincided with a mass strike in Belfast, involving 60,000 workers, both Catholic and Protestant, which pitted them against the Unionist bosses and political leaders in the North. The tragedy of that period is that no serious attempt was made to link up the radicalism of the movements in the south and the north. Instead, the leaders of Sinn Féin, who set up their own parliament, Dáil Éireann, in Dublin, strove at every step to restrain the radicalism of the mass movement in order to placate the landlords, bosses and Church leaders who looked to them to deliver stability and order.[9]

The Treaty with Britain, which ended the War of Independence, fell far short of any radical hopes that had motivated the mass of the population. The Treaty partitioned the country, delivering the North into the hands of the Unionist bosses and leaving the new Irish Free State as a dominion of the British Empire. It was independence on the most cautious and timid basis, on the terms of the British state, which threatened massive violence if the Treaty wasn't signed. So great was the disappointment that Irish republicans split into Pro and Anti Treaty factions and fought a bitter civil war, which the pro Treaty forces, with the help of British arms and munitions, eventually won. Reactionary, conservative nationalism won out in the north and south of the country. Both the potential and the pitfalls of nationalist movements are summed up by this example.

Lenin's support for self-determination developed when imperialism was at its height and when the oppression of small nations by imperialist powers was commonplace. Imperialism remains part of world capitalism. Colonialism now features less. Yet the national question has not disappeared. Nationalism and the demand for a new nation state, as the example of Scotland shows, is as common as it ever was. Partly this can be explained by the collapse of social democratic politics and the inability of capitalism to provide serious reforms due to its ongoing economic problems and because politicians such as Keir Starmer and Nicola Sturgeon can see no other way of operating.

Scottish identity and independence

The nature of Scottish national identity is wrapped up in myths that often make it difficult to unravel the truth from the fiction. For Marxists, the major divisions in society revolve around class and the clash between capital and labour. However, this takes place within the context of national boundaries, with class struggle mediated through the lens of nationalism. Scotland is no different in this respect, with the added complication that workers in Scotland have seen themselves as British while also maintaining a strong attachment to their identity as Scots. In recent years, the British element has weakened considerably and support for independence has grown.

Unlike Ireland, Scotland is not an oppressed nation. It has not been subject to domination and exploitation by a foreign power. In the wake of the Darien disaster—the failed attempt by Scots to set up a colony in Panama which nearly bankrupted the country—the Act of Union of 1707, which brought together the parliaments of England and Scotland, provided the basis on which Scotland's later economic development could take place. For the vast majority of Scots immediately after 1707 little changed. Indeed, it is doubtful that Scotland could even be considered a nation then but "a loose aggregation of small but practically self-supporting communities".[10]

The economic advancement of Scotland in the 18th century can be described by what Leon Trotsky called combined and uneven development. Uneven in the sense that prior to the Act of Union Scotland lagged behind England economically, both because of the backward nature of its economy and because it was prevented from making strides forward by its superior southern neighbour. Combined, because once Scotland had access to English markets and the fruits of empire, it was able to rapidly expand its economy. Scotland between 1746 and 1820 went through an amazing transformation, going from one of the most backward countries to one of the most advanced. As historian Rosalind Mitchison notes:

The clearances

Scotland packed into about thirty years of crowded development from 1750 to 1780 the economic growth that England had spread itself over two centuries.[11]

Such development, of course, could not take place without massive upheaval both political and social. If we look at what is often referred to as the Highland Clearances—though as Tom Devine has pointed out, these also took place in the lowlands and the borders of Scotland and should more properly be referred to as the Scottish Clearances[12]—they also happened for a variety of reasons as Scotland moved from a rurally based economy to an industrial one. The clearing of the land was brought about by new agricultural practices and to make room for sheep and cattle. But the Clearances also provided the labour that would work in the factories and mills of newly industrialising Scotland. There can be no arguing with their inhumanity and brutality. But this was largely carried out by Scottish forces and not some foreign imperial power.

Much of what is considered the underpinning of Scottish identity emerged as part of the Union, not separately from it. The three areas traditionally considered the cornerstone of Scottish identity—the church, the law and education—were strengthened by the Union rather than undermined by it. Of the three, religion was by far the most important, providing the ideological glue which held the country together as a separate unit within a larger union. For most of the two centuries after union, Scotland was largely left to run its own affairs. As Tom Devine explains:

Only after the passing of the education act of 1872, the extension of the franchise to the working class on a larger scale and the creation of the Scottish Office in 1885 was there a decisive movement to a more centralized state. Until then the United Kingdom was probably more decentralized than any other country in Europe.[13]

The important point here is not to see Scotland as an independent country trying to follow its own path in conflict with its English neighbours. Scotland's business class and ruling elite (if these even existed as a separate entity) enthusiastically participated in the Union and happily embraced the spoils of empire. Nevertheless, the fact that there remained after the Union a large aspect of Scottish society which was able to have a uniqueness separate from England is a factor in the development of the Scottish Home Rule movement in the early part of the 20th century and the later drive in support for independence at the end of that century.

Class and nation—reformism in Scotland

Understanding the nature of state and nation does not fully explain the character of the Scottish independence movement itself. Classic nationalism tends to emphasise the deep roots of a distinctive nation stretching back into the mists of time, but the independence movement we see today is by no means an example of classic nationalism. Firstly there was a long gap between 1707 and 1928, when Scottish nationalism as an organised political current began. That year the National Party of Scotland was set up. It merged with another small party to create the SNP in 1934. But even after that the idea languished in the margins until the 21st century.

While the nationalist contribution is important for the Scottish independence movement, until the 21st century, Labour, an unashamed unionist party, consistently took the largest share of Scottish votes, in both Westminster and Holyrood elections. The end of the post-war economic boom in the late 1960s and Thatcher's years as prime minister (1979-90) had destroyed Tory popularity north of the border. After that date both Westminster and Holyrood elections produced a remarkably consistent half to two thirds of the Scottish population voting either for Labour or the SNP. In class terms, many of this group will have been working class. A study of the 1997 general election in Scotland concluded that "Support for the Labour Party was highest in poor urban constituencies".[14] An Economic and Social Research Council study used virtually identical words about the 2014 Scottish referendum. It "found support for independence at 46 percent among those on the lowest incomes, compared to 27 percent for the highest earners. Another survey found Scots in deprived parts of the country backed independence by 58 percent, compared to just 27 percent in affluent areas".[15]

The table below shows the seismic shift that took place within the largely working class segment of the population that voted Labour or SNP.

Labour Party/SNP share of vote in Scotland (%)					
	UK general elections			Scottish Parliament	
	Labour	SNP		Labour	SNP
1964	48.7	2.4			
1966	49.9	5.0			
1970	44.5	11.4			
1974 (Feb)	36.6	21.9			
1974 (Oct)	36.6	30.4			
1979	41.5	17.3			
1983	35.1	11.8			
1987	42.4	14.0			
1992	39.0	21.5			
1997	45.6	22.1	1999	34	27
2001	43.3	20.1	2003	39	20
2005	38.9	17.7	2007	32	33
2010	32.0	19.9	2011	32	45
2015	24.3	50.0	2015	23	47

Source: *UK Elections Statistics 1918-2019*, House of Commons Library, 2020

Of course, Labour and the SNP are not identical. A 2018 study of the party grassroots on the left-right spectrum shows that of the four main parties, Labour supporters see themselves as furthest left, then comes the SNP (followed by Liberal Democrats with Tories furthest right). The same is true of attitudes towards wealth redistribution, the role of big business, and austerity.[16] In terms of the social background of MPs, the Tories have the highest proportion of MPs with a business/commerce background (41 percent), followed by 33 percent of Liberal Democrats, 17 percent SNP and just 6 percent Labour.[17]

Furthermore, not all working class voters in Scotland back either the SNP or Labour. Nonetheless, the pattern is clear enough. 2015 was the tipping point in Westminster terms, while for Holyrood it was 2007.

If the vote now went to a nationalist party, does it follow that the Scottish working class had suddenly fallen prey to nationalist ideology and given up the attitudes that led them to vote Labour previously? For Marxists, popular consciousness is explained by material circumstances rather than the power of persuasion.

Marx wrote: "It is not the consciousness of men that determines their existence, but their social existence that determines their consciousness".[18] From this perspective it was the life experience of working class people in Scotland that led them to look for a new route to achieve their aspirations.

The unchanging beating heart of this process was reformism—the demand for measures to benefit working class people. It was that which motivated people to vote Labour in Scotland before and which motivated them to vote SNP recently. Reformism lies behind the independence movement for many, though not all, even if nationalism provides its external clothing.

But what is reformism? Marx affirmed that: "The ideas of the ruling class are in every epoch the ruling ideas, i.e. the class which is the ruling material force of society, is at the same time its ruling intellectual force. The class which has the means of material production at its disposal, has control at the same time over the means of mental production...".[19] Taken in isolation this statement would suggest that workers will simply accept capitalism and not see any need for left-wing change.

However, the exploitation, oppression and diminished life chances which is the lot of the working class under capitalism does not coincide with the prevailing ideas—that capitalism is a wonderful system which benefits everyone, and so on. The experience of most people is a little like what happens in Voltaire's comic novel *Candide*. In that book, the hero begins by believing "all is for the best in the best of all possible worlds" but experiences one appalling disaster after another. Among those at the bottom of society, consciousness goes in the direction of criticising or even pushing back against the real operation of the system without necessarily rejecting its fundamental precepts. Partial adaptation to, or acceptance of, ruling class ideas is blended with partial rejection and resistance. Reformism could be termed self-limiting resistance.[20]

The interaction of prevailing ideas and resistance born of experience is not just a matter of mixing two concepts but of active contradiction. For example, individuals may be acutely aware of the injustice, oppression and inequality of capitalist society but still accept certain reactionary ideas, such as rejecting trans rights or resenting foreigners and immigration. When reformism is congealed into an organisational form, these contradictions can be stark. Trade union bureaucrats, often elected on the basis of militancy, can sell out or hold back their members. Reformist parties frequently motivate followers with their progressive promises but carry out reactionary policies.

The most successful reformist episode in British political history was the Labour government of 1945-51. It ushered in a raft of reforms such as nationalisation, mass council housing, the NHS and the welfare state. These were clearly an important advance. Yet the existence of capitalism was not questioned even if certain peripheral aspects were tinkered with. The reforms began to be dismantled even before Labour's time in office had ended. Nye Bevan, architect of the NHS, resigned his ministerial post because prescription charges were introduced.

Over the subsequent decades, cut after cut has been imposed in every area of the welfare state and Labour governments have played a full part.

Within reformist organisations such as electoral parties or trade unions, the balance between prevailing ideas and resistance also takes the form of right versus left. Take, for example, the arch anti-communist witch-hunter Frank Chapple, who led the electricians' union for many years, or Mark Serwotka, who leads the PCS civil servants' union from the left. The Labour Party has encompassed reactionary figures from Ramsay Macdonald to Tony Blair, but also left-wingers such as Tony Benn and Jeremy Corbyn. If there is a distinction between them, it is that the former believe in self-limiting resistance while the latter believe in resistance that is self-limiting. From this it follows that reformist organisations operate a "broad church". Though by no means a classic reformist body, this same broad church can be seen in the SNP although the iron grip of its machinery mostly keeps open conflict between the wings in check.

Left and right reformists both accept the capitalist parliamentary system. The Labour Party, the great reformist predecessor to the SNP, can again provide a useful example. Ralph Miliband put it succinctly: "Of political parties claiming socialism to be their aim, the Labour Party has always been one of the most dogmatic—not about socialism, but about the parliamentary system. Empirical and flexible about all else, its leaders have always made devotion to that system their fixed point of reference...".[21]

Uncritical acceptance of this system extends to reformist supporters of independence, although they want a Scottish version. The problem with this is that the British state is not neutral nor likely to concede a breakaway that damages its business and strategic interests. As the Tory George Osborne put it recently:

> Simple. Refuse to hold a referendum. It's the only sure
> way you won't lose one. Yes, the SNP will be in full

cry—but so what? … There's a risk that the Scottish government holds its own plebiscite—but that won't be legal, and the courts will stop the arms of the Scottish state, like the police and civil service taking part. Ask the jailed Catalonian leaders how their illegal poll worked out. The only way you can have legal path to independence is through a referendum that is voted for by the House of Commons… Just say no, Boris, and save yourself a long anxious night in Downing Street.[22]

The idea that the courts could overturn a refusal is doubtful too. The British government's reply is "that the constitution is clearly a reserved matter, and that a vote on a constitutional matter should require an agreement with Westminster".[23]

Another common feature of reformism is the way 'class interest' and 'national interest' are conflated by party and trade union leaders. Class and nation are deemed compatible or even identical. Right-wing leaders interpret this to mean the working class must be subordinated to the country's capitalist ruing class. Left-wing leaders wish the opposite—the capitalist ruling class should be subordinated to working class interests.

Tony Blair's first speech at Labour Conference after becoming Prime Minister (1997) encapsulates parliamentarianism and class/national crossover: "I believe in Britain. I believe in the British people. One cross on the ballot paper. One nation was reborn… Our policy [is] based on the British national interest".[24]

It would be hard to find a Labour politician more hostile to Blairism and the Party's right wing than Jeremy Corbyn (and the feeling was mutual since he was disgracefully suspended and denied the whip). In his last speech as leader of the Labour Party in September 2019, he told conference: "We can bring our country and our people together, which is what I'm trying to do all the time".[25] Corbyn's manifesto in the election that followed declared: "Labour will build a fairer Britain that cares for all, where wealth and power are shared".[26]

Today, in place of Labour, the SNP has the loyalty of the bulk of voters. Presenting itself as social democratic it too conflates the interests of the majority with the cross class institution of the nation. It is an electoral rather than campaigning organisation and the word Scotland appears 348 times in the 50 pages of its last manifesto, where it is conjoined with the word 'people' 93 times.[27] Virtually every utterance of leading SNP politicians performs the miracle of blending class and nation seamlessly.

It must be stressed that comparison of Labour and the SNP only goes so far. The SNP is an even broader church than Labour as it contains many pure nationalists who are not reformists. The same applies to the independence movement in general. It contains these two distinct elements. And, as its names implies, the Scottish National Party's thought process begins with the multi-class concept of nation and then seeks to make it a reality electorally, while the Labour Party still has 'Labour' in its title, which means something to its followers even if its leaders show it contempt.

Reformism is integral to the Labour Party. As one Labour leader put it, the party emerged "out of the bowels of the TUC"[28] and it continues to have deep institutional links with the trade unions. It began with the aspiration for reformist change and took that into the bourgeois institution of parliament where hopes were quickly tamed. The SNP reaches the same point but approaches it in reverse. Its founding notion is acceptance of a prevailing idea of capitalism (the cross class concept of nation) but it sees the benefit of attracting disaffected reformist voters. For the SNP reformism is an electoral choice.

Saying that reformism is an ideology of self-limiting resistance is correct, but that is not the whole story. When released into the world, reformist demands take many forms and have different impacts. The wish for change can be channelled into nothing more than visiting a polling station every few years. On the other hand, there can be active resistance through political campaigning, trade unions, demonstrations or movements.

In sum, when it comes to practice, reformism can go in

different directions. An illustration in the economic arena is the demand for higher pay or equal pay for women and men. If a claim is put in and nothing is done, when turned down the result is likely to be disappointment and apathy. Even when accompanied by successful industrial action, the bosses' control of the means of production is not ended. That is why it is only a matter of time before a new pay demand will need to go forward and the cycle begins again. Rosa Luxemburg used the analogy of Sisyphus, who according to Greek legend was doomed to eternally roll a stone to the top of a hill only to see it roll down once again.[29]

But economic struggle also has the potential to go beyond its initial framework. Withdrawing labour is a collective act which requires self-activity. Challenging your own boss can teach lessons about the power of the working class that go beyond the issue of pay. In contrast to the Sisyphus analogy, Lenin once asked: "Was not the Prussian Minister for Internal Affairs, Herr von Puttkammer, right when he coined the famous phrase: 'In every strike there lurks the hydra of revolution'?"[30] An illustration of the latter is the miners' strike of 1974 that brought down Ted Heath's Tory government. It began as an economic dispute but rapidly raised class wide issues including the nature of the state.

For working class supporters of Scottish independence, indyref2 is a reformist demand. And so, like other demands, it has the potential to lead to passivity or to radicalism. It can be a labour of Sisyphus for, even if independence is won, there is no guarantee of progress. The Scottish boss is no less profit-hungry than the English boss. Alternatively, the hydra of revolution can lurk within it. The balance between prevailing ideas and resistance bred of life experience can be altered in favour of the latter. Everything depends on the level of self-activity, the degree of collective action, and the extent to which class demands are raised and the unity of 'national interest' rejected.

The call for indyref2 is *political* as it involves general class questions—state policy, social justice and so on. But if it amounts only to Blair's version—'one cross on the ballot paper'—this is a passive experience. Being passive will not undermine the prevailing ideas or effect real change.

The 2014 Scottish independence referendum showed the possibility of a different trajectory. The campaign was taken on to the streets and communities and owned by the masses as an expression of their interests. This was radicalising and echoes through to today's politics. This demonstrates that the balance between prevailing ruling class ideas and the push back of lived experience is not constant but can be shaped by active intervention, and that the class component of the independence movement can outweigh the nationalist.

If, as has been argued above, mass support for Scottish independence relies heavily on reformism (though now clothed in nationalist ideology), then what are the theoretical implications? Firstly, the dangers of self-limiting resistance must be recognised. The hopes of working class Scottish voters can easily run into the sand of electoralism. And espousal of the 'national interest' is no more inherently radical in the mouth of a Scottish politician than when a politician at Westminster extols British 'national interest'. This is simply because the Scottish worker has no more in common with the Scottish boss than an English worker does with an English boss. Insofar as independence is conceived as a constitutional process—a rearrangement of capitalist states rather than the overthrow of a state or abolition of capitalism —it is not transformative, however much the Tories might throw up their hands at the very thought. There is a potential cost involved. The slogan of independence can be a rallying point for the Scottish working class. It can also be a bridge which leads those with reformist intentions into the camp of national unity with the Scottish bosses.

Independence, in and of itself, is insufficient to create a different and better society. Johnson & Co were rightly scorned for promising £350 million a week to benefit the British public after Brexit. Promises of nirvana in an independent Scotland are no more realistic if the basis of the country remains capitalist.

However, the other side of the reformist equation suggests the movement for Scottish independence can mean more than that. Firstly, independence is an articulation of working class aspirations at a time when Labour, under Starmer, has more or less abandoned the effort and should be welcomed on that basis alone. While the SNP has shown disdain, huge marches organised by All Under One Banner and the continued existence of large numbers of vibrant Yes groups throughout Scotland shows that independence is far more than a polite parliamentary discussion. Barely diminished since 2014, a renewed campaign could mobilise even larger numbers into self-activity on the streets, in workplaces, and housing schemes. And because the focus is political, it can generalise the demand for change across the working class, in Scotland and beyond.

Secondly, the capitalist state structure which is to be rearranged is the British state. This has an imperial history and worldwide reach and its break up would be significant.

To summarise this section, although the call for independence originated in cross class nationalism, it was taken up by large sections of the working class as a means of delivering reforms. Reformism—that combination of prevailing ideas and resistance—can lead in different directions. Political reformism can divert anger into passivity ('don't rock the boat, but wait for the next election'). It can be demobilising.

Alternatively it can become a source of increased struggle in which the balance moves away from the passive submission to capitalist institutions towards self-activity. By changing the 'being' of participants this can generate a correspondingly more radical consciousness. The hydra of revolution may lurk in the shadows but only if the movement can go further than the reformist idea that independence itself is sufficient to deliver a different kind of society.

Permanent revolution

In the final part of this chapter, we turn from a discussion of nation and class to their interaction. Here the theory of permanent revolution formulated by Trotsky will come in useful. Its application to modern Scotland might seem surprising given that it was developed to solve a question that arose in a very different situation—Tsarist Russia in the 1900s.

Like all Marxist theory, it came out of a particular experience that seemed to contradict the established wisdom. (Marx and Marxists are not exempt from the dictum that being determines consciousness). The official Marxist movement that arose after his death had largely assumed that society must progress through fixed stages, from feudalism to capitalism and only afterwards to socialism.

This prediction was based on earlier historical development. Feudal government was run by autocrats—kings, barons and emperors such as the Tsar—and these were challenged by bourgeois revolutions. England in the 1640s, France after 1789 and the American War of Independence in 1776 showed a rising capitalist class demanding not just economic dominance but a state which would serve their needs. This involved a call for parliamentary style democracy based on a national state.

The puzzle for Trotsky was that Russia was not following this path. It had a developing capitalist class but no real challenge to feudalism came from that source. Instead it came from the working class.

In January 1905 in the capital, St Petersburg, they marched on the Winter Palace intending to present a petition to the Tsar. This was headed by the classic demand of bourgeois revolutions for parliamentary style democracy:

> Elections to the Constituent Assembly be conducted under universal, secret and equal suffrage

However, alongside this were working class demands for:

> Measures against the poverty of the people, and Measures against the oppression of labour by capital.

These could be quite specific:

> An eight-hour working day and regulation of overtime work.[31]

The workers were fired upon in what became known as Bloody Sunday. Subsequently a soviet (or workers' council) was established which, before it was crushed, challenged the Tsarist state. All this was not supposed to happen according to the central tenet of what passed as Marxism.

To make sense of 1905 Trotsky drew on Marx's actual writings during the last great wave of revolutions in 1848. Talking about the bourgeoisie in Germany, Marx pointed to its timidity because if it physically "confronted feudalism and absolutism, it saw [also] pitted against itself the proletariat..."[32] This was not the scenario during earlier bourgeois revolutions because at that time industry had barely taken off so the proletariat was miniscule. Now, in 1848, the capitalists had to weigh the risk of mobilising the proletariat, or working class, to help win its programme, against the irritation of continued aristocratic influence. Therefore, they equivocated and held back. Marx's collaborator, Engels, wrote that the bourgeoisie "attempted an impossible arrangement aimed at postponing the decisive struggle..."[33] With the capitalists so craven in their response, how could the battle against feudalism progress? Marx argued that in confronting that system "the workers, as far as it is at all possible, must oppose bourgeois attempts at pacification... During and after the struggle workers must at every opportunity put forward their own demands ..."[34]

In 1905 Trotsky, who became leader of the Petersburg Soviet, witnessed at first hand both the weakness of the capitalists and the strength of the workers. He wrote that the former presented a "hideous picture of cowardice [and] servility".[35] When faced with Tsar Nicholas II's disastrous Russo-Japanese war, it "expressed the entire spirit of our privileged opposition—compromise instead of struggling...

Organise not for the struggle against tsarism, but in reality to serve it; not to defeat the government, but to seduce it..."[36] By contrast, as we have seen, the workers supported what were bourgeois democratic demands (a Constituent Assembly) but went beyond that to pose their own, the direct democracy of the workers' councils. 1905 suggested to Trotsky that a Russian revolution against feudalism might not stop at the capitalist stage but aim at establishing workers' power and socialism. In that sense the revolution would become permanent. He later summarised this as follows: "The democratic revolution grows over directly into the socialist revolution and thereby becomes a *permanent* revolution".[37]

Thus far the theory was developed for and applied only to Russian circumstances, the key feature of which was combined and uneven development. Tsarist society had archaic and backward social structures from feudal times co-existing with advanced industry, which produced both a modern bourgeoisie and a working class. That peculiar constellation of forces made permanent revolution possible. And in 1917 the theory was spectacularly confirmed when the overthrow of the Romanovs in February was followed by the victory of Lenin's Bolshevik Party with its avowedly socialist programme just six months later. The Russian Empire was known as 'the prison house of nations' because numerous peoples were subordinated to Russian dominance. Yet within a few weeks the Bolshevik government had passed a 'Declaration of Rights' which stated that all these nations were equal and that any which wanted to secede could do so.

The theory also pointed to another conclusion. Although Russian workers could lead the struggle for socialism, the very backwardness that made the permanent revolution possible would also mean the country lacked the resources to achieve socialism on its own. At best social equality in those circumstances could only mean a sharing out of poverty on an equal basis. So at the core of Trotsky's argument was internationalism. A specific situation might enable workers to establish state power, but the revolution had to spread internationally to ultimately create a socialist society. So it must be permanent in this second sense of internationalism. Russia's Bolshevik victory inspired a worldwide Communist movement with mass parties in many countries. However, successful revolutions elsewhere were lacking. This doomed its workers' movement to degeneration and eventually to destruction by Stalinism. The theory had proved its explanatory worth both positively and negatively.

Scotland today has no feudal class to be overthrown and lacks the feature of uneven or combined social development. So it might seem permanent revolution is not relevant here. That would be an incorrect conclusion to draw. It soon became evident that the theory applied beyond the confines of Russia. While the call for a Constituent Assembly and free elections was heard in St Petersburg in 1905 (and repeated in 1917), similar demands (which we shall call 'bourgeois democratic demands' for reasons given later) were raised elsewhere. With most of the globe ruled over by colonial powers, the drive for national independence would be a very important bourgeois democratic demand with wide scope.

First into the fray was China. In the 1920s it was under foreign domination by a range of imperial powers. A movement to end this subjugation emerged under the Kuomintang, a party under the control of capitalist forces. Writing about this Trotsky said: "Every national revolutionary movement is a bourgeois movement". Using the theory of permanent revolution, he predicted: "The Chinese Revolution will be victorious under the leadership of the working class or not at all".[38]

This perspective was put to the test when Chinese workers rose up in Shanghai in 1927, the country's most important port and centre of industry. Trotsky's position was overruled by the bureaucratic clique growing up around Stalin. As a result China's Communists were told to subordinate themselves to the approaching Kuomintang's military forces led by Chiang Kai Shek's nationalists. They did this only to be butchered by

Chiang and the Communist Party was driven underground.

After the Second World War a complication to this picture arose. Both China (1949) and then Cuba (1959) witnessed struggles that achieved national liberation that were not led by the working class. Trotsky's belief that national revolutionary movements could only succeed "under the leadership of the working class or not at all" seemed confounded. Mao's Chinese Communist Party may have had proletarian origins in the 1920s, but decades of Kuomintang repression had forced the few supporters it had left to flee to the remote countryside where it survived as a militarised formation with no real links to the working class. Through the People's Liberation Army, Mao came to power without working class intervention. What happened in Cuba was similar with Castro's 26 July military movement at the fore. Tony Cliff described this phenomenon as an example of "deflected permanent revolution".[39] This phenomenon need not overly concern us here. Circumstances in China and Cuba were very particular and the likelihood of a successful intervention by a third force—neither proletarian nor conventionally bourgeois—is very small in Scotland.

What elements of permanent revolution are applicable to Scotland? Firstly, democratic demands such as for a parliament, or for national independence, are *bourgeois democratic demands*. It is legitimate to ask what makes them specifically 'bourgeois'. Is it not to the benefit of virtually all citizens if they can vote for a parliament sovereign within the state, or if the nation is freed from foreign domination? The problem with seeing such measures as class neutral is that, progressive as they are, if that is all that happens, the critical economic and social power of the capitalists is left intact and unchallenged. The old master, whether it be the feudal lord, colonial boss or Westminster politician, is simply replaced by their local bourgeois equivalent.

Secondly, the modern capitalist class is afraid of mobilising the working class to help win its own programme. It fears the situation will get out of hand and that in the fight for democracy workers will also challenge capitalism. So the bourgeois leadership is left paralysed—too weak to win on its own but too fearful to conjure up the forces that would help it win.

This leads to a third point—that the working class is not limited in the same way. If convinced of the need for radical change, it can take action not only to secure bourgeois democratic demands but to secure its own class interests.

There is a possible objection here. Trotsky regarded the law of combined and uneven development—a rising bourgeoisie pitted against feudalism—as very important for his theory. This has not operated in Scotland since the 18th century. Furthermore, if Scotland is not an oppressed nation, national liberation struggle is not relevant either. If so, how exactly is Scottish independence a bourgeois democratic demand of the sort envisaged by permanent revolution?

The Scottish bourgeoisie espouses independence even though there is no feudal or colonial adversary because the social system is one in which individual units or blocs of capital compete with each other. That wing of Scottish capitalism (along with associated institutions such as the civil service and politicians) favours independence not because it is oppressed by England but because it is in competition with English capital. For the Scottish bourgeoisie, full sovereignty at Holyrood is a path to greater competitiveness. On its own this would not garner any widespread support. So independence is framed in terms of expanding democracy.

For its part, the bulk of the working class supports a Scottish breakaway (though does so for its own very different reasons) which would transfer state sovereignty to Holyrood and local decision making.

Combining these two elements creates a cross class bourgeois democratic consensus for a significant portion of the Scottish population. There is no equivalent in England. Formal parliamentary sovereignty exists in Britain. North and south, voters are systematically ignored whenever their interests clash with capital. It is most obvious each time Labour gets into government. The disappointment that follows usually means it loses the next election. Some years pass and the cycle repeats. From Scotland there is a different perspective. Here the 'democratic deficit' is keenly felt because since the 1970s, the Scottish electorate (sometimes when voting Labour but always when voting SNP) has consistently been at variance with the government elected to preside over Westminster.

The demand for Scottish independence is therefore a bourgeois democratic demand in terms of permanent revolution.

Once understood, a number of perplexing questions can be answered. For example, why is the SNP, which clearly craves an independent Scotland, so hesitant in going about winning it? Why, when All Under One Banner mobilises hundreds of thousands in marches for independence, does the SNP keep them at arms length, or grudgingly send the odd speaker but little more? What Marx said of the German bourgeoisie in 1848 applies here and the theory explains the twin souls of the independence movement.

Finally, when the bourgeois democratic demand for independence is taken up and fought for by the working class, this opens the possibility for a break up of the British state that would be a victory not just in Scotland but in the worldwide struggle against imperialism. There is more. The fight for this has the potential to 'grow over' into something even more ambitious. For the true essence of permanent revolution is about how a socialist challenge to the existing order cannot be achieved in just one country. It needs internationalism rather than nationalism.

Chapter 2

The Formation of Scotland

Donny Gluckstein

Currently Scottish politics is dominated by the SNP. Anyone who witnesses the sea of saltire flags that fill Scottish towns where All Under One Banner demonstrations take place or considers election results might reasonably conclude that this is a consequence of nationalism rooted in "a continuing historical process the origins of which are lost in pre-history". It is argued that this has little to do with "particular economic and social conditions" because "similar economic conditions existed in other parts of Britain, for example in North East England, which did not lead to any significant political action".[1]

This chapter will suggest a very different approach. However paradoxical it might seem, whatever flag the current movement may be waving or whatever party the Scottish population currently votes for, *class* not *nation* has been the predominant factor in historical development.

That does not detract in any way from the significance of the movement for independence. It is pure joy to watch the defenders of the Union panicking over the break up of Britain and the disintegration of a tradition which boasted the largest empire in history upon which the sun never set (and the blood never dried). However, it does no favours for the independence movement to misread the history of Scotland because this leaves it prey to false idols, leaders, and social classes who do not share the progressive goals it aspires to.

It is worth briefly discussing exactly what is meant by 'nation'. Unfortunately, this term is one of the most imprecise in the English language. The conventional view assumes that people occupying a specific geographical area form a fundamental unity on the basis of shared characteristics, such as language, religion, state structure, culture and ethnicity. It is supposed to follow that there is a shared 'national' interest bridging exploiters and exploited, so that 'we are all in this together'.

The relative isolation of Scotland, which is 80 percent uncultivable and lies behind ranges of hills in the cold north of an island itself separated from mainland Europe, would seem to lend itself to such a national consciousness. But appearances are deceptive. Scotland's early history points in the opposite direction. The first signs of human habitation date back 12,500 years, and from around 6,000 years, the cultivation of crops, first developed in the Middle East, was practised. Not long afterwards the Ness of Brodgar temples in Orkney (which predate Stonehenge) made it "the centre for innovation for the British isles. Ideas spread from this place... to the rest of Neolithic Britain".[2] Then, around 2,500BCE the Beaker folk arrived. Originally from the Eurasian steppe, DNA tests have suggested they replaced 90 percent of the local population.[3]

The very name, Scotland, comes from the Romans who identified a tribe, the 'Scotti', who crossed over from Ireland and encountered the Picts, another Celtic tribe. The Celts spread out from the upper Danube, and things did not rest there. The departure of the Romans by around 165AD also saw immigration from Cumbria and by Germanic, Anglo-Saxon and Scandinavian people. A land of clannish, regional authorities emerged with different peoples and distinct traditions linguistically, ethnically and culturally.

Though supposedly there was a single king by the 850s, as late as the 1200s the monarch addressed his "faithful subjects" as "French, English, Scots, Welsh and Gallovidian".[4] By this time, they were mostly ruled over by a class of lords of Norman origin. Unlike England which had been conquered by a Norman invasion, in Scotland King David (1124-1153) invited Normans to take over many areas so as to establish a feudal structure through which control could be better exercised.

Of course, a certain consciousness of place or community, whether this be local, regional or larger, has always existed—both in Scotland and elsewhere. But this does not justify Stuart McHardy's claim that, "The fact that we have a series of significant ritual sites dating from around and before 3000BCE means society here at that time was culturally sophisticated", proving that the "much-vaunted creativity of the Scots from the Enlightenment onwards appears to have deep roots indeed".[5] There is no Scottish chain of historical continuity in ethnic terms. Instead there is a rich seam of migration and variety.

This also means that nationalism has not always existed. Under the feudal system which operated in Western Europe until the 18th and 19th centuries, the ideological bonds holding society together did not depend on the idea of national interest. Indeed, far from a common identity being stressed, qualitative differences in social status were at the heart of the prevailing system of thought. Sanctified by the Christian religion, the metaphorical blue blood of nobles supposedly made them separate and superior to everyone else. It was this claimed fundamental difference between human beings that justified the demand of those at the top for unquestioning loyalty and obedience, irrespective of where they came from.

Things changed with the arrival of capitalism. A new ideology arose alongside modern bourgeois structures such as the unitary state and parliamentary 'democracy'. A supposed shared national interest justified subordination to the new ruling class. Rather than a set of individuals, divinely ordained as superior by birth to run society, symbols like a common language or culture were invoked. But these peripheral symbols hid the reality of class and exploitation no less than the previous belief system. Whatever individuals may themselves think, class is the primary material factor shaping society. It plays a greater role in determining the fundamentals of social life than the nation, which is a belief, an ideological concept, or as Benedict Anderson has put it, "an imagined community".[6]

Nationalism is a political movement that insists the nation (a form of consciousness) is more real and has higher priority than class. For this to be convincing today it has to suggest that the community has always existed. The presence of a Scottish state until 1707 and the continuation of distinct Scottish institutions afterwards is key to making that argument plausible. In the North East of England, for example, these were absent. But it does not follow that having a constitutional history means Scotland's people had a shared interest that negated class.

There is more than one type of nationalism because, not being tied to reality, a community can be imagined in different ways. While all types of nationalism posit the meeting together of upper and lower classes, one version—reactionary nationalism—has the working class subordinated to local ruling class aims (such as war) and uses exclusive concepts like racism to bolster this. So called progressive nationalism suggests the opposite—that the ruling class submerges its private interests into the 'common good of the people'. Such a nationalism can therefore espouse left-wing causes and be inclusive. Both types of nationalism are present in the debate over Scotland today.

The argument of this chapter rejects nationalist interpretations of Scottish history, whether right-wing 'reactionary' or 'progressive'. The former are Anglo-centric and deny Scotland any significant past of its own or they glorify Scotland's history to suggest workers share a common heritage with the Scottish ruling class. But the chapter also challenges the left-wing version of Scottish nationalism. Its more radical supporters are motivated by working class concerns but fail to look behind surface appearances to understand the class mechanisms at work. To criticise left or progressive nationalism in such a way by no means implies support for the unity of the British state, however.

What follows looks at the formation of Scotland both in its historical actuality and in its retelling as myth. Only two key episodes will be covered: the Wars of Independence and the Act of Union with its consequences.

Freedom for whom? Wallace and Bruce

For those British nationalists who treat 'England' and 'Britain' as interchangeable terms, the so called 'Wars of Independence' between 1296 and 1357 are an irrelevance. Many supporters of independence would rightly see this is a travesty and share Stuart McHardy's view that "the point about the closing years of the 13th century and what followed was that it was a battle for survival by the Scottish against a southern invader set on military conquest...".[7] Great battles against English armies indeed took place. These are commemorated in the 'unofficial national anthem', *Flower of Scotland*, which celebrates the moment when Scottish soldiers defeated "Proud Edward's Army, and sent him homeward, to think again".

In 1286 Alexander III died, followed soon after by his only surviving heir, the Maid of Norway. She gained that title having been married off to a son of the Norwegian King. Her name gives a clue as to the dynastic, and therefore non national, character of the struggle for succession. Thirteen competitors claimed the right to be the new king in the 'Great Cause'. One of them was John Balliol. Born in either Galloway, Picardy or County Durham, he held land in Hertfordshire and France as well as Scotland. Another contender, Robert de Brus, had land in Scotland but also held Hartlepool, territory in Essex and, by marriage, in Cumberland. John, the 1st Baron Hastings, also had Abergavenny and held office as the Seneschal (governor) of Gascony and Lieutenant of Aquitaine. The name Floris V, Count of Holland, is self-explanatory as is Eric II, King of Norway. Other pretenders whose names expose their Anglo-Norman roots were Nicholas de Soules, William de Ros, William de

Vesci, Roget de Mandeville and Robert de Pinkeney.

What they all shared was 'nobility'. Society at this time has been described as "intensely hierarchical... Legal rights and duties, a person's very identity, were dependent on their social status...".[8] So academics may talk of this period seeing "a common sense of nationhood"[9] and songs may recall age-old Scots versus English enmity, but what motivated those at the top had nothing to do with nationhood. Land was the key source of wealth at that time, and the wars of 1296 to 1314 were driven by a ruling class desire to control land and exploit the agricultural labour on it. Birth was the key, and where that land was or who inhabited it was of marginal consequence.

Ownership of land was maintained by excluding external rivals, and employing the coercive power of the castle and the dungeon to subdue those who farmed it. This was supplemented by two ideological tools that gave the upper classes control over the rest of the population. The first was another thoroughly non national institution. The universal Catholic Church, headquartered in Rome, sanctified the right of a particular elite group to rule and to do so irrespective of territory, language and culture.

A further element operated in areas not yet fully infiltrated by the Anglo-Norman nobility (mainly the Highlands). This was the belief that all members of a kinship group, or clan, were related. Today all that remains of the clan system are a memory and false emblems, such as recently invented tartans. But in medieval times clan consciousness tended to exclude the broad idea of Scottishness. It led to inter-clan rivalry and so was divisive in itself. Yet McHardy seeks in the patriarchal traditions of the clan an enduring egalitarian tradition underlying nationalism, proof being that even the most lowly took the clan chief by the hand when they met. Unfortunately, the quote he uses suggests the very opposite, as the chief in question considered "seeming familiarity with slaves of so wretched Appearance" contradicted the boast made of "despotic power over his Clan".[10] Thomas Johnston was closer to understanding the clan system when he wrote that "the serf down to the early part of the 14th century, had no rights, no privileges, and no family name".[11] Neither religion nor the clan relied on the concept of a shared interest, which itself would have run counter to the 'god-given right' of the nobility to hold land and exploit wherever possible.

So common commitment to the nation by ordinary people or the elite, as conceived by modern Scottish nationalism, was absent. It neither underpinned the ideological make up of wider Scottish society nor motivated the actions of those who ran it. It was class, in the form of landowners versus those who toiled on the land, that was the basic feature. However, the nobility had a problem—its own greed. With so many eligible competitors in play, the Great Cause had no easy solution. When it appeared the personal ambition of the candidates might lead to outright civil war, it was decided to invite Edward I, King of England, to adjudicate the claims. He selected the one he thought would be the most malleable contender—John Balliol. After a period of subservience, Balliol eventually objected to providing soldiers for England's war with France. Edward then marched armies north to press a claim that he was 'overlord' of Scotland. This aggression earned him the title 'Hammer of the Scots'. An English King, he no more represented the English than the pretenders stood for Scotland. Edward's landholdings included Wales and Ireland, parts of Spain and a considerable part of France. He spent most of his long life fighting to expand his domains, bringing violence, death and heavy taxation for those under him. Like all the competitors, he was keen to establish his right to extract wealth from whoever it might be, but he was better armed than most.

Those around Balliol initially opposed Edward I's rule because they resented his interference in their exclusive rights to exploitation. Their determination proved very limited, however. Balliol's armies collapsed quickly, and most nobles then gave in, inscribing their names on the 'Ragman Rolls', a list of Scottish lords swearing allegiance to Edward so they could continue to enjoy the fruits of other people's labour. But resentment smouldered beneath the surface and it was in this situation that William Wallace emerged as a resistance leader. Although his background is obscure, he was neither an upper aristocrat nor a peasant but probably the son of a minor knight.

Wallace's subordinate status meant he could straddle the classes in Scottish society as war leader. He fought in the name of King John Balliol and was able to gather an army to fight Edward's forces despite lacking the conventional authority of landownership to call up soldiers. Enrolment in the ranks of Wallace's force was stimulated by fear of higher taxes and English conscription. There might also be opportunities to raid and plunder.

The Battle of Stirling Bridge in 1297 was Wallace's great triumph. It was made possible by some peculiar circumstances. His supporters had only light arms and lacked the expensive heavy weapons of the time—knights on horseback. However, this disadvantage disappeared when the large English army arrogantly chose to cross the River Forth via a narrow bridge. Timing its attack carefully, Wallace's smaller force was able to swarm down a hillside to isolate and destroy the vanguard while the rest looked on helplessly from the opposite bank. It is significant that Wallace's troops particularly turned their ire against Hugh de Cressingham. He was Edward's tax collector in Scotland and had ordered the confiscation of all Scotland's wool—then its primary export. Cressingham's skin was flayed and prominently displayed across the country.

Wallace came to prominence because the Scottish aristocracy was so deeply divided by the Great Cause. He was not a 'national leader' in the modern sense. He promoted the claims of one faction of the nobility and his status depended on their accepting him, though he was an outsider. For the victory at Stirling Bridge he was knighted and made a 'Guardian of Scotland'; but his sponsors were careful. Although he had prevented a full English takeover, and that was useful in the short term, other considerations were also in play. Having the crown located in Scotland gave more local influence over the business of exploiting the people, but as is clear from the potted biographies of the contenders given above, this had to be balanced against the benefits gained from landholdings elsewhere. Prolonged outright opposition to Edward might endanger these. So ultimately Wallace's resistance was seen as a bargaining counter by which the various factions might negotiate a better deal with the English King.

The narrow basis of support that Wallace and his followers had within the ruling class game was cruelly exposed at his next major battle in 1298 at Falkirk. Stirling Bridge could not be repeated. The terrain was flatter and so Wallace's infantry formed great 'schiltrons', circles of spears, which the English cavalry could not penetrate. However, this tactic could only succeed if mounted Scottish knights held back English bowmen. As Guardian of Scotland, Wallace's request for cavalry ought to have been met. But in the end the Scottish nobility failed to enter the field, leaving the English to calmly fire arrow after arrow into the defenceless schiltrons. Defeat meant Wallace's value as a bargaining chip was over and he was betrayed to the English by Sir John Monteith in exchange for being made Earl of Lennox.

Wallace was hung, drawn and quartered, but not forgotten. Robert Burns's *Scots Wha Hae* has the lines:

> Scots, wha hae wi' Wallace bled,
> Scots, wham Bruce has aften led;
> Welcome to your gory bed,
> Or to victory!
>
> Now's the day, and now's the hour;
> See the front o' battle lour;
> See approach proud Edward's power—
> Chains and slavery!

The poem was written in 1793, 488 years after Wallace's death and at the height of French revolutionary Jacobin radicalism. Myth-making was already under way and *Scots Wha Hae* was taken up by people who interpreted Wallace's role in light of their own beliefs. The poem was enthusiastically adopted by English Radicals in the early 19th century as a rallying cry in their fight for liberty, democracy and social justice against monarchy, reaction and capitalist exploitation. Conversely, the Wallace Monument (near the Stirling Bridge battlefield) was opened in 1869 by Sir Archibald Alason, author of a deeply conservative critique of the French Revolution. Reactionary nationalism was its inspiration. It is only recently that Wallace, the anti-English and progressive 'national freedom fighter' of the Hollywood film *Braveheart*, has become the dominant narrative. There is no doubting that national myths can be inspirational, but a surer foundation for a successful progressive movement is historical truth. With that meaningful lessons can be learned, real friends and allies identified, and traps avoided.

If this applies to Wallace, who at least had relatively humble origins, it is doubly the case with Bruce. *Scots Wha Hae* links the name of Wallace to Robert the Bruce (1274-1329), implying that the latter battled Edward's 'chains and slavery' on the grounds of freedom. This bears no resemblance to the history. Bruce's pursuit of his grandfather's claim to kingship (in the Great Cause) had nothing to do with defending liberty, as the tortuous record of his political manoeuvring demonstrates. Bruce began firmly on the English side, receiving protection from Edward when the Comyn family, who were important allies of Balliol, seized Bruce's lands. In gratitude Bruce swore fealty to the English King. Yet a year later, 1297, he joined Scottish rebels. What changed his mind? It had become clear that Edward meant to rule Scotland himself and so had no need of an alternative Scottish claimant to the throne. A chronicler quotes Bruce as saying "I must join my own people and the nation in which I was born".[12]

Even if this is accurate, who was included as 'my own people' and 'the nation' was far more restricted than today's understanding and essentially referred to the landowning class alone.

Furthermore, Bruce's loyalty to Scots of any kind was short. On 7 July 1297, in return for a promise of not having to fight Edward's foreign wars, Bruce switched again, though it is not clear if this shift in allegiance went as far as fighting on Edward's side against Wallace at Falkirk. Bruce did benefit from Wallace's defeat though, replacing him as Guardian of Scotland, in another lightning change in loyalty. By 1302 Bruce was back in Edward's camp in reaction to rumours that Balliol would be released and thus re-emerge as the established Scottish monarch.

In 1306 the twists and turns finally ended when Bruce had himself crowned. He did not do this to confer blessings on the Scottish people. A vicious campaign to secure his claim followed. It involved as much of a civil war against other Scots—Balliol, his Comyn family allies and those unfortunate enough to be ruled by them—as against Edward I. Just prior to his coronation, Bruce murdered a prominent Comyn in Church, a heinous crime which earned him excommunication by the Pope. Bruce's campaign included the 'Harrying (a term describing sexual violence) of Buchan'. This was the systematic burning and destruction of a heavily populated area of Comyn land, an act of savagery which, in an age well used to violence, shocked contemporaries but achieved the aim of terrorising his opponents into submission. The description later applied to Edward I's actions in the Declaration of Arbroath (1320) could just as well have been applied to Bruce's behaviour towards many Scots: "The deeds of cruelty, massacre, violence, pillage, arson, imprisoning prelates, burning down monasteries, robbing and killing monks and nuns and yet other outrages without number which he committed against our people, sparing neither age nor sex, religion nor rank, no-one could describe nor fully imagine".[13] As one academic history politely explains, as a result, "Bruce's struggle to secure recognition from Scots was as hard as the war with England".[14] All that tends to be forgotten because of the decisive victory he had over the English army at the Battle of Bannockburn in 1314.

The English defeat was followed by the Declaration of Arbroath. This famous document called on the Pope to back Robert's claim to the Scottish throne against England's pretensions and to overturn his excommunication. It has been held up as evidence of "fierce nationalism", and a clear "statement of Scottish nationalism and patriotism".[15] A famous passage, which clearly inspired the script writers of *Braveheart* when they put a version into Wallace's mouth, states: "for, as long as a hundred of us remain alive, never will we on any conditions be subjected to the lordship of the English. It is in truth not for glory, nor riches, nor honours that we are fighting, but for freedom alone, which no honest man gives up but with life itself".[16]

These sentences have to be put into context, in just the same way we do when we hear US President speak about supporting the 'fight for freedom'. In that situation it means freedom for US imperialism to dominate the world. When the Declaration of Arbroath says 'we' are fighting for freedom, who is this 'we'? A clue is given at the start of the document indicating that it was eight Earls, sundry Lords and "other barons and freeholders and the whole community of the realm of Scotland" who collectively signed. This community of nobles was requesting freedom *for its* tyranny not freedom *from* tyranny. It was a plea to be left in peace to carry this on, free from English interference.

If by any chance there was an intention to conceive of freedom in wider terms, it was, in Johnston's words, that "the tenant was now 'free', but he had to devote his best days of the harvest time to cutting his lord's corn, without recompense or wages, while his own corn rotted; he was free—free to starve... free in name only".[17]

It is useful to compare the Declaration of Arbroath with a near contemporary, and genuine, demand for freedom. The preaching of John Ball inspired the English Peasants' Revolt of 1381. He also talked of 'community', but the meaning could hardly have been more different:

When Adam delved and Eve span, who was then the gentleman? From the beginning all men by nature were created alike, and our bondage or servitude came in by the unjust oppression of naughty men. For if God would have had any bondmen from the beginning, he would have appointed who should be bond, and who free. And therefore I exhort you to consider that now the time is come, appointed to us by God, in which ye may (if ye will) cast off the yoke of bondage, and recover liberty.

He finished by calling on the people to "uproot the weeds that destroy the grain; first killing the great lords of the realm, then slaying the lawyers and justices, and finally rooting out everyone whom they knew to be harmful to the community in future".[18]

With their courts and dungeons, the Scottish earls, lords and barons who signed the Declaration proclaimed freedom for their class but showed no more compunction than their English counterparts in repressing their compatriots. The leaders of the Peasants' Revolt, people like John Ball and Wat Tyler, were executed by the English aristocracy which, as we have seen, included numerous Scottish nobles.

However, even if landowners north and south shared the same class motivation, it does not follow that the situation in each country was identical. When agriculture was the key source of wealth in both countries, natural features such as weather, land quality and topography played an important role. The English economy was more developed, its state could draw on a larger agricultural base and population, and was therefore potentially more powerful than its northern neighbour. Shocks such as the Black Death helped generate conditions for a revolt from below in England, but "Scottish rural society was so largely organised to face war and feud… that it had no conception of itself as divided along other lines by economic interest".[19] Class consciousness was less in Scotland, but this did not mean national consciousness was present. It meant feudalism, with its localism and landlord domination, was all the stronger.

Far from Wallace's Scotland being socially in advance of England at this time, it suffered from a relative social, economic and military backwardness. To defend itself, therefore, from 1295 the Scottish state began the 'Auld Alliance' linking itself to England's rival, France, something that would be important later on. So the historical record shows the maintenance of the Scottish state in the Middle Ages was driven by feudal ruling class considerations. Now that feudalism is long gone, it is fair to ask whether constructing happy myths about the period does any harm. There are no 'competitors' waiting to ravage areas of the country today. Yet it is notable that the SNP supports the retention of the monarchy in an independent Scotland and, though a minor issue in itself, this is connected to a wider ideological stance.

Internal or external colonialism?

If the mythology around Wallace and Bruce is not supported by the historical record, is there more substance for the nationalist cause to be found in the disappearance of the Scottish state in 1707? Burns' poem *Such a Parcel of Rogues in a Nation* is a popular formulation of what many think happened in the Act of Union:

> Fareweel to a' our Scottish fame,
> Fareweel our ancient glory;
> Fareweel ev'n to the Scottish name...
> We're bought and sold for English gold —
> Such a parcel of rogues in a nation! [20]

The poem clearly suggests that Scottish independence was thrown away in 1707 through treason and corruption. A more modern version of this interpretation of the Union is given by James D Young: "Scottish society was pushed into a subordinate role, a victim of 'internal colonialism', with an economy peripheral to the core of English capitalism and civil institutions dominated by 'the conquering metropolitan elite'...".[21]

Once again appearances deceive, since what occurred was another example of ruling class calculation on both sides of the border, which took no account of the interests of ordinary people, Scottish or English. The inclusion of the Scottish state in a British state was not the result of national oppression but a joint venture in class oppression. It is true that if Bruce had lost at Bannockburn, then the sort of colonialism that Ireland experienced might have occurred in Scotland. But that did not happen, and by 1707 the goal of the English state was not one of conquest but of something else.

England's rulers were hostile to having another independent country on this island. As long as the Scottish state was there it could conspire with England's chief geopolitical rival, France, through the Auld Alliance. England pursued two contrasting tactics to solve its problem. One was invasion, which continued fitfully until 1650. The alternative strategy deployed was the forging of an alliance, initially by dynastic means. An example of how the two approaches might combine was the so called 'Rough Wooing' of 1543 to 1551, when an English invasion aimed to force Mary, Queen of Scots, to marry Henry VIII's heir apparent, Edward.

From 1603 the alliance strategy gained an important advantage. Scotland's Stuart King, James VI, acceded to the throne of England as James I. Political expediency motivated the choice that the English state made Philip II, ruler of another of England's imperial competitors, Spain, claimed his daughter was the rightful heir to Elizabeth I.[22] The resulting 'Union of the Crowns' blocked Philip and ensured a smooth continuation of class rule. Such dynastic manoeuvres would be repeated in 1688 with the Dutchman, William of Orange, and then in 1714 with the Hanoverians. Nationalism played no role in these decisions. The decision to have King George in 1714 was taken despite his being 52nd in line to the English throne.

Though the Union of the Crowns meant England and

Scotland had the same head of state, for a number of reasons the two countries diverged in important ways. Firstly, in terms of economic development, they were out of sync. As mentioned above, the effect of climate, character of agricultural land, distance from European markets and the impact of warfare, both internal and external, meant that Scotland was at a disadvantage. As T C Smout puts it, by the end of the 18th century: "Scotland showed in a peculiarly acute form all the evils of a traditional underdeveloped economy... she was poorer and more backward even in her pre-industrial economy than the states to which she most frequently compared herself".[23] While English agriculture was world leading and would soon underpin the industrial revolution, one Scottish observer noted his country still presented "the picture of Europe 400 years ago".[24] One consequence of this was frequent famine. In the 17th century these occurred in 1623-4, 1650-51, 1673-4, 1695-6 and 1698-9. During that last decade hunger may even have killed up to a third of the population.[25]

So called 'natural disasters' always take place in a wider context. Scotland's largely rural economy was controlled by landlords who, since the Declaration of Arbroath, had insisted on their 'freedom' to rule. By the 17th century this meant they had "the reputation of being the most absolute in Britain".[26] The alleviation of hunger during famine depended on the Poor Law, a function overseen by the Church. Since the Reformation of 1560, it had been Calvinist. Johnston points out that the "popular notion that the Scottish Reformation was a vast democratic upheaval is... a travesty of the facts".[27]

Leaders like John Knox mobilised mass resentment at the hypocrisy and greed of the Catholic Church, but the process was shaped by an aristocracy who were after Church property and income, and a weak monarchy ready to "buy allegiance".[28] Once the landowners had pocketed the land, "Knox and his friends suffered speedy disillusionment. There was to be nothing for the kirk... there was to be nothing for the poor".[29] Religious reformers had hoped landlords would cease oppressing their tenants, and part of the Church's funds would go to poor relief, but these wishes came to naught. "The complete failure of Knox's followers and successors to carry out any part of this programme makes the most depressing reading of anything in the history of the Godly Commonwealth", writes Smout.[30] Faced with crop failures, the lords did little, at points banning imports of grain while exports continued. Even those poor relief rules that might have helped were not applied.[31]

A second area of difference was political and social. In the period 1640-1660, England witnessed a successful bourgeois revolution during which civil war broke the power of English feudalism and parliamentary rule replaced Charles I's power. These events were precipitated by rebellion in Scotland during 1637-8 followed by the Bishops' Wars of 1639-40. However, the motive forces in each country were not the same. Urged on by militant popular forces from below, England's political crisis ultimately pitted market-orientated farmers, merchants and 'the middling sort' against royal despotism.

Charles's intentions in Scotland were similar to those in England in being designed to strengthen absolutism. He hoped to centralise power in his hands by bringing Church of England practices into the kirk and threatening the nobility's appropriation of monastic estates. Mitchison describes the Scottish opposition to these moves as "ostensibly a religious revolution, but [it] marked a further secular event, the takeover of the Church by the nobility".[32] So unlike in England, resistance to absolutism tended towards defending feudal arrangements rather than challenging the social system.

As the English Civil War progressed, politics developed in a radical direction. This led to a republic, as well as the radical Levellers' and the Diggers' movements. The nearest Scottish equivalent to these insurrectionary currents was the Covenanters. They were strong critics of Charles I's religious reforms. The lower classes were found among their ranks and they initiated a successful rebellion against Charles which began in Scotland in 1639, a year before the English revolution.

However, the dispute with the Crown fizzled out north of the border, because the popular movement, primarily driven by religion rather than social concerns, allied itself with one wing of the nobility against another.

Led by the Marquess of Argyll, the Covenanters' initial protest against Charles I soon gave way to the 'Engagement', a deal negotiated by a group of top nobles through which Charles made concessions to the Presbyterian religion. Once this was signed, the Scottish establishment quickly switched to supporting the Stuart cause and fighting against England's revolutionaries. The Covenanting movement would split later in the century, with an extremist wing—the Cameronians— breaking away. They lacked the previous close links to the nobility but their motivation always remained tied to the concerns of Calvinism and the Protestant Reformation. Though coming close it never quite reached the social radicalism of, say, Gerald Winstanley of the Diggers.[33]

Scotland's siding with the Stuarts ended when Cromwell took over in 1650. Though his aim was to secure the future of English capitalism, he claimed that conquest meant "the meaner sort... are likely to come into as thriving a condition [unlike] when they were under their great lords, who made them work for their living no better than the peasants of France".[34] Meanwhile, according to one Scottish observer: "Our Nobles lying up in prisons, and under forfaultries, or debts, private or public, are for the most part either broken or breaking".[35] Of course, Cromwell's comment may well have had a large element of rhetoric in it, since capitalism and feudalism are both forms of exploitation, but these quotes do expose the different social structures north and south.

In 1660, after the death of Cromwell, the Stuart monarchy was restored in the shape of Charles II. For a moment the gains the English bourgeoisie made in the Civil War seemed in peril. But in the so called Glorious Revolution of 1688, Charles's successor (James II of England, James VII of Scotland) was overthrown. In his place came William and Mary who headed a constitutional monarchy. They were shortly followed by the Hanoverians. Modern capitalism appeared secure, at least within England. But a problem remained. The Scottish state was still there. Worse still the Jacobites, who were strongest north of the border, favoured the return of the Stuarts and were prepared to use force to achieve that goal. What drove England forward to promoting the 1707 Union was the wish to end potential danger, not any covetous desire for the paltry benefits that Scotland had to offer at the time.

What was happening in Scotland itself? Recurring famines exposed domestic economic backwardness. In 1698 an attempt was made to break out of this by a foreign adventure—the establishment of a colony at Darien in the Panama isthmus. Straddling the Atlantic and Pacific the enterprise was nothing if not ambitious: "Trade will increase trade, and money will beget money [and] this door of the seas and key of the universe… will of course enable the proprietors to give laws to both oceans and to become arbitrators of the commercial world".[36] Mounting the expedition in the first place stretched Scotland's meagre resources to the limit, and Darien was in territory that was both inhospitable and already claimed by Spain.

Success therefore depended on getting some external support. Since the settlers regarded themselves as "subjects of the King of Great Britain",[37] they expected help from the more powerful English. But, as one commentator soon realised, with Scotland setting out to become a rival to its southern neighbour and a continuing security threat, "where the interests of England and Scotland do irreconcilably interfere, the king must act in the favours of England".[38] Deprived of English assistance, Darien turned into a disaster. Anything between a fifth and half of capital in Scotland was sunk into the enterprise and thereby lost.[39]

So the Scottish state began the 18th century facing impasse at home and abroad. This was the context for it entering negotiations for an Act of Union. However, nationalists tend to ignore these difficulties and see 1707 as an English takeover. If so, it is fair to ask what exactly was lost, and by whom? The answer seems to be—very little. The crown had been shared for over a century and Scottish soldiers already acted as a component of British military campaigns. After the Union various Scottish institutions were retained, such as the legal system and the Church of Scotland. So there was no takeover in these areas.

Therefore the biggest change was the dissolution of the Scottish Parliament. How important was this? In today's situation of universal suffrage, parliaments are seen as a mass political arena, but that was not the case in 1707. As Neil Davidson points out, only one in a thousand men could vote in Scotland, a situation markedly less favourable that in England where the figure was one out of 25.[40] The closing of Scotland's Parliament was not a loss to the vast majority of the population. It was unashamedly the tool of a miniscule elite. And the decision about whether it should throw in its lot with Westminster was made by that group alone, and in their own interests.

This is not to deny that the English ruling class were keen to encourage a decision for Union, and this was done through stick and carrot. The stick was Westminster's Aliens Act of 1705. Its passing meant the Scottish would henceforth be treated as foreign nationals in England, their estates confiscated and Scottish imports to England and its colonies banned. Escaping that threat would reap rewards in terms of existing trade, such as in cross border cattle export, tobacco sales and much more. The carrots were numerous—preservation of Church and law, a refund of losses due to the Darien scheme, and the direct bribery of individuals.

However, for Davidson, the most important clause of all declared: "all heritable Offices, Superiorities, heritable Jurisdictions, Offices for life, and jurisdictions for life, be reserved to the Owners thereof…".[41] The contrast with Cromwell is worth considering here. In England the revolution and the centralised state it established broke the power of local lords and created a unified legal system. The capitalist class was able to use this framework to establish a national economy and system of rules in which money rather than birth reigned supreme. We have seen how he predicted bringing the same system to Scotland would benefit the "meaner sort" (i.e. non aristocrats) at a time when the nobles were "broken or breaking". The Restoration stopped this process dead and retention of feudal Superiorities in 1707 confirmed the continuation of feudalism. What such 'superiority' meant in practice was summed up by an observer of the Lowlands, the most advanced area in economic terms:

> The Nobility and Gentry lord it over their poor Tennants, and use them worse than Gally-Slaves; they are all bound to serve them. Men, Women and Children; the first Fruits is always the Landlord's due, he is the Man that must first board all the young Married Women within his Lairdship, and their Sons are all his Slaves… Every Laird (of note) hath a Gibet near his House, and his Power to Condemn and Hang any of his Vassals.[42]

Considering the existing degree of collaboration, the preservation of key institutions and the clause on heritable jurisdictions, the conclusion must be that the Union was, to use modern business terminology, a merger not an acquisition. Unlike in Cromwell's time, no substantial social changes were expected by the English, only the banishing of strategic risk. On the Scottish side, once the ruling class were satisfied their situation was guaranteed, they were willing to give up their exclusive control in Edinburgh and with it their separate state. The Scottish people did not lose an independence they never had. Ruling class cooperation was confirmed by voting on the Act in the Scottish Parliament. The feudal magnates voted 69 percent in favour of Union whereas the barons and burgesses, who were less socially elevated, voted for it in smaller proportions.[43]

How did ordinary people feel about this elite deal? The popular mood was hostility, which on occasion could explode into rioting. One issue was the status of Scottish Presbyterianism within the larger state. Although noble influence was great, Davidson suggests "the kirk was the only institution over which the plebeians exercised any democratic control".[44] But in the end the Church was maintained. There were also a number of social and economic concerns. While some merchants might benefit by being able to sell into England once more, ordinary people would suffer, for as one petition put it, the Act would "bring an Insupportable burden of Taxation upon this Land, which all the Grant of freedom of Trade will never counterbalance...".[45] This was also a time of mercantilism, when much government revenue came from customs and excise. It was rightly feared that the Union would bring rigorous enforcement and the end of smuggling, which kept some essential goods affordable.

These issues imply a class basis for the opposition to the Act of Union. Yet the disappearance of an independent state was the specific issue at hand. This meant, inevitably, that the language employed was often couched in national terms. For example, a leaflet for a mass demonstration in Dumfries talked of how the Scots' negotiators "have been either Simple, Ignorant or Treacherous [by failing to stand] for the Interest and Safety of their Nation".[46] Anti-English sentiment existed. For example, an Edinburgh mob noisily supported the execution of English sailors falsely accused of piracy against Darien traders. Yet this mood was not a sign of Scottish cross class unity as it was accompanied by intense anger against the Scottish elite. As one Scottish noble wrote at the time, "the humour of the commonality are mightily against us".[47] So Burns' later characterisation was apt. He accurately expressed popular resentment against the Union, but it was for two conjoined reasons: English ambitions in combination with the treacherous Scottish 'parcel of rogues', whose merged state represented a new joint enterprise to preserve privilege.

If there was any doubt about the meaning and purpose of the Act of Union it would be clarified by what followed. The elite in both countries gained from 1707. The masses both north and south underwent the brutal exploitation of the industrial revolution. Far from the Union leading to internal colonialism, it facilitated rapid capitalist growth that was the springboard for real colonialism—the most expansionist imperialism the world has ever seen. And now, thanks to the Union, Scottish business had access to a much larger internal market. The benefits to southern capitalists accessing the Scottish market were trivial by comparison. This refutes the idea of national oppression of Scotland by the English. Class was everything.

As Davidson explains, Britain's bourgeois revolution was only fully complete when a Scottish bourgeois revolution swept away the last vestiges of feudalism. This was finally accomplished through the violent suppression of Jacobitism after 1745 (felt particularly in the Highlands and carried out as much by Lowland Scottish as by English soldiers). Davidson's view is that if the feudal elements behind Bonny Prince Charlie's attempt to seize the British Crown had triumphed (and it should be remembered that starting in Scotland his troops got as far south as Derby in 1745), his government would have been subservient to France. Under the *ancien regime,* France was a global bastion of reaction and its domination might have impeded the development of the rising bourgeois class on a global scale.

From the time of Wallace and Bruce up until the Union, the Scottish ruling class had been notorious for its despotism and violent greed. Scotland's post Union ruling class, which now encompassed the magnates and a new breed of industrialists, triumphantly continued that tradition though it was now repackaged as 'business acumen' and much admired by their English and Welsh partners. Capitalism was generally more efficient in exploitation than feudalism, but the ultimate purpose was the same.

Coal production is interesting because output increased 16 times over in the 18th century, using barbaric labour practices that preceded the Union.[48] Thus it was only in 1799 that serfdom, absent for centuries from England, was abolished for Scottish miners. As one collier later recounted, "I was nine years of age; we were then all slaves to the Preston Grange laird…

if we did not do his bidding we were placed by the necks in iron collars called juggs and fastened to the wall...".[49] However, other Scottish capitalists did not rely on such uniquely Scottish methods. Fear of unemployment was a whip that was even more effective than fear of an iron collar.

In the past Scotland had "been viewed condescendingly by its southern neighbour as economically backward" but by 1900 it "outpaced the rest of Britain...".[50] That year the Clyde produced a third of world shipping[51] and 27 percent of the world's coal.[52] In 1852 Scottish iron producers represented 28 percent of British iron output.[53]

So, if anything, the ruling class based north of the border benefitted more from the Union than that based south of it. Indeed, Scotland's economic expansion rested on a higher level of exploitation. Wages were lower than in the rest of the Britain. During the 1840s the gap stood at 20 percent.[54] Rapid industrialisation in Scotland and its consequent intense urbanisation combined with these poorer wages to generate appalling housing conditions. In the 1900s rents in nine of the 15 most expensive local authority areas for housing in Britain were Scottish. The rate of evictions for non payment of rents in Glasgow was 34 times higher than in London.[55] Every measure of life expectancy in Scotland lagged behind England and Wales.[56] At the same time "there were proportionately more millionaires in West Central Scotland than in any other British provincial region" forming "a super rich class merged with the landowning aristocracy...".[57] The shared capitalist state preserved and then enhanced class rule north of the border, which both refutes Scottish nationalist notions of a historical common interest shared by rich and poor, and the British nationalist idea that the Union was a benefit to Scots in general.

The consequences for the rest of the world were even more stark. With Scotland at the forefront of making Britain the 'workshop of the world', the joint state constructed an enormous empire. Before describing the Scottish contribution, it is worth considering what real colonialism entailed and comparing that to the impact the Union had on Scotland. Ireland is the best place to start.

Here, the Crown dispossessed the native (Roman Catholic) landowners and passed their domains on to a settler Protestant elite. Later on the Test Acts meant that only those taking communion in the Church of England could take public employment. Refusing to attend Anglican services could result in fines, property confiscation and prison. Nothing comparable happened to the Scottish ruling class, of course.

Indeed one section of the Scottish ruling class, the landowning nobility in the Highlands, was busily engaged in dispossessing its own tenants during the Clearances (roughly 1750-1860). Marx angrily denounced what was for him a contemporary event: Highlanders' villages were "destroyed and burnt, all their fields turned into pasturage. British soldiers enforced this eviction..." As a result of the actions of the Duchess of Sutherland alone, by 1835 "15,000 Gaels were replaced by 131,000 sheep".[58]

Another dramatic contrast between colonialism and ruling class merger can be drawn by considering the devastating impact that the potato blight had on Ireland and Scotland in the mid 1840s. In Ireland around one in eight of the population of 8.1 million starved to death.[59] Sir Charles Trevelyan, the government official in charge, oversaw this barbarity secure in the belief that for Ireland "the proper business of a Government is... not itself to undertake the role of the landowner, merchant, moneylender, or any other function of social life...". [60] According to Davidson, in the Scottish Highlands, where failure of the potato crop matched or exceeded what had happened in Ireland, "seven people were reported to have died directly from starvation and, after judicial investigation, the number was reduced to two".[61] It was Trevelyan himself who insisted that in Scotland: "The people *cannot, under any circumstances* be allowed to starve".[62] The Clearances were about making profit and so the likes of Trevelyan suffered no qualms of conscience for the fate of Highlanders driven off the land. Famine brought in colonial relations and in this case Scotland would be protected as the part of the colonial power rather than the subject nation.

The example of Ireland is particularly poignant for Scotland's history because the Darien adventure was not the only episode in the country's love affair with empire. Orkney and Shetland were acquired from Norway in the 15th century. Then from 1607, after the Union of the Crowns, the Scottish collaborated with England in the 'Plantation' of Ulster, each country providing the same number of settlers despite the relative population ratio being around 10:1. [63] So even before 1707 the Scottish and English ruling classes were working together to further imperialism (which explains the surprise and disappointment felt by the Darien colonists when they were not supported).

With the Union complete this collaboration resumed, and it was not long before George Washington was castigating "those universal instruments of tyranny, the Scotch" for their role in British efforts to crush US independence.[64] The imperial zeal shown by Scottish forces in particular was remarkable. "During the first half of the 18th century 25 percent of all regimental offices in the British army went to Scots...".[65] Below them perhaps one in four of the Scottish male population of military age were in the armed forces.[66] The consequences were tragic for those under British rule, but the stronger militarism of Scotland also proved destructive for those who participated. This tradition helps explain why, at the outbreak of WWI in 1914, again one in four of the eligible male population in the West of Scotland enlisted voluntarily.[67] Like elsewhere in Britain, poverty and unemployment were undoubtedly a spur, but Scottish enrolment was disproportionate. When the shooting stopped 26 percent of Scottish soldiers were dead, an attrition rate which dwarfed the 11 percent of soldiers killed in rest of the British army. Indeed this put Scotland at the top of the league for casualties alongside Serbia and Turkey.[68]

Scottish involvement in imperialism went further than providing a disproportionate share of the troops to enforce

British rule. The Scottish capitalist class was a willing participant in the plunder that empire brought. Some sections even specialised in the operation, the most important examples being the tobacco trade in Glasgow along with jute manufacture in Dundee. Scottish colonists did not stop with the Ulster Plantation but extended well beyond into America, Canada and into the furthest reaches of British rule. They often combined this with slavery. For example, "Scots were more likely than any other national group to hold slaves in 18th century North Carolina".[69] The same was true in Jamaica.[70] India was another Scottish target via the East India Company and its private army. In 1772 "one-ninth of civil servants and a remarkable one third of all army officers came from Scotland".[71]

Linking all these aspects together was capitalist accumulation: "Scotland invested abroad on a scale per head with no parallel among the other nations of the United Kingdom".[72] So it was that Glasgow came to be known as 'the second city of Empire' and acquired the large numbers of millionaires referred to above. There was a symbiotic relationship between the profits of exploitation extracted from Scottish people at home and the exploitation practised by the Scottish ruling class in the Empire.

It is therefore wrong to equate 1707 with an English takeover of Scotland. It was an agreement between the English and Scottish ruling classes to join forces all the better to plunder at home and abroad. Class considerations therefore were paramount in the construction, execution and results of the Act of Union.

Conclusion

The argument of this chapter must not be taken to imply that Scotland's history is devoid of progressive episodes. Indeed the rest of this book is focussed on how important these have been and can be in the future. The key point here, however, is that these would be forged in opposition to a Scottish ruling class and its state which, after 1707, shared headquarters with its English and Welsh equivalents in London. Even during the period under consideration, the rightly famous Scottish Enlightenment of the late 18th century produced a wide critique of feudal society or *ancien regime*. The insightful power of the Enlightenment owed much to the contrast between the historic backwardness of Scotland and recent advances. Thus when Adam Smith talked of a 'hidden hand' which guides market economic forces independently of the state, this was partly directed against a regime that had been particularly weighed down by feudal remnants. David Hume's writings against religious superstition were an attack on what had been the ideological underpinning of that backwardness.

So far this chapter has sought to demonstrate two main points: a) that Scotland has had a history which is distinct in very important ways from England's, something defenders of the Union deny; and b) that this past does not correspond to mythical portrayals given nowadays by many nationalist supporters of independence, both left and right.

There is a third important lesson. While myths may be inspirational, we do not need to resort to them to argue for independence, as the real history furnishes very good evidence in favour of it. Marx, in discussing religion, understood the benefit it provided its followers. It was "the heart of a heartless world...", "the opium of the people" and may provide comfort, but it will not bring liberation. An independence movement reliant on Wallace, Bruce and a belief that the English people are oppressors will fail to find its true allies and is more prone to domination by social groupings and political factions which do not actually share the aspirations of the rank and file.

The common thread running from the medieval period through to the Union and beyond is that the state, Scottish or British, is an institution to promote exploitation of the vast majority by a ruling class. In the 14th century, Bruce's brutal campaign for kingship successfully maintained a structure within which the local aristocracy could operate, its domination leading to frequent famines and enormous suffering for an exploited and oppressed population subsequently. This is not to suggest that life under Edward I would have been any better. The problem in both countries at that time was feudal class rule.

After the Scottish state fused into the British state, the same basic position applied, though the social system became capitalist. From 1707, and especially after 1745, a confident homogeneous ruling class and state, whose writ ran from Land's End to John O'Groats, spread its tentacles over the entire globe, using the commodities and wealth generated by workers at home and the plunder of resources garnered from a world empire. So, the real history of Scotland shows that an 'imagined community' or shared interest between exploiters and exploited, in either Scotland or Britain, is an illusion. However, a real community of interest does exist. It is one that encompasses ordinary people north and south, alongside those who toil in the rest of the world. Sometimes it is called the 99 percent versus the 1 percent, or the working class versus the capitalist class. Whatever title is used, we can only benefit from breaking up the British state.

Chapter 3

The Making of the Scottish Working Class 1787 to 1850

Charlie McKinnon

In Scotland, the transition from feudalism to capitalism was much later than in England and happened over a shorter period of time. It was characterised by rapid industrialisation and urbanisation. Industrialisation occurred initially in the cotton, linen and wool industries and by the 1840s in coal, engineering and shipbuilding. Urbanisation in Scotland between 1750 and 1850 was the fastest of any country in Europe. In 1750, Scotland was 7th in a league table of urbanised societies but by 1850 was second only to England and Wales.[1]

This had profound social and economic implications for the Scottish population who migrated to the new towns and cities in search of work and a better standard of living. However, once there, they were crammed into overcrowded slum housing and lived in the most squalid conditions. Friedrich Engels noted that 78 percent of the population of Glasgow's 300,000 lived in the wynds (slums) "which exceed in wretchedness and squalor the lowest nooks of St Giles and Whitechapel, the Liberties of Dublin, the Wynds of Edinburgh".[2] They worked up to 14 or 16 hours a day in the new factories and mills in brutal and dangerous conditions. It was in these circumstances that Scottish working class resistance was shaped. The first rumblings of discontent were seen in the Calton Weavers Strike.

The Calton Weavers Strike 1787

On 13 August 1788, James Granger was stripped to the waist and, with his hands tied behind his back, was publicly whipped through the streets of Edinburgh by the common executioner. He was then set free until 15 October to settle his affairs before being banished from Scotland for seven years. Granger was one of the leaders of the Calton Weavers strike, the first recorded industrial strike in the history of Glasgow. The strike lasted from June to October 1787 and began when manufacturers cut the payments for weaving muslin cloth.

On 30 June, 7,000 weavers assembled on Glasgow Green to protest at the wage cuts and unanimously passed a resolution which was published in the *Glasgow Mercury*. It was sent in a letter written by James Mirrie on behalf of a committee appointed by the weavers. He argued that wages had been cut by six and seven shillings per week in November 1786 and that the proposed cut would reduce wages by a quarter. The resolution stated that no weaver would "weave any kind of weaving work at any lower price than paid for the like work since the last breach thereof". It declared that they would help less fortunate weavers if required and that they would not "offer any violence to any man or his work".[3] In a further letter to the *Glasgow Mercury,* Henry McIndoe, acting as secretary for the weavers, defiantly said that the weavers would "exercise their inherent rights to choose, or refuse to have their ears bored to the door posts of their oppressors".[4]

As the strike progressed it became increasingly bitter. A similar strike had taken place in the town of Paisley by silk workers in 1773 when an attempt by silk manufacturers to cut wage rates was successfully resisted by workers. The employers and the authorities were determined that this would not happen in Glasgow and resolved to crush the strike. Strikers went to the homes of other weavers recruited by the bosses to break the strike and removed the webs from their looms, publicly burning them. In response, on 4 July an advertisement appeared in the *Glasgow Mercury* on behalf of the Lord Provost John Riddell and the magistrates which accused the weavers of "going through the streets in a riotous and tumultuous manner" taking the webs from weavers who were prepared to work. It went on to "offer a reward of 20 guineas to any person who will give information of the names of any persons... guilty of the foresaid illegal practices".[5]

On 3 September, the weavers assembled at the east end of Gallowgate with the intention of marching up towards Glasgow cathedral. Troops tried to disperse them but were initially driven back by a hail of stones and sticks. The soldiers opened fire killing six weavers and wounding many more. It was later claimed by the authorities that the Riot Act had been read out before the troops opened fire but it has been established that this is not true.[6] Dozens of weavers were arrested. Five of them were due to stand trial in April 1788 but were declared fugitives, having failed to appear.

Granger's trial took place on 21-22 July 1788 and was the first case of forming illegal combinations in Scotland. Although the Combination Laws had not yet been passed, combinations of workers or trade unions were illegal under Scottish Common Law. Granger was charged with forming an illegal combination, taking part in a riot, seizing the webs of Adam and Daniel Ferguson and being involved in the beating up of the latter. It was clear from the outset of the trial that he could expect no mercy from Lord Hailes, the senior judge. He was determined to make an example of Granger and argued that for the weavers and Granger to "set themselves above the law and to pretend to redress their own grievances was a crime of such magnitude that no punishment was too severe for the perpetrators of it".[7]

In stark contrast to the treatment of Granger and the striking weavers, Colonel Kellett and Major Powlet, who commanded the troops that smashed the strike, were well rewarded by the Magistrates and Town Council. At a lavish dinner in the Tontine

Tavern, they were declared "freemen of the city of Glasgow" and every soldier under their command was given a new pair of shoes and stockings.

Over 6,000 people attended the funerals of three of the murdered weavers—James Ainsley, Alexander Miller and John Page—at Calton cemetery. The families of the victims could not afford a headstone for the graves and it was not until 1836 that one was erected. In 1861 another memorial stone[8] was erected by Glasgow Trades Council in Calton cemetery, with an inscription dedicated to the memory of the strikers who died. The last two lines are particularly noteworthy:

> They are unworthy of freedom who expect
> it from hands other than their own.[9]

This is the key lesson to be learned from the defeat of the Calton weavers. As Marx was to famously write in 1864, "the emancipation of the working classes must be conquered by the working classes themselves".[10] James Granger had clearly come to a similar conclusion, returning to Glasgow after his seven-year exile and taking part in the great weavers' strike of 1811-12.

At the time of the 1787 strike, Lord North's Tory government was heavily influenced by Adam Smith's *Wealth of Nations* (1776) with its strong advocacy of free trade and a free market economy.[11] Adam Smith's book, written at an early stage of capitalist development, did not account for the contradictions built into the capitalist system which drove it to repeated crisis. Part of his analysis, however, his 'labour theory of value', did recognise that labour was the source of wealth.[12]

But Smith was no friend of working people and it was clear where his sympathies lay in any industrial dispute. He argued that workers "always have recourse to the loudest clamour and sometimes to the most shocking violence and outrage". Smith had no empathy or understanding of the difficulties that workers and their families faced in surviving on subsistence wages. He writes "the wages of Labour seem, in the present times, to be evidently more than what is precisely necessary to enable the labourer to bring up a family". Smith goes on to conclude, "A labourer, it may be said indeed, ought to save part of his summer wages in order to defray his winter expenses".[13]

Lord North decided to remove the import tax on French cambrics—a kind of fine, white, plain-weave linen cloth—in 1789, which, according to the *Glasgow Mercury,* could result in up to 30,000 workers being "thrown idle".[14] Hundreds of weavers in the Anderston district of Glasgow protested and burned an effigy of Lord North.

The weavers were in the vanguard of industrial struggle in the early part of the 19th century and were among the most literate and radical of workers. They worked in their homes with control over the hours they worked and, through their craft organisations, could petition Justices of the Peace and town magistrates for increased wages. This right had existed under Scots law since the 17th century and it was not unusual for the judiciary to adjust wages to take account of, for example, rising prices.[15] This had the effect of making industrial conflict less likely. However, as the agrarian and industrial revolutions gathered pace towards the end of the 18th century, the emerging capitalist class was no longer prepared to accept interference in the regulation of wages from the judiciary. Furthermore, industrialisation and technological change led to the setting up of textile factories and many handloom weavers were forced to leave their homes and take up employment in the new factories.

The French Revolution & the Radical Movement

The year after Granger's trial saw the outbreak of the French Revolution in 1789. The ideas associated with the Revolution were an inspiration to Scotland's emerging radical movement. The Revolution was welcomed by the growing number of radical clubs and societies across Scotland. In Dundee, the Revolution Society "pledged the rights of men, an equal representation of the people, and a speedy abolition of the slave trade",[16] and in 1792 the Glasgow Society for Burgh Reform was

*Monument in Edinburgh
to Thomas Muir and the
martyrs of 1793*

presented with a medal from other reform societies which bore the inscription "Men are by nature free and equal in respect of their rights... the deprivation of rights, or the abuse of power justifies resistance and demands redress".[17]

At this time Scotland's governance at both burgh (town or borough) and parliamentary level was based on property qualifications and was characterised by corruption and nepotism. Representation in Scotland was much worse than in England and Wales. In Scotland's 45 constituencies there were only 2,500 voters, about 0.2 percent of the population, and in Edinburgh, Scotland's capital city, there were only 33 voters.[18] In contrast, Cornwall alone in South West England had 44 MPs, only one less than Scotland's total representation.[19] This was largely due to the influence of Henry Dundas, the "minister" for Scotland who wielded the most extraordinary power of patronage. By 1790 Dundas controlled 34 of the constituencies and was nicknamed 'King Harry the Ninth'.

The government's response to the revolutionary fervour spreading throughout the country was to hurriedly issue a proclamation against seditious writings and meetings. However, in May and June 1792, protests against Dundas and the government spread across Scotland. There were eight days of rioting in Lanark and in Aberdeen, Perth, Dundee and in "almost every village in the North of Scotland, the mob burned effigies of Dundas".[20] The celebrations for King George III's birthday resulted in thousands of people taking to the streets to protest in Edinburgh and in Scotland. In Glasgow on 5 June, over 2,000 people burned an effigy of the hated Dundas in George Square.[21]

Unrest continued throughout Scotland for the rest of the year. There were riots in Perth in November where effigies of Dundas were again burned. The anxious sheriff of Perth, David Smyth, wrote to Dundas saying that the "mob" shouted "liberty, equality and no King". In Dundee it was reported that hundreds marched through the streets and a Tree of Liberty was erected with a scroll containing the words "Liberty, Equality and no Sinecures".[22] Trees of Liberty became a potent symbol of the reform movement in Scotland and were erected in many towns across the country in the 1790s.

The tumultuous events in France had not only led to an explosion in the number of reform clubs and societies but also a growth in the number of radical journals and periodicals. Radical literature and pamphlets were widely circulated, prominent amongst them being the poetry of Robert Burns and Tom Paine's *Rights of Man*. Despite being declared seditious, the latter was widely read and was even translated into Gaelic and read throughout the Highlands.[23] In Edinburgh the radical magazine, *The Bee*, published a series of articles in 1792 entitled 'The Political Progress of Britain' which condemned Britain's whole system of government.[24] James Anderson, *The Bee's* editor, was promptly arrested and tried for sedition. The government was further alarmed by the publication of the radical *Edinburgh Gazetteer*, which became the unofficial mouthpiece of the reform societies.

It was against this backdrop that the first meeting of the Scottish Friends of the People society took place in Edinburgh on 26 July 1792. It was the most important of all the radical clubs and societies. Among the most prominent members were the radical Lord Daer and the Glasgow advocate Thomas Muir. Muir is sometimes known as Scotland's Tom Paine and "the father of Scottish democracy". He had a quite remarkable life which reads like a fictional tale from a 19th century adventure story.[25] He died in revolutionary France in 1798 where he was publicly lauded as a "Hero of the French People" and a "Martyr of Liberty". At its first convention in Edinburgh in December 1792, the Friends of the People drew up a series of resolutions on parliamentary reform. It resolved to "restore the freedom of election and an equal representation of the people in Parliament" and "to secure for the people a frequent exercise of their right of electing their representatives". It stated that this should be done by "the proper and legal method… applying by petition to Parliament". There was clearly an attempt to adopt some of the protocol and procedures used by the new French revolutionary government. When addressing the convention, delegates used the term "fellow citizens" as in the French Assembly and its work was organised by way of committees. The minutes make fascinating reading and reflect the divisions and tensions between the more moderate and the more radical delegates. Muir insisted on reading an address from the Society of the United Irishmen which some delegates argued "contained treason or at least misprision of treason". He was forced to withdraw the document.

The convention agreed to expel any members "who may have acted illegally, tumultuously, or in any way to the disturbance of the public peace". On the other hand it agreed to defend any member who was prosecuted by the government for furthering the aims of the society "by the united strength of the Friends of the People". This is one of the earliest written statements of the principle of solidarity and strength in unity. The convention closed with delegates standing to take the oath of the French revolutionaries "to live free or die".[26]

There was a mood of optimism amongst radicals that they could force concessions from the government. This confidence was best summed up by the *Edinburgh Gazetteer*, which boldly asserted early in 1792, "Despotism has now been shook to the centre of the continent and before the conclusion of next summer the Tree of Liberty will occupy the soil that has long been usurped by merciless tyranny".[27]

Repression of the Reform Movement

It is little wonder then that the Pitt government, panicked by events in France and social unrest at home, unleashed a savage repression. The intellectual figurehead of the reactionary backlash was Edmund Burke. In his *Reflections on the Revolution in France* (November 1790), he argued that civilisation would be "trodden down under the hoofs of the swinish multitude".[28] Tom Paine's brilliant pamphlet *The Rights of Man* (1792) was a stinging response to Burke. However, it was the 18th century thinker and feminist Mary Wollstonecraft who launched the first radical attack on Burke in her pamphlet *A Vindication of the Rights of Man* (1790). She was denounced by Horace Walpole, writer and Whig, as a "hyena in petticoats" for her attack in it on Marie Antoinette.[29] As repression gathered momentum, anti-radical groups such as The Goldsmith Hall Association in Edinburgh were formed pledging to "stand by the constitution with their lives and fortunes". They were popularly known as the 'Lives and Fortune Men'.[30] Associations for the Preservation of Liberty and Property against Republicans and Levellers, on the model of the Goldsmith Hall association, were established throughout the country. In Dumfries a group called the Dumfries Loyal Natives distributed anti-radical propaganda and across Scotland monarchist loyalists disrupted radical meetings. Effigies of Paine were burned at loyalist demonstrations and printers who published the *Rights of Man* were attacked.

In 1793-4, the notorious Treason Trials took place in Edinburgh presided over by the vicious Lord Braxfield. Thomas Muir was charged with sedition, distributing seditious works and reading out an address at the Friends of the People Convention from the United Irishmen. Muir conducted his own defence and put up a spirited defence of the reform campaign. He defiantly stated, "Yes, I plead guilty, I openly, actively, and sincerely embarked on the cause of Parliamentary reform, in the vindication and in the restoration of the rights of the people".[31]

Braxfield was determined to make an example of Muir and the other radicals. In a bad tempered and at times xenophobic summing up, he made it clear that his loyalties lay with the ruling class. "I never liked the French all the days of my life", adding "and now I hate them." Turning his fire on the people, he added:

What right had they to representation? A government in every country should be just like a corporation; and, in this country, it is made up of the landed interest, which alone has the right to be represented. As for the rabble, who has nothing but personal property, what hold has the nation on them"?

He accused Muir of "poisoning the minds of the common people and preparing them for rebellion".[32] Muir was found guilty and sentenced to 14 years transportation to a penal colony in Australia. William Fysse Palmer, a Unitarian minister from Dundee, was sentenced to seven years.

Despite this, the second Convention of the Friends of the People met in April 1793 but because of the repression had fewer delegates and some local societies such as Stirling were not represented. Following an invitation from the London Corresponding Society to unite all the parliamentary reform societies in Britain, a British Convention of the Friends of the People met in November 1793.

It responded to the punitive sentences given to Muir and Palmer by adopting much more radical positions. It passed resolutions in support of universal male suffrage and annual parliaments, but this time agreed to organise popular resistance if liberties were threatened.

This was too much for the government, who acted immediately by arresting three key leaders, Margarot, Gerald and Skirving. On his arrest, Gerald exclaimed, "Behold, the funeral torches of Liberty".[33] All three were found guilty and, like Muir, were sentenced to 14 years' transportation to Botany Bay.

During his trial in Edinburgh, Margarot was escorted by supporters to the court bearing a Tree of Liberty "shaped like the letter M", with a scroll inscribed "Liberty, Virtue, Reason, Justice and Truth".[34] In less than a year, over 100 radicals were convicted of sedition and given savage, disproportionate sentences.

Spies and informers had also discovered the so called 'Pike Plot' (1794), an abortive attempt to organise an uprising in Edinburgh. It was led by a former government spy, Robert Watt, who was charged with high treason for trying to obtain 4,000 pikes for the purpose of rebellion.

Watt was found guilty and executed by hanging at Edinburgh's tollbooth. As an example to others he was taken down and beheaded, his head held aloft by the executioner, who declared "This is the head of a traitor".[35]

Government repression intensified in 1795 with the passing of the Seditious Meetings Act and Treasonable and Seditious Practices Act. These made free speech virtually impossible and as such became known as the 'gagging acts'.

They were introduced in response to a huge rally on 26 October 1795 organised by the London Corresponding Society demanding parliamentary reform and the resignation of government ministers. Three days later the King's carriage, on its way to the state opening of Parliament, was pelted by angry demonstrators shouting "Bread, Peace and No Pitt".[36]

The last defiant action of the radical movement in the 1790s came in spring 1797 with the setting up of the United Scotsmen. It was a secret organisation comprising of cells modelled on the United Irishmen and had similar aims to the Friends of the People. Its constitution and rules had been drawn up by the radical weaver and pamphleteer George Mealmaker from Dundee. He was betrayed, arrested and brought to trial in January 1798.

It was alleged that he had planned to establish a Republican government by inciting the army and navy to mutiny. He was sentenced to what had now become the customary 14 years' transportation for convicted radicals. This effectively marked the end of the United Scotsmen as a radical organisation. The intensity and scale of government repression "drove the reform movement back from the streets and parks into silent and sullen resentment".[37] It was not to re-emerge for over a decade.

Such was the scale of social unrest in Scotland during the 1790s it has been suggested "that Scotland was on the verge of revolution".[38] It was certainly an explosive situation with widespread disorder and the government was clearly alarmed. However, the organised working class in Scotland was in its infancy and even the most radical members of the Friends of the People rejected violence and favoured achieving parliamentary reform by petitioning. Hence the unrest was sporadic, uncoordinated and lacked truly radical leadership.

Fightback: strikes, protests and petitions

Scotland's radical movement may have been driven underground but the first decade of the 19th century saw an explosion in the number of strikes. As the factory system developed, the workplace became more polarised and the divisions between workers and employers sharpened. Increasingly workers looked to trade unions to defend their interests and offer protection from a new breed of ruthless bosses. The Calico printers were involved in a long and bitter dispute in 1810-1811 and the paper workers in a Scotland-wide strike.

In 1812, Scotland's weavers again went on strike for higher wages. The strike was supported by 40,000 weavers but after a bitter dispute lasting over two months they were starved back to work. There was also widespread economic distress which fuelled political discontent.

It was made worse after 1815 by the huge increase in unemployment at the end of the Napoleonic wars as returning soldiers sought employment and workers in the armaments industry were laid off. Increased competition for jobs encouraged ruthless employers to cut wages. The Tory government also introduced harsh austerity measures. A shift from direct to indirect taxation led to big increases in the prices of staples such as tea, coffee, sugar, soap and candles. All of this led to widespread poverty and near famine conditions in some parts of the country. Scotland simmered with discontent.

Huge meetings were organised by radicals all over Scotland to demand parliamentary reform. Meeting after meeting echoed the demands of the radicals of the 1790s by calling for universal male suffrage, annual Parliaments and payment for MPs. One such meeting took place at Thrushgrove just outside Glasgow in October 1816, where a massive crowd of over 40,000 agreed to petition parliament for reform. One of the speakers at Thrushgrove was Major John Cartwright, who set up the Hampden Clubs which advocated parliamentary reform and were being established across the country. Scots radicals were influenced by the ideas of William Cobbett and

Joseph Brayshaw and, like their predecessors, by the ideas of the French Revolution and Tom Paine.

The government contemptuously dismissed the Thrushgrove petition. Home Secretary Lord Sidmouth said that the radicals "had parliamentary reform in their mouths but rebellion and revolution in their hearts".[39] It was the failure of the petitioning movement that convinced many radicals in Scotland that 'moral force' would not shift the government and that 'physical force' or armed rebellion was necessary. This was reinforced by the memory of the brutal suppression of the radical reform group the Friends of the People and its successor, the United Scotsmen, in the 1790s.

Radicals in Scotland were further angered by the Peterloo Massacre at St Peter's Field, Manchester on 16 August 1819. Cavalry and yeomanry charged unarmed protestors who were calling for parliamentary reform, killing 15 people and injuring hundreds more.

The bloody suppression at Peterloo triggered a wave of solidarity meetings across Scotland. On 11 September in Paisley, a memorial rally of about 5,000 radicals resulted in clashes between protestors and cavalry which provoked a week of rioting. They carried banners in solidarity with the Peterloo protestors with the slogans "Remember Peterloo", "Hunt and Liberty" and "Arise Britons and Assert Your Rights".[40]

At a mass meeting in Magdalen Yard (now Magdalen Green), Dundee in November, the Radical Laird George Kinloch referred to Peterloo protestors "being hacked down without mercy" and called on the crowd "to be prepared like men to rise in defence of our liberties".[41] In a powerful and fiery speech, he also argued that Lord Sidmouth the government's "spymaster" was guilty of the "highest species of treason" against the people and that dismissal from office would be "far too lenient a punishment for him".[42] This was too much for the government and Kinloch was indicted for high treason. He escaped to France before he could be tried, returning to Scotland four years later in 1822.

The Radical Rising

On the morning of 1 April 1820, crowds of people excitedly gathered on street corners all over West Central Scotland to read a proclamation in the name of 'The Committee of Organisation for forming a Provisional Government'. It contained a strike call urging workers "to desist from their labour from and after this day, 1 April, and attend wholly to the recovery of their rights and consider it as the duty of every man not to recommence until he is in the possession of those rights which distinguish the freeman from the slave, viz that of giving consent to the laws by which he is to be governed".

The proclamation was also a call to arms and urged open rebellion against the government. It appealed not just to the people but also to the army to rebel, "Soldiers, shall you... plunge your bayonets into the bosoms of fathers and brothers?... Come forward then at once, and free your country".[43]

An incredible 60,000 workers across central Scotland obeyed the strike call in what was the first general strike in history, a quite remarkable number given how small the global working class was at this time. In a letter to the Home Office, Glasgow's Lord Provost Henry Monteith noted with alarm, "almost the whole population of the working classes have obeyed the orders contained in the treasonable proclamation by striking work".[44] Every trade and occupation was on strike. Many of them were forced back to work after the first week when it became clear that the rising had failed. However, even as late as July some workers were still out on strike.

The strike and the rebellion that followed were to be coordinated with a rising by English radicals with whom the Scots radicals had longstanding links. The signal for the rising was to be the non-arrival of the London to Glasgow Royal Mail coach. Evidence suggests that the radicals had been stockpiling weapons including muskets, pistols and pikes at locations across central Scotland and were drilling in preparation for the rising. In the event, the rising in England did not materialise, although there were some disturbances in Yorkshire.

Far fewer workers obeyed the call to arms than went on strike, perhaps discouraged by the news that the rising had failed in England. Nonetheless, a small group of 35 radicals led by Andrew Hardie and John Baird marched on the Carron Iron works in Falkirk in an attempt to seize arms and munitions. They were intercepted near Kilsyth by troops of the 10th Hussars and the Stirlingshire Yeomanry and after a brief skirmish, in which both soldiers and radicals were wounded, 20 of the radicals including Baird and Hardie were taken prisoner.

Another group of radicals led by James Wilson marched from Strathaven, near Glasgow, to link up with radicals thought to be planning an attack on the city. One of them, William Watson, proudly carried a banner with the words "Scotland free or a desert".[45] At a meeting at Three Stanes Farm before they set out, one of Wilson's friends, John Stevenson, summed up the mood of the radicals saying, "If we succeed it will not be a rebellion, it will be a revolution and we shall receive the gratitude and thanks of a free and happy nation".[46] They marched as far as East Kilbride on the outskirts of Glasgow but on hearing news that the insurrection had failed, they disbanded and tried to return home. They were intercepted by yeomanry and 12 of them were arrested including Wilson.

A further disturbance took place at Greenock, outside Glasgow, when soldiers escorting radical prisoners came under attack from an angry crowd determined to free them. Ten people were killed by the soldiers, including 11-year-old James McGilp, and another ten were wounded.

The government was determined to smash the rising and make an example of the leaders. In total 88 men were charged with high treason, 24 of them, including Wilson, Baird and Hardie, were sentenced to death. A further 20 radicals were sentenced to transportation to penal colonies in New South Wales or Tasmania and 200 more were arrested and imprisoned. The repression was brutal and widespread with hundreds more being forced to flee abroad, mainly to Canada and America. There would have been more executions and transportations had juries not been so reluctant to convict because the rising had enjoyed such widespread support.

The executions of Wilson, Baird and Hardie were the final act in the rebellion. Wilson was a veteran of the radical unrest in the 1790s and a member of the Friends of the People. His testimony at the trial makes fascinating reading. Before pronouncing sentence, the Lord President of the High Court in Glasgow gave Wilson the opportunity to address the jury. Having been found guilty of high treason, he stood up and defiantly addressed the court. "I have neither expected justice nor mercy here", he said. "I have done my duty to my country. I have grappled with her oppressors... I am ready to lay down my life in support of these principles which must ultimately triumph."[47]

On 30 August 1820, Wilson was executed in front of a crowd of over 20,000. On 8 September in Stirling, his fellow radicals John Baird and Andrew Hardie were also executed for high treason. Baird addressed the crowd from the scaffold saying, "What I have hitherto done was for the cause of truth and justice." Hardie then added "I die a martyr in the cause of truth and justice."[48]

The rising made an impact on the radical journalist Alexander Somerville. He describes how as a school student he played a game called 'Soldiers and Radicals' in the school playground. The children divided into soldiers and radicals according to their class position in society. Soldiers were usually the sons of farmers and tradesmen and the poorer children like Somerville were radicals. The 'soldiers' would shout "ragged radicals" (a term common in the Tory press at that time) and charge the 'radicals' who were usually beaten and taken as 'prisoner'. Somerville supported the radicals whom he describes as "honest working people" who thought that "the country was not governed as it should be that the laws were not made by those who should have made the laws".[49]

There is considerable debate surrounding the Radical Rising. Some nationalist historians perceive it to be essentially a nationalist rebellion.[50] Peter Beresford Ellis and Seamus Mac a'Ghobhainn argue that the rising had an "emphasis on nationhood" with the aim being "to re-establish a Parliament on Scottish soil".[51] Similarly, James D Young has argued that "a major revolutionary movement was planning to set up a Scottish republic".[52]

At first the evidence may seem convincing. In a letter to the Home Secretary Lord Sidmouth, the chief of Glasgow's police James Mitchell writes of the radicals' "audacious plot to sever the Kingdom of Scotland from that of England and restore the ancient Scottish Parliament".[53] However, this was communicated to Mitchell by a government spy, not the most reliable of sources. Some government spies in the 1800s were paid according to the usefulness of their information to the authorities and therefore what was communicated was often exaggerated or simply not true. There is also no cross corroboration from any other source, crucially not from any of the radical testimonies and the letters of Scots and English radicals.

As noted earlier, the Strathaven radicals carried a banner 'Scotland Free or a Desert', and Scottish banners at radical meetings and protests often evoked the memory of Wallace and Bruce and the Covenanters. In addition one of Robert Burn's most famous songs, *Scots Wha Hae* (1793), was sung at rallies and protests. It concludes by invoking the Tennis Court Oath of the French revolutionaries: "Let us do—or die". However *Scots Wha Hae* was the anthem of liberty for both Scottish and English radicals and it is documented as being sung at protests and rallies all over Scotland and England up to and during the Chartist revolt of the 1840s.

Furthermore, the Proclamation that detonated the strike and rising was entitled 'Address to the Inhabitants of Great Britain and Ireland'[54] and refers in the text to the Magna Carta and the Bill of Rights, which are associated with English rather than Scottish history.[55] As Neil Davidson notes, "The adoption of English radical imagery in Scotland was reciprocated by the adoption of Scottish radical imagery in England".[56]

There had also been close links between Scottish and English radicals since the establishment of the Friends of the People in the 1790s. Scottish radicals regularly met and liaised with their English counterparts, as Maurice Margarot did with his attendance at the second Convention of the Friends of the People in 1792. Others such as William Lyon McKenzie travelled between York and Glasgow keeping radicals in touch with each other, sharing information and ideas.[57]

It has also been argued that the rising failed because "it was induced by agent provocateurs a year or two before the radicals were really ready"[58] in order that government forces could crush the revolt and that "the treasonable placards were posted by government agents".[59] However, historians and commentators with diverse political views are agreed that there is no real evidence for this.[60]

Beresford Ellis and Mac a'Ghobhainn also suggest that "the Scottish radical tradition has always gone hand in hand with Scottish nationalism".[61] Young agrees with this and argues that in the period 1770-1820, "the colonial relationship between the two countries (Scotland and England) was a decisive factor in shaping the social and cultural formation of the Scottish working class".[62] The myth that the Scottish working class is more militant than their English counterparts and that this is in some way linked to the colonial relationship between the two countries dates from this period but has no evidence base whatsoever.

However, Neil Davidson has convincingly argued that it was the "specific material conditions under which Scotland entered the process of capitalist industrialisation" that was the decisive factor in shaping the militancy of the Scottish workers in the 1820 rising.[63] We have already noted that Scottish capitalism developed much later than in England and was characterised by rapid industrialisation and urbanisation. Scotland achieved spectacular economic growth in a very short space of time, but there were profound social consequences. Migrant labour from Scotland's rural lowlands, highlands and Ireland flooded into rapidly expanding cities such as Glasgow and Dundee to work in the new factories. They lived and worked in the most brutal and appalling conditions. As Engels observes, "the slavery in which the bourgeoisie holds the proletariat chained is nowhere more conspicuous than in the factory system. Here ends all freedom in law and in fact".[64] Class antagonisms were sharpened in what was a potentially socially explosive situation. Trotsky described how a revolutionary situation developed in Russia in the early 20th century as a result of rapid capitalist development despite the general backwardness of most of the country. This theory of "combined and uneven development", as he called it, is applicable to Scotland in the years from 1750 to 1820 and helps to explain the militancy of the 1820 Radical Rising.[65]

There is no doubt that the rising was the most serious challenge to the British state in the years after the Napoleonic wars. This was a revolutionary struggle against the British state. Central to its strategy was a mass general strike and an attempt at a general insurrection. The Radical Rising of 1820 was a hugely significant event and should be celebrated as an important part of our radical history. The failure of the Radical Rising convinced many radicals of the need to continue establishing trade unions as a means of securing gains for working class people. It also inspired the movement for reform which culminated in the Great Reform Act of 1832 and the Chartist revolt from 1838 to 1850.

In March 1831, the Reform Bill was introduced to Parliament and rejected by the House of Lords despite only extending the vote to £10 tenants in burghs and £10 owners in the counties. There was widespread social unrest in Scotland after the Lords rejected the Bill. Alexander Somerville describes a 10,000 strong protest in Edinburgh where crowds chanted "Up with reform light, down with Tory darkness". Windows not lit with a candle in support of reform were smashed and the Lord Provost was chased by a "mob" who threatened to throw him over the North Bridge.[66] In May 1832, striking workers in Glasgow smashed dummy crowns on Glasgow Green and 120,000 workers marched carrying banners with the slogans

"Liberty or Death" and "Better to die in a good cause than live by slavery".[67] When the Reform Act became law, a poignant notice appeared in the window of the martyred Andrew Hardie's mother's house:

Britons, rejoice, Reform is won,
But 'twas the cause
Lost me my son.[68]

The irony of course is that the new law would not have enfranchised Hardie and did not grant the vote to the vast majority of the working class. As Trotsky notes, "The extension of the franchise was carried out with the specific intention of separating the bourgeoisie from the workers".[69] Widespread anger and disillusionment over the Reform Act led to further militancy and radicalisation which were the seeds from which the Chartist movement grew.

Among the most militant and well organised of the trade unions was the Glasgow Cotton Spinners Union. The employers provoked a bitter and at times violent strike in 1837 by cutting wages. After three weeks, the union agreed to the wage cut but the employers were determined to smash the union and announced a further wage cut of 40 percent. The strike continued with a lockout by employers who brought in scab labour. Five members of the strike committee were arrested and put on trial for an alleged fatal shooting of a scab worker. The trial began in January 1838 and was presided over by Archibald Allison, the Tory Sheriff of Lanarkshire who was notoriously anti-union. Despite there being no evidence to directly link the accused to the shooting, they were found guilty and sentenced to seven years' transportation. Allison was clear that he regarded radical trade unionism in Glasgow and the West of Scotland as a threat to the established order. He brazenly informed a Select Committee on Combinations in the House of Commons that it was necessary to break the rule of law to achieve this. The committee of course wholeheartedly agreed.[70] Allison was right to be alarmed by the increasing militancy of trade unions as 1837 saw strikes by other workers including coal miners, iron miners, sawyers and others.

Despite ending in defeat, the strike did show the extent to which trade union solidarity was developing among workers. The strike was sustained with the help of solidarity collections from workers in the cotton industry in Lanarkshire and Manchester. The strikers were also supported by the Trades Committee of Glasgow, who issued a defiant statement in support of the strike which was printed in the radical press. They condemned both the "greedy capitalists" and a "tyrant government" who were hell-bent on the "destruction of our liberties—the total annihilation of the rights of labour". It urged the workers to "demand their rights and, standing by them still, maintain them, be calm, firm, determined, resolute, make union your guiding star, justice your helm, peace your object and you shall conquer".[71]

Nonetheless the defeat of the most powerful union in Scotland was a major setback for the trade union movement from which it took years to recover. Hamish Fraser rightly argues that, "like the miners' strike of 1984-85, the implications of the defeat of the spinners went far beyond their own union".[72] It also had "a huge effect on class relationships throughout the country".[73] Their savage sentences created enormous bitterness, sharpening class divisions and antagonisms in the workplace.

The Chartist Revolt

It was against this backdrop that the great chartist revolt that shook the British state took place. On 21 May 1838, a huge rally took place in Glasgow in support of the cotton spinners and to launch the People's Charter. The six demands of the charter were: universal suffrage; secret ballots; an end to property qualifications; payment of MPs; equal electoral constituencies, and annual parliaments. The meeting agreed to adopt the Charter and to launch a petition in support.

Chartism in Scotland has been the subject of much debate.

It has been suggested that Scottish Chartism was characterised by 'moral force' and was less militant than English Chartism. It is certainly true that there were some differences. Chartist churches were much more prevalent in Scotland than in England and they tended to support the more moderate wing of the Chartist movement. However, their influence had waned by 1843. Similarly the Chartist temperance movement was stronger in Scotland. Prominent Scottish moral force chartist leaders like Abram Duncan and John Fraser were teetotallers. The danger of the temperance movement was that it blamed poverty and destitution on drunkenness rather than the rapacious capitalist system. A Paisley pamphlet argued that no man "can be a sincere Chartist and Reformer, unless he is a teetotaller".[74]

However, the suggestion that Scottish Chartism was wholeheartedly committed to moral force Chartism alone is simply not true. Scotland was no different from the rest of Britain in that 'moral' versus 'physical' force Chartism was part of an ongoing debate on strategy and tactics that raged within the movement for the duration of the Chartist agitation. It is also true that the most consistent physical force Chartist leaders in Britain, Peter McDouall and John Taylor, were Scottish.

It is important to recognise that many physical force Chartists advocated the use of force only as a last resort. Drilling and display of weapons in public was not just about preparing for a worst case scenario but was also to some degree political posturing to convince the government of their determination and resolve in pursuit of the Charter. Sometimes the lines between the two camps became blurred with many moral force Chartists accepting that they had a right to use physical force in self-defence.

McDouall's attitude to the use of physical force had changed by 1840 and thereafter he argued that weapons should only be used in self-defence. He had an increasing awareness and understanding that the organised working class in the trade unions had an important role to play in the struggle. For McDouall it was class militancy, harnessing the power of the working class, that could be the decisive factor in forcing change rather than arguing for a crude form of insurrectionism.[75]

On 6 December 1838, at a 5,000 strong meeting on Edinburgh's Calton Hill, the supporters of moral force Chartism agreed on a number of resolutions condemning the use of, or appeal to, physical force to achieve the charter. The most vigorous and eloquent exponent of the moral force Chartists in Scotland was Paisley's Reverend Patrick Brewster. Despite the fact that Brewster was a passionate advocate of moral force, his radical views were too strong for the church, who suspended him from the ministry for a year.

Paisley had a very strong radical tradition dating back to even before the Calton Weavers strike in 1787. Hence, even in Brewster's own backyard there were many physical force Chartists. One of the most famous was the radical weaver poet Edward Polin, who opposed moral force Chartists in the town like Brewster and the Provost John Henderson. His radical views were reflected in his poems and songs notably 'In the Days When We Were Radicals' and 'John Henderson My Jo, John'.[76]

It was often the case that at Chartist meetings to discuss the question of moral versus physical force the latter view prevailed. The *Northern Star*, the Chartist newspaper, reported on an attempt by moral force Chartists to remove John Taylor as the Renfrewshire Chartist Union's delegate to the Chartist Convention. As a physical force Chartist, Taylor opposed the Calton Hill declaration. A motion of no confidence in him was moved by Brewster but was heavily defeated.[77]

Taylor wrote regularly for the *Northern Star* under the pseudonym Aristide. In an article in August 1838, he condemned the Prime Minister Lord John Russell and his class as "murdering cowards" and urged people to "take by force that which you have a right to by nature". He added that "universal suffrage and a just government will only be obtained by the sword". Taylor then declared his support for a "Republican form of government, divested of all the absurdities of kings, queens, hereditary legislators, priests and persons". With typical revolutionary fervour he adds, "I am a revolutionist—I confess I never yet heard of a revolution affected by moral force producing any beneficial result".[78]

In the years 1838-39, "the Chartism movement swept over Scotland like a flame".[79] This was true for the whole of Britain, with mass meetings and protests in support of the Charter taking place across the length and breadth of the country. The meetings also elected delegates to the Chartist National Convention. Some Chartist speakers such as George Julian Harney were surprised at how enthusiastically crowds embraced the arguments for physical force. There were reports of Chartist supporters drilling with pikes and swords in Lancashire, Yorkshire and the North East of England. Paul Foot argues that "in the spring and summer of 1839 Britain came closer to an armed revolution than ever since".[80] It is certainly true that the ruling class were alarmed at the scale of the agitation and that it was potentially a revolutionary situation.

On 12 July 1839, the first Chartist petition with 1,283,000 signatures was presented to Parliament. Approximately 18 percent of the signatures were gathered in Scotland, proportionately more than in England and Wales.[81] It was of course defeated in the House of Commons.

The reconvened Chartist Convention voted in favour of a month-long General Strike which was to begin on 12 August 1839. However, the Convention voted in favour of a motion moved by Bronterre O'Brien and seconded by Fergus O'Connor which stated that it was for each locality to decide when and for how long to strike. It was this abrogation of responsibility to give effective militant leadership at key moments that weakened both the strikes and the Chartist movement.

The rejection of the Charter saw the government seize the initiative with mass arrests of Chartist activists across the country. The repression was particularly savage in Wales, where there was anger at the arrest of the popular Chartist leader Harry Vincent. In November 1839, armed Chartists marched to Newport in an attempt to free Vincent but were routed by government troops who killed or wounded at least 20 Chartists. The leaders of the Newport rising were arrested and sentenced to transportation for life.

A second petition was presented to Parliament on 2 May 1842, this time with over 3.5 million signatures, about one third of the adult male population. The petition was again rejected by the House of Commons with only 49 MPs voting in favour of it. Edinburgh's Whig MP, T B Macaulay, contemptuously dismissed the petition arguing that universal suffrage was "utterly incompatible with the very existence of civilisation" because it would result in the confiscation of the property of the rich.[82]

Rejection of the second petition caused further anger and frustration which was fuelled by widespread economic distress across Britain. This led to the first General Strike in British history. It was not called by the Chartist leadership but started in the north west of England as a protest against wage cuts and quickly spread to Scotland. Glasgow masons went on strike for six weeks in June and July and in August 10,000 Lanarkshire coal and ironstone miners struck in opposition to wage cuts.[83] The strike spread to Ayrshire and the Lothians. In Dunfermline weavers were also out on strike over wage cuts.

In Dundee local Chartist leaders supported the strikes and linked them to demands for the Charter. Representatives from 51 of the town's textile mills voted in favour of a national strike for the Charter, which was supported the next day by a mass meeting of over 8,000 workers on Magdalene green. The strike began on 22 August and the following day some of the strikers marched to Forfar to persuade workers there to join the strike. However, the authorities were well prepared and the Riot Act was read before the police and special constables dispersed the strikers. Mass arrests followed, including one of the leaders, John Duncan.

By 1848 Britain was in the grip of an economic downturn which caused widespread unemployment and poverty. In Glasgow on 6 March, hundreds of unemployed met on Glasgow Green to protest at the failure of the city council to provide soup kitchens. The angry crowd then marched towards the city centre looting food shops and a gun shop. Chartist slogans were shouted and cries of "Bread or Revolution" and "Vive la Republique" could be heard in the crowd.[84] The rioting continued in the Bridgeton area of the city the next day before being ruthlessly suppressed by police and the military. It was Wednesday before an uneasy calm descended on the city.

Sixty four people were arrested during the riots, including Peter McDouall, who had arrived in Glasgow to undertake a speaking tour of Scotland. The sentences were harsh and disproportionate with two men, John Crossan and George Smith, being sentenced to 18 years' transportation. Nine others got 10 years' transportation, two got seven years' and 19 got two years'.[85] This fed the growing unrest in the city.

The revolutions that swept across Europe in 1848 gave a much needed boost to the Chartist movement. In April the Chartist leader Ernest Jones, a friend of Karl Marx, addressed huge rallies in Edinburgh, Paisley and Glasgow. At a meeting one evening, Jones boldly declared that he "gloried in being considered a physical force Chartist". He also described Parliament as a "treasonable assembly", adding that they should never again petition Parliament.[86] The arguments over moral versus physical force continued to rage within the Chartist movement. The moral force Chartists prevailed and the movement once again threw itself into the dead hand of petitioning. In April, thousands of Chartists assembled on Kennington Common in London to march to Parliament and present a petition. They were faced by thousands of police and troops but the meeting was in fact dispersed by a rain storm. Parliament duly rejected the petition for a third time, effectively marking the end of Chartism as a mass movement.

The role of women in the Chartist Revolt

The role of women in the Chartist movement has, until fairly recently, been overlooked by many historians, but in fact women played a significant role. Female Chartist Associations were set up all across Britain, 23 of them in Scotland.[87] Women were actively involved in a range of activities including raising money, organising socials, petitioning and so on. More importantly they were involved in the more militant activities such as the strikes of 1842 and 1848 as well as, for example, the Glasgow food riots in 1848. A trawl through the Chartist press reveals many speeches by female Chartists, although their comments often went unreported. Frustratingly, they were often referred to in the press as just 'Miss or Mrs', making identification and further research difficult.

One such woman was Mrs Collie, who spoke at two meetings called by the Female Chartists of Dunfermline in early November 1840. She condemned "a vile and miscreant government" for imprisoning the Chartist leaders and defiantly declared "the victims of oppression are awake… liberty yet shall reign triumphant".[88]

Later that month she led a march in Dunfermline in support of physical force Chartism and, at a meeting of over 1,500, along with Peter McDouall condemned the "Morrisonians".[89] Thomas Morrison was a well-known Fife moral force Chartist and supporter of Patrick Brewster, who made a speech condemning those who advocated physical force. Morrison declared that "the mad O'Connor" (Fergus O'Connor), Bronterre O'Brien and McDouall "spread doctrines subversive of all social order".[90]

One of the most remarkable speeches by any Chartist (male or female) was by 18-year-old Agnes Lennox, Chairwoman of the Gorbals Female Universal Suffrage Association, at its inaugural meeting in November 1839. Hamish Fraser correctly argues that she had a "sharp awareness of class division".[91] It is worth looking at her speech in some detail. She argued that "society is divided into certain classes" and that the working class "are a class upon which all the others depend and without which they would not exist as a state or society". She pointed out that it was the working class who "produce those necessities of life without which the upper classes could not have a being". She considered "the working class as the most useful, the most honourable of all. They could exist as a state, as a society without the others" adding "they are the basement... the pillars on which rests the whole social fabric". She had a warning for the government that the working class may one day "take by violence what they have been unable to obtain by prayer and remonstrance". She reminded the audience that the Reform Bill had not delivered any benefits to the working class and that they "cared little for a government which they are taxed to support, without receiving any benefit in return". She finished off with a rallying cry of "Equal rights and equal laws, the People, and the people's cause".[92]

Lennox was condemned by the Tory press, often in the most sexist manner. Under the headline 'Female Effrontery', the *Glasgow Constitutional* described her as a "brazen-faced jade" and "Miss Impudence". It concluded by saying, "were we her mother ... we would respond with the taws"![93] She was not in any way intimidated by the attacks on her and, in an unapologetic letter to the *Scottish Patriot*, invited Baillie James Campbell, who had argued that "she should be horsewhipped", to a meeting of the Gorbals Female Suffrage Association.[94]

Her sharp class analysis of the workplace and society and her use of the term "working class" were unusual in speeches of even the most militant Chartists. What is even more remarkable is that it was given by an 18-year-old parlour maid speaking nearly 10 years before the publication of the *Communist Manifesto*.

It is also worth highlighting the work of Helen McFarlane from Paisley. More information is now available on her due to the work of *BBC Scotland* researcher Louise Yeoman and McFarlane's biographer, the left-wing journalist David Black.[95] McFarlane was born in Barrhead near Glasgow to a wealthy family. Her father owned a calico printing works and broke a strike by calling in troops at the red dyeing mill he owned in Campsie. After the failure of the Chartist agitation in 1848, Fergus O'Connor argued that the Charter needed to be less radical to win wider support. Radical leaders such as Julian

Harney disagreed; he resigned as editor of the *Northern Star* and launched a new, more radical weekly, the *Red Republican*. Prior to this, in 1849, he had launched a new monthly, the *Democratic Review of British Politics, History and Literature*.

McFarlane was in Vienna during the 1848 Revolutions and was clearly inspired by the revolts that spread across Europe. Soon after, she returned to Britain and threw herself into the most militant section of the Chartist movement, writing for Harney's *Democratic Review* and the *Red Republican*. She was the first translator of the *Communist Manifesto*, which appeared in the *Red Republican* in November 1850.[96] In another article she argued that "Chartism in 1850—is the cause of the producers, and the battle of this one enslaved class is the battle we fight, but it must be fought under the Red Flag, for that is the symbol of the new Epoch, the banner of the Future".[97] Later in the year, in another stirring piece, she stated "We will have a social revolution or none at all. Justice for all, or justice for none. Political power is the means—the reign of Equality, Liberty and Fraternity, is the end".[98]

McFarlane broke from Harney after a disagreement with him and his wife at a Hogmanay party in 1850 attended by Marx and Engels. In a letter to Engels, an angry Marx commented that Harney had broken with McFarlane, "the only collaborator on his spouting rag who had original ideas—a rare bird, on his paper...".[99] McFarlane married Francis Proust, an exiled French revolutionary, but he died on the ship as they sailed for a new life in South Africa. On her return from South Africa in 1854, she met Reverend John Wilkinson, whom she married in 1856, somewhat ironic given her biting criticisms of the Anglican Church.[100]

It is clear that women made a significant contribution to the Chartist movement despite having to overcome formidable obstacles, not least because of the dominant discriminatory ideas of the time in relation to women. Even those male Chartists who welcomed the involvement of women in the movement often did so in the most patronising and sexist way. At the meeting to announce the intention to set up the

Gorbals Female Suffrage Association, one of the male speakers apologised for "the necessity that exists for drawing the female mind from employments more congenial to the tastes and more befitting the close and retiring habits of the women of this country, than the area of politics".[101] Women have always played a significant role in working class struggle but all too often their contributions have been ignored or downplayed.

The lessons of the Chartist Revolt

The Chartist movement was a truly national movement that swept across the British state. The movement in Scotland was no different from the rest of the country in that there were constant debates and disagreements over tactics. The fundamental divide was between moderates and militants. The best elements of the movement understood the need to harness the radical potential of an increasingly militant working class. Moderates on the other hand downplayed class militancy and sought to make alliances with the middle class to persuade the government of the need for reform. The best example of this was Joseph Sturge's Complete Suffrage Union, which sought to distance itself from the militancy of Chartism and favoured 'class unity' to achieve reform.

Chartism may have failed in its immediate goals, but what is undeniable is that it was a major challenge to the British state which had real revolutionary potential. One of the weaknesses of the Chartist movement was that the leadership was drawn mainly from the radical gentlemen of the middle class who at decisive moments, notably the strikes and demonstrations in 1842 and 1848, did not provide the necessary militant leadership that would have taken the struggle in a potentially more revolutionary direction. The vanguard of the movement was the weavers and skilled artisans who had a strong radical tradition. However, all but the most militant of the Chartist leaders failed to link the strikes and riots caused by economic distress with the demands of the Charter, notably in 1842 and 1848. MacDouall was one of the few Chartist leaders who understood that capitalism had led to the creation of a working class that could play a key role in the struggle. He actively encouraged Chartists to join trade unions and sought to harness the potential power of the working class by linking the economic demands of the workplace with the demands of the Charter. When this was done in 1842, the strikes were more widespread and better supported. In Dundee, for example, where 51 textile mills voted to strike, local Chartist leaders not only supported the strikes but linked them to the demands of the Chartists.

However, the lack of a class analysis led many Chartist leaders to narrowly focus the struggle on the aristocracy and landed class. Had they widened the focus of the struggle to also oppose the new capitalist class, they could have drawn hundreds of thousands more workers in the rapidly developing factory system into the fight.

Marx argued that the core demand of Chartism, universal suffrage, "is the equivalent of political power for the working class" and that "its inevitable result, here, is the political supremacy of the working class."[102] Marx's critics have argued that universal suffrage has not led to political supremacy for the working class in Britain or any country. However, as Paul Foot has argued, Marx's view on universal suffrage should not be seen as an isolated demand. "It was rooted in the mass meetings, strikes, demonstrations and uprisings which demanded not just the vote but also, once the vote was granted, a redistribution of wealth."[103]

Perhaps the best summing up of the Chartist revolt comes from Trotsky, who argued that "The era of Chartism is immortal in that over the course of a decade it gives us in condensed and diagrammatic form the whole gamut of proletarian struggle—from petitions in Parliament to armed insurrection".[104]

Dispossession, clearance and resistance

At the top of Ben Bhraggie overlooking the picturesque village of Golspie stands an imposing statue of the Duke of Sutherland. Known locally as 'Mannie' the statue is hugely controversial due to the Duke's role in the Sutherland clearances, widely regarded as the most extensive and brutal episode of the Highland Clearances.[105] For many years there has been a campaign to remove the statue and have it replaced by a Celtic cross. In 1994 there was an attempt to blow it up and it has been attacked with hammers and chisels on many occasions by activists determined to remove or damage it.

The debate surrounding the statue mirrors the debate started by Black Lives Matter (BLM) activists who hauled down the statues of slave owners and slave traders here and in the USA. The campaign to have the Sutherland statue removed has been given fresh impetus by the BLM movement. The on-going controversy surrounding the statue illustrates the strength of feeling about the Highland Clearances that has persisted to the present day. So, what were the Clearances and why is the debate surrounding them still so passionate?

The Highland Clearances—the forced removal of peasants from the land—are often thought of as taking place over the hundred years between 1760 and 1860. However, the clearances continued up until the 1880s, culminating in the Crofters War that resulted in legislation which for the first time gave crofters legal entitlement to land.

Since the publication of John Prebble's *The Highland Clearances* in 1963, there have been many books and articles written on the subject. One of the most important is Tom Devine's *The Scottish Clearances: A History of the Dispossessed*, which looks at the reasons for the clearances and the similarities and differences between the Highlands and the Lowlands.[106] It is important to recognise, as Devine shows, that the Scottish Clearances did not start in the Highlands, as commonly believed, but in the border areas of Scotland and were well underway by the early 1700s.[107] Some of the time frame for the Clearances falls outside the period this chapter covers, but, in the interests of providing a fuller analysis, they will be covered here. There is no doubt that the Clearances in the Highlands were often more convulsive and violent and as such have generated more impassioned debate.

It is difficult to estimate the numbers of people displaced by the Clearances across the whole of Scotland, but it runs into tens of thousands. Sometimes this was done by landlords simply not renewing the lease or by raising rents rather than physical coercion. However, mass evictions were common and many landlords, particularly in Highland areas, did not hesitate to use force. Often the tenants' homes were burned down after eviction to prevent them returning at some future time. Initially landlords favoured compulsory resettlement of the people in coastal areas with a view to developing fishing and kelp production to further boost their profits. When this did not prove to be as profitable as they had anticipated, most of them favoured forced emigration to Australia, the USA and especially Canada. Thousands died on these "coffin ships" from diseases such as cholera and typhus or when the ships sank in storms.[108] Many thousands more migrated to the rapidly expanding cities of Aberdeen, Dundee, Edinburgh and Glasgow in search of work and a better life. Ironically, thousands of Highlanders were recruited into military battalions and used as the shock troops of the British Empire.

It was the rapid development of capitalism, first in England and later in Scotland, that provided the impetus for the Clearances. For landlords, the rationale that underpinned them was the free market ideas of Adam Smith and the Malthusian doctrine of 'overpopulation' in the Highland region. They realised that they could boost their profits by clearing tenants, who had no legal rights to the land, and replacing them with huge sheep farms that could supply the demand for mutton and wool in the rapidly expanding cities in the south. Later, Clearances in some parts of the Highlands were carried out to make way for the introduction of herds of deer to develop hunting estates for the aristocracy.

Marx argues that the Highland Clearances—"the expropriation of the peasants from the land"—was an act of "reckless terrorism" that was "distinguished by its systematic character, by the magnitude of the scale on which it is carried out at one blow".[109] He had no doubt that they were carried out by a ruthless capitalist landowning class that was determined to increase profits with no regard for the human consequences.

It is also true that underpinning the Highland Clearances were a number of racist stereotypes and tropes. William Young, a factor on the Sutherland estate, was responsible for organising the Clearances between 1807 and 1821. He "described the common people as a set of savages, worse than American Indians".[110] Furthermore, Sir Charles Trevelyan, a Treasury official, favoured mass emigration from the Highlands by coercion if necessary. He proposed a scheme for the emigration of 30,000-40,000 people from the Western Highlands and Islands. He wanted to rid the land of "the surviving Irish and Scotch Celts", which might allow the settlement of what he regarded as "racially superior people". He was enthusiastically supported by the *Scotsman* newspaper, which declared, "Collective emigration is, therefore, the removal of a diseased and damaged part of our population. It is a relief to the rest of the population to be rid of this part".[111]

It is sometimes argued that there was very little resistance to the Clearances and that the Highlanders in particular were passive victims who meekly accepted their fate. There were of course significant barriers to coordinating resistance, not least of which was the wide geographical spread of Highland communities and the difficult mountainous terrain. Recent research, however, has shown that, despite rural isolation, there was in fact considerable, courageous and determined resistance.

The Levellers' Revolt & the Ross-shire Insurrection

One of the earliest documented resistances to Clearance was the so-called Levellers' Revolt of 1724.[112] This was a major peasant revolt that took place in the border area of Galloway in protest at the spread of large scale sheep parks or holding areas. Armed gangs of small tenants and cottars roamed the countryside demolishing and "levelling" the walls and dykes used to enclose the sheep. The revolt involved large numbers of people, with groups of a thousand or more not uncommon. It was well organised; resistance was coordinated by local leaders or captains and their demands were published in manifestoes which were posted on church doors.

A contemporary report of the time noted, "Upwards of a 1,000 persons in the shire (Galloway) have their bread taken from them; they are pulling down the enclosures; they nail their manifesto to the door of the Sorbie Church, and when the laird orders the Bedell to tear it down, they tear down the laird's dyke, and the soldiers are helpless".[113] Such was the scale of the unrest that six troops of dragoons were brought from Edinburgh to quell the rebellion. By the end of the summer of 1824, the revolt had been suppressed and the leaders arrested and imprisoned.

As the great sheep farms spread northwards and more and more peasants were thrown off the land their families had occupied for generations, resistance to the Clearances grew. Highlanders referred to 1792 as 'Bliadhna Nan Caorach' (The Year of the Sheep). It was also the year of what became known as the Ross-shire Insurrection. Peasants led by Alexander Wallace, known locally as Big Wallace, were determined to resist the spread of sheep farms.[114] They rounded up 10,000 sheep and began to drive them southwards out of the counties of Ross and Sutherland. Local landlords, panicked by the upsurge in militancy, were aware that radical ideas and activity had increased in Scotland in the wake of the French Revolution and were determined to crush the resistance.

The insurrection was crushed by landlords supported by troops of the 42nd regiment. Authorisation to put down the revolt "to the last extremity" was given by Henry Dundas, who stated that the lower class of people had to learn "that they will not be suffered to continue such acts of violence with impunity".[115] Twelve prisoners were found guilty of sedition at the High Court in Inverness. Two of them were sentenced to seven years' transportation, two were banished from Scotland for life and the remainder imprisoned and fined. Hugh Mackenzie and

John Aird, who had been sentenced to transportation, escaped from prison and, despite a generous reward being offered for information leading to their recapture, were never betrayed.[116]

The Sutherland Clearances

The clearing of Sutherland took place between 1807 and 1821 and was among the most controversial. The driving force behind the evictions was not the Duke of Sutherland but his wife, the Duchess of Sutherland. It was the Duke's fortune that bankrolled his wife's effort to clear the estate with a view to "improvement" that would make the estate more profitable. The Clearances at Strathnaver in 1814 were carried out by one of her factors, Patrick Sellar. He was to directly benefit from the Clearance as he had acquired the land for sheep farming. So violent were the evictions, Sellar was indicted on charges of culpable homicide for the deaths of several highlanders. He stood trial in 1816 but was acquitted of all charges. Highland oral tradition has ensured that his name and deeds have been handed down over the generations and he is widely regarded as one of the most ruthless participants in the Highland Clearances, despite efforts by generations of family to rehabilitate his name. A contemporary poem of the time illustrates the bitterness and anger felt towards Sellar:

> When death comes upon you,
> You will not be placed in the ground,
> But your dung-like carcase will be spread,
> Like manure on a field's surface.[117]

Marx was absolutely scathing about the Sutherland Clearances and the role of the Duchess of Sutherland in particular. He argued that: "The history of the wealth of the Sutherland family is the history of the ruin and of the expropriation of the Scotch-Gaelic population from its native soil."[118] He condemned the hypocrisy of the Duchess for supporting the abolition of the slave trade while at the same time organising the ruthless expulsion of up to 15,000 peasants from the Sutherland estate.[119]

One of the most interesting aspects of the Highland Clearances was the leading role that women played in resisting them. There is well documented evidence of spirited and determined resistance to evictions by women in Arichonan in 1848 and in many other areas.[120] The women typically lined up in rows in front of the men and, armed with rocks and sticks, would physically resist attempts by the police and troops to evict them. Sometimes they were successful and managed to delay if not stop the clearance. But they paid a heavy price for this heroic resistance. Many were arrested and imprisoned and many more were seriously injured by troops who did not hesitate to use rifle butts and bayonets on them.

The Famine Revolt 1846

The misery and suffering of the Highlanders was compounded by famine which swept across the Highlands in 1846 when the potato crop failed. This provoked a remarkable and little-known rebellion in the coastal towns and villages of North East Scotland, brought vividly to life by James Hunter in his book *Insurrection, Scotland's Famine Winter*.[121] Many of the people involved in the disturbances had been cleared from interior Highland areas to coastal locations. They were angered by the decision of local landlords to export grain to more profitable southern markets at a time of famine, which also led to an increase in the price of oatmeal that they could not afford. Evidence suggests that the resistance was well organised and coordinated by secret committees and local leaders such as James Falconer, who played a leading role in the Burghead riots near Elgin.[122] They blockaded harbours, seized grain on its way to the ports and were confronted by the military on several occasions.

In February 1847 in the Highland capital of Inverness, "control of Inverness's streets was surrendered to well organised groups of people who set up and manned a series of roadblocks all around the town".[123] Carts carrying grain thought to be heading to

Inverness harbour were turned back. The blockade was in force for over a week. The Lord Provost of Inverness informed Lord Advocate Andrew Rutherfurd that Inverness was experiencing "violence and disturbance... of a very alarming nature". Such was the scale of the unrest that the *Economist* stated that northern Scotland was "nearly in a state of insurrection".[124]

Ultimately, the disturbances were suppressed by the use of troops, but not before concessions were won from the landowners and the authorities. Some grain shipments were halted and the price of oatmeal reduced. Three men from Hopeman near Elgin—Daniel Sutherland, John Young and John Mann—were charged with mobbing, rioting and assault for their part in the Burghead riot. They were found guilty at the High Court in Edinburgh and given brutal sentences of seven years' transportation. The *Northern Star* summed up the feelings of many Highlanders, describing the verdict as an "infernal mockery of justice".[125]

Could resistance to the Clearances have been more effective?

One of the main weaknesses in the resistance to the Clearances was that they were not linked to wider political demands until the Crofters War in the 1880s. If the struggle to resist clearance and dispossession in the Highlands had been linked to the Chartist movement, it may have been more successful. In November 1840, Julian Harney, one of the most militant Chartist leaders, embarked on a speaking tour of North East Scotland. He spoke at well attended meetings in Aberdeen and Inverness as well as many smaller towns and meetings. Harney emphasised the importance of the collective organisation of the working class linked to political demands, which he regarded as an irresistible force.

His tour gave impetus to the setting up of a Chartist network across the region.[126] There is no doubt that some of those involved in the revolt in the towns and villages of North East Scotland in 1846 had attended Chartist meetings. James Hunter argues with some justification that one of the most militant local leaders of the Burghead riots, James Falconer, had links to Chartism and may have been influenced by Harney's ideas.[127]

The Crofters' Revolt

Is Treasa nu Tighearni
The People are stronger than the Lord
(motto of the Highland Land League)

By the 1880s, although mass evictions had ended, there was still simmering discontent in Scotland's Highlands and Islands, particularly among the crofting community. The crofters had no security of tenure and could be evicted at the whim of the landlord. They were angered at annual rent rises and frustrated that they were not allowed to increase the size of their small land holdings.

These underlying tensions boiled to the surface on the island of Skye in April 1882. The catalyst for the unrest was a dispute over grazing rights. The landlord, Lord McDonald, refused to allow crofters access to the common grazing lands they had had access to for generations. The crofters withheld their rents in protest, which led to the landlord issuing notices for eviction. This culminated in what became known as the Battle of the Braes, where 500 crofters resisted the attempts of the factor and about 50 police officers to collect rent arrears or evict them. By the end of 1882, similar action was taken by crofters in Glendale in Skye. The government moved quickly to quell the dissent and a gunboat was sent to Skye to help with the arrest of three crofters. Another gunboat carrying marines was sent in 1884 to help keep order.[128]

The authorities had hoped to contain the disturbances in Skye but over the next few years, they spread across the Highlands and Islands. Another gunboat was sent to Tiree and, in Lewis in 1887, the authorities sent 500 marines to restore order after crofters invaded sheep farms and slaughtered deer and other livestock.

The crofters were not afraid to use the most militant tactics. As well as rent strikes, there were violent confrontations with police. They destroyed farm fences, occupied old lands now used as sheep farms or hunting estates and killed livestock. In November 1887 in Lewis, up to 1,000 crofters invaded a hunting estate and slaughtered about 200 deer in an attempt to drive them into the sea. The authorities responded by sending in 500 marines.[129]

One of the most significant features of the Crofters Revolt was that for the first time the resistance was linked to a successful political campaign. The spearhead of the political campaign was the Highland Land Law Reform Association (HLLRA), later to become the Highland Land League. It was set up in the 1880s and had strong and influential supporters in urban areas such as Glasgow, Edinburgh and London. After an inaugural meeting in Fraserburgh in 1883, local branches of the HLLRA were set up across the Highlands and Islands. Its three main aims were the redistribution of land, fair rents and security of tenure. The HLLRA was influenced by the Irish Land League, which had some years earlier managed to force concessions from the British Government using tactics such as rent strikes.[130]

In an effort to contain the unrest and appease the crofters, the government set up a Royal Commission in 1883, headed by Lord Napier, to look into their grievances. The Napier Commission collected evidence throughout crofting areas in 1883 and 1884, but, despite reducing rents by an average of 30 percent and arrears by almost 60 percent, the unrest continued.[131]

There was considerable sympathy and public support for the crofters. Books such as Donald McLeod's *Gloomy Memories of the Highlands of Scotland* and Alexander Mackenzie's *History of the Highland Clearances* published in the early 1880s painted a vivid and disturbing picture of the abuse of landlord power and the suffering of the Highland people. For some years, eye witness accounts of some of the most brutal clearances by journalists such as Donald Ross and Hugh Miller appeared in the Victorian newspapers. It is also important to recognise the role that John Murdoch's journal *The Highlander* played in publicising Highlanders' grievances. The tide was turning against landlord oppression in the Highlands and Islands.[132]

By the time of the 1885 General Election, the franchise had been extended allowing more crofters to vote. The HLLRA decided to seize the moment and stood candidates in some constituencies in the Highlands and Islands. Five crofter MPs were elected, including the radical Dr Gavin Clark. He had been a member of the International Working Men's Association and was a friend of Keir Hardie, founder of the Labour Party. His opponents tried to discredit him by branding him a "socialist", "sabbath breaker" and a man who put "popery on an equality with Protestantism". He was also described as a friend of Britain's enemies due to his anti-imperialist views.[133] The election of Crofter Party MPs further increased pressure on the government to solve the Highland problem.[134]

This increasing pressure and the Napier Commission Report led to the passing of the Crofters Act in 1886. Its main provisions were security of tenure for crofters providing their rents were paid, fair rents fixed by Land Courts, and compensation for improvements for crofters who gave up their croft.[135] This was a significant step forward as it was never again possible for landlords to arbitrarily evict tenants as they had done during the Clearances. For the first time in Britain, the government had recognised in law that ordinary people had land rights.

To a certain extent it was a historic victory for the protest movement. However, it is important to set it in its proper context. The Act did nothing to protect crofters with land holdings valued between £6 and £30 or cottars, who held tiny plots of land and hired out their services as land labourers.[136] Furthermore, the new law did not redistribute the land and allowed the crofters very little additional land. The more radical crofters had sought the "abolition of landlordism", but, crucially, the Act left the huge Highland estates under the control and ownership of the landlords.

This remains the case today. The Green Party MSP Andy Wightman has highlighted the fact that about half of Scotland's rural land is owned by 432 landlords. The biggest landowner in Scotland is the Danish tycoon Anders Holch Povlsen, who owns over 220,000 acres across 12 estates in the Sutherland and Grampian mountains. He is closely followed by the Duke of Buccleuch, who owns 200,000 acres. Wightman estimates that ownership of 750,000 acres of the country is held in overseas tax havens.[137]

The Scottish government has made some minor changes to land law, which have led to an increase in community ownership. However, land rights and access to lands deemed private property are still very much restricted in Scotland. Activists can learn the lessons of the past by adopting some of the more militant tactics—such as land occupations and rent strikes—used in the Crofters' Revolt to force the issue of land ownership and land rights further up the political agenda.

The Crofters' Revolt effectively signalled the end of the Highland Clearances. Overall, they were undoubtedly a political defeat but there was clearly significant resistance to the capitalist class. Neil Davidson argues that they were unquestionably a "historical crime" carried out by a rapacious and "triumphant capitalist class" with a "disregard for human life". They were not, he points out, "inevitable" in the sense that the Highlands were peripheral to the profitability and success of capitalism across Britain. Therefore, they were not a consequence of the transition to capitalism but rather of its "established laws of motion".[138]

Continuing Controversy and Debate

Over 140 years have passed since the end of the Clearances in Scotland and yet those carried out in the Highlands in particular still generate controversial debate. Some writers suggest the Highland Clearances are comparable to events such as The Great Hunger (An Gorta Mór) in Ireland in the 1840s, African slavery, the treatment of Native Americans and the Holocaust carried out by the Nazis against the Jews in the 1930s and 1940s. All of these are completely erroneous and fallacious comparisons.

Young argues that "what was happening in the Highlands can be characterised as genocide".[139] David Craig also talks about the "genocide" of the Highland people and suggests that the mass evictions were like "the shipping-off of the Polish and other Jews in cattle trucks".[140] Similarly, Ian Grimble compares the activities of Sutherland factor Patrick Sellar to the Nazi Heydrich, who was responsible for genocidal crimes against Jews in Prague in the Second World War.[141] However, the "rhetoric of genocide.....is profoundly inappropriate".[142] This is to misunderstand the true nature and scale of the Holocaust and belittle its historic significance as the worst genocidal event in human history. What defined the Holocaust was its sheer industrial scale resulting in the brutal extermination of six million Jews. The Highland Clearances were certainly expansive, caused huge suffering and involved the forced removal of thousands of people, but they are in no way comparable to the Holocaust.

By contrast, Michael Fry argues that the Clearances have been greatly exaggerated and that Scottish landowners have been demonised unfairly. For Fry, the infamous Sutherland Clearances were an attempt at improvement for the mutual benefit of landowners and the people.[143] Fry's views created a storm of protest, with some nationalists quick to label him a "Clearance denier".[144]

Conclusion

One of the consequences of Scotland's Clearances was that thousands of people from rural areas migrated to rapidly expanding cities such as Dundee, Edinburgh and Glasgow.[145] There they swelled the ranks of the growing industrial proletariat and took part in strikes and struggles in the textile mills and factories. They were also involved in the great Chartist Revolt.

By the mid-1800s, Scotland's militant radical tradition had been strengthened. Trotsky's view of the Chartist movement can also sum up the making of the working class over the whole period from the Calton Weavers strike in 1789 to the end of the Chartist revolt in 1850. In Scotland, the transition from feudalism to capitalism was faster than in any other country in Europe and was characterised by rapid urbanisation and industrialisation. It was a truly tumultuous period in which an emerging, militant and combative working class was engaged in a relentless on-going struggle against the brutal capitalist system. It included protests, demonstrations, riots, strikes and showed revolutionary intent with attempted insurrections during the 1820 Radical Rising and the Chartist revolt. Working class agitation and struggle was both economic and political in that workers fought not only for better wages and working conditions but also for the extension of the franchise. They not only challenged the bosses but also the legal system and the state.

It is also true that working class agitation and struggle in Scotland during this period should not be seen in isolation from that of the working class in the rest of Britain. Workers north and south of the border were often engaged in common struggles, such as during the great Chartist Revolt. Furthermore, the wider experience of political struggles across Europe, in particular the French Revolution and the 1848 Revolutions, without doubt influenced the radicalism within the Scottish working class. It was the government's contemptuous dismissal of mass petitioning for parliamentary reform between 1790 and 1820 and again during the Chartist revolt that led to some of the most militant elements of the working class being attracted to insurrectionism. However, the failure and brutal suppression of both the 1820 Rising and the Newport Rising in 1839 showed the limitations of this strategy.

As the trade union movement continued to develop, increasing numbers of workers were involved in strikes and struggles against ruthless employers. Engels argued that "as schools of war, the unions are unexcelled"[146] in that workers draw confidence from victories but even in defeat can glimpse their potential power. He argued that the more the factory system develops, "the more the working men employed in it participate in the labour movement; the sharper the opposition between working men and capitalists, the clearer the proletarian consciousness in the working men".[147] In this respect, capitalism sows the seeds of its own destruction. The global working class continues to grow, now making up over 52 percent of total employment worldwide.[148] It is the organised working class that has the collective power to overthrow the capitalist system. The Scottish working class will play its part.

Chapter 4

Red Clydeside

Dave Sherry

Red Clydeside is one of the high points of British and European class struggle. Emerging around 1910 out of a wave of strike action known as the Great Unrest, it flourished as part of the Europe-wide revolt against the First World War.

From the early 18th century, Glasgow's merchants had made vast fortunes from slavery and colonialism, laying the basis for its emergence as the 'Second City' of the empire and a key arsenal for the British state. Together with its European rivals, it brought about the slaughter that began in 1914. Against this, Clydeside saw a rising tide of anti-war agitation, strikes and demonstrations for peace and international solidarity that peaked in 1919—the worst year for the British ruling class since Chartism. Having survived such an existential crisis, their modern counterparts want to eradicate all collective memory of that working class insurgency. That's why alongside the Act of Union, Red Clydeside is the period of Scottish history that is most contested, by those who dismiss it as left-wing mythology and by others who would reduce it to a footnote in the rise of Labourism and municipal socialism.[1]

At the start of the 18th century, Scotland was among the most backward of European nations. Nine out of ten Scots lived in the countryside. Agriculture was primitive, manufacturing almost non-existent. Yet this small, poverty stricken society, perched on the rim of European civilisation, was soon transformed. Neither in Europe nor the rest of the world was the development of industry so rapid or far reaching. England experienced its bourgeois revolution in the 17th Century. In Scotland, the break with feudalism came later and sharper. According to historian Rosalind Mitchison, "Scotland packed into about thirty years of crowded development between 1750-1780 economic growth that in England had spread itself over two centuries".[2]

The rapid urbanisation that followed was unprecedented in Europe and not seen again on such a scale until the forced industrialisation of Russia following Stalin's Five Year Plan of 1928. As a result of this 'Scottish Great Leap Forward',[3] its economy rose to equal and briefly surpass that of England. This was dependent on a massive shift in population towards the central belt, much of it due to the Clearances, the revolution in Scottish agriculture and the Irish Famine.

It was most acute in the Clyde Valley, forging the character and temper of its working class. As Trotsky explained in 1925, "Scotland set out on the road of capitalism later than England; the sharper break in the life of the masses causes a sharper break in political reaction".[4]

Scotland, socialism and mythology

By 1900, Scotland was one of the most advanced economies anywhere, yet trade union and political organisation lagged behind. When the New Unionism exploded in Britain in the late 1880s organising vast numbers of unskilled workers, Clydeside missed out relative to other industrial centres, with trade unionism largely confined to skilled craft workers and mining.

In 1902, when John Maclean joined the Marxist Social Democratic Federation (SDF), its Scottish membership was less than 200, proportionately much less than in England. The Liberal Party dominated electoral politics in Scotland until the end of the First World War. Clydeside was hostile terrain for reformist socialists let alone Marxists. When Keir Hardie first stood as a Labour candidate in mid-Lanark, the mining district where he was born, he polled only 600 votes.[5] To win a parliamentary seat he had to fight West Ham in London's docklands, where the New Unionism had made a far bigger impact. In 1910, the last election before the war, Labour's share of the vote in Scotland was only half its percentage share in Britain.

Average wages and union membership were lower than in England, a big factor in the American Singer Company building its sewing machine factory at Clydebank. Scottish bosses held an advantage they meant to keep by holding the unions in check.

Clydeside before the First World War

Britain's empire spanned the globe. With Herbert Asquith's Liberals re-elected in 1910, political stability seemed assured. But below the surface trouble was brewing. The causes of the Great Unrest were easy to identify. Union membership had trebled since 1890 but wages had fallen by an average of ten percent. Amid spectacular wealth, the great majority of the population experienced grim poverty and brutal exploitation.Over the next four years, strikes engulfed mainland Britain and Ireland, coinciding with the rise of the women's suffrage movement and the Irish Home Rule crisis. In 1913, the military high command and the Tory Unionist opposition threatened mutiny and civil war to thwart Home Rule. The Great Unrest began with strikes, first in the ports, then on the railways and in the mines. As it spread it involved more and more unskilled and previously unorganised workers, including large numbers of women.

Foreign competition forced two big changes on Clydeside. The first was rationalisation and the mechanisation of production. Women and unskilled men fought against the speed-up associated with assembly line production. The best-known example was the Singer strike of 1911. Its assembly lines employed 12,000 mostly unskilled workers. A third of the workforce was female and pay had not risen with profits. Singer was anti–union but the workers organised anyway. A group of women downed tools and within days the whole factory was out. Young Socialist Labour Party (SLP) members, notably Arthur McManus and Tom Bell, influenced by syndicalist ideas, led the strike. There were many unsung heroines among the workforce. Militants like Jane Rae and Fanny Abbot are celebrated but most of the others are hidden from history. The strike was defeated, partly by management skulduggery, partly by inexperience. The SLP activists were victimised but their subsequent dispersal would see them play a key role in the emerging shop stewards movement.

The second big change was the merger of companies. For example, in the Vale of Leven—a series of small industrial villages dotted along the banks of the river Leven between Dumbarton and Loch Lomond—all of the textile dyeing firms combined to form the New Turkey Red Company. It employed 6,000 workers, mainly women. The merger brought a collective bargaining agreement for the male craft unions. Control over the women working in non-union, low-paid grades depended on the regular import of cheap female labour from Ireland. But this source dried up and soon the women grew more assertive, challenging the authority of male bosses and foremen. In 1911, the National Federation of Women Workers joined with the Amalgamated Society of Dyers. Matters came to a head when they brought out the unskilled male and female workers in a strike for a ten percent increase, a shorter week and overtime rates for all. Its victory signalled a growing militancy in 'the Vale'.

That year alone, union membership across Britain grew by 600,000. The following year saw 40 million strike days across Britain. The strikes raged on through 1913. The bitterest was in Dublin, where employers imposed a five-month lockout in a move to smash a new, militant trade unionism. The Dublin Lockout won massive solidarity in Britain. From September 1913 to January 1914, the labour movement on Clydeside devoted its energy to organising the largest collection for the Dublin Lockout outside of Dublin itself. As Joan Smith notes:

The ILP organised marches in support of the strikers and had Jim Larkin speak at a large Sunday night meeting. Govan Trades Council reported that collections were organised inside every local shipyard and factory, around the area's tenements and at Ibrox, the ground of the Protestant football club.[6]

Total War

The outbreak of war brought an abrupt end to the Great Unrest. It also shattered the European socialist movement as its leaders abandoned all pretence of internationalism. 1914 was the first 'total war' with all economic life subordinated to the war effort. Every belligerent state was forced to intervene on an unprecedented scale in its economy, rationing food, conscripting labour and commandeering key firms. Labour and union leaders called it "a war for democracy"—odd given that Britain was fighting in alliance with Tsarist Russia. Labour leader Ramsay MacDonald was a pacifist. When he queried the war, he was deposed by a patriotic trade union bureaucracy and replaced by Arthur Henderson, who was rewarded with a post in the coalition cabinet in 1915. The 'Marxist' leader of the British Socialist Party (BSP), Henry Hyndman, like the labour and union bosses, spoke on army recruitment platforms.

In Glasgow, John Maclean won the BSP branches to an anti-war position. He launched a local paper, *The Vanguard* and, like Lenin, argued it was an imperialist war. "It is our business as socialists to develop class patriotism, refusing to murder one another for a sordid world capitalism".[7] Harry McShane was a member of the BSP, a close comrade of Maclean's and a shop steward at Weir's of Cathcart. In his biography, Harry explained the response of the left in Glasgow:

> Our hopes for an international general strike were unfounded. Every section of the International supported its own country's war effort. Only a few revolutionaries

stood out—Connolly, Lenin's Bolsheviks and Rosa Luxemburg and Karl Liebknecht in Germany.[8]

The anti-war current was small, but it grew by relating to the social and economic issues affecting working class people. Armed with a Marxist understanding and committed to working class internationalism, Maclean rose to the challenge, organising Marxist classes and factory gate meetings.

Proportionately Scotland provided more volunteers than any other part of Britain. Of the 557,000 Scots who enlisted, 26.4 percent were killed, compared with an average death rate of 11.8 percent. Only Turkey and Serbia had a higher death rate. One estimate puts the figure at ten percent of the Scottish male population and 15 percent of all British war dead. Thirteen out of 14 were privates or non-commissioned officers from the working class.[9] A pamphlet by the National Service League conceded, "Want and hunger are, unfortunately, the invisible recruiting sergeants of a great portion of our army".[10] However these high levels of volunteering also underlined the negative aspect of Scottish national self-image as more strongly enmeshed with militarism and imperialism at that point, even than in England.

The leaders of the Women's Social and Political Union (WPSU), the main force in the campaign for votes for women, backed the war. In 1915, when engineering workers in Glasgow and miners in South Wales dared go on strike, the WPSU leaders denounced them as traitors. It was left to the anti-war minority of women, represented by Sylvia Pankhurst's East London Federation of the Suffragettes, to fight the cause. Helen Crawfurd was an anti-war suffragette in Glasgow. She joined the WSPU in 1910 and by 1914 had endured four prison terms and three hunger strikes, including forced feeding. She broke windows at army recruitment offices and fought physically to protect Emily Pankhurst from police brutality and arrest when she came to speak in Glasgow.[11]

But in 1914, she resigned from the WSPU over the pro-war stance of its leaders. Glasgow's abject poverty and dreadful slums drew her to socialism, and she joined the local Independent Labour Party (ILP). In 1915, she helped launch the Glasgow Women's Housing Association. As its first secretary, she rallied working class women behind the Glasgow Rent Strike and won large numbers of them to an anti-war position. In 1920, she led the left grouping that broke from the ILP to help form the new Communist Party of Great Britain.

Glasgow—the first flashpoint

By early 1915, people knew it would be a long, bloody war. The contrast between the sacrifices expected from working people and the profiteering of the employers created massive resentment. Before the war, the skilled engineers were seen as labour aristocrats. The drive to destroy their hard-won conditions pushed them into resistance. In doing so they led the working class into struggle. The first ever shop stewards' movement was born out of the first industrial revolt of the war. Glasgow had a high proportion of skilled workers in big workplaces with a tradition of shop floor organisation. Both Beardmore's Parkhead Forge and J G Weir's of Cathcart, two key arms factories, had functioning shop stewards' committees, which was unusual at the time.

It was an engineer's war as skilled workers were more useful to British capitalism in a munitions factory than in a trench. Crucial was the presence of small groups of socialists in the key factories. Many were revolutionaries, either as members or supporters of the British Socialist Party (BSP) or the Socialist Labour Party (SLP). A few belonged to the bigger Independent Labour Party (ILP). Many rejected parliamentary politics.

The Glasgow engineers' pay claim sparked the first strike of the war in February 1915. Sharp price rises and food shortages affected skilled workers as well as the poor. In engineering, the national pay agreement had expired and local branches of the Amalgamated Society of Engineers (ASE) were for an increase on their hourly rate. The arms firms made big profits. Behind them, ready to confront the munitions workers, stood the enormously expanded wartime state. Union officials had already agreed a 'no-strike' deal, so Maclean and the militants organised factory gate meetings to connect the anger over the wage claim to the bigger question of capitalism and the war. Lord Weir, who owned the Cathcart plant, was also the government's Scottish Director of Munitions. When he brought in American time-and-motion specialists to speed up production, 2,000 workers walked out.

Within days, over 10,000 workers from 26 factories were on strike for a two pence an hour rise. The strike was illegal, but the government was afraid to use the law. Instead, it tried divide and rule. Deprived of 'official' backing and branded 'traitors' by government and press, the strikers set up a Labour Withholding Committee to link stewards from the factories across the city. They stayed out for weeks against the advice of their officials. The committee was eventually forced to organise a united return to work and, although they had won only a limited increase, a new kind of organisation had emerged.

In the next few months, the employers moved to break the movement, this time using the new legislation against shop stewards. Some were threatened with the sack, some were fined and some were sentenced to three months in jail. The threat of widespread unofficial strike action saw all charges dropped and the stewards re-instated. In October 1915, this citywide stewards' organisation established itself as the Clyde Workers Committee (CWC). Three hundred delegates met every Saturday afternoon at the Templar's Hall in Ingram Street. Apart from its secretary, James Messer, and its treasurer, Davy Kirkwood, who were both ILP members, the majority of its leadership were revolutionary socialists.

John Maclean was not on the CWC but his standing meant that he and his close supporters were allowed to attend and participate. It is doubtful whether the Committee would have taken the lead in industrial matters had it not been for Maclean's efforts to show the war served only imperialist interests. The CWC was not an alternative to the unions. Nor was it set up in opposition to them. It originated in the refusal of union officialdom to put itself at the head of the grassroots militancy during wartime. The militants learned that if the Munitions Act was to be opposed root and branch, the workers themselves needed an organisation able to act independently of the official union structures.

As the first leaflet announcing the formation of the CWC in 1915 explained:

> Our purpose must not be misconstrued, we are out for unity and closer organisation of all trades in the industry, one Union being the ultimate aim. We will support the officials just so long as they rightly represent the workers, but we will act independently immediately they misrepresent them. Being composed of Delegates from every shop, and untrammelled by obsolete rule or law, we claim to represent the true feeling of the workers. We can act immediately according to the merits of the case and the desire of the rank and file."[12]
> The CWC pioneered the model militant workers across Britain would follow in the course of the war, laying the basis for the development of independent rank-and-file organisation.

The Glasgow Rent Strike of 1915

Agitation against rent increases accompanied the industrial unrest. During the war, house building ceased yet more and more workers flooded into Glasgow to work in the munitions factories. The landlords raised the rents and served eviction orders on tenants who couldn't pay.

Hardest hit were the elderly, the poor and soldiers' families. Local women formed tenants committees and campaigned against the landlords. Leading ILP members Helen Crawfurd, Jenny Stephens and Mary Barbour, alongside prominent ILP councillors like Andrew McBride and John Wheatley, were demanding rent controls. Maclean urged all the left groups and the CWC to unite on the issue. While the ILP leaders looked to parliament and the council chamber, Maclean argued the rent struggle raised the question of working class power. His distinctive contribution was decisive, helping the women connect the anger over rents with the unrest in the factories.

The first rent strike began in May. Govan rents were raised between 12 and 23 percent. It was a key shipyard and engineering district and in April the eviction of the family of a young soldier serving at the front led to an angry protest. "Mrs Barbour became the leader of a movement such as never has been seen before or since. Every method was used to win the local women and organise them for struggle. Notices were printed by the thousand and put up in windows; wherever you went you saw them—there was scarcely a window without one: WE ARE NOT PAYING INCREASED RENT."[13]

By September, over 20,000 Glasgow households were withholding rents and the strike was spreading across Scotland and to England and Wales. There were demonstrations against the Sheriff Officers and whenever they attempted an eviction, squads of local women stopped them in their tracks.

In October, a demonstration in St Enoch Square called on the Government to act. Reluctant to do so, it promised an enquiry. But on Wednesday 17 November, strike action brought a swift victory. Eighteen munitions workers were summoned to the Glasgow Sheriff court for non-payment. The landlords wanted their wages deducted at source.

Workers from five shipyards downed tools and marched to the Sherriff Court. They were joined by delegations from many other workplaces and by thousands of tenants. Helen Crawfurd, John Maclean and others addressed the huge crowds, insisting there could be no return to work until all of the charges were dropped. The protesters also agreed Maclean should telegram the Cabinet stating: "This demonstration of Clyde munitions workers requests the government to state not later than Saturday that it forbids any rent increase during the period of the war. Failing this, a general strike will be called on Monday,

November 22nd".[14] The Sheriff dismissed the cases and phoned the Cabinet. Scared of an illegal strike, the government agreed to introduce a Rent Restriction Act before the end of the year, tying rents all over Britain to their pre-war level.

According to Lesley Orr, "at the packed rent strike meetings Helen Crawfurd preached the socialist anti-war message".[15] Along with her friend and ILP comrade Agnes Dollan, she organised large public demonstrations on Glasgow Green to encourage working class women to oppose the war. The rent strike brought Maclean to a wider audience.

The Education Authority sacked him for his anti-war activities. Two months earlier he had been charged for a seditious speech at a street meeting. Because his case was heard the day after the rent victory, the authorities were keen not to make him a martyr.

The Sheriff passed a mild sentence for what was a treasonable offence: a £5 fine or five days jail. Maclean refused to pay and went to prison. Some pits in Lanarkshire struck in protest, particularly in the immigrant Irish and Lithuanian communities where Maclean had built a following. Vincas Mickevicius-Kapsukas, a friend of Lenin and president of the short-lived Lithuanian Soviet Republic in 1918/19, was active in Lanarkshire in 1915 and 1916 and did much to establish links between the Lithuanian immigrants and Maclean.[16]

Peter Petroff was a Russian socialist jailed after the 1905 Revolution. He arrived at Leith in 1911. Maclean befriended him and he joined the BSP. Eventually he moved to London to help in its anti-war wing. In autumn 1915, along with his German wife Irma, he returned to Glasgow to work as a second BSP organiser alongside Maclean. Through his knowledge of Trotsky and Lenin, Petroff brought an international dimension to the Clydeside left. Writing in *The Vanguard* about the Zimmerwald Conference of anti-war socialists just held in Switzerland, he highlighted Lenin's call for a new International and this had a big impact on Maclean.

*Tenants picket the Sherriff
officers during the rent
strike in 1915*

The limitations of trade unionism

Maclean sensed that the rent strike raised the prospect of a political strike against the war. The ILP opposed him but on the CWC they were a small minority. The majority of its members came from the small groups to its left and while most of them were anti-war, unfortunately, as Maclean said, "they were inclined to leave their politics at the factory gate".[17] Maclean worked with the CWC but refused to subordinate his socialist politics to trade unionism. Harry McShane recalls that CWC President Willie Gallacher in particular annoyed Maclean.

"He came to speak at Bath Street, where our meetings were at the centre of the anti-war fight. He didn't mention the war. John argued, 'how could any man calling himself a socialist speak at a meeting and not refer to the war?'"[18] Although the ILP presence on the CWC remained small, revolutionaries like Gallacher failed to build an effective alternative to it, with devastating consequences.

German industrial superiority meant British troops were being killed for lack of weaponry. This 'shell scandal' led to the fall of the Liberal Government in May 1915. Prime Minister Asquith was forced into a national coalition with the Tories and Labour. Lloyd George was put in charge of munitions and he embarked on a policy of 'Dilution'—whereby work previously done only by skilled workers could be carried out by semi and unskilled workers in the engineering factories in order to increase production. This became the key battleground.

Contrary to some misleading accounts, the CWC were not opposed to the idea of dilution. They favoured it, as Maclean had done before the war, seeing it as a way of breaking down sectionalism between skilled and unskilled workers. The CWC decided it would accept dilution but only in return for nationalisation and workers' control, the two key principles being: (1) wages should not be determined by gender, previous training or experience but solely by the work performed, and; (2) a workers' committee in each plant should have the power to ensure all agreements were honoured.

Maclean adopted a more offensive position. Previously he'd argued the main engineering union (the Amalgamated Society of Engineers, ASE) should embrace dilution but in wartime he opposed it because it was about more arms production.

He told Gallacher, "It's a contradiction to oppose the war while negotiating with the Government about how quickly and cheaply weapons for the war are produced".[19] Tensions boiled over at a CWC meeting in December. Maclean's supporters called for strike action to halt war production. Maclean arrived late to find Gallacher had ruled their proposal out of order and had then excluded his supporters for challenging his chairman's ruling.

Kirkwood and the ILP leadership were soft on dilution and against outright opposition to the government's plans. Kirkwood was ambiguous, failing to grasp the state was out to smash shop floor organisation. Instead he believed a 'pragmatic' dilution deal, factory-by-factory if necessary, could be agreed with the government. His boasts of increased shell production at Parkhead drew contempt from Maclean. *Forward,* the ILP newspaper, was hostile to the CWC's position. So intent was its editor Tom Johnston on avoiding conflict with the authorities that he refused even to report strikes for fear it might be interpreted as subverting the military defence of the country.

However, ILP member Helen Crawfurd proved—unlike other ILP leaders like Wheatley, Kirkwood and Manny Shinwell—to be a staunch ally of both Maclean and the best elements of the CWC. In December 1915, she was arrested with Maclean and two of the CWC leaders, Willie Gallacher and Arthur McManus, for obstructing North Hanover Street in the centre of Glasgow with a horse and cart while delivering from it anti-war, anti-conscription speeches to a huge crowd in George Square.

Conscription was on the cards and at the end of 1915 the government resolved to defeat the CWC by force if necessary, for it saw it as "a danger to the war effort and the maintenance of social order independently of its desire to obstruct dilution". The first mention of the CWC at Cabinet on November 1915 made this clear: "To obtain a smooth working Munitions Act, this committee should be smashed.'[20] It was decided Lloyd George should visit Clydeside to win support for the war effort and greater dilution. Due to his relationship with union officialdom, it was agreed Labour's Arthur Henderson should accompany him. The pair insisted they would not meet with 'unofficial' bodies during their visit. Instead they insisted they would meet union officials and workers at selected factories as well as at a set piece meeting—a clear snub to the CWC and a crude attempt to isolate them. On 20 December it was announced the two ministers would visit the Clyde that week, but their arrangements were badly botched.

Lloyd George planned to address a mass meeting of munitions workers and union officials on the evening of Thursday 23 December in Glasgow's huge St Andrew's Concert Hall. At the last moment this was postponed to the Saturday, Christmas Day (which at that time was a working day and not a public holiday in Calvinist Scotland) so that he could tour the factories first. The resentment of the union officials at being treated in so off-hand a manner gave the CWC the chance to capitalise on the situation.

Meeting on Thursday 23 December, its leaders agreed to try and force Lloyd George to meet them as a Committee and not on a plant-by-plant basis. When he toured the factories on the Friday, the shop stewards were to refuse to meet him and refer him back to the CWC. Gallacher and Muir toured the factories ahead of Lloyd George and his entourage early on the Friday morning to ensure this would happen. But at Parkhead, Kirkwood broke ranks and met Lloyd George on his first visit of the day, causing a split in the Committee that was papered over for a time. But the cabinet ministers were refused meetings at Weir's and were snubbed by the shop stewards at both the Albion and at Fairfield's in Govan, forcing them to abandon their planned tour. There remained the problem of the Christmas Day event in St Andrew's Hall.

The cabinet members remained confident of winning over the mass of ordinary munitions workers on Christmas Day. The promise of a big police presence reassured them things would not get out of hand. But the politicians were in for a shock. On Friday, news reached Lloyd George that not only would the CWC be attending, they had somehow got control of the event. Caught on the hop, he arranged a meeting with its leaders that evening. Having forced him into a climb-down, they presented to him their Dilution Policy in its entirety. Rejecting its demands, Lloyd George countered: "It would be a revolution and you can't carry through a revolution in the middle of a war!"[21] But he did agree that Johnny Muir could make a statement on behalf of the CWC and that the chair would take questions from the floor.

With 3,000 munitions workers crammed into St Andrew's Hall, the meeting turned into a morale booster for the CWC and humiliation for Lloyd George. Both cabinet ministers received a hostile reception throughout, as *Forward* reported on 1 January shows: "Rising to speak Mr Lloyd George was received with loud booing and hissing. Two verses of the 'Red Flag' were sung before he could utter a word."[22] When it was obvious Muir was not being called to speak, he stood up in his seat and loudly denounced the Munitions Minister's plans. He got rapturous applause from the audience. Repeated disruptions led to the meeting being abandoned, with an angry Lloyd George and Henderson storming off the stage to another chorus of the 'Red Flag'.

The press had been excluded and a ban imposed on all reporting of Lloyd George's humiliation. But like *Forward*, Maclean's report in *The Vanguard* defied the ban: "seldom has a prominent politician, a leading representative of the governing classes, been treated with so little respect. The feeling of servility towards their masters no longer holds with the Clyde workers".[23]

Because the press had been excluded, an official statement was put out giving a thoroughly false account of "a sympathetic hearing for Lloyd George". This statement was widely ridiculed. Humiliating a minister and forcing him to consult over the heads of the union leaders had shown the CWC to be a real threat. The cabinet did not fail to respond. When it did, it exploited the CWC's weaknesses to devastating effect.

1916—the government offensive on the CWC

In January 1916 there was still no sign of an early victory and the flow of volunteers was now down to a trickle. Lloyd George's Glasgow fiasco in December saw the state adopt a much tougher line. On 5 January, Asquith introduced a Conscription Bill in the Commons. There was widespread cynicism on the Clyde and elsewhere that conscription was coming, not for immediate military necessity but for "the military control of industry and consequently the abolition of the functions of our trade unions".[24] In a letter to the Munitions Ministry, its senior officer in Glasgow listed "the gentlemen whose removal from the Clyde district for an indefinite period would go a long way to helping production".[25] Listed were key CWC members Muir, Gallacher, Kirkwood, McManus, Messer and Clark. Maclean and Petroff were also mentioned. By April all of them had been imprisoned or deported from the area.

On 21 January, Asquith announced his Commissioners were coming to Glasgow and three days later they arrived. Throughout January, the cabinet ensured enough munitions had been stockpiled to allow it to withstand a six-week strike—a clear indication of Lloyd George's intention to break the CWC. Before Christmas, the cabinet had agreed contingency plans lest the December visit to Glasgow fail. And because it did fail, these measures were now brought into play. Sir William Weir, whose workers had launched the first strike of the war, had drafted the measures. The hardliner within the Munitions Ministry, Weir, had already pointed out how "government had compromised with the unions since the start of the war. The fallacy was that bargaining and compromise was necessary".[26] The Clydeside engineers had built few links with the rest of the country. Weir's plan was to impose dilution before those links could be properly forged. That meant arresting, imprisoning or deporting the ringleaders and suppressing the socialist press.

Lloyd George knew launching an immediate frontal assault on the CWC would lead to an immediate Clyde-wide strike. So he began with sinister salami tactics.

On 2 January, *Forward* was raided and suppressed for a month. But as its editor, Tom Johnston, truthfully pointed out, "in the files of *Forward* we find no hint of incitement... We declared in our issue of 20 March 1915 we should not touch the subject of strikes during the war".[27] Two weeks later, BSP member Peter Petroff was interned under the Defence of the Realm Act. The munitions official informed his London bosses: "he is a Russian socialist of the most dangerous type. The easiest thing is to have him repatriated—he'll be shot within 24 hours of landing in Russia".[28]

Maclean's *Vanguard* was also seized and shut down. With no socialist press now circulating on the Clyde, the CWC launched the *Worker* in early January, just in time to publish the story for which *Forward* had been raided. Sold in the factories and the streets, readership over its first four issues soared. But as its fifth edition went to print on 2 February, it too was raided and its presses smashed. With no immediate strike response, the authorities followed up with arrests. On 7 February, Gallacher, Muir and Walter Bell, the *Worker's* print manager, were seized. Next day they were charged under the Defence of the Realm Act and refused bail. Maclean was arrested that day too. Others would soon be joining him.

But the court's refusal to grant bail to Gallacher, Muir and Bell did provoke an immediate response. Ten thousand walked out at Weirs, Albion, Barr and Stroud and the Coventry Ordnance works. Significantly, at Parkhead, where Kirkwood was negotiating with the government's Munitions Commission, there was no solidarity strike. But the strikes at the other plants and a demonstration at the court forced the authorities to release the three CWC leaders on bail—though not John Maclean—and the strikes ended.

The Christmas events had revealed Parkhead as the weak link in the CWC. Now, six weeks on, the very same week that Gallacher, Muir, Bell and Maclean were arrested, a unilateral agreement was signed between the commissioners and Kirkwood on behalf of the Parkhead workforce. When the

THE WORKER

ORGAN OF THE CLYDE WORKERS' COMMITTEE

NO. I.   JANUARY 8TH, 1916   ONE PENNY

PREPARE FOR ACTION

Now that the confusion and excitement is over, the workers are vaguely wondering what all the fuss was about, and why the Right Hon. David Lloyd George troubled the Clyde with his presence at all.

Despite the loud-mouthed professions of economy that have been made by members of the Government, public money was squandered in the most reckless manner to secure a favourable reception to the author of the Munitions Act from the men whose liberties he has persistently attacked since the very commencement of the war.

Taxi-cabs unlimited were placed at the disposal of the Trade Unions' Officials who were willing to distribute tickets among their members for the St. Andrew's Hall meeting. To their credit, be it said, out of the 24 or 25 Unions invited 20 refused to have anything to do with the wretched business. They weren't concerned about maintaining the dignity of a falling Cabinet " star," and

sible." It's quite a nice arrangement. If they get all the guns they want and succeed in blowing the Germans across the Rhine, then, little Davie's the man who did it, little Davie takes the credit—and the cash. Little Davey goes up on a pedestal. But, if anything should go wrong anywhere, who is going to take the blame. Little Davey! Not if he knows it. That's where we come in. The politicians, press and pulpit will unite in a clamorous and lying attack on the " drunken, thriftless, shirking" workers who failed to support their brothers in the trenches, because, forsooth, they refused to sacrifice those liberties these same brothers in the trenches are presumably fighting for.

So far as little Davey is concerned, " it's heads I win and tails you lose," all the time. £100 per week for letting us know that guns are needed. What do we get for making them? Let each answer for himself.

Following the demand for guns came the demand for 80,000 skilled men. There was the " imperative necessity" for diluting labour. But what we all wanted to know was the very point the elusive Mr. George carefully avoided, to wit, whether the

to become mere parts of the machine, to be used wherever or whenever they may desire them. But under no condition must these individuals be allowed to relinquish their stranglehold on industry.

" It would be a revolution," said Mr. George in reply to the C.W.C. deputation, " and it can't be done." Why not? Simply because the employers would rather than lose their power ... rather than lose their power ... given for his emphatic " can't be done," is for us as workers to take that power from them. The only way to do it is by organising. Our first business, therefore, is to strengthen our Unions, then to amalgamate them all into one powerful industrial organisation. When that is accomplished the victory will be ours. In the meantime every effort is being made to crush what organisation we have out of existence. It was in pursuance of this object that Mr. George visited the Clyde. He came to " spy out the land." His experience was such that he went home some back again. It was beyond the slightest chance of understanding that the Clyde men ...

The Worker, newspaper of the Clyde Workers Committee January 1916 government's 'dilution men' arrived in Glasgow, the CWC's plan had been to make them negotiate centrally by again adopting a policy of non co-operation at individual plant level. This failed because Kirkwood, as he'd done at Christmas, broke ranks. At his meeting with the commissioners, he was given 48 hours to come up with his requirements for accepting dilution at Parkhead.

It was not to the CWC he turned. Later he confirmed that Wheatley, the local ILP councillor, drafted the deal accepting dilution in return for assurances that Kirkwood would have a say in running the factory. He thought this meant business as usual but, as events would prove, the government had scored a major success. The news that Kirkwood had broken ranks again angered the CWC. Their aim had been a united Clyde-wide fight. Parkhead had torpedoed it, creating resentment in other plants. This would divide the movement. And despite Kirkwood's co-operation, the next flashpoint was Parkhead itself. The owner, Sir William Beardmore, with Ministry approval, reneged on his side of the deal. Soldiers were introduced on the shop floor despite Kirkwood's protests.

Then, on 29 February, as the first group of women arrived to work under the new dilution deal, Kirkwood, keen on them joining the National Federation of Women Workers, met with them. Immediately the owner banned him from doing so again and also banned him from entering another department where a dispute was brewing—thus revoking his right of access to other areas of the plant. This threatened to end effective organisation in the biggest factory on the Clyde and when Beardmore refused to back down, the workforce struck on 17 March.

They were backed by walkouts at Weirs of Cathcart, North British Diesel Engines and at Beardmore's gun plant in Dalmuir—but not at the Albion, where Gallacher was the convenor. Still, the authorities feared these walkouts might spread. On 23 March, Lynden Macassey advised escalation, wiring the Ministry to say, "the whole gang should be removed—we should deport the whole of the CWC".[29] After some hesitation, the authorities acted. In the early hours of Saturday 25 March, Kirkwood and two other Parkhead stewards were seized from their beds. Messer and McManus, the leading stewards at Weirs of Cathcart were also arrested and all five deported to Edinburgh. Banned from political activity, they were forced to report to a local police station three times a day, every day.

Despite his moderation, Kirkwood was too prominent to ignore. Lloyd George was out to break reformist trade union resistance to the war economy, as well as the revolutionary opposition to the war itself.

News of these deportations provoked an immediate rash of strikes. On Monday 27 March, Weirs struck and Coventry Ordnance Works and two other smaller plants came out. Finally, on 29 March, Gallacher brought the Albion works out too. But that same day two more Parkhead stewards and three more from Weir's were deported and next day 30 workers from three of the factories on strike were prosecuted.

Again, the press was banned under the emergency powers from reporting the strikes, the arrests and the deportations. Added to the widespread resentment at Kirkwood's 'go it alone' stance on dilution, this made it much harder to spread the action further, particularly in the absence of a clear call from the CWC. On 31 March, a huge protest against the deportations was organised at Glasgow Green, at which Helen Crawfurd and Jimmy Maxton called publicly for an all-out strike. But by then the movement was losing impetus and there was a slow drift back to work. Yet even at this point defeat could have been avoided.

At a specially convened CWC meeting, a motion demanding the committee call a general strike on the Clyde was tabled. But once again Gallacher ruled it out of order. He then rushed off to London to broker negotiations with the government, but Lloyd George, sensing victory, vetoed them. The CWC failed to co-ordinate a united response to the government attack, letting resentment at Kirkwood get in the way of solidarity. Had the Committee called an all-out strike against both the dilution agreement and the deportations, it could have inflicted a massive defeat on the government and re-asserted its authority.

The trials were held in Edinburgh during April/May. Maclean appeared first to face six charges. Lord Strathclyde imposed a savage sentence of three years penal servitude. Its severity visibly shook the other defendants. Maclean remained in Peterhead prison until June 1917, when under the impact of the Russian revolution, mass working class protest forced his release. Jack Smith, convenor at Weir's, got an 18-month sentence. Gallacher, Maxton and James MacDougall, Maclean's closest associate, were sentenced to a year. The other CWC members were either deported or jailed for three months. The deportees did not get back to Glasgow until the summer of 1917. It would take a year for the movement to recover on the Clyde.

The repression robbed the Clyde of its leadership. Maclean was silenced, militancy subsided and resistance to dilution and conscription collapsed. But it wasn't the end of the CWC. Its defeat was a big setback, but the repression reverberated through the factories, politicising thousands of workers who had been previously indifferent to politics. The government could smash the CWC but not the idea it embodied. The deportations, by forcing some of its leaders to find work in other munitions centres, helped spread the idea. As James Hinton notes: "What was done on the Clyde in 1915-16 made possible the subsequent national development of the rank-and-file movement".[30]

Sheffield and the struggle against conscription

Lloyd George was promoted to Secretary of State for War. He ordered the shelling of Dublin and the execution of James Connolly and other leaders of the Easter Rising. He imposed conscription and pushed for the infamous Somme offensive, where over a million were slaughtered. At the end of 1916, aided by the Tories, he engineered a coup to oust Asquith and became prime minister. As Lloyd George wallowed in the bloodshed, resistance grew. The Sheffield Workers' Committee was built out of unofficial strike action against conscription. In October 1916, Leonard Hargreaves, a young fitter at the Vickers munitions plant, was conscripted despite a pledge not to draft skilled workers. After the horrors of the Somme, conscription was like a death sentence, yet the leaders of Hargreaves' union, the ASE, refused to act. Local shop stewards organised meetings demanding he be returned to civilian life. When the authorities refused, 12,000 engineers struck. The strike spread quickly to other key centres and the government caved in. Shop stewards organisation was established throughout Sheffield and a new scheme introduced exempting skilled munitions workers from military service.

In early 1917, the overthrow of the Russian Tsar brought inspiration. On May Day, 70,000 marched through Glasgow in solidarity with the February Revolution. At the end of that month, 90,000 marched to Glasgow Green to protest against Lloyd George getting the freedom of the city and for the release of Maclean and those arrested in 1916. Two hundred Russian sailors left their warship anchored on the Clyde to join this march and show international solidarity. Russia's Congress of Workers' and Soldiers' Deputies sent greetings to "the brave fighter for the International, Comrade Maclean, expressing hopes that the rise of international solidarity will bring his liberty".[31]

Throughout Britain there was a revival of working class confidence and struggle, accelerated by the events shaking Russia. Although five million workers were away in the army, Britain's union membership was growing dramatically and the number of strike days rising, even though striking meant taking on the police, the army, the courts, the union officials and the Labour Party, as well as the bosses. The rapid growth of the female workforce was a big factor.

In 1914 there were 385,000 women in trade unions. By 1918 it was well over a million and 75 percent of them worked in munitions. A third of the workers in the new aircraft industry were women. In munitions generally, the huge intake of women took part in the growing industrial action alongside the men and independently when necessary.

In March 1917, 10,000 munitions workers struck in Barrow. In May the largest unofficial strike of the war began in Rochdale and spread to Manchester, Sheffield and Coventry. Out of this, the National Shop Stewards and Workers Committee Movement (NSS & WCM) was formed and set up a National Advisory Council (NAC) to act as its reporting centre. But this body was advisory only, holding no executive power. Most of the local centres opposed the idea of national leadership, insisting on local autonomy. This syndicalist prejudice would bedevil the movement in its battles with a highly-centralised state.

With the prisoners and deportees back in the factories, the Clyde revived too. Mass agitation brought Maclean's release in June. Willie Gallacher was released in September and the CWC reformed. Soon it was leading a big wage strike and the government had to concede a 12½ percent increase. In November, a group of women dilutees at Beardmore's were victimised for working to rule and the whole factory stopped, demanding their re-instatement. The officials disowned the strike but the CWC organised a solidarity rally on Glasgow Green and threatened to spread the action. The women won. In January 1918, 10,000 shipbuilders struck over pay and the strike spread to the engineering plants. According to Hinton, "the Clyde was back in the vanguard of the national movement".[32]

The NSS & WCM developed between 1915 and 1918 when the issue affecting everyone was the war. The engineers could have led a struggle to end the war in 1918. Alas their power was never marshalled at a national level. On 5 January, its leaders met in Manchester, demanding, "the government accept the invitation of the Russian government to consider peace terms".[33] In Glasgow, where Maclean consistently denounced the war, this was well received.

At the end of January, a huge Glasgow meeting supported the CWC's call for a national strike against the war. But the Sheffield and Manchester meetings voted narrowly against. The NSS & WCM failed to give a lead and Glasgow did not feel strong enough to act alone. The problem was the lack of national leadership and a party that could organise and act like the Bolsheviks. In February 1918, the NSS & WCM paper

Solidarity published its position:

> If we could only be certain German workers would
> follow suit we would have no hesitation in calling
> for an immediate policy of down tools and damn the
> consequences. But we are not in touch with our fellow
> workers in Germany. It may be that they are willing to
> do the bidding of their warlords.[34]

Yet at the very moment *Solidarity* was voicing this fear,
500,000 German metalworkers struck against 'their warlords'
only to find themselves isolated internationally. The leaders of
the NSS & WCM had drawn back from their challenge to the
state, opting instead for a militant but sectional demand for the
continued exemption of skilled workers from conscription.

But this wasn't the end of it. Maclean argued that if the
national body wouldn't lead on the war, then the Clyde would.
Three months later on May Day, the workers on Clydeside struck
for peace. Ever since his release the previous June, Maclean had
been agitating for strike action and support for the Russian
Revolution. In January, *The Scotsman* reported, "journalist John
Reed would serve as the Bolsheviks' representative in New
York and schoolteacher John Maclean was to fulfil the same
role in Glasgow".[35]

In his new role as Soviet Consul, he now spoke to huge
meetings across Britain, arguing the best defence of Russia
was revolution here. The Cabinet worried about the Clyde and
Maclean's influence. The shipyards were on strike and that
month the Clyde contributed 75 percent of all strike days lost.
Local meetings, several thousand strong, were held by the BSP
and the ILP against the war. Maclean's classes on Marxism were
attracting over 1,000 workers a week. Press reports showed
labour leaders like Ramsay MacDonald were forced to pay
lip service to Lenin's peace policy when speaking to Glasgow
audiences. There was pressure from the local ILP rank and file
for Labour to oppose the war.

In February, the head of the army in Scotland urged the Cabinet to bring another prosecution against Maclean. In April he had been speaking in the Durham coalfield and had returned to Glasgow when he was arrested and charged with sedition. He was refused bail and imprisoned pending trial set for 9 May at Edinburgh's High Court. Before his arrest, he'd been urging the Clyde to strike against the war on Mayday. Glasgow Trades Council took up his call, holding its annual march on a working day for the first time. The strike and the march to Duke Street jail, where Maclean was held pending trial, was a great success. "Few estimates put the number marching below 90,000. Resolutions in favour of ending the war, the release of Maclean and support for the Russian Revolution were passed."[36]

Maclean was brought to trial in Edinburgh on 9 May. In his speech from the dock, he spoke out against the war and capitalism. He ended by appealing to the working class to overthrow it:

> I am not here as the accused, I am here as the accuser of capitalism, dripping with blood from head to foot... My appeal is to the working class because they, and they alone, can bring about the time when the whole world will be in one brotherhood, on a sound economic foundation... That can only be obtained when the people of the world get the world and retain the world."[37]

Sentenced to five years hard labour, he went on hunger strike and a campaign for his release was launched. Lenin told the Russian Trade Union Congress, "They imprisoned him because he exposed the object of the war and spoke out against the criminal nature of British imperialism—this time not only as a schoolteacher, but as the Consul of the Soviet Republic".[38]

In November 1918, the German Revolution toppled the Kaiser and ended the war. Weeks earlier, with Maclean on hunger strike and subjected to force-feeding, the Gorbals Labour Party selected him as its candidate in the snap Christmas elections. It did so in defiance of Labour's national leadership. At first the state couldn't decide whether Maclean was more of a threat in or out of jail. Soon the campaign for his release extended across Britain with 10,000 gathering in London's Finsbury Park and Labour's National Conference calling for his release. The Cabinet realised granting his freedom and a pardon was the only way of defusing the protests. So, they released him a week before polling day. Maclean returned to Glasgow a hero and huge crowds gathered at Buchanan Street station to greet him off the train from Aberdeen. The newspapers estimated 100,000 lined the streets to see him—many had struck work to do so.

As the war ended, Britain experienced an explosion of strikes and mutinies in its army and navy. Lloyd George worried: "the whole of Europe is filled with the spirit of revolution. The whole existing order is questioned by the mass of the population from one end of Europe to the other".[39] In such a crisis the state has to rely on its armed forces but at the end of 1918 the British ruling class wasn't sure it could. Disaffection and delays in demobilisation meant thousands of conscripted soldiers were in revolt. At Folkestone, 12,000 soldiers mutinied and refused to return to France. The boats sailed empty while the troops formed a soldiers' union. Another 4,000 demonstrated at Dover. The revolt spread to the navy. In Milford Haven there was a mutiny on board HMS Kilbride. Sailors hoisted the red flag, declaring: "Half the navy are on strike and the other half soon will be".[40]

The movement spread to troops still abroad. In Calais they struck demanding immediate demobilisation. Strike committees were elected in the camps and the surrounding area. Attempts were made to crush the rebellion, but the troops sent to restore order joined the striking soldiers. The government was terrified mutinous soldiers might unite with striking workers. A report to the Cabinet warned, "the danger must be obvious to anyone who has studied the events in Russia. Evidence can be obtained of a determined effort to emulate the Bolshevist movement".[41]

In 1919, Britain was embroiled in Ireland's war for independence as well as colonial revolts across the globe. The Chief of the General Staff feared "the loss of Ireland to begin with, the loss of Empire in the second place and the loss of England itself to finish with". He told the Cabinet, "A Bolshevik rising was likely".[42] The head of Special Branch warned, "February 1919 was the high watermark of revolutionary danger".[43] To cap it all, in May the police went on strike in London and Liverpool. On average, 4.5 million working days had been lost to strike action during each of the war years. In 1919 this figure would soar to an incredible 34.5 million.

The Forty Hours Strike

Glasgow was hit harder and sooner than most towns as shipbuilding and engineering were run down as the war ended. By the end of January 1919, unemployment in the city had rocketed from a wartime average of 0.5 percent to 11 percent. Soldiers promised a land fit for heroes returned instead to lengthening dole queues. At the 'khaki' election in December, the Liberal-Tory coalition was returned. Workers drew the conclusion they would have to fight for change themselves. The issue on which the CWC chose to stand its ground was shorter hours.

1919 started with a bang. The CWC rejected a deal that the ASE engineering union leaders had struck with the Employers Federation offering a reduction in the working week from 54 hours to 47. This deal surrendered the morning meal breaks and guaranteed workers would produce in 47 hours as much as they had been producing in the much longer wartime hours, when overtime was rife. With two and half million servicemen being discharged, the rank and file wanted a much bigger reduction in hours to absorb unemployment—and with no detriment and no speed-up. The CWC favoured a 30-hour week but held workshop meetings and a huge delegate conference, finally agreeing on an all-out strike for a 40-hour week—the Scottish Trade Union Congress' (STUC) position—with no loss of pay and no worsening of conditions.

The ASE union leaders responded by attacking the shop stewards who had also incurred the wrath of the government. Nonetheless, a strike date was set for Monday 27 January with the support of the Glasgow Trades Council. Maclean agreed on the need for a fight but argued to wait and link up with the miners. They were balloting on a national strike for a 30 percent pay rise, a 30-hour week and nationalisation of the industry. There were a million miners and they were in powerful position to defeat the government. The CWC ignored Maclean and failed to contact the NSS and WCM. He feared that by going it alone, the local leadership was spurning the opportunity to mount an all-out attack on a weak ruling class. Nevertheless, he campaigned for the 40-hour strike and toured the coalfields urging miners to join in.

Maclean's wariness about the officials would prove prophetic. Although represented on the joint strike committee, the CWC would be hamstrung by officialdom. Chairing the strike committee was Manny Shinwell, official of the Seafarers' Union, chair of Glasgow TUC and a leading ILP member. Before the strike, Shinwell went to great lengths to stress the reformist aims of the officials, "this movement is not revolutionary; it is attributable solely to the fear of unemployment".[44] Worse, on the eve of the strike he addressed a meeting of local sailors in Glasgow warning of mass unemployment if action were not taken to restrict foreign labour. Hours later, a riot ensued at the yard where he had spoken. Thirty or so black, Asian and Arab sailors were chased and assaulted by an armed mob of white sailors, the first of a number of race riots in British ports in 1919.

The 40-hours strike was key to the developing revolutionary movement. The War Cabinet knew it and prepared for the worst, putting troops on standby for dispatch to Clydeside. But it was the union leaders, not the army, who would do the real damage. While local officials like Harry Hopkins, the ASE District Secretary, and Tom Bell, President of the Iron Moulders, backed the strike, the TUC and the ASE leadership opposed it. Hopkins was suspended from union office for joining the strike committee. When all attempts to halt it failed the bureaucrats looked to apply the brakes whenever and wherever they could. This didn't deter the rank and file. Within days the Clyde Valley and much of the central belt was at near standstill. Barrow and Belfast were out. The Belfast strike had begun two days earlier, involving 60,000 workers. On Clydeside, the strike was built through mass picketing. They marched from factory to factory closing all in their path. Two thousand Albion workers marched on Barr and Stroud. John Brown's in Clydebank and Beardmores in Dalmuir were picketed out. On Wednesday, picketing at Singer saw 11,000 men and women walk out.

On the second day, a conference of strikers' delegates was held in Glasgow. They came from as far away as Dumfries, Dundee and Alloa, as well as Belfast, Barrow, Grimsby and Rugby. The same day, 5,000 strikers marched through Dumbarton picketing out Dennystoun Forge and Babcock and Wilcox. The local paper reported, "no strike demonstration like it was ever seen in Dumbarton".[45]

Contrary to some accounts, the strike was not about the self-preservation of a skilled, male elite. The mass picketing involved large numbers of women, young people and ex-soldiers. It built organisation among the unemployed for the first time, laying the basis for the Scottish Unemployed Workers' Movement. The war had brought a dramatic rise in women workers, especially in munitions, but now it was the women who were the first to be sacked. The Federation of Women Workers supported the strike. In Clydebank, a meeting of women workers voted to join the strike and picketed the apprentices out. Similar activity came from women in Bridgeton, Partick, Govan and Dumbarton.

Mass meetings every morning decided where to picket and the local unemployed helped spread the strike. Local committees sent a delegate to the strike information office in Glasgow at 11am to report the news from their area, then they returned to the local district to report to their committee by 2.30pm, then back to Glasgow by 4pm. By such grassroots ingenuity, lines of communication were maintained and a daily bulletin was produced centrally by the strike committee. Sold on the streets and round the doors for a penny, its readership was over 20,000. In Dumbarton, trams were only allowed to run if strike bulletins were displayed prominently in their windows. The strikers were also kept informed by daily mass meetings in the localities and big meetings were held regularly in George Square in Glasgow.

National negotiations between the miners' leaders and the coal owners were on-going at the start of the 40-hour strike. The Cabinet was desperate to avoid joint action by the Triple Alliance of miners, rail and transport unions, hence Maclean's call for unity. In the coalfields the first walkouts came in Fife. On 23 January a strike that began in Cowdenbeath quickly spread and within days 10,000 miners were marching to the union HQ in Dunfermline, demanding the stoppage be made official. In Lanarkshire the news from Fife was enough. On 27 January, thousands of Lanarkshire miners responded by ignoring appeals from their officials to stay at work until the national miners' ballot was known. Instead, they threw their weight behind the CWC. Their strike spread and mass picketing brought out all of the many pits in Shettleston, Cambuslang, Blantyre, Hamilton, Bellshill, Carfin and Holytown, birthplace of Keir Hardie. On Wednesday 29 January, 15,000 strikers held a mass meeting in Hamilton, outside the headquarters of the miners' union.

> An immense mob like a swirling flood poured into the quiet streets of Hamilton to get the officials to proclaim the strike in the name of the union. They took possession of the union offices. At a joint meeting of the local executive and members of Miners' Reform Committee it was decided the strike be declared official. That meant that all the 50,000 Lanarkshire miners were out.[46]

To escape the pressure from the rank and file, the local executive fled to Edinburgh at the weekend and, from a safe distance, recommended a return to work. Some pits ignored them and continued the unofficial strike.

The Red Flag and Bloody Friday

The 40-hours movement is remembered for the battle of George Square, five days into the strike, which became known as Bloody Friday, but most accounts ignore the tremendous ingenuity and initiative shown by the ordinary men and women who built it. On Monday, the first day of the strike, a packed meeting of 3,000 was held in St Andrew's Hall in Glasgow with an estimated 30,000 other strikers left outside. At the end of the meeting, the strikers joined up to march through the city centre to George Square. A huge red flag was famously hoisted up the municipal flagpole in front of the City Chambers. The resulting jubilation led to the boisterous singing of the 'Red Flag'. This event appeared in all the newspapers at the time and became the iconic photograph of the Red Clyde.

Workers at the two key power stations had just joined the strike, threatening electricity supplies to the city. On Wednesday morning, two days before Bloody Friday, there was a mass protest at Pinkston power station. It was followed by a short march to George Square. As it dispersed, a delegation chosen and led by Shinwell went into the City Chambers to meet the Lord Provost, leaving Gallacher outside in charge of stewarding. Without Gallacher's prior knowledge, Shinwell asked the Provost to get the Cabinet to intervene and respond to the strikers' demands. Shinwell was looking for a get out and when Gallacher learned of his initiative he was sceptical, but the Provost had agreed to wire the Cabinet.

So, there would be another march and rally on Friday to hear the cabinet's response and demonstrate the strength of the strike. Coming hard on the heels of the red flag incident and the threat to the power supply, the Cabinet made their own plans. Churchill was shrewd enough to use Shinwell's request to further widen the rift that already existed between the Joint Strike Committee, the ASE officials and the TUC. Feigning

Bloody Friday
George Square, Glasgow,
January 1919

neutrality while plotting with the rest of his Cabinet on how to break the strike and jail its leaders, Deputy Prime Minister Bonar Law, Tory MP for Glasgow City Centre, wired the Lord Provost with these deceitful words:

> The government are unable to entertain requests for intervention made by local members of unions, whose official representatives are acting for them in conference with the employers. Such action by the government could only undermine the authority of those chosen by the men to represent their interests and would destroy that co-operation between employers and employed on which hopes of industrial peace rest.[47]

Yet the government felt 'able to intervene' against the 'local members of unions' when 60,000 strikers and supporters gathered on the Friday to hear the cabinet's reply. Some activists, including Maclean, saw it as a trap set by the state to make its pre-planned military response appear justified afterwards. There is enough evidence from abinet papers and two Cabinet meetings held earlier that week to show this was the case. Churchill had already argued the best strategy was "a judicious use of force at an opportune moment combined with support from the union leaders".[48] On the eve of Bloody Friday, the *Evening Times* reported what Churchill had to say about the strike at the Cabinet meeting earlier that day:

> The situation in Glasgow had been brewing for a long time. The disaffected were a minority and there would have to be a conflict to clear the air. We should be careful to have plenty of provocation before taking strong measures. By going gently at first we should get the support of the nation and then troops could be used more effectively. The moment for their use had not yet arrived. Meantime DORA [the Defence of the Realm Act] was in force and some of the leaders should be seized.[49]

Scottish Minister Sir Robert Munro, justifying Churchill's 'strong measures', insisted it was "a misnomer to call the situation in Glasgow a strike, when it was a Bolshevist rising—there were no more than 10,000 malcontents and public opinion supported the quelling of disorder".[50] This was before there was any disorder! Churchill went on to say the War Office would take all necessary steps for placing troops in the vicinity. The Deputy Chief of the Imperial General Staff told the Cabinet six tanks and 100 lorries were going north by rail that night.

Next morning, 60,000 strikers and unemployed, including many ex-soldiers, marched into George Square to await the response to their demands. Government figures indicate another 25,000 men and women were crammed into the side streets. Reporters from all the major British and European press were there to witness and record the events—including the war poet Siegfried Sassoon. There is no doubt the authorities provoked the confrontation that followed.

The police used the pretext of keeping the tramlines open to launch an unprovoked attack on a section of the crowd. The *Daily News* reporter who was present wrote, "I have no hesitation in saying that the baton charge to clear the way for a tram car was the beginning of the trouble".[51] But the police explanation for the riot, peddled by the *Daily News*, doesn't bear scrutiny. The baton charge took place outside the City Chambers, but as one historian has pointed out, "no tramlines ran along the east side of the square in front of the City Chambers in 1919. Nor were there any in North Frederick Street".[52]

Gallacher, addressing the crowd when the police attacked, and Kirkwood, who came out of the City Chambers to calm the crowd, were both bludgeoned on the head by police truncheons. Gallacher was arrested and charged with incitement to riot. The wounded Kirkwood would be arrested and charged later that evening. But the strikers gave us good as they got and then some! Eventually the police were overwhelmed. Harry McShane's section commandeered a delivery lorry and fought back by hurling its empty bottles at the charging police. "The police charged but the crowd stood; when that happens the police are lost". After a pitched battle in North Frederick Street, the police gave up. "Finally they ran for it and we ran after them".[53]

In George Square, the crowd chased police back inside the City Chambers from where the Sheriff of Glasgow appeared to read the Riot Act. But the crowd would only disperse when asked to do so by their leaders. Kirkwood and Gallacher, heads now bandaged, came out onto the balcony of the City Chambers and appealed to the crowds to line up and march to a rally at nearby Glasgow Green. The police regrouped and tried to stop the march en route but were again routed. "When we got there the police were lined up ready to attack us. But the ex-servicemen pulled up the park railings, spikes and all, and the police ran for their lives".[54]

Gallacher had been arrested and the Riot Act read. Shinwell and Kirkwood were charged that evening. Hopkins would be arrested too. The "opportune moment for the judicious use of force" that Churchill was anticipating had arrived. Overnight both Scottish and English troops held on standby were flooded into the city, "young lads of 19 or so who had no idea of where they were or why they were here. The authorities did not dare use the local regiment at Wyndford barracks in case they supported the strikers. Next morning, Glasgow was like an armed camp. The city bristled with tanks, machine guns and howitzers".[55]

There is no doubt that Bloody Friday was an attack pre-planned by the police and an excuse to call in the army. That Glasgow could be under armed occupation without prior planning between the government and the military was inconceivable. Violence and armed repression was the Cabinet's reply to the strikers' demands. Ten thousand troops were brought in and deployed in George Square and at other key locations across the city, notably the power stations. The City Chambers were surrounded by barbed wire with howitzers protruding from the buildings. Machine guns were sited on the rooftops of surrounding buildings, including the Post Office. The Cattle Market was requisitioned for the tanks and heavy artillery that arrived a day later.

Contrary to some accounts, the arrival of the military did not lead to the immediate collapse of the strike. The strike continued into the second week but the mass picketing, which had seen flying pickets of up to 5,000, was set aside, showing the local leadership were on the back foot. Attacks on the strike by a hostile press were stepped up. The TUC sent out a letter to all its affiliates, openly attacking the strike and calling for order to be restored so that "the hands of the responsible leaders of the trade union movement may be strengthened and the unions governed in an orderly fashion".[56] False stories about the ending of the strike started to appear, furnished to the press by the government and the ASE leaders. A boycott of the *Daily Record* was called, but the key lay in spreading the strike wider afield and an immediate resumption of the mass picketing. The strike had already spread across Scotland and south to Barrow and Tyneside.

In Belfast, the action was even more solid than Glasgow. There, where the strike for shorter hours had begun two weeks earlier than on Clydeside, the city was firmly in the hands of the strikers. In his vivid account of the events, Kieran Allen writes:

> On 14 January, 1919, 20,000 shipyard workers downed tools and marched to Belfast City Hall for a mass rally. Within days they were in effective control of the city....the *Manchester Guardian* noted that 'the strike committee have taken upon themselves, with the involuntary acquiescence of the civic authority, some of the attributes of an industrial soviet'. Electricity was only allocated with the workers' permission and no traffic could travel down the major streets without workers' permits. The authorities became terrified because they were facing similar upheaval in Glasgow and elsewhere. The loyalist labour organisation, founded by Edward Carson to co-opt workers became irrelevant, while the Orange Order decided not to take

sides. Despite Belfast's sectarian history, the leader of the strike committee, Charles McKay, was a Catholic and the majority of the strikers were Protestant.[57]

After Bloody Friday, delegates were belatedly sent from Glasgow to some of the English centres to try and spur on the threatened strikes there. But it was far too little and too late. Maclean had given prior warning of the risk of 'going it alone'. Writing after the event, J T Murphy, one of the leaders of the national shop stewards' movement, underlined Maclean's point. "The CWC's greatest mistake lay in the fact that it had done nothing to prepare the movement beyond the Clyde. Although it was represented on the National Committee of Shop Stewards, it had not even acquainted this committee with its plans."[58]

Murphy was right to highlight this blunder, but, as we noted earlier, the shop stewards movement nationally shared the same cavalier attitude towards centralised organisation. Throughout the second week of the strike, hopeful reports of it spreading to London, Sheffield and Manchester appeared in the strike bulletins. Barrow was already on strike and in London and some cities in the North real attempts were made to bring workers out. Shipyard workers on Merseyside, Tyneside, and Hull did come out on unofficial strike. Coventry and other Midlands towns saw action too. But the movement lacked national leadership and co-ordination.

The ASE executive did its utmost to hold back or sabotage the action, but, on the Friday, electricians threatened to black out London and engineers in Sheffield, Manchester and Tyneside were poised to take unofficial action too. Over the weekend of 8-9 February, the executive responded by publicly announcing the end of the strike and suspending its District Committees in Glasgow, London and Belfast—the three most militant areas. The government and the press ramped up the propaganda and the confusion led to a number of ASE branches voting to return to work. On Monday 10 February, the Glasgow evening newspapers announced that the strike was over, forcing the hand of the Joint Strike Committee. It decided to suspend the action and recommend a return to work on an understanding that an official campaign for 40 hours would be launched in due course. It was a trick by the bureaucracy to end the strike and do a deal with the bosses.

The majority on the Clyde returned to work on Wednesday 12 February. In Belfast the strikers held out until the union officials forced them back on 20 February. While the 40 hours was not achieved, workers returned with their working week reduced from 54 to 47 hours and on much better terms than the officials had negotiated a month earlier. But this was cold comfort. The 40-hours strike was a missed opportunity to inflict a hammer blow on the ruling class. Instead, the government and the bosses were given a breathing space and time to regroup. John Maclean was right at the time when he argued the strike was defeated "more by lack of working class maturity, than batons, tanks and machine guns".[59] It was not the police or an army on the streets that broke the strike. The ASE national leadership did everything to undermine the fight— refusing to make it official, suspending the most militant district leaderships and threatening the other English districts who supported the action. Instead of representing their members, they turned on them. Alongside the TUC, they encouraged the government and the bosses to refuse even to talk to the Joint Strike Committee on the grounds that an agreement had been made with the ASE executive and they could not go back on it.

Of course the presence of troops, machine guns and tanks was intimidating, but if there had been strikes in every city and in every industry, not just in two or three engineering centres, then the government would have been powerless. So why then was the strike eventually isolated? The answer lay not in the strength of the government but in the shop stewards' political ideas. While they understood the need for the self-activity of the rank and file, they'd forgotten what the CWC was all about when it was launched in November 1915—its ability to act independently of officialdom.

After the first week, the CWC played no independent role in the 40-hours movement. It merged its forces with the Joint Strike Committee, chaired by Shinwell, and went along with the abandonment of picketing, allowing the strike to be conducted as an industrial dispute rather than a challenge for power. Shinwell's involvement throughout had been to confine the action. Although charged and later imprisoned for simply being there on Bloody Friday, as Jimmy Maxton truthfully told the 1919 ILP conference, "Shinwell, far from being an inciting factor in the 40 hour movement, was there all the time as a restraining element among the strikers".[60]

In 1919, a national rank-and-file organisation capable of independent leadership when the officials failed it was lacking. So too was a revolutionary organisation that could develop the movement into a challenge for power. Mass pickets had shown the power of the working class, but, shorn of determined leadership from within its own ranks, the officials could re-assert their influence. Committed to negotiating within the framework of capitalism, they were able, in conjunction with the Cabinet, to safely steer the ship of state through what John Maclean had called "the rapids of revolution".

To see how close Britain came to major civil disorder and revolutionary upheaval and to appreciate how much it relied upon the union leaders for its survival, one only need read the Cabinet discussions of the time. Three weeks before Bloody Friday, Lloyd George warned his Cabinet, "1,500 soldiers had arrived in Downing Street. The attempt to stop them marching on Whitehall was without success". The chair of the Imperial Staff added, "the soldiers' delegation bore a dangerous resemblance to a Soviet".[61] On the eve of Bloody Friday, when the Cabinet was discussing the use of troops in Glasgow, General Childs agreed that this tactic had worked in the past but warned, "Then we had a well-disciplined and ignorant army whereas now we have an army that is educated and ill-disciplined".[62] In Glasgow, they gambled and sent in the army but that wasn't what ended the strike. It didn't even end the picketing. It was the local strike leaders, under the influence of the local officials, who called it off. In the second week of the strike, the Cabinet itself came to realise just how much they needed the union leaders.

From now on the Cabinet's main tactic would not be the deployment of troops. In the official trade union machine, they had found a much more reliable ally. Churchill explained this to his Cabinet colleagues as early as 4 February, a week before the strike ended. "The trade union organisation was imperfect, and the more moderate its officials the less representative it was but it was the only organisation with which the government could deal."[63] By trade union organisation, he meant its bureaucracy.

Revolution?

In *Revolt on the Clyde*, Gallacher wrote "we were leading a strike when we should have been leading a revolution. A rising was expected, a rising should have taken place. The workers were ready and able; the leadership had never thought of it".[64] He was wrong. It was not a revolution, at least not yet. Harry McShane was clearer: "we regarded the 40-hours strike not as a revolution but as a beginning. Other things would follow. From the end of the war we were hoping for the formation of a revolutionary party. We thought it only a matter of time before we'd have a revolution in Britain."[65] Even Lloyd George conceded, "the Russian Revolution lit up the skies with a flash of hope for all dissatisfied with the existing order. 'In Russia', they claimed 'the workmen had formed a separate authority co-ordinate with the government—why not Britain?' This was the question being asked in every workshop and on every street corner."[66]

Had the local leaders led the 40-hour strike as revolutionaries, acting independently of the officials and not simply as union militants, they could have won a decisive battle. That in itself would have raised the stakes against a worried ruling class and moved revolution right up the agenda. After all, the Clyde was affiliated to a Britain wide network of workers' committees in Sheffield, London, Barrow, Belfast and the other engineering and mining centres across Britain. But as we know, those links were ignored until after it was too late. If the strike committee had maintained the mass picketing when the troops arrived, if the victors of George Square had marched to Maryhill barracks to fraternise with the local garrison instead of being sent by Kirkwood in the opposite direction to Glasgow Green, and if delegations had been sent out to the coalfields and to England in advance of the strike, it would have overwhelmed a panicky ruling class.

John Maclean had wanted the strike delayed by weeks so that a million miners stretching from Kent to Wales and to Scotland could be part of it. The unofficial action taken by the Lanarkshire and Fife miners during the 40 hours strike had shown the rank and file were up for the fight. In the second week, much more effort should have been put into extending the strikes to other areas. At the start of 1919, Europe was ablaze with revolution. Ireland and large swathes of the British Empire were in open revolt. The army was stretched to breaking point occupying Ireland, Germany, Turkey, Iraq, Palestine and the West Indies. It was also engaged in clandestine operations in Russia, trying to topple the new workers' government and growing sections of it were in open revolt.

On Mayday 1919, two months after Bloody Friday, 150,000 marched through Glasgow singing the Irish anthem along with the Red Flag. That evening McLean shared the platform at a huge rally with Irish Republican Constance Markievicz. Victory in the 40-hours strike in February would have deepened the existential crisis of the British state. At any rate the failure of the 40-hours strike did not stem the floodtide of working class revolt that followed in its wake. For every day of 1919, an average of 100,000 workers would be on strike. But it was their union leaders that saved the government.

The miners and railway workers were the biggest threat. Here the state dared not attack but had to rely on reformist union officials disarming the movement. The potential existed for workers in all the key industries to fight together, but that raised the question of leadership and the focus turned to the

Triple Alliance. Formed in 1914, it could have co-ordinated action in the biggest and best organised sections—the miners, the railworkers, the dockers and other transport workers. But the conservatism of its leadership meant the potential was never harnessed. The leadership saw its role as bargaining with the capitalists and the government not wresting control from them.

But the miners were up for a fight. In January, their Annual Conference voted for a 30 percent wage rise, a six-hour day with a five day week, and nationalisation of the mines under workers' control. When these demands were rejected, the Miner's Federation organised pithead ballots and its million members voted six to one for all out action.

Presented with this ultimatum in February, the government was in trouble. Coal stocks were at rock bottom and the Triple Alliance could halt all movement of coal. Concessions could be made on wages and conditions, but nationalisation was another matter—forced by mass struggle from below, it would widen other workers' horizons.

The government was desperate to avoid a strike so played for time by offering an enquiry into pay, conditions and hours—the Sankey Commission. The leaders of the Triple Alliance delayed the strike pending the outcome of this enquiry—a big mistake. As John Maclean argued, "Government's never compromise unless they have to—now is the time to break British capitalism for good".[67] Sankey offered higher pay and reduced hours but no nationalisation. At a famous meeting with Lloyd George, the union leaders were told what was at stake:

> Gentlemen, you have fashioned in the Triple Alliance a powerful instrument... we are at your mercy. The army is disaffected and can't be relied upon. We've just emerged from a great war. The people are eager for reward of their sacrifices but we are in no position to satisfy them. If you carry out your threat you will defeat us. But if you do, have you weighed the consequences? The strike will be in defiance of the Government and its

success will precipitate a constitutional crisis. For if a force arises in the state which is stronger than the state itself, then it must be ready to take on the functions of the state or withdraw and accept the authority of the state. Gentlemen... have you considered, and if you have, are you ready?[68]

"From that moment", said miners' leader Robert Smillie, "we were beaten and we knew it".[69] Terrified at the prospect, the leaders of the Triple Alliance threw in the towel and tried to sell it to the miners as a victory. The Government's only hope had been to avoid a confrontation it could not win. But its strategy worked because the union leaders toured the coalfields convincing a narrow majority to accept the deal.

This was a major turning point. It postponed the day of reckoning to a time that suited the coal owners and the British establishment. That would finally come in May 1926, in the General Strike. Lloyd George knew in such a crisis the union bosses would always settle for the status quo rather than risk revolution. In 1919, the ruling class owed the union leaders a great debt of gratitude. Tory leader Bonar Law put it in a nutshell, "Trade union organisation was the only thing between us and anarchy—without it our position was hopeless".[70]

The missing link in 1919 was bold, independent, revolutionary organisation inside the British working class. Had the Communist Party (CPGB) been formed before 1919, it could have grown sufficiently to take advantage of the great opportunities. But it wasn't launched until the end of 1920, when the tide had turned in favour of the employers. In 1920, unemployment in Glasgow soared to 16 percent and quickly thereafter to 25 percent, sapping working class confidence and workplace organisation. This enabled the employers to launch a vicious counter offensive that broke the back of workplace organisation and the powerful movement that had developed between 1910 and 1920.

John Maclean and Scottish nationalism

The failure to make the breakthrough in 1919 and his increasing isolation led John Maclean to call for a Scottish Workers Republic. According to his daughter, "there is little evidence that he took the question of Scottish Nationalism seriously until 1920".[71] Until then he had looked to a British Revolution.

As a supporter of Irish freedom and one of the few British socialists to have defended the 1916 Easter Rising, he saw how by 1920 the fight for Irish independence had shaken the British Empire. He believed a similar fight for a Scottish Workers' Republic could challenge it even further. But he underestimated the differences between Scotland and Ireland, never properly taking into account the contrasting roles played by the Scottish bourgeoisie and their Irish counterparts in relation to British imperialism. While the Irish were prepared to fight a war against British rule and occupation, the Scottish ruling class was a partner in Empire

In 1920, he was arguing a similar fight in Glasgow could tear the Empire apart. But he was not a nationalist. He was for workers' power based on soviets, not a bourgeois parliament in Edinburgh. His arguments for the break-up of the British state were never presented in nationalist terms.

> We can make Glasgow a Petrograd—a revolutionary storm centre second to none. A Scottish breakaway would bring the empire crashing to the ground and free the waiting workers of the world. English labour is bound to respond to our call if we in Scotland strike out boldly for political conquest.[72]

Underlying his call was the centrality of class struggle and anti-imperialism. Yet his notion that workers in Glasgow were ready to seize power was wrong, saying more about his own isolation than it did about the balance of class forces. By then the movement was as weak on Clydeside as it was in Sheffield. The CWC had been broken by mass unemployment and the victimisation of its leadership. Even if a Glasgow soviet had come to pass, only one thing could have saved it from the barbarism inflicted on rebel Dublin in 1916 by the British State—solidarity from the English cities that Maclean insisted lagged behind the Scots.

Lenin had wanted Maclean to play a leading role in the new Communist Party of Great Britain but in the negotiations he was sidelined. Eventually he refused to join because of his political differences with those who came to lead the CPGB—notably Willie Gallacher and Theodore Rothstein. Maclean was head and shoulders above them, but his decision to stand aside cut him off from the most class-conscious workers and the one organisation which did try to face up to the task of rebuilding the movement. It was a mistake on his part, depriving the new party of Britain's leading revolutionary. Maclean died at the end of 1923. He was only 44, his death the result of poverty, physical exhaustion and the treatment he had to endure in prison. Ultimately his weakness was his failure to build a party that could draw on his great strengths. He was still highly regarded among the Scottish working class, as shown by the tens of thousands who lined the streets for his funeral. But sadly, his Scottish Workers' Republican Party, founded towards the end of his life, numbered its membership in dozens and its electoral support in hundreds.

Some on the Scottish left look back and defend Maclean's refusal to join the CPGB. Often they confuse the new party of 1920 and the Third International to which it belonged with the deformed caricatures both subsequently became after Lenin's death, the isolation of Russia and the rise of Stalinism in the mid-1920s. Those who led the October Revolution never meant it to be confined within the borders of Russia.

Maclean, like his great contemporary James Connolly, left nothing behind in the way of political organisation. None of this diminishes his significance. Mistakes are inevitable; the key thing is to learn from them. Like Lenin, Maclean broke with the rotten politics of the Second International without ever falling into the trap of syndicalism. A consistent anti-imperialist, he argued the war was a repartitioning of the world between the great powers and could only lead to further imperialist conflict and he was proved right. Maclean is a giant who can still speak to us now.

Red Clydeside & the ILP—myth and reality

During the Centenary of the 40-hour strike in 2019, the Scottish press carried articles debunking "the myth of Red Clydeside created and fostered by the far left".[73] If these and other hostile accounts down the years are to be believed, the battles led by revolutionaries during and immediately after the First World War were rear-guard actions to defend privileged labour aristocrats, the 40-hour strike was simply an industrial dispute and Bloody Friday was a storm in a teacup. This sleight-of-hand is not new. It began with C A Oakley's semi-official history of Glasgow, *The Second City.*[74] First published in 1946 and reprinted on numerous occasions since, it was an ever-present in Glasgow's popular municipal libraries. Its author dealt with Red Clydeside by excluding from his definition of it everything that occurred before the end of 1922.

Oakley had an axe to grind. As Chairman of the Glasgow Chamber of Commerce in the period of the Cold War, he was worried, along with Glasgow's politicians, that the city's red reputation and its association with industrial unrest was bad for business and would scare off new investment—particularly from the USA—in a region where, even in the boom years of British capitalism, traditional industries were in steady decline. To not mention Red Clydeside would be unthinkable, so he resolved his dilemma by painting it pink—focusing on the electoral swing to the left and ignoring the events that produced it—the munitions strikes, the rent campaigns, the anti-war struggles and the great demonstrations and marches; not to mention the Russian, German and Irish revolutions and the 40-hours strike at the end of the war.

In this highly moderated version, it was reformist politicians like Wheatley, Shinwell, Kirkwood, Maxton and Johnston, who, especially in the three years after 1919, created a mass Labour vote and did so through patient work in the local communities around the provision of housing and other municipal services. John Wheatley, the ILP Councillor associated with the 1915 housing campaign, later a key figure in the 1924 Labour government, opposed Maclean's call for strike action against the war. In 1916, he and Kirkwood sabotaged the CWC by brokering a separate dilution deal with the government officials at Parkhead Forge. In response to Maclean's attacks on the pair, Wheatley countered by claiming it was "pragmatism rather than socialism" that won the Clydeside ILP its haul of Westminster seats in the 1922 general election.[75] He made cheap jibes at Maclean's expense, belittling the Russian Revolution and Maclean's anti-war activity. "At our meetings we talked local politics, advocating the needs of the near east of Glasgow rather than the far east of Europe".[76]

There is no denying the importance of the Glasgow ILP during those years. With the crushing of the CWC in 1916 and Maclean imprisoned for over a year, it became the main beneficiary of the growing radicalism generated by the February Revolution in Russia and the growing anti-war mood. From early 1917, the ILP in Scotland grew from 3,000 members in 117 branches to 9,000 members in 192 branches by the end of the war. It was an expansion that happened nowhere else in Britain, as Labour Party membership declined. But it left Scotland with a third of the ILP's total British membership. In the continuing absence of any revolutionary current of national significance during the explosive struggles of 1919, the ILP became the electoral beneficiary of the movement's containment and defeat.

In 1920, Labour took a third of the seats in Glasgow's municipal election. But the real electoral breakthrough came in the 1922 Westminster election when Labour increased its vote to 32 percent and 29 seats on Clydeside. The Irish vote had swung behind Labour as Lloyd George's policy of repression in Ireland destroyed its traditional allegiance to the Liberals. The breakthrough was made in nearly all the industrial areas which had working class communities of Irish descent.

But to see the ILP as the legacy, the crowning achievement of Red Clydeside, is preposterous. It dismisses the mass movement and ignores the international dimension. It also ignores what shortly became of the ILP. The left electoral gains on Clydeside in 1922 were real enough but they were a product of mass struggle and the anti-war mood. 1922 was a temporary electoral victory not the defining moment nor the take–off point for the movement. Rather, 1922 signalled the beginning of its safe containment in the orthodox vault of parliamentary politics.

Working class men and women had struck terror in the hearts of the British ruling class during the war years and even more so in 1919. In comparison, Wheatley, Kirkwood, Maxton, Shinwell and the others who went to represent them in Westminster were but a pale reflection of that earlier militancy. Helen Crawfurd, a brave anti-war socialist who became increasingly disillusioned with the ILP, could see the rightward direction it was taking. Hence she ditched them to play a leading role in the belated formation of the revolutionary CPGB and wrote about it in her autobiography, which sadly went unpublished after she died in 1954.[77]

The dreaded 'Clydeside Reds', who came to shake up Westminster and capture the state, were soon playing the parliamentary game. In his memoirs, Labour's Philip Snowden recalls how "It was rather amusing to see the Labour members, whose advent to parliament was expected to outrage all conventionalities, performing parliamentary customs with more correctness than the Tories".[78] Three of them ended up in the House of Lords!

After a parliamentary debate where Kirkwood attacked Tory leader Bonar Law's unemployment policies, the latter buttonholed him in the corridor to say, "You Clyde boys were pretty hard on me today but its fine to hear your Glasgow accent. It's like a sniff of the air of Scotland in the musty atmosphere of this place". "What could a man do in the face of such a greeting?" was Kirkwood's hapless response.[79] According to historian Iain

S McLean, "Red Clyde had left the streets to sit in parliament. But the press of 1919 registered genuine fear and hatred at the 'Bolsheviks' of George Square; the press from 1922 offered no more than condescending indulgence to Maxton and Kirkwood. From the beginning the Scottish rebels were treated as colourful curiosities, not threats to public order."[80]

Winston Churchill, who with Bonar Law was instrumental in Kirkwood's arrest and trial in 1919, wrote flattering comments in the foreword to Kirkwood's memoirs, published in 1935. By then the bold Davy was First Baron Kirkwood of Bearsden. Earlier, to show "no bad feeling", Churchill, then a government minister, agreed Kirkwood be "put in charge of a munitions factory", rekindling his ambition of 1916 when he sabotaged the CWC in exchange for a worthless promise of a "say in running Beardmores". In his memoirs Kirkwood explained why he broke ranks with the CWC:

> We were all scared as the thundering masses of Germans tramped their way towards the coasts. That night I went to John Wheatley. In thirty minutes he drafted the scheme, which became the basis for the whole of Britain and worked perfectly till the end of the war. The extremists attacked us for having agreed increased production. Maclean made me the theme of innumerable speeches.[81]

In 1920, Antonio Gramsci, leader of the Turin factory council movement, connected the example of working class power which had emerged in Russia with the experience of workers in a number of other countries:

> We say the present period is revolutionary because we can see that the working class in all countries is tending to generate from within its own ranks and with the utmost energy, proletarian institutions of a new type—representative in basis and industrial in arena.

We say the present period is revolutionary because the working class tends with all its energy and willpower to found its own state.[82]

There is no doubt Red Clydeside was part of what Gramsci described. The institutions he referred to—soviets or workers' councils—existed here in embryonic form. The events of those years can inspire those fighting to change the world today, provided we learn the lesson that workers need to organise themselves in a revolutionary party capable of generalising the struggle into a challenge for workers' power.

Red Clydeside was not the only notable event in the inter-war period. During the nine-day General Strike of 1926 some areas in Scotland played the same leading role in the British working class that was seen on Clydeside during the war and in 1919. The 1926 General Strike strike was in defence of miners' jobs and Britain was covered by a network of Councils of Action. Eleven of the 140 Councils formed Workers' Defence Corps, but the most ambitious of these was in Methil, Fife, where a 700-strong Workers' Defence Corps was set up under former NCOs. This meant that police attacks on pickets such as seen elsewhere were minimised. Unfortunately, the strike was sold out by the TUC General Council—a serious setback for all workers, but the experience of the Second World War revived the labour movement in both trade union and political forms. This laid the basis for Labour dominance in Scotland, which is the starting point of the next chapter.

Chapter 5

The Decline of the Labour Party in Scotland

Dave Sherry & Julie Sherry

In the latter half of the 20th century, Scotland became a bastion of the British Labour Party. In every general election from 1959 until the earthquake of 2015, when Labour in Scotland collapsed from 41 Westminster seats to just one, Labour always held the most Scottish seats at Westminster. For those 55 years, Labour also dominated the most important local councils, while its activists dominated at every level of the structures of Scotland's powerful trade union movement.

These networks of power and influence dominated working class communities in the big cities and in countless towns and villages built around mining and industry. Especially during the worst of the Thatcher years, Scotland seemed like a bulwark against the Tories' right-wing policies. But over the last 30 years, Labour's vote in Scotland has gone into steep decline and shows little chance of recovering.

There have been many attempts to explain this reversal and some of that story is bound up with the reasons for the rise of the SNP. Tom Devine and Gerry Hassan, for instance, have written extensively on the changes in voting patterns and the general disillusionment with the Blair leadership of the Labour

Party that came to be expressed in Scotland (if not elsewhere) in the growth of support for the SNP.[1]

This key shift is covered in the following chapter, 'Rise of the Independence Movement'. But there is a deeper explanation below the surface. Support for the politics of Labourism, the notion of gradual change through the existing institutions of capitalism, rests on a material basis. Reformism is an expression of the desire for change combined, to varying degrees, with a lack of confidence in workers' ability to achieve change through their own efforts. The decline of Labour in Scotland is bound up with the outcome of working class struggles in the decades since the 1960s and the role of the Labour Party within those struggles.

From the wave of workplace occupations in the 1970s to the heroic defensive battles of the miners' strike and other struggles in the 1980s and on to the fights by public sector workers for equal pay and against privatisation in the 2000s, Labour politics have either (i) diverted or derailed the potential of these movements leading to a series of unnecessary defeats and setbacks, or (ii) represented the opponents of workers in the form of Labour governments at Westminster, Labour-led administrations at Holyrood and at local council level.

This chapter examines the key moments of working class struggle during this era and the legacy of Labour politics in Scotland. It also looks to the alternative strategies that emerged in this period and their lessons for today.

Labour in office 1964-70

By 1964, the Tories had been in power for 13 years. In 1955, they'd polled 50 percent of the Scottish vote. The long post war boom meant Tory leader Harold Macmillan could tell voters "you've never had it so good". In 1959, they won a third election in a row but in Scotland Labour won most seats. During those Tory years, half a million people left Scotland, 90 percent of its population growth. By 1964, unemployment, low by present day standards, was double the rate south of the border and would have been greater but for high emigration. With a tenth of its population,

Scotland had a quarter of Britain's long-term unemployed. Scotland's economy, based as it had been on traditional heavy industry, now lagged behind Britain as a whole. This would feed into support for Labour. Eventual disillusion with Labour would feed into support for the SNP. It was not national consciousness but working class discontent driving both processes.

Labour won the 1964 General Election. Scotland's contribution was decisive, returning 43 Labour MPs and securing Harold Wilson a wafer-thin majority. Scottish voters aside, Labour's victory was down to a widespread feeling, including among some sections of big business, that the Tories could not revive a flagging economy. Wilson had promised "a new Britain forged in the white heat of the technological revolution" and "a planned growth of incomes". He looked more capable of arresting Britain's decline than the Tory Prime Minister, old Etonian Earl Sir Alec Douglas-Home.

It soon became clear that Labour's new 'left' management was as committed to capitalism as the discredited Tories. But in 1966, Wilson called another election, winning easily with a majority of 96 seats. Labour took 49.9 percent of the Scottish vote and 46 seats—compared to 48 percent across Britain—its biggest ever percentage share. Egged on by the establishment and right-wing union leaders, Wilson looked to modernise Britain by taming shop floor militancy and boosting productivity.

Yet *Tribune*, voice of the Labour left, greeted the 1966 victory with the incongruous headline: 'Socialism is Right Back on the Agenda!' What was really on the agenda was a government that doubled unemployment, introduced racist immigration laws, imposed a wage freeze, backed US genocide in Vietnam, sent troops to Ireland, made more cuts to social services than the previous three Tory governments combined and to cap it all, tried to introduce anti-trade union legislation.

The number of trade union shop stewards had increased during the post-war economic boom but generally they were apolitical. There wasn't a 'shop stewards movement' as in the First World War but the tradition of do-it-yourself reformism on the factory floor expressed workers' growing self-reliance and self-assertiveness. Having suffered no serious defeats for a generation, it was a strong, confident working class that was confronted with the sudden politicisation of industrial relations as Labour tried to restore British capitalism. The attempts by governments and employers to shackle the shop stewards in the late 1960s and early 1970s led to the biggest class confrontations for half a century.

A compliant TUC did not oppose Wilson's wage controls but groups of workers did and were sufficiently well organised at rank-and-file level to fight independently of their union leaders. A prominent example was the strike by 400 machinists at Fords Dagenham over equal pay which forced the company to negotiate directly with the women. It also forced Labour employment minister Barbara Castle to introduce an Equal Pay Act. More importantly the strike—following the Abortion Act of 1967—inspired others to fight and raise the banner of gender equality and women's liberation.

Unions like the Transport and General Workers' Union (TGWU) spoke in militant terms and left wingers were elected to leading positions. Leaders of the new white-collar unions set their sights on growth and took militant action to gain recruits. The 1968 TUC Conference reflected the changing mood by voting seven to one against wage controls. Labour responded by attempting to legally shackle the militants. 'Red' Barbara Castle was won over by the bosses' arguments. In 1969, she published a White Paper, *In Place of Strife*, which attempted to curb workers' right to strike. The government proposed fines on trade unions which refused to hold strike ballots or agree to a 28-day "cooling off" period before strikes.[2]

A letter to Harold Wilson reports on a meeting with Vic Feather, leader of the TUC: "Feather insists there is no belly for a fight. He says that people who say there must be no legislation at any price are just a few of the romantics."[3] It looked like Castle's Industrial Relations Bill would sail through parliament but it riled hundreds of thousands of rank-and-file activists into resistance. Now economic struggles flowed into political ones. A sizeable minority of shop stewards were linked to the Communist Party of Great Britain (CPGB), whose strongest base was Clydeside. At this stage, the CPGB was still arguing for a degree of independence from Labour.

1968: a watershed

International events also had an impact in encouraging revolt and increasing the popularity of radical ideas, far to the left of the Labour or Communist parties. 1968 showed how the world could be changed by rebellion from below, especially after the May events in France. Called in response to police attacks on student protests in Paris, a massive general strike led to virtually every French workplace being occupied under workers' control. It was also the year the black ghettos of the USA exploded after the assassination of Martin Luther King and the year of the Prague Spring, when Czech students and workers fought the Stalinist monolith and were crushed by Russian tanks, causing upheaval and decline in the world's Communist parties.

1968 also saw the rise of the movement against the US war in Vietnam, the Women's Movement, the Gay Liberation Movement and the Civil Rights Movement in Ireland. Revolutionary ideas flourished, especially among young workers and students. The slogan of the International Socialists (forerunners of the Socialist Workers Party)— *Neither Washington nor Moscow but International Socialism*— chimed with the times. But the vacuum left by the decline of the Labour and Communist parties also produced a sinister development. Tory MP Enoch Powell, looking for a scapegoat, made his "rivers of blood speech" in Birmingham in April 1968, calling for tougher immigration controls. Alarmingly, a group of London dockers struck and marched in support of Powell after his sacking from the Tory shadow cabinet.

Then, in February 1969, for the first time since 1926, an overtly political strike took place when 150,000 workers marched in Glasgow and Liverpool against Barbara Castle's White Paper. On May Day, the unofficial, CP-led Liaison Committee for the Defence of Trade Unions called a strike of half a million workers under the slogan 'Kill the Bill'. The shutdown of all the newspapers meant no one could ignore what was happening. Now Labour left MPs and some union leaders sided with the revolt—even though they objected to the May Day strikes. The Labour cabinet split and Wilson and Castle had to abandon the anti-trade union bill. It was a great victory for the rank and file. Strikes against wage controls spread from traditionally militant sectors to groups of workers who had rarely if ever taken action before.

A six week strike by trawler men began in Aberdeen. Bin workers in London struck and the strike spread to other parts of Britain. Pressure from below forced the National Union of Teachers (NUT) to call its first–ever campaign of industrial action. In January 1970, militancy spread to women clothing workers in Leeds, with 25,000 on strike for equal pay. Despite the official policy of wage controls, average real wages across the working class rose by ten percent between 1967 and 1970.

Turning the tables at East Kilbride

Typical of the spirit of 1969 was a historic battle in East Kilbride, when workers at the Birmingham Sound Reproducers (BSR) factory, which made record player turntables, walked out for equal pay, union recognition and an end to management intimidation and sexism. The factory had opened in 1964, attracted north by substantial grants, a modern factory and an untapped female labour source. BSR was aggressively non-union; only its skilled, male toolmakers were union members. Earlier it had closed its Derry plant, dismissing its workforce and re-opening it a week later under another name. Most workers were re-employed but not the shop stewards.

By 1969, BSR East Kilbride was booming but demands for union recognition and equal bonus pay were ignored and women began joining the union. Then, in June, management sacked a tool room worker. When other workers walked out in protest they were sacked. So they picketed the factory and began recruiting women to the union as they came to and from work.

When BSR tried to buy the women off with a paltry bonus they walked out and joined the craftsmen and the Amalgamated Engineering Union (AEU) immediately made their strike official. What followed was the most bitter recognition dispute of its era. In October, 50,000 local AEU members struck for two hours in solidarity.

Weeks later, 200,000 workers across central Scotland staged a one-day strike, with 3,000 coming to demonstrate at East Kilbride. At another mass picket, Bernadette Devlin, newly elected as an independent socialist MP for Mid Ulster, addressed the strikers. Then, in November, there were 47 arrests on the picket line, most of them women. *The Evening Times* reported, "A number are charged with breach of the peace. They were taken to the police station after another sit down outside the factory and a flour bomb battle with the police."[4] All 47 were released after 200 women marched from the picket to the police station, promising that if the strikers were not released hundreds more would besiege it.

After 14 weeks, the strikers in East Kilbride returned to work, having won equal pay. Management tried to humiliate them on their return. "One foreman said, 'if I tell you to clean the toilets, then that's what you'll do', so we marched out on strike for another week until we were given our old jobs back. We got 100 percent trade unionism and union recognition throughout the factory."[5]

Disillusionment with the Labour government grew and so did the SNP—from 2,000 members in 1962 to 100,000 in 1968. At the Pollok by-election in 1967, the SNP took 28 percent of the vote allowing the Tories to capture a safe Labour seat. A bigger shock came in November when the SNP won its first by-election, overturning a big Labour majority in the former mining seat of Hamilton. The May 1968 Council elections saw the SNP poll 30 percent with a strong showing in Glasgow, where the Tories, with fewer seats than Labour, were able to form an administration with SNP support.

Labour had promised much but ended up attacking its supporters. In the 1970 General election, it paid the price. Heath's Tories won because Labour voters stayed home in droves. Its vote slumped from 48 to 43 percent. Scottish results for Labour were better; they retained 44 seats and the SNP threat receded.

1970–74: How to topple a Tory government

Ted Heath's Tory manifesto was far to the right of anything since 1945. Initially he was successful, using unemployment and the weakness of some union leaders to inflict defeats on the power workers and the postal workers. Legislation was introduced to sell off council housing and end rent subsidies. Thatcher gained notoriety by axing free school milk. Home Secretary Maudling introduced imprisonment without trial in Northern Ireland and was behind Bloody Sunday, when the British state assassinated 14 civilians at a civil rights march in Derry.

The post-war boom was over. By 1971, redundancy was the Achilles heel of an otherwise strong trade unionism. Labour had introduced the Redundancy Payments Act, to encourage workers and union leaders to accept sackings without a fight. The demands adopted by the unions—'last in first out', 'voluntary redundancy', ' better redundancy pay', 'early retirement', 'natural wastage'—were inadequate.

While strike days rose 25 percent between 1965 and 1970, the number of strike days fighting redundancy fell by half, despite the fact that job losses were increasing. "Unemployment is the chief weapon of economic policy", wrote *The Times* in April 1971. "The market would weed out" inefficient industry— "lame ducks" as Heath called them—providing leeway for profitable growth elsewhere.

In June, Upper Clyde Shipbuilders (UCS), the consortium owning four of Glasgow's five shipyards, was allowed to go bust. Here was a 'lame duck' the Tories could exploit for their purposes. Industry minister John Davies announced, "nobody's interest is served by injecting public funds into UCS".[6] Two yards were to shut with 6,000 of the 8,500 workers sacked. These measures would destroy another 30,000 jobs. Unemployment on the Clyde was already 40 percent up on the previous year.

Upper Clyde Shipbuilders and the Right to Work

The government was taken aback by the anger and militancy of the response. Mass meetings in every yard voted to occupy if sackings went ahead. A hundred thousand workers took part in a one-day strike and a huge march through Glasgow—the biggest since Red Clydeside. The action at UCS would not be as militant as the first signs indicated. The occupation became a 'work-in' whereby workers continued to work with supervisors in charge, ensuring orders were completed and ships handed over to the government liquidator.

The campaign was run as a Scottish popular front rather than a confrontation with government. The work-in stressed the importance of Glasgow's shipyards to the *Scottish* economy and the demand for a Scottish assembly—instead of encouraging workers to confront the Tories directly.

In 1972, as negotiations over the future of the yards dragged on, many workers lost faith in the campaign. One thousand four hundred had left to seek work elsewhere by the end of 1971. The percentage of redundant workers who were 'working-in' fell from 48 to 14 percent between October 1971 and June 1972.[7] Eventually, in late 1972, the shop stewards would agree to proposals that kept the yards going but with a much-reduced workforce.

Nonetheless the refusal to simply accept redundancies shook the Tories and galvanised other workers. It turned the tide against a government hell-bent on attacking working people and signalled redundancy was not inevitable. UCS became a symbol of resistance. Jimmy Airlie, Amalgamated Engineering Union (AEU) shop steward and chair of the UCS work-in committee, told the *BBC News* cameras, "The only way we'll be beaten is if we're starved into submission. It's the responsibility of the labour movement to see that does not happen because it's not only our fight, it's the fight of every man and woman in this country—the fight for the right to work."[8]

The response was as dramatic as Airlie's appeal. On 10 August, a meeting of 1,300 shop stewards from Scotland and the North of England endorsed the work-in and called on workers everywhere to give financial support and backed a call by the CP's Jimmy Reid for another strike and demonstration in Glasgow. On 18 August, 200,000 Scottish workers struck for the day and there was another huge march through the city with representatives from every workplace in the West of Scotland and big delegations from south of the border. Thousands of workplaces organised weekly levies. Money and messages of support poured in from all over the world.

The work-in continued into 1972 and the Tories were forced to announce a £35 million package to save three of the yards. The negotiations dragged on until October, when the remaining John Brown yard at Clydebank was taken over by the American-owned company Marathon. Concessions on demarcation and job losses would return to haunt the movement; meantime the Tories were forced to retreat.

UCS was an important turning point. As Roger Rosewell noted: "Despite its leaders' efforts to confine the struggle, there's no doubt the ideas raised by UCS will spread within the movement."[9] Soon others facing redundancy were occupying too. First came the torpedo plant in nearby Vale of Leven, two months after the UCS work-in started. It was a smaller workforce with a big percentage of women workers. Facing closure they launched a full-blooded occupation and seized the plant. "The workers held a mass meeting, marched through the factory and padlocked the gates. Other Plessey plants are refusing to handle any machinery removed from Alexandria."[10] Plessey walked away but the occupation forced the Scottish Development Agency in 1972 to acquire and convert the site into an industrial estate, providing jobs for the former Plessey workforce.

Occupation was used as a tactic to improve wages and

*Jimmy Reid and UCS
workers*

conditions and it spread from blue- to white-collar and public sector workers. Millions got involved in campaigns of civil disobedience, in resistance to the government's Industrial Relations Act and its Housing Finance Act. Over 200 factory occupations occurred between 1972 and 1974. Most attained their objectives.

In 1972, the miners' strike smashed Tory wage controls. Flying pickets were key and the turning point was the battle at the Saltley depot in Birmingham, with its huge stockpiles of coal. Police were mobilised to smash the miners' picket. In response, 100,000 Birmingham engineers and car workers struck in solidarity and 10,000 marched to Saltley to join the miners and shut the depot.

Heath had to concede the miners' claim in full. 1972 was a great year for the workers but not every fight ended in victory.

The national building workers' strike that summer was the biggest since the 1920s. It erupted over low pay and the widespread use of casual labour known as 'the lump'. Three hundred thousand struck, thanks to flying pickets and a call for £30 for a 35-hour week. While it is still remembered for the 'Shrewsbury 24'—a group of strikers in North Wales who were fitted up by the building industry bosses, the police chiefs and the Tory cabinet, and wrongly prosecuted for conspiracy, including Ricky Tomlinson and Des Warren who were jailed— Scotland was at the centre of it. The big construction firms offered local agreements that fell short of the full claim, but Scottish union officials saw this as an easy get-out and recommended acceptance. A mass meeting of 4,000 strikers in Edinburgh rejected it but in the end the officials were able to push through local deals and the strike fizzled out as different companies settled.

The Tory Housing Act

Heath's Housing Finance Act provoked resistance north and south of the border. Councils were ordered to scrap rent subsidies for the poorest tenants. Non co-operation was punishable by withholding council funds, imposing fines and disqualifying councillors. Scottish tenants took part in the rents strike that spread across Britain.

Although Labour in Scotland opposed the Act, it ruled out extra parliamentary action. In the council elections of 1971, Labour had won back control of Glasgow Council but it wasn't prepared to defy the law; nonetheless 20 other Scottish councils pledged they would. But the rebels collapsed one-by-one and in January 1973 Clydebank was the only council in Scotland still resisting the Act.

Jimmy Reid, one of three Communist councillors, assured tenants in February, "in no circumstance will we implement this Tory Rent Act. We are answerable to no courts—only the working class of Clydebank".[11] A month later, all three voted with Labour to implement the rent increases.

Two thirds of Scotland lived in council housing so the impact of defeat was severe—one of the reasons for an SNP resurgence that forced devolution onto Labour's agenda. Labour's Scottish Council reluctantly set up a devolution working group in January 1973.

Proof of an SNP revival came when it polled 30.2 percent against Labour's 32.7 percent in the Dundee East by election. That year, Margo MacDonald overturned a 16,000 majority to capture the safe Labour seat of Govan in a by-election. Days before, Scottish Labour had announced its opposition to devolution. Wilson ordered a U-turn. Faced with rising support for the nationalists, he decided, despite opposition from his Scottish executive, Labour must steal the SNP's clothes.

In the summer of 1972, the Tory Industrial Relations Court's imprisonment of five trade unionists was rescinded in spectacular fashion. Spontaneous mass walkouts forced the TUC to threaten a general strike. The Pentonville Five were released and the government humiliated.

On May Day 1973, two million workers struck and 120,000 marched through London to demand the scrapping of the anti-union laws and Heath's wage controls. A militant working class was about to scrap the government. In November, the crisis it had been dreading arrived.

Oil prices quadrupled following the Arab-Israeli war, forcing Heath to jam the brakes on the economy. *Phase Three*, his third attempt to hold wages below price rises, had encountered more resistance than the previous phases. It was defeated by a group of workers whose union had rarely taken action.

An unofficial strike by a few hundred Glasgow firefighters achieved more in a few days than all the union leaderships put together. The union officials had opposed the strike, suspending the Glasgow Fire Brigade Union Committee for calling it; yet they led it to a victory that improved the pay and conditions of every firefighter across Britain—a turning point in the union's history.

Chris Harman highlighted its importance: "The lesson is not lost on millions of other workers. Power station engineers and ambulance workers are emulating the firefighters. Public transport workers in London are planning strikes. And above all, of course, is the miners' national overtime ban."[12]

Heath had rejected the miners' pay claim. In response to their overtime ban he imposed a ten-day shut down of industry followed by a three-day week. In February, a national pithead ballot returned an 81 percent majority for an all-out strike. Heath called a general election for the end of February amid power cuts and blackouts. "Who runs the country?" was Heath's slogan. On 28 February, voters confirmed what the wiser elements of the ruling class already knew and Heath was defeated at the election.

'The least bad government'

Harold Wilson was elected on a manifesto to the left of anything Labour has come up with since—promising a "massive and irreversible shift in the distribution of both wealth and power in favour of working people and their families".[13] Chancellor Dennis Healey promised, "we'll squeeze the rich until the pips squeak". But after a brief period of reforms the new government turned against its own supporters. The bosses' magazine, *The*

Economist shrewdly noted, "with one proviso, namely, that it can introduce some sort of incomes policy sometime soon, this government of Labour men and consensus measures could prove to be the least bad government Britain could have".[14]

With only 37 percent of the vote and 17 seats short of an overall majority in Parliament, Wilson at first had to make concessions. Workers' power had finished the Tories. Heath's anti-union laws and wage controls were scrapped. The miners' demands were met in full and Michael Foot became employment minister—a sop to the left on the TUC. But the new government, the Confederation of British Industry (CBI) and the TUC were all agreed on one thing: strikes had to be curbed. Labour was prepared to bail out the bosses and their system, while the TUC—left and right—was ready to police the rank and file.

For the minority Labour government, its Scottish seats were crucial to its survival. Although Labour recaptured Govan in the February election, its vote in Scotland fell to just 36.6 percent. By contrast, the SNP captured seven Westminster seats, forcing Labour to take seriously its electoral threat. Immediately Wilson promised a White Paper on devolution. The union block vote was mobilised at a Special Scottish conference in August to overturn the recalcitrant Scottish executive and push through support for a Scottish Assembly. In October, Wilson called a second general election, securing an overall majority but only by a margin of three. Labour's vote share in Scotland fell slightly while the SNP's jumped to 30.4 percent, capturing 11 seats and coming second in 35 others.

Labour now pressed ahead with its Social Contract. Crafted by a joint TUC/Labour committee, union bosses used it to enforce 'voluntary' pay restraint. The architects were the left union leaders—Jack Jones of the TGWU and Hugh Scanlon of the AUEW. Activists were confused and loyalty to Labour and the left officials became a serious impediment to the struggle. The revolutionary left had grown with the upturn in struggle but not enough to outweigh the influence of the CP and its supporters. If UCS underlined the popular front pretensions of the CP, the strike wave following Labour's return to office showed the danger of the left seeking top positions in the trade unions at the cost of building a rank-and-file movement.

Angry at the wage squeeze, workers began to strike, especially throughout central Scotland where a series of 'unofficial' stoppages exploded at the end of the summer. The strikes involved bus workers, lorry drivers, schoolteachers, distillery workers, bin workers, car workers, council electricians, workers at Hoover and Rolls Royce, as well as many light engineering and assembly plants where a majority were low paid women. Even Ladbrokes betting shop staff struck. But national and local full-timers fought to push their members back to work.

Prominent CP members, including the secretary of Glasgow Trades Council and the TGWU district officer, intervened to urge compromise or surrender. During the dustmen's dispute, they told the strikers to get back to work and negotiate. When the Labour Council used the army to break the strike, the council electricians who maintained the depots and incinerators walked out to join the bin workers' picket.

The powerful Glasgow Trades Council could have mounted a campaign against the use of troops by involving the whole movement: it was national news. Instead it organised a local, token demonstration that kept well away from the rubbish dumps and incinerators where the troops were working.

At the end of the march, the TGWU officials ordered the strike committee to call a mass meeting and accept a return to work, despite the fact that the dispute was of tremendous national significance.

In the end, the movement for better wages that had grown in the Scottish strike wave faded. Although most won increases, the Social Contract survived its first serious test. What could have been a successful campaign against wage controls was never developed because the main organisation capable of giving it direction failed to do so. Individual CP members played a positive role in many of these struggles but as a political force the party failed, insisting that the Social Contract would be headed off by left officials and politicians rather than by mass action from below. It sacrificed a living movement for conference hall manoeuvres. In the Scottish strike wave, the emergence of a real rank-and-file movement was within reach. At one point, five strike committees were holding separate meetings in separate rooms in the same building—the Glasgow Trade Union Centre in Carlton Place. The Social Contract could have been defeated.

Solidarity with Chile

On a brighter note, the confidence, self-activity and class-consciousness that typified the strike wave against the Social Contract led—only weeks later—to a historic act of international solidarity by workers in both East Kilbride and Rosyth. The 2018 Glasgow Film Festival featured the premiere of the moving documentary, *Nae Pasaran*—the story of how, in 1974, workers at Rolls Royce, East Kilbride refused to repair the fighter jet engines used by Pinochet's junta to overthrow the elected government in 1973. The boycott lasted four years but the workforce never knew the real impact of their solidarity until the making of the film, 40 years later; that they'd grounded Pinochet's air force and brought inspiration to trade unionists being held and tortured in his jails.

John Keenan, a leading shop steward at East Kilbride during the boycott, appears in the film with some workmates.

> After the coup our factory voted unanimously to condemn it and to support the Chile Solidarity Campaign and the refugees fleeing repression and torture—many of whom came to Scotland. In October 1974, we'd been on strike against Labour's 'social contract'. On returning to work we discovered there were Chilean air force jet engines to be inspected and rebuilt at East Kilbride. Our works committee recommended the workforce refuse to inspect or work on them. Every section meeting voted to back our call. Local management was annoyed but

reluctant to take us on. In parliament Tory leader Ted Heath tried to force Harold Wilson to instruct our union to lift the boycott but at that point Wilson didn't want to take us on either.

We'd later discover the Chilean air force got a court order for the engines to be released. While the AUEW had a formal policy on Chile, the Executive Council member for our district—a right-winger—instructed our works committee to lift the boycott, under pressure from the company and his cronies in the Labour government. So we called a mass meeting and it voted to continue the boycott and ignore the official. It was the courage of the ordinary workers that mattered. Without them we couldn't have done a thing. It shows what real working class unity might achieve.[15]

The same year the Chilean submarine *O'Brien* docked in Greenock so that key components could be repaired and sent back to Chile as spares. When these parts arrived at the naval dockyard at Rosyth, the shop stewards refused to release them, informing the Ministry of Defence: "No future Chilean Navy work will be done in Rosyth dockyard until the fascist *junta* is removed and a democratically elected government is in power and human rights restored in Chile."[16]

How Labour weakened the movement

The Labour government encouraged widespread incorporation of workplace convenors and senior shop stewards into partnership, productivity and planning agreements with management. This top layer were soon detached from the rank and file—a process that weakened organisation and helped bring about the biggest fall in real wages for a generation. When world recession brought a doubling of unemployment, militancy collapsed and strikes hit their lowest level since the 1950s. The union leaders' loyalty to Labour and their hold over most of the shop stewards meant struggles were increasingly dependent on the officials.

Until 1974, the CP played a dual role, initiating actions like UCS while limiting them to retain control. With Labour in office, it became more of an obstacle, blocking initiatives like the National Rank and File Movement and the Right to Work Campaign against unemployment. The CP's reluctance to criticise the left union leaders led it to oppose unofficial strikes against the Social Contract.

In 1976, Dennis Healey pushed through welfare cuts amounting to £8 billion (£87 billion in today's money) in response to demands from the International Monetary Fund and an investment strike. Monetarism in Britain didn't begin with Thatcher. Nothing she did matched the carnage wrought by Labour in the mid-1970s.

"The toughest monetary policy yet seen was pursued by Callaghan and Healey", wrote one right-wing commentator, "they were successful; unemployment shot up to a new post-war record of 1,635,000."[17]

This triggered an explosion of strikes, protests and marches. Dundee saw the biggest action yet against the cuts. A one-day stoppage across the city produced an impressive display of working class power. Early in the morning, workers from the major factories, shipyards, hospitals, offices and depots assembled outside their workplaces. Then, from every corner of Dundee, trade union feeder marches converged in a protest rally in the city square. A week later Glasgow schoolteachers and bus workers struck in big numbers, protesting against the cuts to education and public transport. Glasgow abandoned its tenement housing renovation programme, closed its public toilets and cut its refuse service to the bone.

Teacher training and recruitment was also slashed. In response, every teacher training college in Scotland occupied, starting at Jordanhill College in Glasgow. The college occupations built links with one other and the wider movement. Trainee teachers occupied the City Chambers. Others spoke to lunchtime factory gate meetings, shop stewards' committees, union branches and even major union conferences, calling for a class-wide fight against education cuts. Occupations spread across Britain and only the summer holidays brought them to an end.

Alas political organisation lagged behind. The revolutionary left had grown, playing a key role in initiating important united fronts—the Right to Work Campaign, local anti-cuts groups, the Anti Nazi League and Rock Against Racism—all crucial given the rise of unemployment, racism and the Nazis of the National Front. But it was too small to counter the conservative influence of reformist ideas at work and in the unions. The feeling among a growing minority, that workers had the power to run society, began to ebb away and there was a shift to the right.

When Callaghan replaced Wilson in 1976, he called those who opposed wage controls "small bands of disrupters" and the TUC was ready to deal with them. In March 1977, there were three key strikes against wage controls but the leaders denounced them as "greedy", encouraging other workers to scab by crossing picket lines. At the end of 1977, the firefighters got the same treatment. The Wilson cabinet ordered troops to break their national strike but the TUC General Council voted *not* to organise solidarity. Seven weeks into the strike, the TUC and the union leaders cobbled a deal and sold it to a majority of members before Christmas.

In 1978, after two years on strike for union recognition at Grunwicks film processing plant in North London, migrant women who'd been sacked for standing up to a ruthless boss were told by the TUC and their own union Apex the dispute could not be won. Consequently, all official support was withdrawn—despite their having been mass pickets of trade unionists outside the factory and postal workers refusing to deliver Grunwicks' mail. The Tories and the National Front saw that by turning growing discontent against black and Asian people, they could grow and win votes. The right-wing press helped by demanding tougher measures against immigrants and Labour's Home Secretaries—first Roy Jenkins then Merlyn Rees—hastened to comply.

No post-war Tory government had managed to cut real earnings for workers and neither would the Tories under Thatcher. Labour's success in doing so couldn't last. Eventually the union leaders, left and right, couldn't hold their members back any longer. But when struggle erupted at the end of the Labour government during what became known as the 'Winter of Discontent', it was bitter, sectional and did not lead to the generalisation and confidence that had marked the early 1970s.

Labour's final acts were to mess up Scottish devolution and agree a *Concordat* with the General Council of the TUC in February 1979—a blatant attempt to further undermine union rights and return to the wage-cutting that had preceded the 'Winter of Discontent'. The demoralisation it created among its own supporters led to defeat in the election of 1979. Labour got its lowest share of the vote in any election since 1931. Barbara Castle's *In Place of Strife* had opened the door for Edward Heath: Callaghan's *Concordat* paved the way for Thatcher.

The Tories didn't win north of the border. Labour's share of the Scottish vote was up 5 percent on October 1974. For the SNP the election was a disaster. It lost nine of its 11 seats and its vote slumped from 30 to 13 percent. At that point in Scotland, the SNP could attract working class votes on the basis of a protest against Labour's anti-working class policies, but when the choice was between a Tory and a Labour government at Westminster, then many of those voters returned to Labour.

The baleful legacy of UCS

UCS, celebrated as a victory, ended with major job losses and concessions that had repercussions for shipbuilding and the wider struggle in Scotland during the Labour government and long into the Thatcher era. This was not inevitable.

UCS demonstrated some of the complexities and the shifting sands of the time. Jimmy Reid and Jimmy Airlie's popular front strategy, invoking a Scottish national interest, was pulling in one direction. But the spread of the occupation tactic across Britain illustrated the interaction and unity of the

British working class movement in spite of that.

UCS had prompted new developments throughout the working class. But if any party in Scotland benefitted, it was the SNP. In October 1973, a year after the work-in ended, Margo MacDonald won the Govan by-election. Part of the explanation lies in the way that the CP and the Scottish TUC conducted the UCS campaign. Scottish nationalism was not confined to the ballot box or the SNP.

Focusing on a Scottish People's Assembly meant looking to the great and the good: church leaders, SNP and moderate Tory politicians, Scottish businessmen and celebrities. In the midst of a class struggle that was rocking the Tories, the CP promoted a top-down, cross-class alliance to "save Scottish jobs and defend Scottish industry". If the aim was to steal the SNP thunder, then it failed. The STUC and the union leaderships applied this 'pan-Scottish approach' for the next 20 years with dire consequences. As the global crisis deepened, coal, steel, shipbuilding and engineering, as well as the car, print and newspaper industries, were ruthlessly downsized or axed.

The UCS work-in petered out 14 months after it began. Three of the yards were saved as a result of Heath's U-turn but while his cabinet retreated from its target of 6,000 redundancies, it succeeded in cutting the workforce and its terms and conditions. The Clydebank yard—renamed Marathon—made concessions no other yard in Britain would have accepted, including a no-strike agreement. Instead of forcing the Tories to keep the Clydebank yard in the consortium, the shop stewards helped them persuade Texan businessman Wayne Harbin to take it over. He did so only after the Tories gave him £12 million public cash and the stewards conceded his demands. Govan Shipbuilders—the new name for the other yards—agreed to a 120 percent increase in productivity with a reduced workforce. The unions agreed 'no strike' pledges and gave management the right to impose overtime. This became the model for elsewhere, paving the way for an onslaught. In 1977, Labour nationalised the industry and British Shipbuilders re-allocated

*Shipyard workers at
the Robb Caledon yard
in Leith occupy to halt
closure 1984*

work on an order of Polish ships to Govan after workers on Tyneside refused to concede to their terms and conditions. Everyone expected Govan to defy this crude attempt to divide and rule. Yet its shop stewards agreed to take the work. Jimmy Airlie, who, in 1971, asked, "are other yards going to accept our orders and let my men starve?" was singing a different song in 1977: "If Newcastle are losing six ships through disputes, we will build them; if not us then the Japs will."[18]

The 1980s

Nationalisation reduced shipyard jobs by a third in six years, including the run-down of the lower Clyde yards in Inverclyde and the closure of the Robb Caledon yards in Dundee and Leith. The last lower Clyde yards closed under Thatcher in the late 1980s after the failure of yet another 'UCS-style' campaign backed by the STUC. Appealing to "all sections of the Scottish people for support", but ruling out strikes or occupation, it failed to save anything.

The 1970s ended with a Thatcher government that had no mandate in Scotland. Support for the SNP had fallen back but it would rise again as North Sea Oil production increased. Some working class voters in Scotland were fluctuating in their allegiance, showing increasing hesitancy with Labour by sometimes turning to the SNP as a protest vote in by-elections, which were seen as less decisive than general elections.

Electoral support for the Nazi National Front (NF) had grown dramatically in parts of England, but Scotland was not immune as the far right tried to exploit the war in Ireland and anti-Catholic bigotry in addition to its hatred of black and Asian Scots and immigrants. In response, the Anti Nazi League grew significantly in Scotland in the late 1970s, especially among young workers and school students.

In opposition, Labour moved left under Michael Foot. He led a series of regional protest marches against unemployment. At the Glasgow event in 1981, over 150,000 marched through the city to hear him address a monster rally in Queens Park. It was a time of factory closures, soaring unemployment and inner city riots. There were no riots in Scotland but groups of young unemployed Scots joined the Right to Work Campaign, leading local protests as well as joining big national demonstrations at the Tory and TUC conferences in Brighton and Blackpool.

But the level of workplace resistance was falling. The late 1970s had seen a spate of Scottish factory closures under Labour, including Massey Ferguson and Monsanto in Ayrshire, BSR in East Kilbride, Rolls Royce in Blantyre, Singer in Clydebank and Goodyear in Glasgow. In Thatcher's first two years, Scotland lost a fifth of its workforce. Corpach pulp mill, Invergordon smelter, Linwood car plant, Burroughs in Cumbernauld, Rowntree–Mackintosh in Edinburgh all closed, while British Shipbuilders, British Steel and multinationals like Timex and Hoover axed thousands of jobs.

The steel strike of 1980 was Thatcher's initial foray against the unions, pre-planned while she was in opposition. But first came the Social Security Act of 1980, which slashed welfare payments to strikers' families. Steel presented an ideal opportunity: a workforce that had never been on national strike and an undemocratic union, the Iron and Steel Trades Confederation (ISTC), with leaders that were weak and right-wing.

Yet the workforce put up a real fight that lasted 13 weeks and was remarkable for the militant tactics of a supposedly 'moderate' group of workers. The Tories couldn't win an outright victory yet the workers didn't win either. The ISTC "threw BSC a lifeline", to quote its right-wing leader Bill Sirs, snatching defeat from the jaws of victory. There then followed a rapid run down of the steel industry. Next came attacks on the civil servants, the health workers and the train drivers. The TUC stood aside while unions were taken on one at a time and beaten.

Scotland, like Wales, Yorkshire, Kent and elsewhere, still had a significant mining industry and a militant workforce. Scotland had 15 coalmines before Thatcher came to power in 1979; just two when she was forced out in 1991. Yet her first move against the miners in February 1981 was stopped in its

*Workers from the Plessey
Occupation in Bathgate
march through the town
1982*

tracks by swift action from below. Her closure plan sparked walkouts and flying pickets fanned out from the Welsh coalfield. Soon the Scottish pits were idle. Faced with a national, Britain wide strike, the Tories had to back off and bide their time.

Linwood and Lee Jeans

In early 1981, the labour movement suffered a hammer blow when a mass meeting at Linwood car plant rejected a shop stewards' recommendation to occupy the factory and prevent its closure with the loss of 8,000 jobs. Hopes of a struggle against unemployment, which would have galvanised Clydeside as UCS had done ten years before, were dashed. Linwood had a militant record. Its occupation would have fired others. Instead it closed without a fight.

At the same time, 240 women at Lee Jeans in Greenock occupied their factory after its bosses threatened closure. Most were teenagers with no experience of unions. American multinational Vanity Fair owned the factory, one of 40 it owned worldwide. Its bosses wanted to shut Greenock and move the work and machinery to its Irish plant and receive more state aid. They reckoned without the women, who fought like their lives depended on it. Inverclyde with high unemployment offered no other future for its young female workforce. One 20 year old had been made redundant from five previous jobs. The occupation lasted seven months and while their own union did little to help, the women won solidarity from other workers.

Pat Clark, a platers' steward in the nearby Scott Lithgow shipyard, was involved in the campaign: "I remember a yard union meeting at which the workers had little interest in the business and were more concerned about what we should be doing to support the sit-in that had begun the day before. We agreed a weekly levy of 50p to support the occupation and raised this with the joint shop stewards' committee. Soon every shipyard and engineering worker on the Lower Clyde was donating to the levy for Lee Jeans".

Helen Monaghan led the occupation. She knew the

leadership of her union, the Tailor and Garment Workers, wished they would go away. It was two months before it got round to making their dispute official. Delegations from the occupation toured workplaces around the country, initiated by the Right to Work Campaign. It also organised nationwide pickets of Vanity Fair's shops and outlets. The bosses won a court order to evict the strikers but on the appointed day a thousand other workers came to defend them. Pat Clark recalls how "shipyard and engineering workers downed tools to attend a rally at the occupied factory. We'd heard the bosses were coming to evict the occupiers but suddenly the VF Corporation weren't up for it. Helen Monaghan told us, 'we didn't know when we occupied where help would come from, but we hadn't long to find out. Without the support of trade unionists we wouldn't have lasted this long and with your support we'll keep fighting."[19]

Dockers refused to handle Vanity Fair goods. Even though the women's own union withdrew official support, their occupation stopped the closure and saved 140 of the jobs. Lee Jeans had an impact on other women workers. Over the next six months, a further six similar factory sit-ins took place, mainly involving women workers, including at Plessey in Bathgate and the Loveable Bra factory in Cumbernauld.

CND against Trident

The Campaign for Nuclear Disarmament (CND) began with marches to the Aldermaston nuclear weapons base in Berkshire in the early 1960s but the focus soon shifted to Clydeside during the anti-Polaris campaign. Thatcher's decision to base Trident missiles at Faslane was met by widespread resistance that continues to this day. The anti-Trident campaign of the early 1980s led to a massive resurgence in CND, surpassing what happened two decades earlier when Scottish CND grew out of the anti-Polaris campaign at its base on the Holy Loch. Easter 1982 saw the establishment of the Faslane Peace Camp and a huge two-day protest that marched from Faslane to Clydebank, camped overnight there and then marched to Glasgow. It culminated in an enormous rally in the city and led to a growth of new CND groups across Scotland.

But the faltering industrial struggle, the defection of Labour's 'Gang of Four' to form the SDP and the wave of jingoism surrounding Thatcher's victory in the Falklands helped the Tories to an easy election win in 1983.

Neil Kinnock replaced Michael Foot and Labour moved sharply back to the right. Kinnock championed 'new realism' and expelled the left-wing Militant group, opening the way for the defeat of the wider left in the party. He launched his attack just as the resistance to the Tory onslaught on local government from a group of left Labour councils was collapsing. These had included Liverpool, Manchester, Sheffield, Edinburgh and Ken Livingstone's Greater London Council. The balance of forces had shifted considerably since 1974 but it wasn't all Thatcher's doing; she extended Labour's anti-union policies and the monetarism it pioneered when Healey capitulated to the IMF in 1976.

The Miners' Strike in Scotland

Some of Thatcher's achievements were real. She forced the working class further onto the defensive, inflicting a serious defeat on the mining communities. But like Wilson in 1974, the union bosses helped her out. She could not have beaten the miners without their hostility to Scargill's leadership. We now know that on at least two occasions her government was close to defeat but the union leaders failed to deliver the action needed to shut down steel.

In July 1984, walkouts in the docks caused a run on the pound. The TGWU could have turned it into a battle alongside the miners that could have broken the government. Even the pit deputies' union, NACODS, could have turned the tide in November 1984, but its leadership refused to call strike action after a big yes vote. These powerful unions, along with Liverpool Council who had been defying the cuts, were literally bought off, their leaders settling with government and leaving the miners to fight on alone.

Scotland had lost 40 percent of its miners between 1974 and 1984. When the strike began, nearly half the remaining pits were already in dispute over closure threats, including a strike at Polmaise colliery. The 1984 strike began solidly in Scotland thanks to mass picketing by a rank and file that knew what was at stake. Stopping steel production was key but the National Union of Mineworkers (NUM) leaders in Scotland, Wales and Yorkshire broke with Scargill, conceding British Steel and ISTC union leader Bill Sirs' claims that steel production must continue. Sirs, a staunch supporter of 'new realism', had gone along with the destruction of 100,000 jobs after 1980. If he wouldn't fight for his own members, he was hardly likely to fight for the miners. This didn't deter the NUM area leaders from seeking alliances with the local ISTC leaders. Their approach had the opposite effect to that intended.

Rather than closing the steelworks, it saw NUM Scotland giving 'dispensations' to supply coal to Ravenscraig, the major steel plant, and it was here the first confrontation took place. When rail unions halted emergency deliveries because convoys of scab lorries were driving imported coal with police escorts from Hunterston on the Ayrshire coast to Ravenscraig, the miners were unable to stop them without practical solidarity from the TGWU. In May, 1,000 pickets clashed with the huge police presence at Ravenscraig. Fifty two miners were arrested. Next day, mounted police attacked the pickets and 65 miners were arrested. Miners travelling from Fife had a taste of what the state was up to in Nottinghamshire, when police halted eight coaches en route for Ravenscraig, arresting 300 miners. The pattern of police violence followed by mass arrests was repeated at British Steel's Hunterston coal terminal.

Steel union leaders instructed their members to work with scab coal and cross picket lines. Steelworkers who supported the miners were isolated. Tommy Brennan, the Ravenscraig union convenor, declared: "Our people will use any coal that comes into this plant."[20] The Scottish NUM backed down, agreeing a deal to allow 18,000 tonnes of coal for the plant every week, three times more than needed to keep its furnaces safe. Mick McGahey, Scottish NUM leader and prominent CP member, claimed it was "in the interest of Scotland's industrial future". The strategy was a disaster and miners knew it. "The only way to win is by stopping steel," said a picket at the height of the controversy. "First they'll chop us, then they'll chop Ravenscraig." A local steelworker worker told *Socialist Worker*, "There's no guarantee this place will stay open—even less chance if the miners are defeated."[21]

The lesson that there was no separate Scottish workers' interest from that of the British working class was painfully underlined by this episode. But equally, the damage done by union bureaucrats elsewhere, invoking the British national interest was shown during the Great Miners' Strike.

In 1986, after defeating the miners, the Tories shut Gartcosh steelworks. In 1990, they privatised British Steel and imposed redundancies at Ravenscraig and in 1992, the huge Motherwell plant closed without a fight—a devastating blow. At each turn of the screw, the STUC and the steel union leaders called for public support to save 'our Scottish steel industry', instead of building working class resistance and practical solidarity. Of all the Scottish popular fronts between the 1970s and 1992, it was only UCS that achieved any success because it took place during the rising class struggle of 1971-2. Each example thereafter, from Singer to Ravenscraig, occurred in a period of defeat, which the STUC campaigns helped extend by their failure. There were exceptions, when workers seized the initiative to win or save some jobs through taking action and solidarity from others.

Thatcher's supporters claimed she'd crushed the unions; she tried but failed. The Tories, by their own admission, needed the union bureaucracy to beat the miners but victory was won at a terrible financial cost to the ruling class and the reputation of the police. The all-out war on the mining communities cost billions, creating a bitterness that erupted over the Poll Tax. Despite the myth of Thatcher's invincibility and the lack of leadership from the unions, workers did resist and fight. Strikes and occupations never disappeared off the radar, even in the grimmer aftermath of the miners' defeat. Scotland, like other parts of Britain, saw important battles which inspired great acts of solidarity from other workers and the wider community. A notable example was Caterpillar.

Caterpillar: revenge of the pink panther

Occupations that don't win can still make a difference. In January 1987, Caterpillar called a press conference in Glasgow to announce the sudden closure of its profitable Uddingston plant and the loss of 1,200 jobs. When the shop stewards found out, they hijacked it. Union convenor John Brannan arrived to tell the press and TV cameras the factory "was now under workers' control and would stay that way until the jobs were saved". So began a 104-day occupation, a marvellous example of workers' ingenuity.

The recent miners' defeat was an excuse for the leaders of the Amalgamated Union of Engineering Workers (AUEW) to do nothing to win the solidarity action against Caterpillar that would have forced a climb-down. Despite official passivity, the workers mounted a terrific fight. They defied the law, stayed solid and won widespread support.

There had been a spate of local closures either side of Christmas, including the nearby Gartcosh steelworks. Before the Christmas shutdown, Caterpillar had announced a massive £63 million investment in the plant, the site chosen to produce the company's new model.

The about-turn in early January left the workforce bitter and with no option but to occupy. Over 100 shop stewards from across Lanarkshire gathered in Motherwell to organise support. A campaign run by the workforce meant they were able to raise £20,000 a week, every week, to sustain the struggle. Delegations toured Britain, speaking to workplace and union meetings. Caterpillar was a beacon of resistance for a dispirited movement.

The role of socialist shop stewards and the influence of *Socialist Worker*—sold inside the plant for years—made a difference. The occupation looked outwards and won support internationally. Shop stewards travelled to Belgium and France to set up links with Caterpillar workers there. They won support from Caterpillar workers in the USA, who were also under attack.

The French and Belgian plants held a stoppage and threatened an indefinite strike if moves were made to evict the occupation. Despite the AUEW leadership, dockers and lorry drivers imposed unofficial embargoes on the movement of Caterpillar goods. Although the majority of the workforce was male, involvement in the miners' strike taught them the importance of setting up a women's support group. It was crucial in holding the occupation together and in winning mass support throughout the community, including a local march, 10,000-strong. Every week Caterpillar workers and supporters held street collections in Glasgow and the local shopping centres. Huge cash collections outside Celtic and Rangers football grounds helped. In many Scottish towns there was a Caterpillar Support Group.

During the strike, the 'Pink Panther' appeared—a huge tractor assembled from spares held inside the occupation but painted pink to distinguish it from Caterpillar yellow. The workers agreed to donate it to Scottish War on Want. The gesture had a serious purpose. The new banner hung over the front of the occupied factory summed it up: 'Caterpillar workers say we can and we will, help to feed the world'. The Pink Panther was driven ten miles into George Square, where it was parked throughout the occupation. Caterpillar served an injunction to prevent it being handed to War on Want.

Eventually the AUEW withdrew all support. In the end, the workforce went back in April, having forced enhanced redundancy terms and a longer stay of execution. The factory finally closed in November. Its impact was one reason why the Tories lost so many of their Scottish seats despite winning the 1987 general election.

*STUC-called Glasgow
demo against the Poll Tax*

1987 and Labour's feeble fifty

The Tory vote in Scotland in the 1987 general election fell to 24 percent, compared to 42 percent across Britain, and they held only 10 Scottish seats. Labour had fought the election in Scotland on a promise to make the Poll Tax unworkable. Fifty MPs and 42.4 percent of the vote, compared to 31 percent across Britain gave it the mandate to do so. However, despite opposition from within its ranks, Labour's leadership made clear its intention to abide by the law. A Scottish Labour Party conference in Govan Town Hall in March 1988 refused to back a non-payment campaign. Labour ran the biggest Scottish councils and they implemented the Poll Tax without a murmur. Of course the SNP lambasted Labour's 'feeble fifty' Westminster MPs but Angus, the only SNP-controlled council, co-operated and implemented the tax from the outset.

Broadcaster James Naughtie insisted the 'feeble fifty' argument "was bound to have resonance in a Scottish population tired of voting Labour and ignoring the Conservatives in large numbers, but getting nothing from it".[22] He was soon proved right by the SNP's spectacular by-election victory at Govan in November 1988, which threw Labour into crisis. Ex-Labour MP Jim Sillars ran a clever No Poll Tax campaign, overturning a 19,500 Labour majority with a swing of 33.1 percent. In the previous Govan election, the SNP had finished fourth. Treating the Scottish working class like guinea–pigs by implementing the tax a year ahead of the rest of Britain only fuelled the non-payment campaign. Local groups formed and came together in the Anti–Poll Tax Federation, led by Tommy Sheridan. Copying the tactics of the Glasgow rent strikers of 1915, 'No Poll Tax Here' window posters appeared in working class communities. The Federation called a 20,000–strong demonstration in Glasgow. When sheriff officers tried warrant sales, local fast-response networks mobilised to harass and stop them and occupy the debt collectors' offices in protest.

In April, *Scotland on Sunday* estimated there were 850,000 non-payers in Scotland. Sheridan was jailed for defying a court order and trying to halt a warrant sale. Later, in 1992, he was elected to Glasgow City Council to represent Pollok. When the Poll Tax came to the rest of Britain, mass non-payment took off, with 11 million defying the law. It culminated in the biggest riot of the century when police attacked an anti-Poll Tax march of 250,000 in London. That same day, 40,000 marched in Glasgow. Some leaders of the Anti-Poll Tax Federation attacked the London rioters; instead they should have toasted them because the riot led to Thatcher's demise. Sheridan was a member of Scottish Militant Labour, a grouping driven out of the Labour Party by Kinnock's right-wing witch-hunt and now gravitating towards a form of left-wing nationalism, which would crystallise in the Scottish Socialist Party in 1996. This takes nothing from the impressive movement that was built, but does illustrate the risk of seeing the interests of Scottish workers as separate from the British working class.

Labour now led the Tories in the polls by 24 percent, but Kinnock blew it. Labour disassociated itself from the campaign and Kinnock condemned the advocates of non-payment as "toytown revolutionaries".

Worse was to follow. In 1991, he joined with the Tories in backing US President George Bush Senior in launching the first Gulf War against his old pal Saddam Hussein. In the build up to war, 100,000 marched through London in opposition, but Kinnock stood with US imperialism. Many Labour MPs opposed the war, but obedience to the leader outweighed principle for all but a minority. Labour failed to argue for delaying the war, avoiding calling a parliamentary debate during the conflict. The 1992 general election should have been a cakewalk for Kinnock but Peter Mandelson guided their campaign.

The ditching of one principle after another and Labour's backing for the war were supposed to win voters, instead it handed "a remarkable victory to the Tories. To win by such a margin was totally unexpected".[23] The British vote in the 1992 general election was 42 percent Tory and 34 percent Labour. But Major was returned with only 23 percent of the Scottish vote. The gulf between British wide and Scottish voting was widening though still within a conventional two-party structure. A growing 'democratic deficit' would increasingly prise this open and ultimately lead to Labour's demise, something it was rushing towards in a flush of soft nationalist enthusiasm. The concept of national interest—in this case a Scottish version—tended to trump class politics.

Two days after the 1992 general election, thousands gathered in George Square for a rally called by Scotland United, a new body initiated by the STUC. Campbell Christie, STUC general secretary, demanded a Scottish parliament, telling the crowds: "We're here to tell the nation, the Tory government and the world we are not prepared to accept the election result. Representing the 75 percent in Scotland who voted for constitutional change, we are not prepared to allow 23 percent, the Tories, to rule us."[24]

Scotland United involved the unions, Labour MPs and prominent Scots. The SNP participated, jettisoning its policy of boycotting campaigns that didn't back full independence. Donald Dewar, Kinnock's man in Scotland, attacked the Labour MPs who took part for collaborating with the SNP. Yet opinion polls showed 80 percent support for a Scottish parliament. Kinnock dismissed it as "the noise of the Scottish chattering classes".[25] In December, the SNP held a march of 25,000 in Edinburgh during its hosting of the EU leaders' summit.

Kinnock's defeat brought a leadership contest in 1992: the choice being John Smith—a Scot and Labour MP for Monklands East or Brian Gould, with the Labour left so demoralised that it didn't stand a candidate. Smith won with 91 percent of the vote. Major's divided Tories stumbled on despite Michael Heseltine's hugely unpopular pit closure programme, which Major was forced to delay. Monster marches on Parliament enthusiastically took up the NUM call for a general strike. Even the *Sun* headline asked, "Is Major a goner?" The TUC did nothing. No further demonstrations were called and the chance to end Tory rule was squandered. A year later, all remaining pits were either closed or privatised. *The New Statesman* lamented, "here, out of the blue, was an opportunity—not given to oppositions even once in a decade—a monumental gaffe by government. Inertia amounting to intellectual and political paralysis appears to have seized Labour".[26]

Russia, the Eastern bloc & the end of history

In 1989, the year of the Eastern European revolutions, US State Department adviser, Francis Fukuyama published *The End of History*, claiming the collapse of the Stalinist states meant "the ultimate triumph of western liberal democracy, the unabashed victory of political and economic liberalism"[27] and the death of socialism. He claimed it would bring "a peace dividend and the end of the nuclear arms race".[28] The opposite happened: a convulsive change that gave rise to a new era of imperialist wars and an ever-deepening global crisis of capitalism.

The outer empire of the USSR crumpled at its westernmost frontier in Berlin and then unraveled eastwards from the Baltic States to the Caucasus. Workers' struggle played a central role in sweeping away regimes that the old left defended as 'deformed' or 'distorted' workers' states. Instead these were state capitalist dictatorships modeled on Stalinist Russia and based on exploiting workers as ruthlessly as their western counterparts.

The left was in turmoil—not least in Scotland, where the Russian Revolution and its isolation and degeneration had loomed over the Labour movement since the 1930s. It was not only the Russian Empire that dissolved in 1991, the CPGB dissolved too. All of this fed the prevailing mood of 'new realism' and a fashionable notion that class struggle and socialism were dead. Founded as a revolutionary organisation in 1920, the CPGB's long drift rightwards accelerated in the 1980s when its magazine *Marxism Today* proclaimed Thatcherism unstoppable. It advised the Labour left to ditch Arthur Scargill and Tony Benn for Neil Kinnock. It advised Kinnock to do a deal with David Owen and the SDP. By 1992 the Party was over.

Timex

In early 1993, a bout of industrial struggle cut through the pessimism on the left. There were walkouts in the Post, at Fords and at Yarrow's naval yard on the Clyde, where a mass meeting rejected a rotten wage offer recommended by the officials and shop stewards. The workers rejected yet another compromise before returning to work with an improved deal. But the most important of these disputes was Timex. Not only did it underline the growing prominence of working class women, it was arguably the first real challenge to both TUC 'new realism' and the STUC's Scottish popular front.

The 1945 Attlee government attracted new industries to 'Scotland's depressed areas', nowhere more so than Dundee. Boosted by grants and tax concessions, multinationals were drawn to new purpose-built industrial estates around the city. The name most associated with this was Timex, a US company that brought jobs for large numbers of women who'd worked in the fast-disappearing jute industry. What would happen now the post-war boom had ended? Would the first factories to suffer not be those overseas outposts?

So it proved for Dundee. In the recessions of the 1980s and early 1990s, multinationals slashed jobs, cutting their Dundee operations and forcing the unions onto the back foot. Before Christmas 1992, Timex announced a round of sackings. In January, its Thatcherite manager, Peter Hall, sent out letters detailing who would be sacked and who would stay. The workers refused to open their letters and occupied the canteen. In response, Hall promised negotiations and they returned to work on the basis they would consider fair lay-offs but had balloted overwhelmingly in favour of strike action in the event of compulsory redundancies.

Negotiations never materialised and Timex refused conciliation. A frustrated workforce walked out on strike at the end of January. In mid-February, they returned en-masse only to be told they would have to accept a pay cut and lower pensions. When they refused, they were locked out and scabs brought in. Picketing of the plant began with regular delegations of supporters travelling from across Scotland to back the predominantly female workforce. In April, local workplaces stopped work and marched to join the pickets. A solidarity rally was held outside Timex with 6,000 in attendance. In May, 5,000 trade unionists travelled from all over Britain to another mass picket. It took a huge police presence an hour to get a busload of scabs through the gate.

Unfortunately their national union officials, Gavin Laird and Jimmy Airlie of UCS fame, were spineless and more worried about union assets than their members. In August, Timex, unable to break the strike, abandoned the plant. Like Caterpillar, the right-wing leaders of the Amalgamated Electrical and Engineering Union (AEEU) washed their hands of the Timex workforce. By complying with the anti-union laws and refusing to organise a blacking campaign, they allowed Timex to walk away. While the strikers didn't win, they hadn't surrendered and didn't feel defeated. Many were angry, though, at the betrayal.

It wasn't the only sell-out that year by the leaders of the AEEU. During the Timex dispute, Gavin Laird and Jimmy Airlie were busy foisting a rotten deal on their members at Hoover Cambuslang. It froze wages, cut overtime and bonus rates, denied pay and pension rights to new workers and weakened the shop stewards' ability to represent members. Even worse, it allowed Hoover to announce the closure of their Dijon plant, sacking 600 French workers. To their credit, the French responded by occupying the factory. US-owned Hoover had held secret talks in advance with Laird and Airlie, while the Cambuslang workforce were kept in the dark and presented with an ultimatum on the day of the mass meeting: "Accept the deal or Cambuslang closes today."

Playing off Scottish against French engineering workers did not embarrass Airlie: "We have secured one of the best pieces of news on the Scottish industrial front for years."[29] It would have taken a grim imagination to work out what Airlie's 'bad news' might look like. Many leaders of the STUC and the Labour Party in Scotland shared Airlie's outlook. For years they insisted national unity—Scottish and/or British—not industrial action, is what would save jobs, despite a dismal record to the contrary. Hoover finally closed its Cambuslang operation in 2005.

But the women at Timex helped stir other workers into action and the period following the Timex dispute saw a continuing revival of struggle, the victory of the railway signal workers' strike, which broke the Tories' 'pay norm' in 1994, being a prominent example.

Tony Blair and New Labour

Tony Blair became Labour leader in 1994 after the death of John Smith. Straight away he threw down the gauntlet to the left and the trade union movement, announcing he'd fight to remove the party's symbolic Clause IV, which had called for public ownership of key industries. It signaled his determination to reject class politics and all talk of socialism, persuading enough of the party it was necessary to move decisively towards Tory policies under New Labour. After Clause IV was removed, Shadow Chancellor Gordon Brown revealed in whose interests any New Labour government would act:

> The Labour Party is now the party of modern business and industry. For the first time it has set down its commitment to a market economy, to living with the rigours of competition and to nurture enterprise. Now with our clear statement of aims, no one can ever again question our commitment to a healthy and successful private sector, or to competition and enterprise.[30]

In the 1980s, Kinnock had moved from unilateral to multi-lateral nuclear disarmament. New Labour seemed to have abandoned disarmament completely. In opposition, Gordon Brown demanded financial prudence for social spending but the £22 billion Tory Trident project was never questioned; neither would the coming wars in the Balkans, Afghanistan and the Middle East.

Glacier

On a brighter note, November 1996 saw workers at the Glacier engineering factory in Govanhill occupy against sackings. Owned by a multinational car components firm, Glacier had sacked its entire Glasgow workforce after they refused to accept new unsafe working practices, changes to their contracts, a reduction in their wages and an attack on union organisation. Instead of walking out or relying on their officials, the workers occupied and locked out the management. Two years earlier, they had been locked out themselves after taking strike action. This time they decided to turn the tables. They defied the law and won solidarity, touring workplaces to win financial support.

They led a solidarity march of 3,000 supporters through the local area. They maintained the occupation over Christmas and workers' families held a party inside the plant on Christmas day. Management caved in and the workers won a complete victory against a multinational company, celebrating by marching back into work under their engineering union banner. As the 1997 election drew closer, the union leaders grew ever more reluctant to countenance such action, arguing it jeopardised the chances of a Labour government. That's why in 1996 an important strike of Liverpool dockers, fighting for their jobs, was shamelessly abandoned by the TGWU.

Corrupt and split on Europe, Major's was a zombie government. Labour had maintained a sizeable lead in the polls ever since Black Wednesday, 1992, when Britain had to withdraw from the European exchange rate mechanism despite throwing 30 billion pounds sterling away in an abortive attempt to protect it. Labour's lead continued under John Smith with the Tories getting only 29 percent in the 1994 European elections, their lowest share ever in a national contest. This was *before* Blair became leader. When the complicated two-tier local authority structure of regions and districts was dissolved in 1995, the Tories failed to win control of a single local council in Scotland. In 1997, Labour won handsomely, wiping out the Tories in Scotland, not because of Blair but because the Tories were corrupt, incompetent and universally despised. During the election campaign, the *Sun* claimed Labour would do the unions' bidding. Blair replied, saying that after whatever changes Labour made, "we will still have the most restrictive union laws in the Western world", one promise he did keep.[31]

Before Blair, Labour leaders made promises and then sold out after being elected. Blair was the first Labour leader to sell out *before* he was elected. The few decent promises New Labour did make—to take the railways back into public ownership; to fund public services; to end sleaze; to introduce an ethical foreign policy—were all broken. When asked what was her greatest achievement, Thatcher said: "Tony Blair and New Labour".[32] It is important to remember in the face of the Blairite claims that the 1997 election victory was down to his right-wing policies, that "New Labour was not embraced enthusiastically. Only 31 percent of the total electorate voted for Blair. His big win was helped by Tory collapse, tactical voting and the peculiarities of the first-past-the-post system".[33] At first, many Labour voters were prepared to believe New Labour's election anthem: 'Things can only get better'. After 18 years of Thatcher and Major, it was a reasonable expectation but instead, for most people, things got worse.

By the late 1970s, Glasgow was the city with the biggest share of council housing anywhere outside the Eastern bloc. If Thatcher had threatened to sell it off cheaply to an unelected quango and hand over its school building programme and long-term maintenance to private contractors under lucrative Private Finance Initiative (PFI) scams, then the Labour council and the STUC would have been up in arms. But Gordon Brown and former Labour lefts Frank McAveety and Charlie Gordon, who had switched to become New Labour council leaders, led this privatisation bonanza, spending millions on propaganda to blackmail Glasgow's council tenants into reluctantly accepting a stock transfer. A recent study highlights just how right wing the Glasgow Labour-controlled council had been, even before Blair. After he became Prime Minister and Brown his chancellor, privatisation went into overdrive:

> Given recurring claims of Glasgow's militant history and its strong socialist and trade union traditions, it may come as a surprise that over the past three to four decades, Glasgow was dominated by Labour-led administrations that eagerly embraced the pro-market doctrine associated initially with Thatcherism. Prior to the 1980s, politics in the city were dominated by the failing management of long-term social problems, not least in relation to housing provision. That Glasgow was a city in decline for much of the period from the 1950s to the early 1980s reflected a growing crisis at a Britain wide level.
>
> In 2000, the Council embraced the controversial Private Finance Initiative funding scheme to build new schools and in 2003, despite a vigorous public campaign of opposition, it transferred all its housing stock to the new Glasgow Housing Association.[34]

The death of John Smith had put a question mark against Labour's commitment to a Scottish Parliament. Smith saw it as "the settled will of the Scottish people".[35] It remained to be seen if the commitment would survive Blair's leadership. It did, not because Blair was a democrat but because he needed Scottish votes and Donald Dewar was able to convince him that granting devolution would see off the SNP and scupper Scottish independence. Both were proved wrong along with those who designed the new system of voting for Holyrood— the additional member system. It was deliberately framed to stop the SNP getting an overall majority and to ensure coalition governments. In the Scottish Referendum in September 1997,

Scottish delegation to the
European Social Forum in
Florence 2002

74 percent voted 'Yes' to a Scottish Parliament with 63 percent voting to grant it limited tax-raising powers. Consequently, Labour would rule Scotland in coalition with the Liberal Democrats until 2011.

After two decades of growing inequality under the Tories, New Labour did nothing to reverse it. Indeed, after a decade of Blair and Brown, the gap between the very richest and the poorest in British society was the greatest ever. Peter Mandelson made it clear New Labour was "intensely relaxed about people getting filthy rich". During Blair's tenure in office, he never allowed the income tax rate to rise above 40 percent, while his chancellor Gordon Brown cut Capital Gains Tax for the rich.

Throughout the 1990s, wars accompanied the break-up of the former Yugoslavia, the most extreme example of the collapse of the Eastern bloc. The Balkan wars marked the start of the doctrine of 'humanitarian intervention', western imperialism's cover for intervention in Eastern Europe and later the Middle East. NATO's Kosovo intervention and its bombing of Serbia in 1998-99 was the start of Tony Blair's career as a warmonger. His hawkishness exceeded President Clinton's as he searched for a leadership role for 'cool Britannia'. He thought he'd found it in military adventures overseas. At this time, NATO, the military wing of the USA and Western Europe, began incorporating the states of the former Warsaw Pact. Western military organisation now extended to the borders of the Balkan states.

The Kosovo war, with its horrific cluster bombing— supposedly to protect 'civilised values' rather than grab power— was waged for the same sordid reasons as most previous wars; its strategic aim was to assert Western control while minimising the influence of Russia in its former spheres of influence. But by the late 1990s, a new global movement against war and for social justice began to emerge. Those affected by globalisation and neoliberal economic policies, ranging from trade unionists to ecological campaigners to the indigenous peoples of Latin America, began to protest at their impact. Then came Seattle. In the dying weeks of the old millennium, a huge demonstration against the World Trade Organisation brought together protestors from all sorts of backgrounds and they all learnt in action. As one demonstrator put it: "I went to Seattle to save the turtles and came back determined to overthrow capitalism."[36]

The movement would spread to huge demonstrations in Melbourne, Prague in 2000 and Genoa in 2001, and the anti-capitalist movement merged with the biggest international anti-war movement ever seen in the aftermath of the 9/11 attacks and the build up to the Iraq War. London would see Britain's biggest, most diverse anti-war demonstration ever on 15 February 2003 and on the same day 150,000 besieged Tony Blair at the Scottish Labour Party conference in Glasgow. When the G8 came to Scotland in 2005, 350,000 marched through Edinburgh and 10,000 marched through Gleneagles.

Disillusion among Labour supporters increased throughout the Blair and Brown governments. Brown would be the third Labour leader in succession born and educated in Scotland and, like Smith, represented a Scottish seat. These three followed on from other Scots like Keir Hardie, founder of the Labour Party and Ramsay MacDonald, its first prime minister. In 1997, New Labour won the general election with 13.5 million votes. At the next election in 2001, its vote fell by 3 million. Another 1.1 million voters had departed by 2005, a further million by 2010. Over the same period Party membership slumped from 405,000 to under 180,000. This marked decline was especially true in Scotland, where a political sea change was coming:

> The transformation in the 1990s of old Labour into New Labour, which seemed to embrace a free market philosophy and failed to reverse Thatcherite reforms, triggered much disenchantment among the party's supporters in Scotland. Evidence covering the period between 1997 and 2001 demonstrated declining support for the proposition that New Labour looked

after class and trade union concerns but increasing agreement with the view that the party primarily looked after the concerns of business and the affluent in society.[37]

Labour, the crisis and austerity

What happened in Scotland between 1997 and 2017? The Labour Party went from over 1.2 million votes in Scotland, with 56 out of 59 seats and 45 percent of the vote in 1997,[38] to a humiliating landslide defeat in 2015 of just 700,000 votes, one seat and 24 percent of the vote following the 2014 referendum.[39] In the 2017 general election, Labour did manage to regain six seats, claw back around 10,000 votes and shift to 27 percent of the vote.[40] By the 2019 general election, Labour had plummeted even further, with another 200,000 votes lost, just one seat, and a mere 18 percent of the vote in Scotland.[41] Looking back over Scotland's political landscape during those two decades throws light on the factors that combined to produce the spectacular cataclysm of the 2014 referendum and the 2015 general election. But it is important to stress that this process is far from a uniquely Scottish experience. The rupture in Scotland, the dramatic bottoming out of the Labour Party and the rise of the independence movement, was one of many examples of the sharp polarisation produced by the crisis of capitalism.

Across Europe and beyond, the mantra of austerity politics was played out in the wake of the 2008 crash and the bailout of the banks. It produced profound and savage attacks on working class people, like in the Spanish state and in Greece. In Britain, it saw the emergence of a big anti-cuts movement, culminating in the biggest strike since 1926 on 30 November 2011 when 2.6 million public sector workers struck against an attack on pensions. It was a working class response to a generalised class assault. For many it was about so much more than simply an attack on pensions. The failure of the Labour Party to effectively identify with this mood or provide any effective opposition, alongside the pacifying role played by the trade union leadership, proved to have a serious impact when it came to 2014.

The weakness of Labour's opposition to austerity at both national and local level; the desperation for an alternative to the Tories' agenda and the absence of a lead from the union leaders; the lived experience of Scottish Labour's track record of corruption, scandal and infighting;[42] its role in outsourcing and privatising council services, and its attacks on workers' conditions and pay, all of these factors combined to weaken labour's fifty year hold on Scottish politics. The final straw was its rush to wrap itself in the Union Jack alongside David Cameron in the 2014 referendum.

Through its dominance of the Convention of Scottish Local Authorities (COSLA), Labour's fiefdom, Glasgow City Council, had pushed through New Labour's neoliberal strategy that led up to the austerity years under Tory rule, and continued in this vein in the devolved public sector, provoking a wave of disputes. Council workers, especially large numbers of low paid women, were told the money wasn't there for services, pay or conditions and the private sector was increasingly brought in. Meanwhile billions of pounds were found to fund a war for oil and for nuclear weapons that the population opposed.

As the polarisation deepened, we began to see a global pattern: the fracturing of the mainstream centre politics of the establishment. Unquestionably dominant before the crash and through the era of neoliberalism and war, the old establishment was now proving incapable of holding the ring. The fast-paced drama unfolding on Scotland's political stage from the end of 2014 into the 2015 general election was a reflection of this wider process. Across Europe, the US and elsewhere, came the rise of racist populism and the far right, but we also saw the emergence of mass left parties, from Podemos in the Spanish state to Syriza in Greece, from Corbynism to the movement behind Bernie Sanders in the US.

The SNP's politics differ significantly from these formations, which were expressions of rising left reformism. But it remains the case that millions were looking for an alternative. The potency of the independence movement was born out of this, with the SNP as the beneficiary in the schism. While in the Spanish state and Greece, left reformism emerged from outside the existing social democratic Labour-style parties as new political formations, in England and Wales it grew inside the Labour Party and in the US it found expression in the Democratic Socialists of America (DSA), which orientated on the Democrat Party. This polarisation came in the midst of an era of mass political movements—from the anti-capitalist movement to the anti-war movement—and at a time of a significant political upturn that these global movements reflected. These events certainly shaped a layer inside the current leadership of the SNP, who actively opposed the Iraq war, pushed pro-migrant and anti-racist rhetoric, and have rather successfully cloaked themselves as the antithesis of the Tory austerity agenda. So the SNP can appear to fit into this category, embodying in Scotland the force of left reformism that has emerged out of the crisis elsewhere. Yet the SNP is a thoroughly neoliberal party. In the current global capitalist climate, it can be defined as a progressive neoliberal, nationalist party. It is neither a new force created by the pressures and polarisation of the crisis nor does it share the social democratic roots of the Labour Party, with its links to the trade unions and notions of socialism. Nor does Sturgeon's leadership represent a far-left socialist force inside the SNP, as Corbyn did within the Labour Party or as the Democratic Socialists of America (DSA) have within the Democrat Party.

The demise of Labour in Scotland and the rise of the SNP to power came as the independence movement rose—a mass movement motivated by class issues—and was widely adopted as the way to fight austerity and resist Tory attacks. The SNP at the same time provides a space which south of the border is being squeezed, as is the centre political ground. As well as its new found mass of working class supporters, it can adequately provide a political home for a liberal middle class in Scotland, or those who see themselves as progressive capitalists: those who perhaps abhor the racism and jingoism of the likes of Boris Johnson, identify with the anti-war movement and its legacy and are pro-migration but whose interests are in business and profit. This space is something of an anomaly, or at least relatively rare in the current global picture, given that the rapid acceleration of capitalism's triple crisis doesn't leave much room for dreams of supposedly more progressive capitalist models to dazzle for too long. We can expect this contradiction to quickly sharpen for the SNP in power, particularly if independence is won and the ability to blame Westminster policies for attacks on the working class disappears.

The central problem is that first two decades of the century have been marked in Scotland and in Britain by the stubborn fact that workers' struggle and confidence to fight back has remained historically very low in the face of a tsunami of attacks to make us pay for the crisis of capitalism. Yet the upside is that these years have also been defined by big explosive political movements and increasing politicisation among working class people. It is here that not only the hope lies but also the seeds of an effective strategy for revolutionary socialists who see the potential and necessity for a mass movement of workers' struggle and revolution. As Rosa Luxemburg eloquently describes in her pamphlet *The Mass Strike*:

Every new onset and every fresh victory of the political struggle is transformed into a powerful impetus for the economic struggle... After every foaming wave of political action a fructifying deposit remains behind from which a thousand stalks of economic struggle shoot forth. And conversely. The workers' condition of ceaseless economic struggle with the capitalists keeps their fighting energy alive in every political interval; it forms, so to speak, the permanent fresh reservoir of the strength of the proletarian classes, from which the political fight ever renews its strength, and at the same time leads... now here and now there, to isolated sharp conflicts, out of which public conflicts on a large scale unexpectedly explode... In a word: the economic struggle is the transmitter from one political centre to another; the political struggle is the periodic fertilisation of the soil for the economic struggle."[43]

The anti-war movement

The historic anti-war movement that burst onto the global stage, reshaping the political landscape in Britain and in Scotland in the early 2000s, culminated in the biggest demonstration in Britain's history in 2003. It led to the formation of the Stop The War Coalition (STWC), which shaped the political decade. In Scotland as elsewhere, people marched in their thousands and their millions against the war. A vibrant, colourful and determined movement galvanised around the slogan 'Not In Our Name', with large school student walkouts, a flourishing of STW groups on campuses, a challenge of the deeply class divided army recruitment strategies in schools and universities, and occupations against Israel's occupation and attacks on Palestine.

Coming on the back of the anti-capitalist movement, the mass anti-war movement fundamentally challenged and shaped people's consciousness on the nature of the system itself. Bush and Blair—and as a result the face of New Labour—were widely despised as war criminals. The role of imperialism, oil and wars for profit was exposed, as was the nature of a ruling class that Blair-face lied and undemocratically ignored mass expressions of public opposition in order to let the bombs out.

Throughout those years, the continued presence of the anti-war movement on the streets was a huge part of the political landscape. The politically charged buoyancy of the mass movement that exploded merged with other battles provoked by Blairism. The Fire Brigade Union (FBU)'s strike in 2002 merged with the rising mood of resistance to the Iraq war and reflected a shift that had taken place since the late 1990s in a section of the trade union bureaucracy identified as the 'Awkward Squad'. This group of emergent left union leaders rejected the Blairite partnership with the bosses and their enthusiasm for playing a role in STW breathed life into the unions. Despite incredible support for the strike from the movement, the inevitable immense pressure was brought to bear and the FBU leadership called off the strikes choosing to put nation before class. The strike was both a sharp example of the fusion of politics and economics and of the enormous gap left by the absence of independent rank-and-file organisation in the unions and the role played by the bureaucracy.

Stop The War was a major part of the 'Make Poverty History' monster march through Edinburgh in 2005 during the G8, having overturned a police decision to ban the STW rally, and at the major demonstration at Gleneagles where the G8 was being held. In Scotland, the question of Trident nuclear weapons, based at Faslane on the Clyde with a permanent peace camp in opposition, was bound up in this. The campaign to get rid of Trident was an integral part of Scotland's anti-war movement. Glasgow STW ran a campaign of protests at Prestwick Airport exposing the fact that the US government was illegally flying bombs for Israeli forces' use in Lebanon in and out of Prestwick. Protesters boldly occupied the airport and ran their own inspection of the planes. Following the action, the decision was made that US military flights carrying bombs to Israel would no longer use civilian airports in Britain.[44] As was the case across the rest of Britain, Ireland and other parts of the world, the demand for justice for Palestine became a common sense of the movement—because it was fought for by socialists and anti-Zionists within the movement.

In recent years, there has been a conscious and, tragically, relatively successful move by the right, particularly within the Labour Party, to undermine and weaken the movement that challenges the atrocities of the Israeli state and champions the rights of the Palestinians. Unlike elsewhere in Europe, the battle for the movement to stand in solidarity with the Muslim community and reject the Islamophobic rhetoric of the 'war on terror' was critically important—a lasting strategic legacy of the anti-war movement in Britain, and in Scotland. This built unity, and drew the line in the sand that shaped the landscape for years to come. In those years, Islamophobia would be increasingly used as the thin end of the wedge in a polarised, crisis-ridden Britain experiencing a rise in establishment racism and a growth of the far right. The contrast to having fought for and won this strategic alignment of the movement can be seen in France, where the left had failed to seriously take up the question of Islamophobia as a racism that must be opposed. The anti-war movement brought new generations to anti-imperialist politics, and many to socialist ideas and organisation.

The 2008 crash and the onset of austerity

The economic crisis hit in 2008, triggering the collapse of the banks, the huge bailouts that were promptly awarded, and catastrophic consequences for working class people. It was akin to an enormous meteor hitting the ocean, so devastating that the crashing waves from its impact continue to emanate, growing larger and moving more rapidly the deeper it goes. In Britain, across Europe, in the US, and reverberating around the world, the fact and moment of the bank bailouts was already accounted for by the ruling class: 'Working class people will pay, austerity will be the method, and we can use racism to divide them'. By 2010, the legacy of the Iraq war and disillusionment with the New Labour's neoliberalism—Private Finance Initiatives (PFI) and housing stock being sold off, corruption, the outrage of the MPs' expenses scandal, anti-union laws— paid off for the Tories. After 13 years of New Labour in power, the 2010 election delivered a hung parliament, the 'Con-Dem' coalition and a Tory-led government. In Scotland, there was no seat change, and Labour took 42 percent of the vote keeping 41 out of 59 seats.[45] As the Tory onslaught unfolded, this would contribute to the sense of undemocratic Westminster Tory rule imposing increasing carnage in Scotland.

The onset of austerity was a deeply uncertain time; battle

lines were being drawn and it remained to be seen whether working class resistance might emerge and from where it might appear. In those early days, the shock of huge closures and redundancies started to hit, and the question was posed about what working class people and, crucially, the trade unions were going to do about it. A poignant reflection from a Woolworth's worker, Jayne Maltman, as the company collapsed in 2009 captures the huge contradiction of the class tensions in the situation.

> We found out on TV in late November that we were going to close. We just carried on as normal, and it wasn't until we actually came out and we were all upset when we signed our last bits of paper that we thought, 'Well, why did we go quietly?'[46]

Surely 30,000 shop workers could have been a force to be reckoned with had they been organised, had their union leadership called action?

As the crisis, and the strategy to make working class people pay gathered pace, flashes of resistance did begin to emerge. Workers at the Visteon car plants in Belfast and in Enfield, north London occupied in April 2009, followed by workers at Vestas wind turbine factory on the Isle of Wight in July that year, both in a stand to defend jobs. In Scotland, a major flashpoint was the job cuts announced at Diageo's Johnnie Walker, where 900 jobs were set to go from the factories in Kilmarnock (700) and Glasgow (200). There were clear signs of the tremendous support and expectation for a serious fightback—such as an 87 percent vote in a consultative ballot supporting a strike,[47] and a monster solidarity demonstration through Kilmarnock of 25,000 people (over half the town's population at the time).[48] The Johnnie Walker factory was of great significance within the town—as locals explained throughout the dispute, "everyone is related to someone who works there". At the march, current Unite general secretary Len McCluskey (at the time an assistant general secretary in the union), Labour MP Des Browne and Scotland first minister Alex Salmond spoke to the huge crowd. Their focus was placed firmly on pressuring the company for an "alternative business plan".[49]

Workers who were part of attempting to organise in the Kilmarnock factory and put pressure on union leaders to call a strike pointed out that Diageo CEO Paul Walsh personally took home £5 million,[50] and that Diageo's operating profits had come in the previous year at £1.86 billion.[51] They raised demands for Unite to urgently facilitate mass meetings across the plants, where plans for a strike and the option of occupation could be discussed among all members.

Working alongside Socialist Workers Party members and with solidarity and support from other trade unionists organised through the newly formed Right to Work campaign who were leafleting the plants with their demands, the workers organised a busload from the Kilmarnock factory to join a solidarity meeting. They met and exchanged ideas and experiences with the occupying workers at Visteon and Vestas factories, as well as with workers from the Prisme factory in Dundee who had recently occupied and Communication Workers' Union (CWU) postal workers, who in Scotland were among the branches that took unofficial action that autumn to jumpstart a national strike to defend pensions.

There was huge potential and desperate need for a fight that could have been a defining moment for working class people everywhere. Yet the role played by union leaders was to work alongside politicians, stall and then demobilise. They pushed through a deal that meant that not a single job in Kilmarnock or Glasgow was saved. The only concession from Diageo was an increase in redundancy payments to £9,000 instead of £5,000. Despite a resounding vote to strike, Unite released a statement saying "the issue has been settled and it has been settled to the satisfaction of our members. The campaign will be stood down".[52]

Both the SNP and Labour were focussed on making Scotland, and Britain in the latter's case, business-friendly in this volatile moment in the onset of the crisis. While Salmond and the SNP hired a consultancy firm in an attempt to develop the 'alternative business plan', the Labour affiliated trade union bureaucracy kept the campaign on the ground and in the factories—expressing the strength of the union without ever intending to allow it to be used.

In July, local Labour MP Des Browne called for the Scottish government to bail out Diageo with £1 million of tax payers' money to try and save jobs. It appeared more an attempt to score political points attacking Salmond and the SNP for "sleeping on the job" [53] rather than focus on encouraging and supporting the workers, their families and the wider working class movement to utilise the force shown on the streets and in the factories and mount a serious fight.

After Browne's call for a bailout for Diageo, he did later argue, more correctly, that "this is a very profitable business that has increased profits and is seeking to make even more profits".[54] The money was already there but the bosses at Diageo were not going to give it up willingly, certainly not without a fight they couldn't ignore. But the focus for the Labour MP as well as the local council was on meeting with Diageo bosses to find 'viable' 'alternative solutions' and urge patience as "it would be unrealistic to expect that to be done in a couple of hours".[55] The focus was pointed upwards at convincing a particularly shrewd and callous management at Diageo—who were not even in crisis and were simply using the economic climate to boost their already huge profits—to save the jobs. The union bureaucracy line was very much shaped by its close ties to the Labour Party, and certain defeat was snatched from the jaws of a potential victory for the hundreds of workers, the local community and the wider trade union movement that was ready to go into battle.

The pessimism of the trade union bureaucracy

This period was marked by an overwhelming pessimism from weighty figures in the trade union bureaucracy, at a time when they urgently needed to inspire confidence for mass and militant action. This is summed up by the then joint general secretary of Unite, Derek Simpson's remarkable setting of the tone on the *Andrew Marr Show* in August 2010. At a moment when Mark Serwotka of the Public & Commercial Services (PCS) union and Bob Crow of the Rail Maritime & Transport (RMT) union had called for mass coordinated strikes, Simpson stressed that a 'Greek-style' response to austerity—where already a wave of general strikes was happening—was not on the agenda here:

> I don't think that's the nature of the British public. We don't have the volatile nature of the French or the Greeks.[56]

Yet, by 2011, the anti-cuts movement was getting into its stride. Half a million marched on 26 March that year on an enormous and hugely significant Trade Union Congress (TUC) demonstration that had seen the STUC, union branches, workplaces and activists across the whole of Britain mobilise to fill coaches and trains and deliver a mass visual collective representing the force and potential power the unions and organised workers could bring to bear against the Tory onslaught.[57]

The year had begun on the back of a combative and determined student movement resisting the hikes in tuition fees and the removal of Education Maintenance Allowance (EMA). It led occupations, the smashing up of the Tory headquarters by thousands of students and supporters at Millbank in London—where a sizeable contingent of students who had mobilised and travelled from Scotland played their part—and a series of street battle demonstrations against the police kettles and horses.

Then the impact of the Arab Spring and the Egyptian Revolution shook everything. Union conferences throughout 2011 saw union leaders and delegates express heartfelt solidarity with the students who had taken the lead and stressed that the unions must fight austerity. The whole movement was fired by the inspiration of Egypt. That summer, there were riots in the streets of London, riots in the streets of Birmingham—in a cry of rage against institutionalised racist violence in the wake of the police murder of Mark Duggan. This moment exploded like a pressure cooker as austerity hit hard across working class communities.

Across Britain, the organised working class entered the fray in a serious way. Three unions played a decisive role: the PCS, the then National Union of Teachers (NUT)—now the National Education Union (NEU) and the largest teachers' union in England and Wales—and the University College Union (UCU). It was a combination of the growing mood for a serious fight against austerity among masses of workers, the role of socialist activists within these unions, and the willingness of their leaders to seek to build strikes in response.

This led to a strike of some 700,000 workers on 30 June against the Tories' flagship attack on pensions that would mean workers across the entire public sector would have to pay much more in pension contributions, work longer and get lower pensions. In an increasingly politicised and class divided situation, workers in the larger public sector unions like Unison, the General & Municipal Boilermakers' union (GMB) and Unite were asking, 'Why are we not striking too?' Pressure from below led to the spectacular, historic strike of 2.6 million public sector workers on 30 November that year.

In 2011, the pension strikes had shown the potential to deliver mass, powerful and political strikes. Tens of thousands took to the streets in marches all over Britain and Scotland. In Glasgow 20,000 marched, 15,000 in Edinburgh and 10,000 in Dundee, as well as mobilisations of thousands and of hundreds across towns, cities and villages all over Scotland.[58]

Striking teachers in the Educational Institute of Scotland union (EIS), with remarkably strong turnouts and well-organised picket lines, shut 2,670 of Scotland's 2,700 local authority run schools on the day.[59] The strike day also demonstrated how the experience of more days on strike could swiftly lift the confidence of workers in their own collective power and rapidly accelerate and deepen levels of organisation that could deliver such action.

Across the unions who struck, membership figures skyrocketed for the strikes, [60] and layers of new activists emerged. The feeling of marching out on strike together, joining workers from public sector workplaces all across your town and city in the streets, and knowing this was happening everywhere, had a big impact in showing workers how they could defeat austerity.

So the frustration across the movement when the pension strikes were quickly sold out after the magnificent November strike was profound. A number of left union leaders opposed the deal and the calling off of action, showing the demarcation within the TUC general council. Some of the left union leaders were calling for more action, while the big guns in Unison, GMB and Unite lined up behind the deal.

The years that followed still saw a stream of national, regional and sectional strikes at various moments across the NUT, PCS and UCU, as well as a national strike by the Fire Brigade Union (FBU) over an attack on their pensions in 2014. The CWU postal dispute against the privatisation of Royal Mail mobilised impressive mass national and regional rallies with unit reps (i.e. from every workplace) and the union delivered a near unanimous strike vote, but the action wasn't called. The union leadership championed a "ground breaking deal" and "new way"—what was essentially a partnership deal with management.[61] Despite this, the CWU has uniquely maintained its incredible organising strength at workplace level coupled with a political method that puts anti-racism at the heart of the union's organising. It has delivered in a series of disputes including big strike votes since—though none of these have yet led to a national strike in Royal Mail.

Despite the absence of any significant independent rank-and-file action in any of these unions, there were several examples of a kickback through this period following the sell-out of the pensions strike and before the rise of Corbynism. Towards the end of 2014, Unison members garnered enough support to win a recall conference where a vote was also won to essentially censure the leadership for their role in selling out the pay dispute in local government that followed the pension strikes. [62]

In early 2015, FBU members also won a recall conference where they too, reprimanded their leadership for backing off from their pensions fight.[63] In the Unite leadership election of 2013, the rank-and-file left candidate Jerry Hicks won an astonishing 36 percent of the vote in the biggest union in the country, and despite Len McCluskey being seen and supported as the left candidate.[64] While it was not a period of mass rank-and-file strikes from below, there were repeated examples reflecting the level of politicisation and a growing sense there needed to be a general strike—or a generalised fightback against the Tories. Any time workers were balloted for strikes, support was demonstrated time and time again.

It is important to note that all of this union activity, both in its successes and its failures, was taking place at a time when support for the SNP and independence was surging. The notion that the fate of the working class is dependent on nationalism rather than common class action north and south is refuted by this. But equally, the idea that there cannot be a challenge to the unity of the British state at the same time and that somehow the two are incompatible is equally disproved.

Grangemouth: a defining moment

One isolated example where serious rank and file action forced a huge victory was the 'sparks' dispute with the major construction companies in 2011-12. The electricians fought against the Building & Engineering Services National Agreement (BESNA) pay attack. Their action stopped a 36 percent pay cut and other attacks on their working conditions. [65] Unofficial rank-and-file strikes shut down sites at 5am every Wednesday for six months in key centres across Britain. Glasgow was a centre of the dispute.

A particularly heightened moment was when Unite balloted electricians officially for a national strike and a strong strike vote was delivered. At Scotland's Grangemouth oil refinery, workers decided at a mass meeting that they would not be crossing electricians' picket lines. As Scotland's only oil refinery, a strike there would have meant petrol supplies would have dried up in a few days. The threat of a strike at Grangemouth—one of the most powerful and solidly-organised workplaces in the country—was a central factor that led to the collapse of the BESNA, and is a stark reminder of the power organised workers hold in the system.

Such a threatening show of strength at a moment when the ruling class across Britain, in both the public and private sectors, were striving to drive down pay and roll back conditions did not go unnoticed. It should not have come as a surprise, though it was an audacious and nasty move, that Ineos billionaire boss Jim Ratcliffe—one of Britain's wealthiest individuals—moved to crush this bastion of workers' power the following year. He threatened to close the plant if the workers resisted a package of savage and calculated attacks, not just on pay and pensions but crucially trying to blackmail the workers into signing a no strike deal in order to save jobs.

When Unite held its strike ballot, workers at the plant returned a vote to walk out, and they organised to refuse to sign the deal on the advice of the union. In the wider trade union movement, across Scotland and beyond, many activists were well aware of the kind of moment that was coming and were organising to deliver solidarity, poised in the event of a high stakes pitched battle that everyone would have to get behind. Yet again, at another potentially transformative turning point in the class struggle and with such huge stakes, the union leadership failed the workers fundamentally.

Instead of leading a struggle, the Unite leadership folded and pushed a deal that left the workers with their pensions slashed and their pay frozen. Worse, McCluskey signed up to a no strike deal—a devastating blow that reverberated across the movement. This let SNP leader and first Minister Alex Salmond off the hook. Salmond knew that if he rebuffed the workforce, he would have little chance of winning the Independence Referendum due in September 2014. On the crucial weekend when matters hung in the balance, Grahame Smith, STUC General Secretary, said the behaviour of Ineos was "disgusting" and called for Salmond to consider nationalising the plant—just as the Westminster government had done with the banks. Unite should have fought and demanded every union back the STUC call for nationalisation to save the jobs.

Just weeks later, Ratcliffe twisted the knife to finish the job and slashed hundreds of jobs anyway and thousands of pounds from the remaining workforce's shift pay.[66] Ratcliffe explained why he moved to smash the union at Grangemouth. His words, in the article 'Grangemouth: The Battle with the Union and why we trail behind Germany', published on the Ineos website after appearing in the *Sunday Telegraph* in late 2013, underline how this dispute was really a question of who would blink first:

> On Grangemouth site this year, Unite threatened a strike three times—in February, July and October. In February, the union demanded a pay rise of 3.9 percent... we had no option but to accede as... a strike... would simply have been too damaging. In late July, Len McCluskey telephoned the site personally and demanded the reinstatement of Stevie Deans... again, a strike would have been too damaging at that time... In October came the straw that broke the camel's back... I maintain that '70s-style union behaviour leads to ruin.[67]

It was agreed Ineos would receive some £134 million grants and loan guarantees from the British and Scottish governments to back its investments after the Grangemouth deal was imposed on the workforce. And according to SNP MSP Joan McAlpine, Alex Salmond also negotiated a deal to reduce the cost of Ineos's gas supply by £40 million.[68]

The trade unions and the Labour Party

The role that the trade union bureaucracy played through the past decade has been defining, both in its failure to provide a lead and mobilise mass struggle on the scale that could have defeated the attacks and also in what came out of that politically, from the rise of Corbynism to the collapse of Labour in Scotland. Both cataclysms came in the aftermath of a strike movement against austerity that was squandered, and each provided the hope of an alternative strategy for that movement other than overcoming the trade union leaders' inertia.

The focus of the leaders of the big unions in particular was consistently, first and foremost, getting Labour re-elected. The actions of the union bureaucracy—or its inaction—was also deeply shaped by the complete failure of the Labour centre-right to correctly interpret what had happened in their election defeat and to their vote, and what that reflected amongst their working class base.

What should have been learned was that working class people were crying out for an alternative to austerity and growing inequality and poverty. Yet the whole argument that has flowed into the debates around Corbynism and the way forward for Labour to win a general election has been shaped by an interpretation that concluded that you can't be too radical or push socialist policies too much because you will alienate large sections of workers who are supposedly to the right of this.

This rubbed off on those union leaders who were so fixated on working with a Labour leadership that always demanded compromise. It found echoes in arguments around immigration—with the then Labour leader Ed Miliband's racist 'immigration controls' mug for example. And it became the deeply mistaken mantra of the Labour right and some trade union leaders that has been central to the defeat of Corbynism as well as the pessimism from the bureaucracy on the willingness or ability of workers to strike.

That's not to say there were not clashes between Miliband and those union leaders. During Miliband's leadership,

McCluskey took on the mantle of 'Red Len' and made it his mission to "reclaim Labour" from the right-wing politics that continued to dominate the leadership of the party. He was willing to clash with Miliband, warning him that if he adopted an "austerity-lite" programme then "he'll be defeated and he'll be cast into the dustbin of history".[69] He argued publicly and throughout the wider movement that Labour can be reclaimed by convincing more and more union—and specifically Unite—activists to join the party, fight for Unite policies and get more union members selected as candidates for Westminster, Holyrood and the local councils.[70] And it wasn't merely rhetoric to make the headlines—every branch secretary in Unite was written to and urged to promote this Labour Party recruitment drive.

McCluskey's line on the Labour Party leadership contest was a decisive factor in Ed Miliband's election, but there is little evidence that Unite or any other union had any influence on Labour policy. As Labour councils implemented cuts, Unite's Labour councillors mounted little in the way of opposition—and in a few instances where they did, they were suspended with little or no support from the union. McCluskey was openly critical of Labour's failure to repeal the anti-trade union laws, and Miliband's support for the public sector pay freeze and opposition to strikes.

The Labour right retaliated, accusing McCluskey of trying to rig the composition of the parliamentary party and local councils through the union's sponsorship of candidates. This blew up in Miliband's face, culminating in the fiasco of the candidate selection at Falkirk in Scotland, where Unite was accused of signing up local people to the Labour Party without their knowledge in order to ensure the selection of a favourable parliamentary candidate. Both the candidate Karie Murphy and local party chairman Stevie Deans (Unite convenor at Grangemouth) were suspended from the Labour Party in the furore. Unite was cleared in the end of any wrongdoing. Yet, with the events in Falkirk as a flashpoint, McCluskey headed up a significant collision between the trade unions and the Labour

Party around issues of funding for the party and representation.

Meanwhile Dave Prentis, Unison's general secretary, also criticised Miliband for backing the public sector pay freeze in 2012—a major attack that followed in the wake of the union leaders selling out the pensions dispute. Prentis accused Miliband of "falling into the Tory trap" and of "breathtaking naivety". Yet his words reveal the expectation and misplaced trust union leaders like him invariably place in the Labour leadership:

> Our members needed hope and a reason to vote Labour. They have been snatched away. In the past year Labour has struggled to get its message across to show that there is an alternative to the Coalition's savage cuts in our public services and the attack on the living standards of millions of ordinary people.
>
> We were told by Ed Miliband to be patient, to prepare for the long haul and that their economic plans needed to be cautious. And we hoped, as the economy worsened, Labour's voice would get louder, more forceful and that Ed Miliband would step up and speak out against the tearing apart of communities and families as they face insecurity and uncertainty.[71]

Disastrously, and true to their historic role, the union leaders of the largest unions prioritised looking to Labour to challenge austerity instead of mobilising the enormous power of the workers they represent—workers who had voted repeatedly for strike action whenever they were balloted.

Labour in power: Blairism and betrayals

For many working class and therefore 'Labour heartlands' voters, stomaching the shameful role of New Labour in government—from the Iraq war to the advancement of the Thatcherite neoliberal agenda—felt a repugnant necessity. The Tories' onslaught on the public sector and systematic dismantling of the welfare state rampaged on, as the rich continued to line their pockets. So it was common sense for many across the trade union and wider movement to continue to hang on by a thread to the Labour Party as their only political option despite deep frustration and anger. This was exacerbated by the absence of a serious fightback led by the unions. Yet as the years of savage Tory rule ground on and with an increasing ineptitude from Labour in opposition, this did not remain static.

Given that the resilient Labour 'heartlands' had long sat stewing in a slowly brewing bitterness, it was only a matter of time before that was bound to bubble over and douse out the flame that had kept it burning so long. As in Scotland in 2014/15, this dynamic also applies to the 2019 election south of the border, if producing drastically different results.

The perennial let down by Labour at a national level, which had a profound impact, was reinforced by the experience on the ground with Labour–controlled councils. In the 2017 council elections, Labour lost its 40-year majority on Glasgow City Council.[72] It was a dramatic moment in the city as well as nationally. Yet it is revealing how for so many it naturally rolled off the tongue to say in the wake of the result that it was a long time coming. It was not a surprise for that dam to have finally broken. The result reflected the dire judgement of Scottish Labour's leadership. Instead of seeking to relate to the clear anti-Tory anti-austerity mood that was motivating the surge in support for independence amongst Labour's old working class base, it decided to belligerently push a reactionary defence of the Union. Unsurprisingly, that seemed to largely benefit the Tories. At the same time, the 2017 council election result was a reckoning of Labour's rotten role in Glasgow City Council over the previous two decades. The bitter resentment towards Labour council leader Frank McAveety and his predecessors' betrayals had finally surfaced.

The Blairite leadership in the council had provoked a trail of bitter, combative strikes in response to their neoliberal onslaught. As late as November 2016, McAveety—quite incredulously given the proximity of the looming election—went on a frenzied offensive that provoked three simultaneous strikes.[73] First at council-run firms Cordia and Community Safety Glasgow (CSG), and then with the council's IT workers, a larger group, when he announced they would be privatised. This came on the back of inspiring strikes that had won solidarity from the movement, with strike tours across the whole of Britain and the north of Ireland that had started unofficially in 2014 with a walk out against a victimisation that won.

This was followed by a 16-week strike by Glasgow homelessness case workers in 2015. These are but a few of the many examples. McAveety had led Labour's transfer of Glasgow's entire council housing stock out of public hands, tried to scrap public holidays for council workers and free school buses for the poorest children. His funding cuts also gutted mental health services. In his previous reign as council leader in 1997-99, he championed anti-union laws and trashed workers' conditions with a 'sign or be sacked' ultimatum.

In 2004, under the leadership of fellow Blairite Charlie Gordon, Glasgow City Council and Scottish local authority body COSLA found themselves faced with a vibrant and determined strike of nearly 5,000 nursery nurses who had gone into direct conflict with the New Labour project of smashing up national bargaining. It was the biggest and longest-lasting strike in Scotland since the 1984-5 miners' strike. Involving nursery nurses across Scotland, it saw mass demonstrations at the Scottish parliament and when COSLA refused to come to the negotiating table to discuss a national deal, over 2,000 nursery nurses made their point by marching with a table to the COSLA offices in protest. Glasgow saw unofficial demonstrations where the strikers were joined by parents and supporters. The majority of parents refused to cross picket lines and many became involved in the picketing and raising support.

In the end the Unison national leadership decided a national agreement was not possible and, to the anger of masses of strikers, went for local deals. The Glasgow nursery nurses in particular felt they were left to fight alone and the struggle ended with the last group of nurses in Glasgow going back to work after 14 weeks of all out strike.

From 2007 to 2009, council leader Stephen Purcell waged war with four further strikes on his hands as workers fought to defend national bargaining in Single Status Agreement disputes in the council. To many working class parents in Glasgow, Purcell made himself a hate figure, trying to close 25 primary schools and sparking a mass campaign across the city, including the widely-supported occupation of the Wyneford and St Gregory schools in Maryhill. For decades, a procession of Labour leaders had passed on the baton in their race to implement the neoliberal 'modernisation' agenda.

When the dam broke for Labour in Scotland, this toxic mixture—Labour's crass response to the rising independence movement, its two-decades long war on jobs and services, its failure to act as a serious opposition to Tory austerity, its zeal for privatisation—brought about its stunning demise.

"It's no fur me it's fur the weans"

One of the Tories' flagship attacks was the despised Bedroom Tax and it sparked a furious resistance. Like their 'Workfare' programme, which was also defeated by protest, much to the fury of the Tories, [74] the Bedroom Tax was a deeply ideological attack, aimed at demonising the poor with the divide and rule tactic of distinguishing between a 'deserving and undeserving' poor. But the Tories had bitten off more than they could chew.

The tax was designed to punish people for "under occupying", and was set to drive around 100,000 people into rent arrears by April 2013, when tenants with so-called spare rooms could lose as much as £80 a month from their housing benefit. It sharpened the already appalling housing crisis across Britain. Councils and housing associations had a shortage of one bedroom properties and the attack would result in many of the poorest being pushed into the private rented sector, where cut-throat, racketeer land-lords have profited from the demise of council housing

Across Britain, the attack gave birth to a strong working class response and a new movement. Scotland was where it became the most developed, turning out the biggest demonstration during the year-long revolt. Thousands took to the streets from housing schemes and working class communities in a fiery and determined fight. Out of this, the Scottish Anti Bedroom Tax Federation was formed. It helped organise the many emerging grassroots groups from all over Scotland; it held delegate conferences of hundreds and embedded itself into the trade union movement by winning affiliations and practical support—especially among the housing trade unions.

Over the course of a year from early 2013 to early 2014, the movement against the Bedroom Tax expressed the deep anger against austerity that was creating the potential for a powerful fightback that mobilised working class people and showed how to win. In February 2014, the Scottish government was forced to announce it would budget an extra £15 million and pay the Bedroom Tax for all the 76,000 households it would affect in Scotland. This was a significant blow to the Tories and a major victory in the fight against austerity.[75]

The spirit, energy and confidence that came from the movement and its victory in Scotland flowed into the emerging independence movement. Back in 2011, at a strike demonstration in George Square, a newspaper photograph caught a woman striker, with her child, holding a placard that read "It's no fur me, it's fur the weans". That poignant image embodied the wider politicisation and class generalisation. The sense of dignity and clarity that found its expression in the need to get out on the streets, to take part in the strikes, to challenge the Tory agenda, not as resistance to this or that particular attack but in the knowledge that it was a class battle we were fighting.

That sentiment was on display from the outset in those early independence demonstrations. Support for independence swelled because it was widely adopted as the means to 'end Tory rule', to 'end austerity' and to imagine the possibility of a different society. Hence the Hope Over Fear mobilisations in particular were so reflective of the profound influx of working class communities onto the stage of history. For the Labour Party to so badly misunderstand this, and to attempt to dismiss it as a reactionary nationalist movement, is another stark reflection of its isolation—its inability to identify with its traditional base, the working class people it was supposed to represent.

Labour after the referendum

Labour at a British wide level was failing to relate to the anti-austerity mood. The Scottish Labour leadership in particular responded to the independence movement that had emerged as a result of this failure in an appalling manner. The Scottish Labour Party as an institution was a bastion of the right in the party. Johann Lamont presided over the referendum and Labour's role in the No Campaign, but her reign as Scottish Labour leader started in 2011, at the height of the anti-austerity movement. Her track record was consistently awful.

In autumn 2012, she launched an ill judged attack on the SNP for introducing free prescription charges—something that was celebrated throughout Scotland's working class communities, and something longed for south of the border. Infamously, Lamont said, "Scotland cannot be the only something for nothing country in world".[76] She wasn't a lone voice—she was defended at that year's Scottish Labour conference, with Labour's shadow Scottish secretary Margaret Curran arguing that Lamont's speech was about "facing up to the truth". Labour's then deputy leader Harriet Harman added, "How pleased we have all been to see the smile wiped off the smug, arrogant face of Alex Salmond".[77]

Perhaps the best way to sum up how huge swathes of Labour's working class base in Scotland felt about its leadership during the referendum campaign is to recall the hilarious moment when hapless Labour politicians from all over England travelled up to Scotland to get behind the No campaign in what was presumably intended as a show of real force. They were followed—and filmed—by a man carrying a boom box and playing Darth Vader's *Imperial March* from Star Wars. The Youtube video, entitled "Empire Strikes Back as 'imperial masters' gather in Glasgow" went viral and captured a widespread feeling of the betrayal by Labour in lining up alongside the Tories in what became known among activists as the 'bitter together' campaign.[78] After the referendum, Lamont resigned, unsurprisingly. Polls suggested up to 40 percent of those who had voted Labour in 2010 and in the last Scottish election had voted Yes, and places where Labour's support had previously had its strongest base correlated with the areas with the highest Yes votes.[79]

As the referendum drew closer and, the polls showed 51 percent support for Yes just a month before the vote,[80] the British establishment panicked and the 'Better Together' campaign for a No vote became widely known as 'Project Fear'. A 'British Together' march of 15,000 the following week organised by the anti-Catholic Loyalist Orange Order, that celebrates Scotland's role in the colonial oppression of Ireland, laid bare the reactionary nature of the campaign to defend the union and the racism and bigotry it mobilised. Here indeed was a reactionary nationalism—British imperialism.

While the march had no official Labour support, and these forces represent a fringe, there were some Labour councillors on it and, of course, Labour certainly has had its Loyalist Labour voting base. Ian McNeil, Aidrie South councillor for Labour, for example, is also an Executive Officer of the Orange Order Scotland, which, in July 2019, was the only salaried role in the organisation.[81] He is a member of Loyal Orange Institution of Scotland and of the Aidrie St John Freemasons.[82]

At the 2017 council elections, members of the Orange Order won seats both as Tory and as Labour candidates. Grand Master of the Grand Orange Lodge of Scotland, Jim McHarg, said at the time that the organisation was looking to stir the Unionist population in Scotland. He said that a "huge number" of Orange Lodge supporters were Tories, but that most of the Protestant Order's members were Labour supporters, and that the majority of Orange Order councillors voted in were Labour. He claimed that the Orange Order had more politicians in Scotland than it had at any time in the past 20 years. [83]

Much as establishment racism in general opens up a greater space for the forces of reaction, Scottish Labour's backward, right-wing, pro-union campaign allowed the bigots and racists of the Loyalist organisations to gain more of a foothold during the height of the No Campaign.[84]

Scottish Labour may have been successful in their desperate efforts alongside the Tories to rescue the British state and the Union Jack from defeat, but in doing so they sealed their own demise. For any left activists in Scotland who couldn't bring themselves to leave the party, or support the SNP, they may have felt some relief at Lamont's resignation in the wake of the referendum.

They must have been horrified to see her replacement was Jim Murphy, arch Blairite, defender of heinous acts by the Israeli state, notorious for his role in backing the War on Terror and the bombing of Iraq. His method of addressing the breakdown in trust in Labour was patronising and smacked of someone who had no grasp of how to relate to disillusioned working class Labour voters. For anyone familiar with Armando Iannucci's TV series *The Thick Of It*, they may have thought they had tuned into a new series when watching reports of Murphy's "100 town tour" with his Irn Bru crate soapbox and his appeal to "trust Labour, not the nats".[85] Surely it was meant as satire?

At the time of the referendum *Socialist Worker* Scotland correspondent Raymie Kiernan, reporting from the count in Glasgow, wrote "the sight of Labour politicians celebrating with the Tories at referendum counts will not be forgotten". After a sobering night for Labour in Scotland seven months later in the 2015 general election, Labour's shadow foreign secretary Douglas Alexander, having lost his own seat to 20-year-old Mhairi Black of the SNP, acknowledged, "Scotland has voted to oppose the Tories, but hasn't trusted Labour to do so".[86]

Corbynism, independence and Trident

Following the 2015 general election—an unbridled disaster for Labour in Scotland, and down south an indictment of Miliband's lacklustre opposition—we saw the emergence of Corbynism within the British Labour Party. His crushing, unexpected victory in the leadership election came only months after some Labour MPs had lent their nominations to Jeremy Corbyn merely to expose his supposed lack of support. They thought it was a laughable prospect that he would get anywhere near ending up a serious contender. On 15 September 2015, Corbyn walked off the podium from his victory speech as leader of the Labour Party and onto a mass demonstration of tens of thousands in solidarity with refugees. It was a moment that transformed the whole atmosphere of the class divided politics in Britain.

It was the mass rallies, the socialist policies, the manifesto pitched for the many and not the few, and above all the challenge to the rich that swung Corbyn's vote in the 2017 general election. He delivered the biggest rise in support in a campaign for any party in British electoral history. It can be plausibly argued that the slight bounce in the Labour vote in Scotland in 2017 (an increase of 10,000 votes, winning 3 percent more and regaining six MPs) can be attributed to some renewed enthusiasm from Labour's old base, including many who had voted Yes, inspired by Corbynism. But the key headline here was Labour's inability to make any real comeback despite the dramatic positive change in leadership nationally. This was an election where the SNP lost half a million votes. The average increase in the Labour vote across Britain was 5,883 per constituency. In Scotland, it was 550. [87]

While many ex-Labour voters who had drifted away in the wake of the referendum would likely have been drawn to the essence of Corbynism, and would have welcomed the change in leadership, there were two insurmountable problems facing the Labour Party in Scotland. Firstly, the Scottish Labour leadership was still dominated by the right. After Lamont and Murphy, it was difficult to see how anyone could be as bad as Kezia Dugdale—Corbyn's nemesis in Scotland. When she became the Scottish leader in 2015, she tried to have Corbyn removed and then attempted to claim that the slight improvement in Scottish Labour's fortunes in 2017 was down to her leadership when in reality it was a result of Corbyn's. Her real impact was, as analysis produced by Momentum showed, quite the opposite. It argued that:

> By not challenging effectively the Tories' record in government since 2010 and focusing on the SNP, Scottish Labour's strategists tacitly oversaw the Scottish Tories increase their vote by approximately 5,500 in the average constituency.[88]

This hardly comes as a surprise given Dugdale actually encouraged voters in some parts of Scotland "where the Tories might be better placed", to vote for them rather than Labour to keep the SNP out.[89]

The second hurdle that Labour was incapable of clearing—not without a fundamental policy change that would mean civil war in the party—was a political gulf that had opened up along two key faultlines; independence and Trident.

Unless the Labour Party shifted its position on independence, many of its old voting base were not coming back. Corbyn appeared to relate to and understand that class issues were motivating factors at the heart of the independence movement. His aim genuinely seemed to be to find a way to focus on the class issues in and of themselves, in a way that previous Labour leaders had failed to do. He was hounded in the Labour Party by the right for saying in 2017, "if a referendum is held then it is absolutely fine, it should be held" and that he "didn't think it was the job of Westminster or the Labour Party to prevent people holding referenda".[90] He then formulated a Labour position of not blocking a second referendum from Westminster but for its MSPs to oppose it should it reach Holyrood.

At Labour's 2018 conference in Liverpool, Corbyn continued to try and bridge the gap, avoiding as much as he could further alienating his potential base in Scotland but without opening up another front with the Labour right. This method was very much the story of Corbyn's leadership, always trying to balance the contradiction, to be on the right side of the argument while also conceding to the right-wing.

Even the new Scottish Labour leader Richard Leonard, who was far closer to the left than his rotten predecessors and had backed Corbyn, couldn't let Corbyn's attempt to soften the position towards the independence movement go unchallenged. Days after John McDonnell had said Labour would not block a vote on a second referendum, Leonard went public arguing that Labour should block another referendum from Westminster.[91] Nicola Sturgeon seized on this, tweeting that "normal service resumed" and that Leonard was attempting to "out Tory the Tories on #Indy".[92]

Leonard had emerged as Scottish Labour leader clearly stationed in the Corbynista camp of the Labour Party—a dramatic shift in this sense from his woeful right-wing predecessors. There was a shift to supporting more left policies and standing with left campaigns. The language of Scottish Labour shifted much more to identify with the left, class-based politics put forward by Corbyn.

Yet Leonard remained dogged in his opposition to a second referendum and his defence of the British state. After three years as leader, Leonard's days were numbered. Firstly, there had been no shift in support for Labour in Scotland under his leadership; it sat at an underwhelming 18 percent. Secondly, the collapse of Corbynism made it easy for the right to push him out. Leonard's resignation came in January 2021, after the 18th consecutive poll showing majority support for Scottish independence.

The other key faultline is Trident, which for 40 years has faced consistent opposition, both in the form of the permanent peace camp at Faslane and in the form of major demonstrations, particularly during the high points of the anti-war movement.

While the SNP abandoned their long held opposition to NATO in 2011 and faced quite a backlash from delegates and their wider base, it remains an anti-Trident party. The Labour Party gave up its disarmament position in 1987 under Neil Kinnock.

Corbyn's own credentials in opposing Trident are solid in the sense that he is the vice president of the CND, which he has been a member of since he was 15 years old, and he was the chair of the Stop the War Coalition from 2011 to 2015. Yet as the leader of the Labour Party, he did not move to challenge the Party's position on Trident, and despite the extraordinary tussle with General Sir Nicholas Houghton. The chief of defence staff, when asked if a Corbyn election would be a problem for the military beause Corbyn had said he would not be willing to press the nuclear button, had eerily responded, "well there are a few hurdles to cross before we get to that".[93]

No Labour manifesto under Corbyn would include a policy of opposition to Trident, whereas the SNP was very vocal in 2019 that scrapping Trident would be one of its key demands should a minority government be the outcome of the general election.

The collapse of Labour in Scotland has been a spectacular train crash. When it hit, it happened very quickly, but in truth it was the culmination of forces that were in play since Labour's election in 1997, like Blair's Iraq war, Ed Miliband's advocating of 'austerity lite', and decades of Scottish Labour's dismal record in running major councils.

When it came to the fight against austerity and the paths it could follow once union leaders scuppered the opportunity for mass working class resistance and strikes, the notion of breaking with Westminster and Labour's betrayals altogether found much greater purchase. This schism had taken place before Corbynism emerged, with questions of independence and Trident being so central to the movement. Even Corbyn's projection of socialism couldn't turn back the tide. With the profound assault Keir Starmer has launched on the left in the Labour Party, the already flimsy prospects for any kind of Labour revival in Scotland seems doomed.

While the SNP managed to soak up the widespread anti-Tory, anti-austerity mood and continues to do so, the wider polarisation caused by the deep triple crisis of the system will see this space narrow. For while in Scotland, the general pattern—polarisation and the collapse of the political centre—has had its own local peculiarities, it is not immune to the threat of the far right.

Though the terrain is different, the challenge is just as urgent as in the US against Trumpism or south of the border against Johnson. Hence socialists must place themselves at the heart of the movement for independence, knowing the blow it could deliver to the ruling class across Britain. We have a critical role to play in fusing this movement with the anti-racist movement that has mushroomed in the wake of Black Lives Matter. We must also campaign for the independence movement to fan resistance to the impact of the Covid-19 crisis, the looming economic crisis and the accelerating climate chaos. The heightened political consciousness in these movements can prepare the ground for workers' collective action to emerge. Within this process, it is socialists who can raise the vision of a struggle that can take on the system and go beyond the limits of what the trade union bureaucracy, the Labour Party or the SNP are capable of delivering.

Chapter 6

Racism and Anti-racism in Scotland

Charlotte Ahmed & Henry Maitles

Racism is a constant feature of capitalism, rooted in the historical development of the system, from slavery, through colonialism and beyond. While the defeat of Donald Trump is a blow for racists and fascists across the world, his legacy of racism and enabling the far right continues.

In Britain politicians and the media have been deliberately ratcheting up their attempts to divide opposition in the face of the government's callous mishandling of the Covid-19 crisis. As the pandemic continues with its disproportionate impact on Black and ethnic minority communities, the stoking up of Islamophobia and the scapegoating of refugees and migrants is increasingly being used to whip up division.

In the US, the Black Lives Matter movement saw the biggest anti-racist protests since the Civil Rights movement. This movement went global, generating a wider anti-racist consciousness and a deep questioning of institutional racism and the role of slavery and colonialism in shaping the experience of black people. In Britain this mood was epitomised by the tearing down of the Edward Colston statue in Bristol, similar agitation against colonial statues and street names in Glasgow,

Edinburgh and other towns across Scotland, plus a growing agitation for the decolonising of our education system.

With their much vaunted 'civic nationalism' and 'welcoming of refugees', successive Scottish governments and even some on the Scottish left would have us believe that Scotland, compared to England, is relatively free of structural and institutional racism. The friends and family of Surjit Singh Chokar, Imran Khan, Sheku Bayoh, Mercy Baguma, the detainees in Dungavel detention centre and countless other victims of racial assault and racial injustice over the last 30 years know otherwise.

Karl Marx insisted, "The ideas of the ruling class are in every epoch the ruling ideas; that is the class which is the ruling material force in society is at the same time its ruling intellectual force".[1] This of course includes racist ideas. Propagated from the top down, they are always challenged by anti-racists. The myth that Scotland has been less racist than Britain generally is linked to notions of a progressive nationalism, discussed elsewhere in the book. Like the rest of Britain, racism in modern Scotland is bound up with slavery and empire.

It's not just about the past. The racist institutions of the British state remain intact in Scotland. True, there have been positive statements, for example, welcoming and inviting greater numbers of refugees. But too often the government and some of its supporters simply throw up their hands, saying Scotland does not have the power to take action, that it's London's fault. Westminster is truly culpable but that's a poor excuse. The SNP have been governing Scotland since 2007, having won three Scottish Parliament elections and three Westminster elections in a row. Yet the Holyrood government continues to tolerate the detention of asylum seekers imprisoned at Dungavel, denied their human rights, while it condemns racist Tory policies. Increasingly, Police Scotland operates without proper scrutiny and accountability for its actions and, in the case of Sheku Bayoh, with impunity. The present government devoted much of its energy to keeping Scotland in the anti-immigrant, Fortress Europe, contradicting its own anti-racist, pro-immigrant aspirations.

Yet there is a tradition of resistance to racism in Scotland, reaching back to the early industrial revolution and the rise of the working class. This confusion of ideas can be explained by what the Italian revolutionary Gramsci called 'contradictory consciousness'. Workers who are continually taught to believe 'too much' immigration is bad can also see that the non-white person working and living alongside them is a co-worker and someone to be protected from racism.[2] Even in the grimmest of situations, this can be true. Himmler, writing in Nazi Germany in 1938, five years after Hitler came to power, complained that the problem with Germans was "each one has his decent Jew"[3] and didn't want him/her subjected to violence.

There's a myth that Scotland has always welcomed refugees and migrants. Yet, as this chapter will show, often people arriving here faced and continue to face resentment and aggression. So, for example, Jewish children of the kinder transport remember their experiences positively, yet there was clear opposition to immigration of adults. For example, Glasgow University and the medical establishment opposed foreign (Jewish) doctors being allowed entry.[4]

We need to challenge the myths and look to build on the real tradition of anti-racist activism as an essential part of the movement for independence. Collective action and the role of socialists and socialist ideas can be decisive in shaping events.

Scotland and slavery

Scotland's role in slavery and empire, previously buried under a mountain of lies and evasions, has belatedly and gradually been uncovered. Angus Calder's pioneering *Revolutionary Empire,* first published in 1981, was a good, early start, challenging the orthodox, Anglo-centric account of empire and dispelling the amnesia over the role Scots played in colonialism and slavery:

> The Pakistani who sells me my paper most mornings
> is part of the same process of history as myself, and

salient in it is the disturbing figure of John Johnstone, arch-profiteer from the Rape of Bengal after the battle of Plassey: even the habitual warmth, in portraiture, of Henry Raeburn could not soften the sharp features of that cynically rapacious fellow-Scot.[5]

Scots played a key role in the British Empire, greater comparative to their relative population size than their English counterparts. Glasgow's merchants in particular benefitted. Their profits laid the basis for Clydeside's rapid industrialisation and Glasgow's claim to be the Second City of the Empire. Neal Ascherson, in reviewing Tom Devine's recent work, refers to Scotland's paradoxical Victorian apogee of industrial triumph and mass emigration:

> Devine asks the big question: where did it all go? Why has contemporary Scotland benefited so little from those billions of intercontinental profit? And why do the Scots—once, per capita, so much more involved in the empire than the English—now affect amnesia about it, sharing none of England's imperial nostalgia? Could it be true that the immense profits from slave-worked sugar and tobacco plantations made Scotland's industrial take-off possible?[6]

In *Scotland's Empire*, Devine is cautious about this ugly problem but fresh research hardened his views. Ascherson writes that capital inflows from "the slave-based economies were of fundamental importance in the first textile-dominated phase of Scottish industrialisation".[7] As for the slave trade itself, it's true that Glasgow did not send slave ships to Africa and the Caribbean as did Bristol and Liverpool. But Scots abroad were managing and financing the trade in disproportionate numbers. The Scots seldom competed directly with the English, establishing "distinct and almost exclusively Scottish fiefdoms: the fur trade, the tobacco trade, the jute industry, the opium business in China, the 'hedge-banking' outfits in Australia, the executive levels of the East India Company".[8]

By the late 19th century, Clydeside had near-world domination in shipbuilding, locomotive production and heavy engineering. Colonial enterprise was a pattern of near monopolies from Scotland's regions and Ascherson shows the scale of it:

> The Hudson's Bay Company was staffed by Orcadians; its Canadian rival, the North West Company, was run by Highlanders; the sugar plantations of Jamaica were packed with younger sons of Argyllshire lairds; the great trading houses of South-East Asia were mostly family businesses from Aberdeen and north-east Scotland; the outflow of foreign investment was cornered by Edinburgh solicitors. The myth that the Scots were closer to indigenous peoples than the English has been well punctured. They were indeed closer—by the length of a slave-driver's lash. ...The same myth suggested Gaelic emigrants had a special rapport with traditional societies. In fact, Highlanders behaved with sometimes genocidal savagery—the Gaelic vigilantes who carried out the Warrigal Creek massacre of Australian aboriginals in 1843.[9]

Since the murder of George Floyd, the Black Lives Matter rebellion has forced millions to reconsider the 400-year history of racism, slavery and imperialism. Here in Scotland, it has accelerated the unearthing of the ugly role that many Scots played in it.

The legacy of slavery in Scotland

Glasgow's Victorian and Edwardian splendour derived from the proceeds of slavery. Tobago Street, Jamaica Street, Otago Street, India Street, the Virginia Mansions, the Kingston docks and countless other streets and buildings are named after the outposts of slavery. Glasgow's Museum of Modern Art was the home of the Oswald family, who were enriched through slavery. Oswald Street is named after them. Headstones in the graveyards of Jamaica and Antigua bear a succession of Scots names like Campbell, Mackinnon, Baird, Duncan and Malcolm. How and when did this happen?

After the Darien disaster, Scotland's failed colonial venture into Central America in the 1690s, key sections of the Scottish ruling class concluded that their commercial interests lay in union with England. Darien was final proof they lacked the economic muscle to compete with their stronger southern neighbour. So a section of the nobility and the late-emerging, land-owning and merchant bourgeoisie favoured the union and a stable Protestant, Hanoverian succession. With few opportunities at home, upper- and middle-class Scots travelled the world seeking their fortune, emigrants and mercenaries par excellence. Later, thousands of their poorer compatriots were forced abroad by their landlords and masters.

After the Act of Union, the Scottish merchant class, free to trade with the colonies, lost no time in establishing its own lucrative share of the slave trade. Before the American War of Independence its main focus was the tobacco trade in the plantations of Virginia and the Carolinas. By 1796, Scots owned 30 percent of the sugar plantations in Jamaica, including the slaves. Scots traders specialised in tobacco, sugar, cotton and rum—commodities reliant entirely on slavery. Although the slave ships did not operate through Scottish ports, the products of the trade did. "In one year, 1758, Scottish tobacco imports from the American colonies exceeded those of London and the English ports of Bristol, Liverpool and Whitehaven combined."[10]

As profits rolled into Glasgow, service industries grew up to support the trade. Dundee specialised in the manufacture of cheap linen, sacking and packaging fabrics from jute. The linen was used to make clothes for slaves. Profits were reinvested in a variety of manufacturing enterprises in and around Glasgow, as well as the dredging and deepening of the Clyde to allow more and bigger trading ships to reach the city. The single biggest industry benefitting from the slave trade was linen manufacture. It employed at least 230,000 men, women and children in the 1780s, a huge proportion of the population.[11]

The American Revolution saw the focus of Scotland's trans-Atlantic trade shift to the Caribbean and the sugar plantations. More profits were made from importing sugar, refining it and exporting it to Europe. The fashion for sweet tea fuelled a rapid increase in demand for both commodities. Tate & Lyle became a huge employer in Greenock, and Glasgow became famous for its genteel tearooms.

By 1815, 65 percent of all goods exported from Scotland went to the West Indies.[12] Scots dominated the sugar plantations in Antigua, St Vincent and Jamaica. Rape and sexual exploitation was rife on the Scots–run plantations, evidenced by the proliferation of Scots names in the plantation records and the Caribbean graveyards. Scots participated in the establishment, maintenance and brutal coercion of the slave trade. Their plantations were ruthlessly efficient, reducing food rations and clothing to save money. Death rates among slaves were higher than those of the tobacco and cotton plantations.[13] Many died within three years of arrival. The lack of family facilities and the unrelenting, back-breaking labour required contributed to the soaring death rates.

But there were slave rebellions and fear of revolt mounted among the slaveholders. By 1750, 85 percent of the population of British West Indies were African slaves. Between 1655 and 1813, there were 16 slave rebellions in Jamaica. Some 50,000 slaves took part in the Baptist revolt there in 1831. The rebellion lasted 11 days and was brutally suppressed with hundreds executed. But it proved a turning point. Historian Hilary Beckles describes a '200 Years' War'[14] between slaves and slave-owners in the British Caribbean, culminating in the great Jamaican revolt of 1831—the death knell of slavery throughout the British Empire.

Scots also participated directly in the brutal task of

procuring and transporting slaves. The previously mentioned Richard Oswald owned the slave fort on Bunce Island off the coast of Sierra Leone. Tens of thousands of African slaves passed through it on their way to plantations in America and the Caribbean, some of them owned by Oswald.

In 1833, slavery was abolished in Britain, but only after slave rebellions and decades of campaigning. Scotland's slavers were generously compensated by the state and their profits financed the rapid agricultural and industrial revolutions that transformed the country.

However, there were also many Scottish anti-slavery proponents. In *The Wealth of Nations* published in 1776, Adam Smith argued slavery was both morally repugnant and ultimately inefficient:

> From the experience of all ages and nations, I believe, that the work done by free men comes cheaper in the end than the work performed by slaves. Whatever work he does, beyond what is sufficient to purchase his own maintenance, can be squeezed out of him by violence only, and not by any interest of his own.[15]

Of course, Smith was extolling free enterprise, but his attack on slavery, combined with the powerful influence of the French Revolution and the zeal of Christian reformers, gave a fillip to the growing abolitionist movement in Britain, particularly in Scotland. Although there were few slaves in Scotland and accounts of the brutality of plantation life were suppressed, the issue of slavery became a political issue.

The Abolition Act was finally passed in 1833. Several Scots were prominent in the leadership of the movement. Zachary Macauley from Inverary and William Dickson from Moffat witnessed slavery in the plantations and were passionate abolitionists. The Glasgow Anti-Slavery Society was formed in 1822 and became one of the most active in Britain. Women played a prominent role in the abolitionist movement that spread throughout Scotland. Many leading figures in the Church—but not all—took a principled position on slavery as "inconsistent with the spirit and principles of the Christian faith".[16]

Yet many Scots who witnessed slavery in the colonies subscribed to the ideas of 'scientific' racism, a thoroughly *unscientific* theorisation invented to justify the rise of capitalism, slavery and the subjugation of the colonies. This was a glaring contradiction within the dominant themes of the so-called Scottish Enlightenment, the period at the end of the 18th and into the 19th century, in which the ideas generated by the American and French Revolutions, of reason and scientific discovery as against religious superstitions and the proclamation of universal human values, were eagerly discussed and developed by a range of Scottish intellectuals and scientists. One of the most prominent philosophers of the Scottish Enlightenment, David Hume, for instance, who claimed to stand for the values of a universal humanity, could write:

I am apt to suspect the negroes to be naturally inferior to the whites. There scarcely ever was a civilized nation of that complexion nor even any individual eminent either in action or speculation. No ingenious manufacturers amongst them, no arts, no sciences.... Such a uniform and constant difference could not happen, in so many countries and ages, if nature had not made an original distinction betwixt these breeds of men. Not to mention our colonies, there are Negroe slaves dispersed all over Europe, of which none ever discovered any symptoms of ingenuity.[17]

Hume, in his writings, condemned slavery in ancient Rome but was involved in encouraging friends to invest in slave plantations in Grenada.[18]

The recorded comments of a Scottish woman who travelled from Edinburgh to Antigua in 1774 are illuminating. Janet Schaw felt uncomfortable with the inhumane treatment of slaves she witnessed when she first arrived in Antigua. In time, however, she reconciled this with the belief that African slaves do not feel pain and demonstrate indifference to their suffering in a way that Europeans would not.[19]

Even as increasing numbers of Scots were beginning to campaign against slavery, the Scots actively participating in the trade and the plantations developed no such scruples. The developing revolutionary ideas of liberty, equality and fraternity did not extend to all. But masses of ordinary Scots played an active part in the movement against slavery. In 1788 and 1792, petitions were sent to Parliament protesting against it. In 1792, a third of all the petitions were from Scottish groups.

In Scotland's central belt, where thousands of jobs were dependent on exports of cotton goods, pro-slavery voices were well represented in civic society, usually by businessmen. Newspapers such as the *Glasgow Courier* and the *Edinburgh Review* carried articles defending slavery and published accounts of travellers who claimed slaves were very happy on the plantation.[20]

In 1792, in the wake of the French Revolution and the mass circulation of Tom Paine's popular pamphlet, *The Rights of Man*, there was mass rioting in Edinburgh, triggered by King George III's birthday celebrations. It spread throughout Scotland in protest at the corrupt establishment at Westminster and its venal placemen in Edinburgh, notably Dundas, Prime Minister William Pitt's key man in Scotland. Known disparagingly as 'Henry the Ninth, King of the Scots', Dundas held direct control over all political appointments, including colonial appointments. He became President of the East India Company and acquired a notoriety for using his considerable patronage to bribe politicians. In this way, Dundas was responsible for delaying the abolition of slavery in Britain.

Wealthy Scots held a huge financial stake in slavery. Compensation paid to former slave owners ran to billions in today's money, a sum rivalled only by the bailout of the banks after the 2008 crash and the subsidies to big business during the coronavirus of 2020.

Recent research has shown that significant land ownership in Scotland derived from slave transportation, ownership and investment in the plantations and compensation paid to slaveowners when slavery was abolished.[21] An estimated 1.2 million acres (33.5 percent of the West Highlands and Islands) was bought with this slave money. Further, it shows how many traditional landowners (what we might call clan chiefs) married into slavery-derived wealth. The research suggests that these two groups were also responsible for some of the largest clearances of people from their land.

With British slavery formally ending in 1833, the attention of the abolition movement turned to the US and its slave-owning southern states—enterprises from which many in Britain still profited. The extent of the abolition movement in Ireland, England and Scotland is shown by accounts of a speaking tour undertaken by the great African-American abolitionist Frederick Douglass in 1845. He wrote that "Scotland is a blaze of anti-slavery agitation—the Free Church and Slavery are the all-engrossing topics".[22]

The Free Church split from the Church of Scotland in the Great Disruption of 1843 over state interference in Church affairs, but it needed money for its new enterprise and found many donors in the Presbyterian churches of the slave states in America. This incensed abolitionists, who launched a campaign against the Free Church using the slogan 'Send Back the Money'. Douglass toured Scotland speaking to large, raucous gatherings in bigger centres like Greenock and Paisley but also in smaller towns like Arbroath, Ayr and Montrose. They included songs, poems and the constant refrain of 'Send Back the Money'![23] Douglass, and other US abolitionists, were welcomed everywhere and at one point he considered settling in Edinburgh.

The campaign featured petitions, public meetings, posters, pamphlets and street graffiti ('Send Back the Money' was painted in red on the sides of the Free Churches), newspaper articles and debates. Ultimately the issue was resolved by the victory of the northern states in the American Civil War, a war in which many Scots fought, on both sides. It is estimated that about 50,000 people of Scottish origin fought in the Union Armies, many American citizens. There were no Scots regiments like the famous Irish Brigade. However, two divisions of largely Scots volunteers, the 79th New York State militia and the 65th Illinois Infantry, both fought at the key battle of Gettysburg in 1863, a resounding Union victory. It is difficult to find accurate estimates of the numbers of Scots who fought for the South. Most would have been second or third generation immigrants.

The Civil War had a big impact in Britain. The Union organised a blockade of southern ports to stop the export of commodities such as cotton and the import of munitions and food. Confederate agents in Britain organised the purchase of blockade-running ships, finding willing suppliers among Clydeside's shipbuilding magnates, who first supplied second-hand paddle steamers then started building state of the art ironclad ships for the Confederacy. There were 27 shipyards on the Clyde at the time.

The effective blockade of the Confederacy devastated the British cotton industry. Particularly affected were Lancashire and Renfrewshire. Mills closed and thousands were laid off experiencing real hardship. These had been centres of Chartism, the first working class political movement. The shipping, finance and mill bosses sided with the southern slave states. In Manchester, public meetings and marches were held to support the Union. In 1862, a huge meeting of cotton workers took place in Manchester Free Trade Hall and voted to support an embargo on goods from the Confederacy, including cotton.

There was no corresponding class action in Scotland. The large crowds attending abolitionist meetings, mainly working class people, did so largely as conscientious objectors, influenced by religious and moral ideas. In terms of class consciousness, Manchester was ahead of Glasgow at this point.

As the profits from slavery diminished, the profits from

the empire in the East began to flow in.[24] Huge fortunes were made.[25] No wonder that the Indian sub-continent was called 'the Jewel in the Crown'. Scots were involved in every aspect of this. Devine writes that:

> The Scots became prominent in the East India Company long before their position was further enhanced during the long reign of Henry Dundas as President of its Board in 1784. Many were from landed backgrounds and Scottish administrators, merchants and army officers returned home with the accumulated profits of their Asian enterprise. They sometimes used these fortunes to invest in estate improvement and road building.[26]On the Isle of Lewis there is a monument to James Matheson, then the second biggest landowner in Britain. A Liberal MP representing the electors of Ross and Cromarty, he became Governor of the Bank of England and Chairman of the P&O shipping giant. He also bought the Isle of Lewis for £500,000. The inscription on his monument says he was "a child of God, a consistent Christian".[27] It does not tell us that his mass eviction of tenants led to 'the Crofter Wars' that continued into the 1880s, nor that he accrued his massive wealth smuggling opium into China.

Illegal though it was, opium generated huge revenues for the British in India, where it was grown, and substantial income for the London government. Britain simply waived the rules and 12 million Chinese became opium addicts. When the Chinese tried to stamp out the illegal trade, Matheson persuaded the British to launch a war of reprisal. Thousands were slaughtered and ports were bombarded in what became known as gunboat diplomacy. As a sceptical British naval officer put it, "the Chinese must submit to be poisoned with opium or be massacred for defending their own laws in their own land".[28] Finally, the British army stormed Beijing forcing the Chinese to submit and concede Hong Kong as part of the spoils. Matheson became co-founder of the Jardine-Matheson Bank that came to dominate Hong Kong.

Poverty and land clearances instigated by the likes of Matheson fuelled Scottish recruitment into the army and navy. There was a conscious effort to create Highland regiments and make them the backbone of the imperial army.[29] They acted as the shock troops of empire from the Siege of Quebec to the slaughter of Kandahar. In 1857, the Great Indian Rebellion was crushed by mainly Scottish regiments. The brutal repression that followed imposed direct rule from Britain, as opposed to the regime of the East India Company. The poverty inflicted on the Indian population increased and famines occurred frequently. Millions were starved to death throughout the remaining decades of British rule in India.[30]

In Scotland, as elsewhere, the 2020 Black Lives Matter movement has inspired a flurry of popular agitation to decolonise education, change street names and topple the statues commemorating the 'Great Men' who prospered from slavery and defended it. One of the most prominent was the aforementioned Sir Henry Dundas, whose imposing statue dominates St Andrew Square in Edinburgh's New Town and who has streets named after him in Glasgow and many other Scottish towns. The ongoing campaigns to highlight the racism of those connected with slavery or racist ideas forced the decision to rename the Hume Tower at Edinburgh University.[31] It further led to debate as to whether there should be re-namings or plaques explaining the context of the times.

We need more of this to challenge racism and reflect the new Scotland. Not everyone in the independence movement might agree but as the Russian revolutionary Lenin argued "... every nation possesses a bourgeois culture (and most nations a reactionary and clerical culture as well) in the form, not merely of 'elements' but of the dominant culture".[32] Scotland is no exception. Its dominant culture incorporates elements of racism from its slavery and imperialist past. It means, unfortunately, Islamophobia in the wake of the Iraq war and the anti-immigrant, hostile environment rhetoric from Westminster finds an echo here; but not without challenge. Amid the celebrations of the 2014 Commonwealth Games, itself a relic of imperialism, there were lectures, exhibitions and discussions exposing the real legacy of empire in Scotland. An impressive antidote to the brazen attempt to whitewash empire was South African opera singer Pumeza Matshikiza's wonderful rendition of Hamish Henderson's great song 'Freedom Come All Ye' Her performance was viewed by one billion worldwide. Henderson's song refers to Nyanga, one of the oldest black townships in Cape Town, where Pumeza grew up. Describing the event afterwards, she said: "The song is not one I was even aware of until I was given it to rehearse but it is so beautiful. I love what the song stands for—freedom for all regardless of race, social standing or nationality".[33]

Irish immigration into Scotland

Scotland was never oppressed like Ireland. While its ruling class benefited from the union with England, Ireland's economy was driven backwards. Scottish forces were at the forefront of British imperialism, not least in Ireland itself. It can be argued that Ulster was a Scottish colony during the 17th century. In 1603, James I and VI of Scotland recruited Scottish Presbyterian settlers to establish loyal 'plantations' in Ulster to crush its Catholic population and use it as a Protestant bridgehead for the subjugation of the whole island. At the start of the 19th century, Ireland's population was eight million. During the 1840s it fell by an estimated three million—two million dying of starvation and one million emigrating. Not only did Scottish troops help police this genocide but Scottish capital played a big role in developing Ireland's one area of industrial development—Belfast and its hinterland.

The Great Hunger (An Gorta Mór) between 1845 and 1849 led to a massive growth of the northern cities of Belfast and Derry as the poor fled the devastated countryside and there was a rapid increase in Irish immigration to Scotland. At the same time, thousands migrated from the Highlands and Islands following the Clearances and the potato famine that ravaged the North and West of Scotland in 1846. The wealth from the slave trade was now being used to drive industrial development in Scotland. Throughout the 19th century, thousands of Irish people were driven into the industrial revolution that was gathering pace in the Scottish lowlands. Along with the victims of the Scottish Clearances, much of the unskilled heavy labour that transformed Glasgow from a small trading port into a key centre of heavy industry came from Ireland. They built the roads, canals and railways and laboured in the mines, mills and factories that made Clydeside such a powerhouse of capital accumulation.

With Manchester in mind, Engels claimed the industrial revolution would have been a more gradual affair but for the human raw material provided by Irish immigration.[34] This was equally valid for Scotland. By 1851, 7.2 percent of its population was Irish compared to 2.9 percent in England and Wales. In Glasgow, the Irish immigrant population had grown to 19 percent and would increase as the city tripled in size between 1851 and 1911. Poverty was shared between Scottish and Irish, but not equally. "The Irish constituted the most abject part of the population, prepared to tolerate a lower standard of life than all but the very poorest of the workforce".[35] While this is true, it would be more appropriate to use the word 'forced' rather than 'prepared'.

Since the Reformation, Scotland had been overwhelmingly Calvinist, with some remaining Catholic communities in the Highlands and Islands. The newly arrived Catholic Irish were regarded with hostility and suspicion. Between 1847 and 1880, there was a rise in sectarianism and a growth of the Orange Order—first established within Scottish regiments who had been used to suppress the United Irishmen revolt in the 1790s—in the West of Scotland.[36]

Divide and rule meant systematic discrimination against

Irish Catholics at work. Often it was 'No Irish Need Apply', except when Irish labour was being deliberately hired to break strikes or drive down wages. This in turn saw sections of a rapidly growing working class develop an antagonism towards Irish workers. Karl Marx, then resident in London, pointed out that this hostility served only the ruling class: "This antagonism is the secret of the impotence of the English working class... It is the secret by which the capitalist class maintains its power. And the latter knows this".[37] Marx's insight applied to Scotland just as much as England.

But working class solidarity was hard fought for in the factories, mines and shipyards over the next decades. Influenced by socialists like John MacLean, James Connolly, Helen Crawfurd, Mary Barbour, Agnes Dollan and Harry McShane, the working class in Scotland, as elsewhere, united to fight intransigent bosses. Throughout the Great Unrest of 1910 to 1914, strikes over wages and conditions united workers across the sectarian divide. For example, there was the Belfast Dock strike of 1907 and huge support for the Dublin lockout of 1913. Led by Jim Larkin and James Connolly, these strikes inspired a wave of solidarity in Britain, nowhere more so than in Glasgow. In the immediate post-war period, Clydeside became a key centre of solidarity with the Irish struggle for independence.[38]

Sectarianism did not disappear after the high tide of Red Clydeside and the First World War but it was relatively diminished. The bigotry of sectarian unionism continued to express itself in the Church of Scotland, in some trade unions and in Protestant organisations like the Scottish Protestant League, discussed below.

Today, it emerges from the shadows, often in association with racism, fascism and British nationalism. The rivalry between Celtic and Rangers is still a flash point. Neil Lennon, Northern Irish-born former manager of Celtic, was sent bullets and an explosive device by loyalist criminals from Ayrshire. There is considerable debate about the influence of sectarianism in Scotland today. A report commissioned by the Scottish government concluded that perceptions of sectarianism's prevalence being widespread were not backed by empirical evidence on issues like housing, employment and educational outcomes.[39] But there is no room for complacency and not surprisingly, age, gender and class influence the extent to which people experience sectarianism today.

The SNP government responded by enacting a bad law that criminalised a section of society—young football fans. The ridiculous 'Offensive Behaviour at Football' Act of 2012 was repealed in 2018. Yet the police continue to identify 'football risk groups' and act with impunity—an approach that apportions blame 'evenly to both sides' when the evidence shows this is not the case. Until 2020, hundreds of Orange Order marches took place, disrupting services and bringing violence and intimidation in their wake. During the Referendum campaign of 2014, groups associated with the Orange Order attacked independence protesters. Loyalist groups rioted when a local Republican band marched in Govan in 2019.

During lockdown in 2020, in response to the Black Lives Matter movement, loyalist and fascist groups gathered in Glasgow's George Square to 'protect the Cenotaph' even though it was never under threat. They used it as a pretext to attack young anti-racists gathered there to protest against the detention of asylum seekers. At the subsequent Stand Up To Racism demonstration in George Square, 1,500 anti-racists gathered safely and peacefully to support Black Lives Matter. The police decided to kettle hundreds of them, claiming they were a 'football risk group'.[40] So the police powers were used against peaceful anti-racists, not against violent fascists.

The legacy of anti-imperialism in relation to Ireland, Britain's oldest colony, is still present in Scottish political life. But in the mass movement for independence, sectarianism can be isolated further by a campaign that puts internationalism, anti-racism and pro-immigration at its heart. During the successful campaigns against the Scottish Defence League and attempts to spread the influence of the racist Football Lads Alliance into Scotland, Stand Up To Racism supporters leafleting all of the Scottish football grounds were heartened by the positive response of the great majority of fans—especially at Tynecastle and Ibrox—stadia that the far right have previously targeted.

We cannot rely on laws to protect us from bigotry and racism. History has shown racism and sectarianism is best challenged and defeated when socialists and the working class act and lead the way.

1880-1920: immigration controls or fair wages?

Historically Scotland has been built on immigration, benefitting from the contribution and diversity that newcomers have brought. That remains the case today. Yet the trade union leaders' attitude to Jewish immigration at the end of the 19th century and the first two decades of the 20th is perhaps summed up by dockers' union leader Ben Tillett's infamous welcome: "We know you are our brothers, but we wish you had not come".[41] Some parts of the trade union movement reflected the widespread anti-immigrant mood of the period from 1880 to 1920. Millions of Jews had to uproot themselves and their families from the 'Pale' (the Jewish settlement area in Eastern Europe) and move west, fleeing Tsarist persecution in the Russian Empire and antisemitic pogroms in hundreds of towns and cities. In 1898, a Tsarist official had promised Russia's 'Jewish problem' would be solved by one third emigrating, one third converting and one third being killed.

Initially the British trade union leadership's reaction to the bosses' attempt to use migrant labour to undercut wages was to blame the exploited migrant worker rather than the bosses. Breaking from that backward approach depended upon effective trade union organisation becoming established, especially amongst the immigrant workforce.

Iron, steel and mining unions in the West of Scotland complained their wages and conditions were being undercut in areas where first Irish and then Lithuanian Catholic immigrants were employed. The Ayrshire, Lanarkshire and Fife coalfields saw initial hostility towards the new migrants and the Lanarkshire union officials even promised support for strikes protesting at a Lithuanian presence in the coalfields. There had been major discussions on these issues at Glasgow Trades Council, which wrote to the TUC. The pathetic response complained "there was no law prohibiting the importation of foreign labour".[42]

Clearly, trade unions wanted immigration controls to protect, as they saw it, Scottish workers. At the 1892 TUC Congress, import restrictions and immigration controls were linked. The resolution asked for government contracts to be purchased in Britain rather than abroad and demanded a ban on "foreign labour during strikes, lockouts or any trade disturbance".[43]

Some leading socialists and union leaders, such as Keir Hardie and Ben Tillett, were not immune. Hardie had been against Irish immigration in the middle of the 19th century. He told the 1899 House of Commons Select Committee on Immigration and Emigration that there was a strong dislike between Scots and foreigners. In response to a question about whether Scottish trade unionists wanted a total immigration ban, he replied: "Yes they would... Strong diseases (immigration of destitute aliens) require strong remedies... to prohibit their importation".[44] When an overtly racist MP on the Committee questioned him, Hardie conceded, "every foreigner throws one British workman out of employment".[45] When another MP pointed out that the emigration figure for Scotland that year was 1,500 greater than immigration, he claimed: "It would be much better for Scotland if those 1,500 were compelled to remain and the foreigners be kept out".[46]

As another example, Henry Hyndman, leader of the Social Democratic Federation (SDF), characterised Eleanor Marx as having "inherited in her nose and mouth the Jewish type from Marx himself". Satnam Virdee comments that in England the dominant socialist imagery of the time put the Jews in a double-bind that represented them simultaneously as capitalist parasites and sweated labour.[47] Sadly this applied to Scottish society too.

There was a sharp divide on the 'Jewish question' between socialist internationalists like Eleanor Marx and James Connolly and reformists like Ben Tillett and Keir Hardie throughout the course of the 'new unionism'. In May and June 1891, Ben Tillett and Tom Mann sent letters to the *London Evening News* demanding immigration controls against Jews. Keir Hardie's paper, *Labour Leader*, printed this astonishing, antisemitic statement: "Wherever there is trouble in Europe, wherever rumours of war circulate and men's minds are distraught with fear and change and calamity, you may be sure that a hook-nosed Rothschild is at his games somewhere near the region of the disturbances".[48]

Hardie was contradictory, arguing at the time to restrict foreigners but to let in those who fled from religious or political persecution. That would have applied to the great majority! Encouragingly there was widespread dislike of Tsarist policies and sympathy for persecuted Jews. So for many trade unionists, the key issue became one of challenging the exploiters rather than their Jewish victims. Gradually Hardie softened his position, explaining "where a foreigner was employed, it ought to be at the recognised trade union rate of wages for that employment".[49] By 1905, he had stopped blaming migrants as the cause of society's ills. At a rally in Glasgow that year, he argued a clearer mainstream social-democratic position: "the whole explanation of the distress is due to unemployment" and his solutions were "higher wages and reduced hours".[50]

Unionisation of immigrant workers made a significant impact on the trade union movement. It led Glasgow Trades Council and other union bodies to change their tune from anti-immigration to fair wages campaigns. The change can be attributed to the solidarity and militancy of unionised migrant workers. In 1889, Glasgow Trades Council wrote to the Town Council in 1889 calling for an improved minimum wage as the solution.[51]

Clearly the push for wage clauses was more progressive than the call for immigration controls, yet, at the end of the day, the level of union organisation and the involvement of socialists, both generally and among the new migrants, would largely determine whether there would be a fight for general pay increases rather than call for immigration controls.

It was crucial that there was socialist opposition to immigration controls. When unions called on the government to control the immigration of 'alien workers', Eleanor Marx—a "bred-in-the-bone internationalist"[52] —boldly stood against them. At a mass protest meeting called by Jewish trade unions in East London in 1895, she issued a leaflet arguing: "Jews! The English antisemites have come to the point where the English workers' organisation calls on the government to close England's doors to the poor alien, that is, in the main, to the Jew. You must no longer keep silent".[53]

Many members of the SDF left wing in Scotland agreed with her and saw little sense in remaining in such an organisation, leaving the SDF *en bloc* to launch the Socialist Labour Party (SLP).[54] Its most influential figure in Scotland then was James Connolly, who played a vital role in its formative days, travelling across Scotland and addressing dozens of meetings on behalf of the organisation. Connolly was both clear and forthright about the dangers of immigration controls and antisemitism to both Jews and the labour movement.[55] Although John Maclean remained in the SDF and its successor the British Socialist Party (BSP), he broke politically from the Hyndman leadership's increasingly nationalist outlook. Maclean always opposed racism and worked hard to build links with the Irish and Lithuanian mining communities. When Maclean was jailed after the 1915 Glasgow rent strike, a number of pits in Lanarkshire struck in protest, particularly in the Irish and Lithuanian communities. Years earlier, a branch of the Marxist Lithuanian Social Democratic Party was founded in the mining community of Bellshill, an area of Lithuanian settlement, where Maclean had built a following. His links with the Lithuanian community grew and he campaigned in their defence when families were threatened with starvation and deportation at the end of the war.

1919: Race riots in Glasgow

At the end of January 1919, just as the British state was planning to deploy troops and tanks to Glasgow fearing the looming 40-hour strike would threaten revolution, out of the blue racism within the working class movement came to the fore. The events of 1919 are detailed in Chapter 4, including this ugly and less well known race riot in the week before the strike began. It was the first in a series of race riots in a number of British ports during 1919. It was triggered by the words and deeds of Manny Shinwell, Scottish full-time official of the National Seafarers' Union, Chair of Glasgow Trades Council and a local Independent Labour Party (ILP) councillor. Later, Shinwell would move further to the right, becoming a Labour cabinet minister and then a member of the House of Lords.

On 23 January, just days before the strike started, Shinwell addressed a meeting of seafarers warning of mass unemployment if action were not taken to restrict foreign sailors on British ships. He called for British jobs for British workers, even although most of the black sailors were union members. Shortly afterwards near the depot where Shinwell had spoken, African and Asian seafarers were viciously attacked by a mob, both in the street and in their lodging house.[56] Some were injured and wounded but, in a classic example of institutional racism, the 30 victims were arrested and tried in court. Incredibly only one white sailor was charged and that was for police assault. As Henry Bell points out: "Whether Shinwell incited the riot cannot be said with certainty but the aim was quite clearly to stir up racial tensions within the workforce and the riot that followed made bosses reticent to hire non-white crews on Glasgow ships and led to the widespread deportation of black sailors".[57]

Then, as now, some union leaders blamed foreign workers for lowering wages and stealing jobs. Shinwell's actions show that even in the high points of class struggle it is vital to combat racism, particularly when it comes from a union leader. At the same time on Clydeside there was a strong socialist current vigorously opposed to racism. Leading activists like Arthur MacManus from the SLP, John Maclean, Willie Gallacher and Harry McShane from the BSP and Helen Crawfurd from the ILP argued it was a dangerous diversion for workers.

In an article entitled 'Race, Riots and Revolution' published in *The Socialist*, the SLP attacked the leaders of the Seafarers' union for scapegoating black and Asian workers and condemned Shinwell for deflecting the anger away from the real enemy. The Clyde Workers Committee made its opposition to racism absolutely clear. While Central Scotland was on strike for a cut in working hours, there was a mass strike in Mumbai docks. The CWC's daily Strike Bulletin proudly proclaimed: "A victory here in Scotland will help our comrades in India, who are with us heart and soul".[58]

Support for immigration controls persists in the higher echelons of the trade unions still. In 2019, Len McCluskey, leader of Unite, intervened in the British general election arguing against freedom of movement. His argument, similar to that expressed by Mannie Shinwell a century ago, opens the door to racist ideas. Socialists have consistently opposed this kind of dangerous ambivalence since the late 19th century onwards.

Combating racism and fascism in the 1930s

The economic crash of 1929, the ensuing world crisis and the rise of fascism challenged the labour movement and in particular the Jewish community throughout the 1930s. The immediate problem in Britain was the rise of the British Union of Fascists (BUF) which, from 1932 onwards, modelled itself on German Nazism and Italian fascism.

When Sir Oswald Mosley launched the BUF, there was fierce opposition throughout Britain. In Edinburgh in June 1934, there were fights between Blackshirts and anti-fascists and in Glasgow the fascists were 'trapped' in their city centre office by a hostile crowd of some 2,000 following a BUF public meeting. The BUF continued to hold meetings in Glasgow and Edinburgh, many of which involved physical opposition from the left and the trade unions.[59] Monty Berkley, a Communist Party member in the 1930s, remembers:

> William Joyce (later ridiculed as Lord Haw-Haw for his radio broadcasts from Nazi Berlin,) came to speak at Queens Park Recreation Ground and we held a counter demonstration... The Labour League of Youth, the Young Communist League and other youth organisations, all agreed to disrupt the meeting. I had the privilege of taking one of the platform legs and throwing the platform up in the air. We were chased by the police but got away.[60]

Morris Smith, secretary of the Glasgow Workers Circle, a group of left wing and left Zionist Jews, recalls that the BUF met regularly at Queens Park gates in Govanhill but "never got a chance as they were howled down. They never got a turnout and I don't think they recruited anyone. The line then was we had to stop them appearing on the streets".[61]

It is important not to overstate the impact of the BUF in Scotland. Its membership remained low. At the high point of BUF national membership in 1935, estimated at 50,000, there were approximately 50 members in Glasgow and 80 in Edinburgh.[62] The BUF newspaper, *The Fascist Week,* claimed in 1935 that there were active organisations throughout Scotland from Dumfries to Wick.[63] Despite this exaggeration, it is true there was some activity outside Glasgow and Edinburgh.

Motherwell was a big coalmining and steel centre, 15 miles east of Glasgow. Despite having elected the first ever Communist to parliament in 1922, by 1934 the town had an active BUF branch and it was bizarrely granted leasehold of the tennis courts at Calder Park in Motherwell![64] Its Scottish organiser claimed the branch was making great strides and

Lady Mosley visited the town in 1934 and spoke at the tennis courts. In nearby Wishaw, there was also BUF activity, but there was also strong local opposition.[65] In October 1934, the Motherwell Communist Party, "out in full force and in matters of numbers... easily superior to the Fascists", stopped the BUF meeting, forced their speaker off the stage and held a meeting of their own. The police did not intervene as "the audience, swelling in number... wanted to listen to the Communist for the rest of the evening".[66]

There was a sustained attempt to build the BUF in Aberdeen from 1936 until 1939.[67] Its meetings were heckled and broken up by opponents. In 1937, a BUF rally in Aberdeen had to be abandoned and its members protected by the police as a crowd of about 8,000 chanted, "Down with Fascist murderers...Mosley shall not pass...One, two, three, four, five, we want Mosley dead or alive".[68] There were arrests but the bail was collected from the huge crowd who "were almost fighting for copies of a leaflet issued by the CP". Similar events occurred in 1937[69] and throughout 1938.[70]

Following a BUF rally in Dumfries, a town with little left influence, Finlay Hart, a Communist Party full-time organiser, recalls that in the area "...we held a meeting to set up an anti-fascist committee and then a branch of the Party and the following year we had a member elected to the town council". Hart maintains labour movement activity helped ensure people were not attracted to the BUF. He says the BUF did not grow "because of the strength of the labour movement. For the unemployed there was the National Unemployed Workers Movement".[71]

It is assumed, from the strong British unionist stance of present day fascist groups, that there is an affinity between fascism and Orangeism born out of a mutual hatred of Irish republicanism. In Scotland, in the 1930s, there were two significant Protestant, staunchly unionist, organisations—the Scottish Protestant League (SPL) in Glasgow and Protestant Action (PA) in Edinburgh.[72] Until very late in the 1930s, both were vehemently anti-BUF. While it was on the rise across

Britain, the extreme Protestant organisations in Scotland opposed it and by the time they'd moved closer to fascism, the BUF was in decline.

There was widespread Scottish trade union support for the anti-fascist struggle in Spain during the 1930s, with a large number of Scots volunteering in the International Brigades and this is still celebrated. Although the Republicans failed to stop Franco, the role of the International Brigades helped to inspire the successful struggle against Mosley's Blackshirts in the 1930s.

Antisemitism today

There is less antisemitism today compared to Islamophobia and anti-Roma racism in Scotland, but it still exists and is once again on the rise on the far right. It has to be combatted but the issue has been confused by the International Holocaust Remembrance Alliance's (IHRA) erroneous and dangerous examples of antisemitism, which equate criticism of the Israeli state and its Zionist origins as racist and opposition to its oppression of the Palestinian people as tantamount to antisemitism. The Tories, the media and the BBC cynically exploited the IHRA definition to attack Jeremy Corbyn, the wider left and pro-Palestinian activists as antisemites.

Here, Keir Starmer and the new right-wing leadership of the Labour Party have, as in most things, fallen into step behind Johnson and the Tories. Disappointingly, the SNP leadership and the Scottish government have done so too. Many of their supporters and some of their elected members who disagree with the IHRA definition are unhappy at this. When the Equalities and Human Rights Commission (EHRC) published its report on antisemitism in the Labour Party, there were, given the media barrage, surprisingly few examples. Jeremy Corbyn was suspended for pointing this out and, even when reinstated, had the whip withdrawn in Parliament so that he could not sit as a Labour Party MP. And all-out attack on the left in the Labour Party is underway, with hundreds of members suspended for supporting Corbyn and gagging orders imposed on local Labour

Party branches. In Scotland, Corbyn supporter Richard Leonard has also been forced out as leader of Scottish Labour.

This attack on the wider left has serious consequences. The absurd charge of antisemitism has been used to attack Palestine solidarity and undermine support for the non-violent Boycott, Divestment and Sanctions (BDS) campaign. Both Labour and the SNP adoption of the IHRA 'working definition' of antisemitism has given unwarranted legitimacy to a wider suppression of free expression and right to protest over Palestine and western imperialism in the Middle East. The narrative of this 'new antisemitism' is aimed at the left, the Muslim community and social movements including Black Lives Matter and the anti-war movement.

This false equation of criticism of Israel with antisemitism has also given the far right and the fascist movements a free pass. Antisemitism is used by Trump and the far-right leaders in Hungary, Poland and elsewhere to attack Jewish financiers as 'globalists' who undermine national economies for personal gain—a notion that was the centrepiece of Hitler's *Mein Kampf*.

Antisemitism is a reactionary ideology and socialists oppose it. But we reject the absurd notion that criticism of Israel, anti-Zionism and support for BDS equals antisemitism.

Asian immigration

There has been an Asian presence in Scotland for centuries. However, large-scale immigration from Asia to Scotland did not occur until after the Second World War. The numbers settling in Scotland were far less than in England.

Some settled to work in the jute mills of Dundee, others in the newly expanding public services, notably public transport and the NHS. Students entered Scottish universities and colleges. At first, Asian immigrants were employed largely in retailing and catering rather than industry.[73] The Asian experience in Scotland is not as well documented as it should be. For the same reasons that Scotland's role in slavery was largely hidden, the belated acknowledgement that racism has been a big problem is long overdue.[74]

Most Asians settling in Scotland arrived from Pakistan and some from Bangladesh. Most settled in Glasgow. Many were housed in sub-standard tenement properties on Glasgow's southside, like successive waves of immigrants before them. The stark inequalities of the pre–war slums continued after many skilled workers' families had been moved out to the post-war new towns around Glasgow. Councils were ill-equipped to provide for the needs of their new citizens, who spoke a different language and practiced a different religion. Their daily privations were real but went unrecorded.

As Black Lives Matters shows, tragedy can spark reappraisal and ignite activism. In 1998, 16-year old Imran Khan was stabbed to death in a school on the south side of Glasgow. Racial tension had been developing there for a while, but the authorities were reluctant to accept this was the case. That same year, Surjit Singh Chhokar, a young waiter, was murdered in the street in Overtown, near Wishaw.

These racist murders shocked many in Scotland. Anti-racists, socialists and trade unionists organised solidarity for the bereaved families and made sure that the cases did not disappear from public view. Incredibly it took 18 years of campaigning to deliver justice for the family.[75] But constant campaigning made sure fascist groups like the British National Party (BNP) did not make an electoral breakthrough in Scotland when they attempted to exploit racial divisions.

The Macpherson report, published in 1999 in the wake of Stephen Lawrence's murder, exposed widespread institutional racism in society and in the police. Evidence proves this was and still is the case in Scotland too.[76] The lack of action over the deaths of Imran Khan and Surjit Singh Chokar demonstrate this. The Sheku Bayoh case and the mishandling of other recent racist attacks and incidents show that apart from the rhetoric nothing has really changed since the MacPherson report was published over 20 years ago. A November 2020 report, by former Scottish Lord Advocate Dame Elish Angiolini, shows that there was a persistent problem with racism, sexism and homophobia in police culture.[77]

The political representation of Asian Scots has increased but only marginally. Only in 2021 has Anas Sarwar become the first person of colour to lead a major political party in Scotland. Islamophobia has recently been highlighted and a cross party report has been commissioned by the Scottish Parliament. Reports are all very well. The urgent question is what is to be done? Most Scottish Muslims have suffered racism on such a scale that it leaves them scared, bullied, frightened and excluded—a sobering account of daily life for Muslims today. Their experience fits into the long pattern of immigration to Scotland—racism and fightback.

'New' immigration

We are witnessing a huge migration of people across the globe—fleeing war, famine, climate devastation and persecution. In 2003, the number of refugees in the world was estimated at 10 million.[78] By 2020 it was 80 million.[79] Over the last 20 years, migrants from the new EU member states and from Turkey and other countries outside Europe have arrived in Scotland. In each of those years bar one, there has been a net inflow and this is to be welcomed.[80] Polish delicatessens, Turkish barbers, African supermarkets, Chinese restaurants, Syrian patisseries and other enterprises have become part of the streetscape, even as more traditional businesses have closed.

Schools have also been transformed with pupils from many countries being taught alongside Scottish children and at least 20 languages being spoken in some schools. The 2011 census showed 16 percent of people in Scotland do not give their ethnic origin as Scottish.[81] The largest non-Scottish group identify as 'other British', the second largest 'Polish', although there has been a considerable return to Poland following Brexit and the recent upturn in the Polish economy.

For a time, Britain's policy was to encourage dispersal of migrants and refugees, housing people in different parts of the country away from London. Not all regions of Britain accepted this policy but Scotland did. In common with previous immigration, the new migrants have tended to settle in particular areas where previous immigrants have stayed. In Glasgow, for example, this has been primarily in Govanhill, where Irish, Jewish and Asian immigrants had previously settled and then moved on as their economic circumstances improved. This has led to overcrowding and poor conditions—primarily caused by landlordism and the lack of repair and investment in new, affordable public housing. It has also led to sporadic campaigns demanding 'a clean-up of the area', which have peddled or encouraged racism, blaming the victims of overcrowding and unfairly targeting recently arrived migrants.

Refugees were mainly housed in hard-to-let high-rise council flats in deprived areas of the city. The approach of the Scottish Labour government at the time was generally positive but it was inadequately resourced. The campaign, 'One Scotland, Many Cultures' was refreshingly so. Scotland needs immigrants. It has an ageing population plagued with chronic ill-health. Encouraging immigration is one way for the new Scottish parliament to assert its independence from Westminster and serve the needs of the Scottish economy and public services.

A case study of the Roma community in Govanhill shows this well. Historically one of the most persecuted groups in Europe alongside Jews, they were targeted by the Nazis for extermination in the 1940s. They currently suffer abuse and racism in most European countries, including violent attacks and discrimination, notably in Hungary but also in Germany, France and Italy. As Stefan Harda argues, "Disproportionately affected by poverty and discriminated against in employment, education, health care, administrative and other services, they face considerable obstacles to a full enjoyment of human rights and fundamental freedoms".[82]

Harda's study found discrimination in every aspect of life—employment, housing, benefits, health services (through language issues) and educational achievement. As well as institutional racism, Roma also suffer racism at personal and community levels. The Govanhill Law Centre found that some local housing office staff routinely refer to Roma people as "gypos, scum, beggars, suicide bombers, thieves and paedos". A whistle blower highlighted a culture of hostility: "almost as if there is a competition to see who can make the most outrageous statement for a cheap and nasty laugh".[83] One young campaigner, giving evidence to the Scottish government, talked of discrimination against Travelling People in Scotland becoming the last form of "acceptable racism".[84]

In 2019 and again in 2020, vandals destroyed a Roma Holocaust memorial in Glasgow dedicated to those murdered during the Second World War. The Romani Rose Tree Memorial was planted in Queen's Park on Roma Genocide Memorial Day on 2 August 2019 by young people from the Govanhill community but the plaque has been ripped from its podium in a senseless act of vandalism. Local residents reported it had been "violently destroyed" in November 2019 and again in June 2020.[85]

However, wherever there has been racism there has been anti-racist activity. Among many positive responses has been International Roma Day in Govanhill and the Govanhill International Carnival. Both have Roma at their centre, with a strong anti-racist theme. Both events are popular, having become established in the locality, attracting support from mainstream politicians and trade unions. They provide talks, films, walking tours and workshops. Local socialists and community activists in the area worked together to engage the wider community and develop these activities.

The acceptance of migrants and refugees by Glasgow City Council was laudable in principle but in practice there has been a lack of resources, a lack of political will at the top and a failure to engage with local people. Here we highlight some examples of racism and how anti-racists responded.

First, the racist murder of Firsat Dag in August 2001 just two weeks after his arrival in Glasgow. Alongside other asylum seekers, Firsat had been housed in the badly deprived

Sighthill area of the city. The hardship and deprivation of this working class community had been ignored for years. Housing conditions were appalling with repairs non-existent. No one had spoken to the residents of the tower blocks, where many refugees were suddenly housed. It was predictable that tensions could develop and they did.

Firsat's murder sent shockwaves through Scotland. The migrant community demonstrated in fury all the tensions and frustrations boiling over in a spontaneous expression of solidarity. Some local residents also demonstrated, feeling that the refugees were getting preferential treatment while locals were abandoned. It could have been a flash-point for fascists and hard-core racists to exploit in order to establish a local presence based on hatred and division.

Community activists and local anti-racists worked hard to ensure that any racism was nipped in the bud and there was a concerted campaign to both condemn the scapegoating and demand increased investment in the area. A key point was when asylum-seekers and local residents marched together on the City Chambers to demand improved conditions. Billy Singh, a community activist in Sighthill, said: "If anything good can come out of somebody's death, then Firsat Dag did not die in vain. His murder has galvanised the community, both local people and refugees, into one voice fighting for the same social improvements".[86] A local festival was organised to showcase local talent, culture and food. The local schools reported that the new arrivals had brought a new positivity after years of decline.[87] A tragedy that could have seen the resurgence of racism was turned into something much more inspiring.

The intervention of socialists was crucial in arguing for unity—particularly so given the fact that the media peddled lies about refugees getting £5,000 cheques and claiming Firsat Dag was a 'bogus' refugee, not a genuine asylum seeker.[88] Campaigners demonstrated outside the *Daily Record* in protest at its coverage. The police reported that one year later, racist incidents were down 56 percent in the area. Sighthill was crucial in demonstrating that racism could be defeated and that solidarity between new and existing communities was vital.

This would be tested in towns and cities across Scotland over the next few years as refugees from the Iraq and Afghan wars came to Scotland. The Stop the War Coalition (STWC) organised activity across Scotland, uniting different communities on an unprecedented scale.

The huge Scottish demonstration held in Glasgow against the Iraq war in 2003 coincided with the two-million-strong march in London and the hundreds of other mass demonstrations across the world. It was one of the biggest political demonstrations ever to take place in Scotland. Thousands of young Muslims took part in political activity for the first time.

Another effective anti-racist campaign was inspired by the action of 'the Glasgow Girls'—young Drumchapel school students who made national headlines in 2005. Their successful fight against the detention and deportation of their friend Agnesa Murselaj led to them campaigning vigorously across Glasgow, organising pickets to stop the arrest of their friend's family and forcing a meeting with first minister Jack McConnell, that eventually overturned the deportation. It was a model of how to deal with deportations and Home Office raids. As Roza Saleh, one of the Glasgow Girls, put it: "We definitely raised awareness of the dawn raids. Locals didn't know that children were being detained and deported. People got really angry about it, saying 'these are our weans' and that gave us a boost knowing we had that support from our community".[89]

A third example was the campaign to halt the eviction of asylum seekers in 2018. Serco, the multinational given the contract to house asylum seekers in Glasgow, first announced it was issuing eviction notices to tenants who had been denied the right to remain in Britain. Following legal challenges, which Serco initially won, there were protests at Serco's Glasgow HQ and at each and every attempt they made to change the locks. Robina Qureshi from Positive Action in Housing (PAIH) proved that people were being intimidated into leaving their homes and that Serco were changing people's locks to force them out. She warned that if unchallenged, Serco would leave 300 people destitute. "Are people going to be dragged out and their belongings dumped in the street? Anecdotal evidence tells us that vulnerable, frightened people, both men and women, will be manhandled onto the street."[90]

Large protests organised by Stand Up to Racism, Living Rent, PAIH and the trade union movement forced Serco to back off. It then lost the contract, but it was only a temporary victory. The problem remains and local activists have had to respond to further attacks on asylum seekers.

In June 2020 during lockdown, there was a stabbing incident at a Glasgow hotel where asylum seekers were being temporarily accommodated. Police responded by shooting dead the assailant. Police Scotland seems to have wrongly assumed it was a terrorist attack and flooded the area with armed officers. It emerged that Mears, the private company that profits from the outsourcing of housing and care services, which had taken over the Serco contract, removed all asylum seekers from their homes into city centre hotels, ostensibly to help with the Covid-19 lockdown. Yet they carried out no risk assessments, withdrew their daily allowance and failed to provide sufficient food. Little wonder that in these circumstances an asylum seeker became distressed and it is unacceptable that he was shot and killed.

Far right elements tried to exploit the tragedy by calling for asylum seekers to be deported. They launched a violent attack on a small group protesting in support of the refugees. However, the most important response was a socially distanced, 1,500 strong rally organised in George Square by Stand Up to Racism alongside refugee support groups and trade unions. It challenged the false narrative, highlighting the inadequacy of the hostel arrangements as well as making clear that refugees were welcome in Glasgow and that the Scottish government should act rather than hide behind the excuse of Home Office culpability.

Institutional racism is rife throughout Scotland. Although the

SNP government is consistently anti-racist and pro-immigration in words, it has so far failed to increase black and minority ethnic involvement in government and in key institutions like education. The detention centre at Dungavel still incarcerates people who have committed no crime. The family of Sheku Bayou still waits for justice, years after his death in police custody. The campaign led by his family is widely supported throughout the trade unions and by politicians and campaigning bodies such as Stand Up to Racism and Black Lives Matter. There is no immunity from racism for asylum seekers or for Roma, but wherever it happens, local communities, trade unions and left political organisations can push it back.

Conclusion

Scotland is no more immune from racism than anywhere else. Racism grows from the ideology that suits the purposes of the ruling class. It emerges from a system based on the exploitation of the vast majority of human beings by a tiny minority because it is only a tiny minority who benefit from the division of the working class. We need to organise all those who want to challenge it wherever it exists but ultimately we need to end the system that breeds it. The only alternative to capitalist barbarism is the socialist revolution

As the crisis of the system intensifies, the political polarisation is accelerating. We live in an epoch of extremes. In his final book, *Marxism at the Millennium,* Tony Cliff, who had then been a revolutionary socialist for two thirds of the 20th century wrote: "The 1990s has been like watching a film of the 1930's in slow motion".[91] In the 20 years since, the film has been speeding up.

This means adopting the tactic that has proved most effective in practice—the united front. While this is not the place to examine Germany in the 1930s, we have to grasp the scale of the defeat and the horrors that followed. The failure of what was a powerful German working class movement to unite and join forces, allowed Hitler's Nazis a path to power. As late as November

1932, the major parties of the German left—the Communist Party (KPD) and the Social Democratic Party (SPD)—achieved a bigger combined vote and more seats in the election than the Nazis. Even at that late stage, if they had utilised the tactic of building a united front to crush Hitler, the history of the 20th century would have been completely different. Understanding the horror of the 1930s and learning the lessons to ensure it never happens again is as important now as ever.

This means mass anti-racist campaigning that draws in the social weight of trade unions, faith organisations, anti-racist politicians across the spectrum, and all anti-racist campaigners, to unite the different strands and develop unity. In Britain, as elsewhere, the tradition of building broad anti-racist united front work has seen off—at least for now—the threat of far right movements, such as the 15,000 who marched with fascist 'Tommy Robinson' in the summer of 2018. The united front method has meant the anti-racist movement has pushed back the threat by isolating and defeating the fascists and the far right. But as the crisis deepens the challenge is getting tougher.

In Scotland groups like the fascist Scottish Defence League (SDL) failed to garner the forces that emerged in England, for example in 2009 or 2018. Similarly, the outcome of the 2019 general election produced different results either side of the border—with a cabinet that reflects a deliberate intensification of state racism and the 'hostile environment' at Westminster, and a pro-immigration, rhetorically anti-racist Scottish government. But it would be a huge mistake to think it can't happen here. The same polarisation that produced Trumpism, and that drives the growth of the far right is at work in Scotland too.

Fighting for the breadth and unity of the united front has its own historically specific challenges for us now. Islamophobia has been used as the sharp end of the racist wedge, by mainstream conservative parties, by racist populists parties like UKIP, and by the hardened fascists and the racist right. Islamophobia promoted from the top has opened the door to these sinister forces to promote older forms of racism, for example antisemitism. Anti-racist campaigning that imposes preconditions—for example, opposition to Israel—on participants in the movement will inevitably limit it to a smaller layer, rendering it unable to unite the breadth of Jewish communities and Muslim communities alongside others in a powerful united movement in opposition to both Islamophobia and antisemitism. Similarly, while many anti-racists may well identify with the movement for Scottish independence, any mass anti-racist campaigning strategy that excludes, alienates or fails to reach out to those who oppose independence will be too narrow for the task ahead.

Many of Scotland's newly arrived citizens found that they too wanted to get involved in the fight for independence. The Tory years of austerity preceded by Tory and New Labour backing for US imperialism and its 'war on terror' made people receptive to the idea that something better was possible through Scottish independence. People fleeing here from countries blighted by years of war and imperialist domination found common cause with the Yes campaign. This included people from Afghanistan, Somalia, Iraq, Eritrea, Turkey, Syria, Poland, Romania and Catalonia.

All Under One Banner has organised huge demonstrations, including the biggest ever political demonstration in Scotland in Edinburgh in 2019. Its marches always include migrants who support independence and groups, like 'Asians for Independence', that sprang up in the run up to the 2014 referendum. Now Scotland, All Under One Banner and other campaigning groups need to ensure the campaign for indyref2 is inclusive of migrant communities and carries a strong thread of visible anti-racism at its heart.

Potentially this movement can unite a broad coalition of activists with anti-racism as one of its core principles. It will mean challenging the pro-business, pro-'Fortress EU' stance of the SNP and the idea that migration is good so long as it benefits the economy, rather than a cornerstone in the building of a more equal, fairer society.

*Refugees welcome here
demonstration,
George Square, Glasgow
June 2020*

*Kill the Bill demonstration,
Buchanan Street, Glasgow,
April 2021*

Whether in favour of the union or opposed to it, there is a place in the anti-racist campaigns for all who want to fight racism. The post-Covid-19 recession will result in the potential for scapegoats. We must not let them divide us.

It is the task of socialists to insist that racism and the legacy of slavery and imperialism are exposed and contested. The explosive BLM movement and the vast numbers it has shifted into an active and conscious alignment with the anti-racist movement represents a qualitative shift. This is not an optional extra to be left to professionals and politicians but a task for the whole working class. This is not automatic, but has to be fought for. As Lenin argued, socialists have to act as "the tribune of the people, able to react to every manifestation of tyranny and oppression, no matter where it appears, no matter what stratum or class of the people it affects".[92]

This is a key task for us now and we have a fantastic opportunity to push for real change in Scotland. The high incidence of Covid-19 in black and minority ethnic communities is a result of structural racism throughout Britain and needs to be exposed and challenged. We want statues down, plaques put up, more black and ethnic representation in our institutions, an end to police racism, an end to detention of refugees and migrants, a decolonisation of the curriculum and a museum of slavery in Glasgow. But such reforms will not be enough to eradicate racism with its deep roots in the capitalist system built on slavery and imperialism. Independence in a capitalist form is thus not enough. As Angela Davis put it: "Racism can't be separated from capitalism".[93]

Chapter 7

A History of the Independence Movement in Scotland

Bob Fotheringham

Why the history of the independence movement and not the history of Scottish nationalism or even the SNP? The answer is relatively simple. Until the late 20th century Scottish nationalism as a political force has been relatively weak. As recently as the 1966 British General Election, around 95 percent of votes in Scotland went to unionist parties.

Since its inception in 1934, the SNP has had a profile in Scottish politics. At moments like the 1967 Hamilton by-election victory, it looked on the verge of a breakthrough. However, it was really only after the arrival of the Scottish Parliament in 1999 that the SNP began to play a significant role in the political landscape and only after the 2014 referendum that it became the dominant political party. Support for the party has flourished as support for independence has increased, though the two are not synonymous. We need to look beyond nationalism to understand why support for Scottish independence has grown in recent years.

Between 1746 and the end of the Second World War, there was no real political challenge to the Union and for a long time after 1945 this remained the case. The decline of Empire and the collapse of the Scottish economy after the First World War stimulated a reformist class–consciousness and its organised expression in the Labour Party in Scotland was consolidated in the following decades. Of course, this did not mean that there was not a strong Scottish identity throughout this period. Separate legal and education systems, a strong association with Presbyterianism and a clear difference in language and culture underscored this.

Language is a case in point. There is debate about whether Scots is a language different from English. The Kirk, a driving force behind the development of universal education in Scotland, made sure Scots children were taught standard English.[1] It is conceivable that had this not been the case, the Scots language would have deviated even further than it currently does. Nevertheless, it is significant that when crossing the border from England to Scotland there is an immediate change in dialect and accent which does not occur when crossing from England to Wales.

The formation of the Scottish Football Association in 1867 and the existence of a Scottish national football team was another element in fostering and maintaining a sense of Scottish identity throughout the 20th century. But the trappings of Scottish identity—tartan, the elaboration of a clan system and the Highland Gathering—as well as what is identified as Scottish culture, developed as part of Britain and not separate from it.[2] Scotland's middle classes, its employers and its landed aristocracy enthusiastically supported the growth of the British Empire and played a central role in it.[3] Empire shaped Scottish identity and had widespread popular support. As shown earlier, rapid industrialisation transformed Scotland's economy from one of the most backward in Europe into one of the most urbanised and advanced anywhere in 100 years. This could not have happened without the Acts of Union and the markets provided by Empire.

The modern independence movement begins with the formation of the Scottish Home Rule Association in 1886, which lasted until 1914.[4] A Home Rule Act passed its first reading at Westminster but was scuppered by the onset of war. Support for home rule in Scotland was partly as a consequence of Liberal support for home rule in Ireland. Though the Scots and Irish differed in religion, rural communities shared a common experience, particularly in the Highlands, at the hands of oppressive landlords. Irish agitation had won an element of land reform. An upsurge of struggle in the Western Highlands in the mid-1880s—the Crofters' Wars—brought land reform to the fore and was central to the movement for home rule.

Importantly, this shaped the formation of the Scottish Labour Party. Two of its prominent founding members, James Keir Hardie and Robert Cunninghame Graham, were enthusiastic Home Rulers.[5]

Nicola Sturgeon, in her speech to the 2019 SNP Conference, quotes Jimmy Maxton, left-wing Labour MP for Bridgeton from 1922 until his death in 1946, whom she describes as "one of the great figures of the Labour movement" and whose position on Scottish home rule was presented by her as a "modern day definition of independence."[6] Much of the ambiguity and mystification that characterises the SNP's version of independence is contained in Sturgeon's quote from Maxton:

James Maxton, one of the great figures of the Labour movement, spoke about the campaign for Home Rule back in the 1920s.

His words are worth quoting in full—so indulge me:

"Give us our parliament in Scotland", he said.

"Set it up next year. We will start with no traditions. We will start with ideals ... men and women will spend their whole energy, their whole brain power, their whole courage, and their whole soul, in making Scotland into a country in which we can take people from all nations of the earth and say: 'This is our land, this is our Scotland, these are our people, these are our men, our works, our women and children: can you beat it?"

The Home Rule movement was for a Scottish Parliament within the existing Union. The powers it would have were those concerning "purely Scottish affairs", while war, foreign affairs, national defence, immigration and the collection of taxes would be left to Westminster.

In the period during and after the First World War, many of the key individuals who could have provided support for Home Rule had led the working class agitation and the then potentially revolutionary socialist action in Glasgow around Red Clydeside. These included Highland and Irish workers, driven from their homes and rural communities to work in the factories and shipyards of the Clyde. This is in contrast to Ireland where the failure of the Home Rule movement led directly to a revolutionary nationalist struggle for independence from Britain.

Another reason Home Rule failed to make significant progress at the time was because support for the Union was popular with working class Protestants. During the 19th century Liberalism, had been the dominant parliamentary force in Scotland and it only began to decline because of the rise of the Labour Party and an identification with class politics, but also because of the Liberals' association with Home Rule for Ireland. While it would be wrong to characterise Scottish politics as defined by sectarian divisions, they can't simply be dismissed. Working class support for unionism and the Tories, the Conservative and Unionist Party as they were known in Scotland, shows this to be the case.[7]

Formation of the Scottish National Party

The Scottish National Party was formed in 1934 as an amalgamation of the National Party and the Scottish Party.[8] The former can be broadly defined as emerging out of the pro-home rule section of the Scottish labour movement, while the latter was a split from the Cathcart Tory Party.

Its founding was at the depth of the depression, when the long-term decline of British capitalism was evident. The First World War—the product of growing imperialist rivalry—saw

US capitalism become the dominant world power. At the start of the 20th century, the Clyde was building one fifth of the world's shipping. By the 1930s, its shipyards were closing and heavy engineering was in severe decline. British capital's global reach, which had sustained a Scottish identity as an intrinsic part of Empire, came under threat. The formation of the Scottish Party was a consequence of growing disillusionment among Tories in Scotland in response to a perceived disinterest by Westminster in the plight of the Scottish economy.

Prior to 1914, Home Rule was popular within the Scottish labour movement. After the war, most on the left focussed on class struggle and the belief that socialism was the only way forward. Many who led the illegal strikes, the rent struggles and the anti-war agitation on Red Clydeside helped launch the Communist Party. Others joined the Labour Party, seeking reform through the ballot box as an easier road to change society. By the 1930s, the experience of working class defeat and economic decline led many former supporters of home rule to accept that only centralised control of the British economy could resolve Scotland's social and economic problems. Like Northern Ireland and parts of northern England, the Scottish economy had suffered disproportionately compared to the Britain.

Almost alone on the left in supporting independence was John Maclean, renowned for his fierce opposition to the war and his commitment to the Bolshevik Revolution and workers' power. Maclean did not join the Communist Party but instead launched his Scottish Workers Republican Party in support of Scottish independence and the break-up of the British Empire. As a result, some claim Mclean as part of a nationalist tradition in Scotland, but this misrepresents everything he stood for. Maclean's support for independence stemmed from the failure of the movement to seize the revolutionary opportunities of 1919 and from the vicious ruling class counter offensive of the early 1920s. MacLean believed Scotland, like Ireland, was a weak link in the capitalist chain and that working class revolution was more likely in Scotland, based on his estimation of the Clydeside working class movement,[9] a far cry from the constitutional nationalism of the SNP.

The future nature of the SNP can be gauged by the fact that the left-wing rebel and poet Hugh MacDiarmid was expelled from the National Party prior to its amalgamation with the Scottish Party and that the vast majority of leadership positions in the new party were given to former Tories.

SNP: The road to power

Scottish academic James Mitchell, writing in a book edited by Gerry Hassan, identifies the 1967 SNP by-election victory in Hamilton by Winnie Ewing as a "new era in Scottish politics" when "the SNP had finally broken through". Published in 2009, it is understandable why he might think that.[10] The SNP had been able to attract a significant number of young Scots, as did the Labour Party Young Socialists, during the exciting anti-Polaris campaign on Clydeside in the early 1960s. But the really dramatic advance of the SNP came much later with the Scottish Parliament in 1999 and the establishment of an SNP minority administration in Scotland in 2007.

This gave the SNP, despite the obvious limitations of the Scottish Parliament, the platform to present an alternative political narrative. A separate parliament meant people could vote for parties supporting independence, such as the Greens and the Scottish Socialist Party (SSP) as well as the SNP, while voting for other parties in a British General Election. The new parliament also represented the beginning of a sustained shift in working class votes from Labour and, to a lesser extent, from working class Tory voters, to the SNP and support for independence. The unintended consequence of Labour establishing a Scottish Parliament was the 2014 Independence Referendum and despite the No vote, it heralded a sea change in Scottish politics.

The preceding period had, nonetheless, played an important role in leading to the establishment of the Edinburgh parliament and in increased support for independence. SNP by-election victories and the winning of various council and Westminster seats in the years before that were important for keeping independence a live political issue. Undoubtedly, SNP victories, such as Winnie Ewing in 1967 and Margo MacDonald in 1973 in Glasgow Govan, garnered media attention without achieving a sustained SNP breakthrough.

Often overlooked is the election of Gordon Wilson, MP for Dundee East from 1974 until 1989. Wilson was on the right of the party and coined the slogan, "it's Scotland's oil". As SNP leader, he led the expulsion of seven left-wing 79 Group members (including future leader Alex Salmond) from the party in 1982. His tenure as MP in a thoroughly working class constituency predated the wider working class support for the SNP that would come in the new millennium.

Both Dundee parliamentary seats were solidly Labour during the post war period. Glasgow was still returning a few Tories to parliament until the mid-1970s. Dundee saw a big influx of Irish immigrants into the city in the 19th century, but unlike Glasgow and the West of Scotland, Irish immigration into Dundee came from the South of Ireland. It lacked Protestant immigrants from the north. The bitter Protestant sectarianism in the west was largely absent in Dundee. In 1922, Edwin Scrymgeour stood on a pro-temperance, pro-working class and socialist platform. Hailing from the radical wing of Scottish Calvinism, he was able to unseat Winston Churchill as MP for Dundee by winning a substantial vote from Dundee's immigrant Catholic population.[11]

The 1964-70 Labour government is often portrayed today as left wing and committed to socialist planning. Distance lends considerable enchantment to this view, as those who lived through it can testify. In fact, Labour imposed wage controls, villainised shop stewards' organisation and tried to introduce legislation to break it—all to restore profits. Harold Wilson's government represented a break from post-war economic and social reform, paving the way for Heath's Tories. The relative decline of the British economy impacted disproportionately on Scotland and other regions across Britain because of their over dependence on traditional heavy industry. Labour found it increasingly difficult to deliver reforms for working people and keep the bosses happy.[12] It opted for the latter, the beginning of an employer's offensive on jobs and living standards. Gordon Wilson's election victory in 1974 was one of the first signs of Scottish working class disillusionment with the Labour Party.

The debacle of the 1979 Devolution vote

In March 1979, Scotland voted in the referendum on Devolution and a Scottish Assembly. Throughout the 1970s, rising support for the SNP led the leaders of both the main British parties to conclude Scotland should be offered the choice of devolution. Though it was Labour that initiated the referendum, it was Tory Prime Minister Ted Heath who had first presented the idea with his "Declaration of Perth" in 1974.[13] Once back in power, Labour under Harold Wilson—a supreme opportunist—established a Royal Commission on Devolution and the subsequent Kilbrandon Report recommended a Scottish Parliament with limited powers.

The minority Labour Government's Devolution Referendum was only possible with the support of eleven SNP MPs. But in 1978, right-wing Labour MP George Cunningham proposed a spoiler amendment which rigged the vote—the notorious 40 percent rule—which when carried in the House of Commons, meant a Scottish parliament would only be established if at least 40 percent of the entire Scottish electorate voted for it. Cunningham's motivation here was to use this as a way of undermining and damaging devolution. On the day, 52 percent of those voting voted in favour, but, with a turnout of only 64 percent, the numbers failed to meet Cunningham's rigged threshold.[14] Opposition to devolution, from both the left and right of the party (left-winger Robin Cook was a prominent opponent),[15] highlighted Labour's inability to come to terms with the growing attraction of working class Scottish voters to the idea of self-government and the right to determine their own future. More importantly it tied Labour to a failing union and its long-term negative impact on the lives of the people they were supposed to represent.

In the aftermath of the vote, the SNP brought a motion of no confidence in the Labour government and this was taken up by the Tories. The British Parliament voted in support of the motion by one vote, with SNP support.

Labour's accusation, "Tartan Tories", stems from the SNP's promotion of the 1979 no confidence motion. Although Labour/ SNP rivalry predates this, it became more bitter after it. In truth, both the SNP and Labour suffered as a consequence of the referendum and the no confidence vote. Labour's election defeat led to 18 years of Tory rule, while the SNP lost all but two of their 11 Westminster MPs in the General Election. The SNP blamed Labour for failing to follow through on devolution despite the fact that there was a majority in the vote for an Assembly. Labour members, on the other hand, many with little enthusiasm for devolution, blamed the SNP for bringing Tory rule.

The truth was more complicated. Labour lost in 1979 largely as a consequence of the fact that a Labour Government which had been elected on the basis of "squeezing the rich until the pips squeaked" had squeezed its own supporters instead. By 1979, it had spent five years attacking strikes, sacking workers, cutting wages and reducing public services. Labour voters in 1979 abandoned it in droves—although it performed much better in Scotland, where the SNP was reduced to two seats.

As far as the SNP were concerned, the reality was that there was little enthusiasm from its members for devolution in 1979. Neil Ascherson, in his book *Stone Voices*, makes it clear that it was not just the failure of Labour. There was also a lack of passion from SNP members to campaign for a form of home rule which fell well short of full independence.[16] Within the pro-independence camp, the 1979 devolution campaign seems to only have been supported by those on the left; by Margo MacDonald who had won the Govan by-election in 1973, by Jim Sillars who had left the Labour Party to form the short-lived Socialist Labour Party and the then young SNP activist Alex Salmond.

While the 40 percent rule was a democratic outrage, there were major problems with the campaign itself. While the Scottish working class undoubtably supported devolution, it was far from the dominant issue concerning them. Many on the left, not just in the Labour Party, opposed devolution because they believed that it was the first step to full independence and that this would undermine working class unity across Britain. As Neil Ascherson points out, in 1979 "party and class loyalty were far stronger than feelings about self–government".[17]

In the aftermath of the devolution defeat, it was hardly surprising that it led to a great deal of discussion and debate within the party. One consequence of this was the formation of the 79 Group, which included Margo MacDonald, Alex Salmond and recent SNP member Jim Sillars.[18] Though the reasons for the failure to achieve devolution were complex, for Margo MacDonald they were clear: "while working class Scots voted yes, Scotland's middle class voted no".[19] The 79 Group had three guiding principles: nationalism, socialism and republicanism. To achieve independence they proposed direct action, including mass strikes and civil disobedience. The group were successful in winning a measure of support within the SNP, but were, however, unable to win mass support outside. Jim Sillars and five other members of the 79 Group broke into the Edinburgh Royal High School Building (the proposed site of the Devolved Scottish Parliament) in October 1981. They were arrested but avoided prosecution on a technicality.

The group became involved with nationalist groups from Northern Ireland to discuss "common issues, such as unemployment". This led Winnie Ewing to describe the group as pro-IRA and "a naked and open conspiracy" to take over the party. When SNP leader Gordon Wilson went on the offensive the following June at the party's conference, a number of 79 Group members walked out in disgust. The conference voted to proscribe the group by an overwhelming majority. After attempting to reform as the Scottish Socialist Society, seven members, including Alex Salmond, were expelled from the

SNP. Most were later readmitted after agreeing to accept the discipline of the party majority.[20]

How should the experience be viewed? The 79 Group was an attempt to give a radical edge to the demand for independence and to engage with wider working class forces. However, its view of socialism and republicanism was confused and confusing, rejecting as it did "the state controlled paternalism of today's centralist Labour Party". There was an irony in this because the failure of the 79 Group allowed what was essentially a right-wing leadership of the SNP at the time to reassert 'centralised' control of the party. While the SNP has been keen to position itself as a left of centre Social Democratic organisation, this should be seen as a very much watered down version of social democracy with the SNP committed to keeping business interests on board. It also led to some in the 79 Group, such as Alex Salmond, to make peace with the leadership and accept what was essentially a conservative pro-capitalist approach to an independent Scotland's economic future.

From 1979 to the Scottish parliament

In September 1997, Scotland voted 74 percent in a 60 percent turnout in favour of establishing a devolved Scottish assembly.[21] While the yes vote was considerably greater than in 1979, the turnout was lower; hardly overwhelming approval for a Scottish parliament, let alone a ringing endorsement for independence. However, it did represent, in the words of Labour's former leader John Smith, "the settled will of the people of Scotland". More importantly it enjoyed clear majority support in Scotland's working class communities.

So, what were the factors which brought it about?

From 1979 to 1997, Scotland voted Labour in four different general elections and ended up with a Tory government. The Labour vote averaged 41 percent and the Tory vote averaged 26.82 percent. (The British Tory average was 40 percent and Labour was 35 percent). With the SNP and Liberal Democrats averaging 17 percent and 16 percent respectively, this meant that the peculiarities of the first past the post system led to Labour in Scotland winning the majority of seats. The failure of Labour to use its clear mandate to mount an effective challenge to the Tories, especially Thatcher's hated poll tax, led to Alex Salmond dubbing Scotland's Labour MPs as the "feeble fifty".

The Thatcher years saw crucial working class defeats such as the miners' strike and the collapse of what had been Scotland's industrial base, although the process was begun under a Labour government. By the mid-1990s, shipbuilding was a shadow if its former self, coal mining was effectively ended and the closure of the Ravenscraig Steel plant in 1992, under John Major's government, led to the end of large-scale steelmaking in Scotland. It was clear the Tory Party did not represent the views of the great majority of the Scottish population.

A key milestone was the imposition of the poll tax on Scotland in 1989. Thatcher had announced an alternative to collecting local rates with a new community charge, which replaced a property-based tax with an individual flat rate tax for every adult. This was to be introduced in Scotland a year earlier than in England. Widely condemned as a tax on the poor, the Church of Scotland called it "morally indefensible". The Labour Party had fought the 1987 election on the basis of opposition to the poll tax but, when it was enacted, the Labour leadership refused to break the law. As a result, a mass campaign of non-payment saw 850,000 people refusing to pay. The SNP condemned Labour's lack of action and, in dramatic fashion, Jim Sillars took Govan from Labour in the November 1988 by-election. The poll tax was eventually defeated by a demonstration of 200,000 and a riot in central London in March 1990, with 50,000 marching in Scotland on the same day. The London riot forced the Tories to remove Thatcher as leader and she was eventually driven away in tears from Downing Street in November 1990.[22]

In the 1992 General Election, the Tories were surprisingly returned to power, further alienating the majority of Scots from Westminster. The Tories won only a 25.6 percent share of the vote in Scotland, considerably less than the 42 percent achieved nationally.

Scotland's industrial decline hammered its traditional industries of shipbuilding, mining and steel. However, Thatcher's era saw a major decline of many of the light engineering jobs which had been established in Scotland after the war, symbolised by the closure of Timex in Dundee after a long struggle by its predominantly female workforce.[23]

In electoral terms, for the SNP from 1979 to the establishment of the Scottish Parliament, it was a mixed bag. Their vote never went above 20 percent. There were, however, notable results which highlighted their potential threat to the mainstream parties, particularly Labour. Jim Sillars was able to capture Govan in a by-election in November 1988 with a 33 percent swing.[24]

The growing distance between Scotland and the British state as represented by the Tory Party was highlighted in 1992 After the Tories had been returned to power, a Scotland United Rally was held in Glasgow's George Square with 3,500 attending at short notice. The rally was addressed by the STUC General Secretary, who called on "Scottish political parties to sink their differences and unite to fight for a multi-option referendum on constitutional change; Scotland United, he added, represented the 75 percent of Scots who had not voted for Major's party". Also attending were George Galloway and Denis Canavan and musicians Pat Kane and Ricky Ross.[25] In December, 30,000 turned up for a march and rally organised by Scotland United to coincide with a European Summit held in Edinburgh.[26] In the 1997 General Election, the mood in Britain was for an end to Tory rule and Labour under Tony Blair came to power with a 43 percent share of the vote. In Scotland, the vote was 46 percent for Labour with the Tories dropping to 17.5 percent with no MPs elected. The SNP took 22 percent of the vote and their representation doubled from three to six MPs.

One of the first decisions of the incoming New Labour Government in 1997 was to hold a referendum to establish a devolved Scottish parliament. A major strategic aim of this was to shoot the SNP fox and ensure full blown independence would not have a realistic chance of success. Throughout the period the Tories were in power, the SNP vote averaged around 17 percent, creeping up to around 22 percent in 1997. However, past by-election victories had shown that the SNP were capable of winning working class support from Labour.

The Scottish parliament was established with an additional member voting system where voters had two votes, one for a first past the post constituency and another for a regional list. As far as proportional representation goes, it is almost certainly one of the least effective. Its aim was to guarantee Tory representation in the Scottish parliament and that the SNP would never gain an overall majority, thus ensuring there would not be a majority in parliament for independence. This was to prove otherwise.

Having elected a Labour Government in 1997, it came as a shock to working class voters in Scotland that New Labour was a slightly more humane version of the Tories. Under Blair, levels of poverty across Britain hardly changed while the gap between rich and poor widened.[27] Privatisation of public services, notably the NHS and council housing, was considerably expanded while PFI was introduced for the construction and maintenance of schools, hospitals and other public buildings.

The Scottish parliament provided the SNP with a platform to hammer home its message that under Tory or Labour things only got worse. It also showed that a parliament in Scotland could act differently from a British government whether Labour or Tory. Interestingly the early examples of this came under the Labour/Lib Dem Scottish Executive coalition, which held office from 1999 to 2007. It introduced free social care for the elderly, a ban on smoking in public places and a graduate endowment to pay for students' university fees. When the SNP formed a minority administration in 2007, they abolished university tuition fees for first degrees, removed prescription charges, abolished bridge tolls and froze the council tax.[28]

The establishment of the Scottish parliament also allowed

the potential of representation from parties to the left of the mainstream. In 1999, both the Scottish Socialist Party and the Greens won one MSP each and in 2003 the SSP won six and the Greens seven seats. Three independent left-wing independence supporting MSPs were also voted in.

The run up to the Scottish parliamentary election in 2003 coincided with the attack on the twin towers in New York and the decision of the US government, supported by a great majority of the British parliament, to launch an invasion of Afghanistan and then illegally invade Iraq in March 2003. The American action was supported by the Blair government and led to the development of the huge Stop the War movement in Britain as well as a worldwide anti-war movement. In February 2003, up to two million demonstrated in London against the planned invasion of Iraq with over 100,000 marching through Glasgow the same day. The justification for attacking Iraq was based on fabricated evidence by Bush and Blair that Iraq had weapons of mass destruction. It proved to be a lie.

Under the leadership of John Swinney, the SNP had supported the US invasion of Afghanistan.[29] In autumn 2001, it worked with the anti-war movement, with Alex Salmond in particular condemning British involvement in the invasion of Iraq. This, along with long standing opposition to Britian's Trident Nuclear missile programme, helped cement the notion that the SNP were a radical left of centre opposition to the mainstream British parties. The SNP was not the only electoral beneficiary of New Labour's accommodation to neoliberal capitalism and its alliance with American imperialism. However, when the SSP imploded in 2006, the SNP were able to capitalise with most of the working class votes which had gone to the SSP in 2003 being transferred to the SNP in 2007.

The SNP is not a socialist party and has never claimed to be. It looks for support among working class communities and from big business. It has no formal links with the unions but makes every effort to appease finance and big business by promising that an independent Scotland would safeguard inward investment and profits. The SNP has always been supportive of the oil and petrochemical industry and reduced taxes on Scottish airports.

The SNP has won working class support by using the issue of independence and a number of significant but, in reality, minor reforms as a way of presenting a radical alternative to the failed policies of successive British governments. At the 2011 Scottish Parliament election, the SNP surprised even themselves, winning an overall majority of seats. After all, the voting system established under Blair and Donald Dewar was designed to ensure this could not happen. The fact that the SNP were able to overcome this hurdle underlined the widening gap in voting patterns between Scotland and the rest of Britain. Undoubtedly the financial crisis of 2009/2010, the role played by Gordon Brown and New Labour in bailing out the banks and the austerity programme launched by David Cameron's newly elected Tory-led coalition further alienated Scottish working class voters from supporting the mainstream British parties.

The seismic voting shift to the SNP in 2011 gave it a clear mandate to hold a referendum on Scottish independence. David Cameron, Prime Minister of the Tory/LibDem coalition, agreed to provide the powers to enable the Scottish Parliament to hold a referendum on independence, supremely confident he could easily win it and crush the independence movement. With support for independence languishing at around 30 percent in all the polls, Ruth Davidson, Tory leader in Scotland and close ally of David Cameron, arrogantly encouraged Alex Salmond to "Bring it on!". Salmond originally wanted increased devolution powers for Scotland on the ballot paper as well as independence but wanted others such as the STUC to argue the case rather than openly call for it. To do so would have provoked conflict with the 'fundamentalist' wing of his party. In any case, what the SNP presented to the voters was widely described as 'Independence lite', a timid proposal which meant keeping the pound, keeping the monarchy and staying part of NATO. The Devo-Max option, Salmond's original plan B, was ruled out by the Unionist parties, who wanted a straight choice between the Union and separation, even though most Scots at the time would have voted for increased federalism as a way of avoiding full blown independence.

The 2014 independence referendum

For those involved in the Yes campaign, 2014 was a unique and inspiring event. Scottish journalist Iain Macwhirter, in his book *Disunited Kingdom—How Westminster Won a Referendum and Lost Scotland*, catches the mood of the campaign:

> There was an eruption of political activity in towns and cities across Scotland. The town hall meeting was revived after three decades of decline. In Glasgow's George Square in the days and weeks before the referendum there had been, as one observer put it, "a wee whiff of Tahrir" as thousands of people gathered singing songs, waving flags, and talking politics.[30]

From the beginning, it was clear that this was a campaign that departed from the normal. The Scottish government won the argument that the voting age should be 16 and not 18, as is the case with political elections in Britain. This meant that many young people, most of them at school, became engaged with discussions around the issue of independence. Far from lowering the level of the debate, the involvement of young people enriched it. After all, any decision about the future of Scotland would affect them most of all.

Apart from the change from 18 to 16, it was decided that the electorate roll used to vote in the referendum would be the same as the one used in normal parliamentary elections. If you were Scots and lived outside Scotland, you did not get a vote. If you were not Scottish by birth, you were entitled to vote even though you had only lived in the country for a short period of time. This was important because it cut across the notion that there was some sort of "ethnic" or "racial nationalism" that defined who was able to participate in the referendum. A Scot was simply one who happened to be living in the country at the time.

The campaign itself is best described as having three separate elements: the official Yes campaign, the opposition to independence called Better Together, and a multitude of rank-and-file organisations who campaigned enthusiastically for yes. On the surface, the official Yes campaign was an amalgamation of different groups which supported independence including the SNP, the Greens and the Scottish Socialist Party, as well as a number of well-known figures in Scottish civil society and cultural life. However, in practice it was very much the vehicle for the SNP's pitch for independence. This can be illustrated by the fact that during the campaign an organisation called Trade Unionists for Independence were refused the use of the official Yes offices in Glasgow because it would not confine its activity to simply campaigning for a yes vote. As part of the campaign, those involved wanted to ensure that the case for Scottish independence should be put in a way that improved the conditions and rights of workers in Scotland by, for example, ensuring that independence would lead to the repeal of the Tories' anti-trade union laws. This did not chime with the needs of the official campaign and the group was duly told to stop using the office for meetings.

The SNP's case for independence was largely put in a document called 'Scotland's Future', a Scottish government white paper published in November 2013.[31] The main radical aspect of the document came from the fact that it committed an independent Scotland to the removal of the Trident nuclear base. Apart from that, 'Scotland's Future' is in many ways quite a conservative document. It committed Scotland to keeping the Monarchy, Scotland would keep the pound and take its share of the British state debt, it would apply to join NATO and the EU and it would cut corporation tax and airport duty.

The SNP's emphasis was that Scotland could be a successful capitalism open for business as usual. There is no inherent reason why Scotland could not become a capitalist nation state like many other countries of a similar or smaller size, but that was not why most Scots had come round to supporting independence. Rather they wanted an end to austerity and cuts and greater control over their lives. Yet the SNP leadership was obsessed with making the pro-business case and keeping on board supporters like Brian Souter, financial backer of the SNP and owner of the anti-union Stagecoach Group. Souter had opposed the Scottish government's move to scrap Section 28, a Tory law banning Local Authorities from promoting homosexuality. From the outset, the official campaign shunned the case for a radical break from the British state and British capitalism.

During the campaign, two set piece debates took place between Alex Salmond on behalf of Yes and former Labour Chancellor Alastair Darling putting the case for Scotland remaining part of Britain. The first debate was dominated by whether it was possible for Scotland to keep the pound as its currency. Salmond insisted that this was a reasonable way forward even though this would have meant much of the economic policy of an Independent Scotland being decided by the Bank of England. Alastair Darling made it clear that, as far as he was concerned, any British government would not allow this to happen. No matter how insistent Salmond was that an independent Scottish government had the right to use the pound and that this was in the best interest of both countries, Darling and George Osborne the Tory Chancellor at the time simply said that it would not be allowed. When asked what the alternatives were, Salmond kept repeating the same argument. This failure to even consider another option considerably undermined Salmond's economic case.

The second debate by contrast was generally considered to be one in which Salmond did much better. He went on the offensive over defending the NHS, ending zero hours contracts, defence of the welfare state and opposing foreign wars. In other words, Salmond, in this debate, pitched the argument for independence to its most obvious supporters in Scotland, the working class communities who had suffered under the Tories and New Labour. The effect was immediate, with support for independence taking a boost in the opinion polls.

The Unionist campaign was called Better Together, though it was soon dubbed Project Fear. Instead of presenting a positive case for Scotland remaining part of the Union, it was an entirely negative operation, claiming Scottish independence would mean economic Armageddon, destroying jobs, services pensions and perhaps civilisation itself. The British Cabinet, the Labour Party, the CBI, the Bank of England, the representatives of the EU and even the President of America all had their say: the only way Scotland could remain part of the EU was by voting to stay part of Britain.

While the Tories were part of Better Together, they were smart enough to leave it to Labour politicians like Darling, Gordon Brown and Douglas Alexander to make their case. Arch-Blairite Jim Murphy was voted leader of the Labour Party in Scotland. He announced he was giving up his Westminster seat to stand for the Scottish parliament at the first opportunity. He set out on a '100 towns in 100 days' tour of Scotland and then cancelled it, claiming he was "pursued by a gang of Yes thugs". It was mostly nonsense, but it was a story that the British media were happy to milk as yet another negative example of the Yes campaign and an indication of where independence would lead.

Unfortunately, the case against independence was also put by sections of the left in Scotland and the majority of trade union leaders, claiming that independence would divide the working class of Britain and weaken its capacity to organise and resist the bosses. For some unions it was about defending jobs, for example the GMB opposed the scrapping of Trident mainly for that reason. Unions opposed independence despite the fact that large numbers of their own members and many prominent trade union officials supported Yes. It is also worth noting that the RMT openly supported Yes and Unite, which was formerly rabidly anti-SNP, took a neutral position. This was an indication that on the ground many union members were much more enthusiastic about Scottish independence than some of their trade union leaders.

Only weeks away from polling day, with the vote too close to call and at least one poll showing Yes in the lead, Prime Minister Cameron and Better Together panicked. Gordon Brown, the *Daily Record* and the Queen were summoned to save the day. Devo-Max was suddenly back on the table. Greater powers for the Edinburgh parliament had been ruled out on the ballot paper; now, at the eleventh hour, Scotland was promised them in abundance if it would just vote No on referendum day.

However, the main story of the 2014 Scottish referendum campaign must be about how a grass roots movement developed independently from the main campaign. It enthusiastically took to the streets, meeting halls and communities of Scotland and embraced the Yes movement as a way of changing their lives for the better. Hope over Fear, Radical Independence Campaign, Women for Independence, Labour for Independence, the Socialist Workers Party and a myriad of Yes groups across the country campaigned on a daily basis, putting forward the positive case for Scottish independence. This was a real organic rank-and-file movement which flourished and grew throughout the course of the campaign.

One of its most positive aspects was the inclusive and diverse nature of the Yes movement. Historically, Scotland's black and minority ethnic communities have passively supported Labour in Scotland as they have in other parts of Britain. One of the great experiences of campaigning for a Yes vote in areas like Pollokshields and Govanhill was how many individuals from a wide range of ethnic backgrounds, including refugees and immigrants, came together and worked their socks off for a Yes vote. There was an attempt by the media and politicians to smear those supporting independence as anti-English, but it was confounded by the large numbers of English people, now resident in Scotland, who threw themselves into the Yes campaign.

The outcome of the vote was a major disappointment. Scotland voted against independence by 55.3 percent to 44.7 percent, with an overall turnout of 84.6 percent, which was historically one of the highest in the history of Britain. The momentum was all with Yes. In the year prior to the referendum, backing for Scottish independence stood at only 29 percent. However, the voting only tells part of the story. Support for independence was at its highest in working class constituencies across Scotland and strongest within the central belt, with Glasgow and Dundee coming out solidly for Yes. More affluent and middle-class areas voted no, even though some had a strong historical association with the SNP such as Angus and Perthshire.

The aftermath

While it is important to recognise the positive support given to independence by working class voters in 2014, it is also essential that some of the weaknesses are acknowledged. Support for independence in Scotland grew out of years of defeat—socially, politically and economically. Working class voters, after years of Tory governments, the defeats of the miners and other industrial workers and the destruction of Scotland's industrial base, transferred their support to independence and with it the Scottish National Party. One of the consequences of the 2014 vote was to cement the SNP as Scotland's dominant political party. In the period after the referendum, SNP membership grew to over 120,000, making it one of the largest per capita in the world. Large numbers of socialists and activists believed that the only way forward was to throw their lot in with the SNP and campaign for independence. Tommy Sheridan, a well-known but controversial figure on the Scottish left, called for a vote for the SNP.

But, was uncritical backing for a nationalist party looking for cross class support necessarily the best way of achieving independence?

In November 2014, a month after the result, the Radical Independence Campaign (RIC) held a conference in Glasgow just as the SNP were electing Nicola Sturgeon as their new leader. The RIC had made an important contribution to the independence campaign, carrying out mass canvasses in working class communities and helping to mobilise support for independence. On the morning of their conference, 4,000 attended to discuss the outcome of the vote. Later in the afternoon, the problems for the left in Scotland were summed up by the fact that after lunch the vast majority left to hear Nicola Sturgeon's acceptance speech at the SNP conference at a larger venue 100 yards from the RIC conference.

While most of the left in Scotland had played a positive, decisive role in winning support for a Yes vote, it also played an important role in developing support for the SNP. This was in part a consequence of the historical animosity between groups on the left. RIC and Hope over Fear ran completely separate campaigns, even though they were talking to and winning support from essentially the same people. But it also came about because far too much faith was placed in the SNP and independence *per se*.

The 2015 General Election was another watershed moment in the development of the independence movement. The SNP took 56 of 59 seats with 50 percent of the popular vote—a damning indictment of Better Together, particularly the role played by the Labour Party

After the referendum, the SNP faced a number of electoral challenges. Ruth Davidson, former BBC Scotland journalist, became the darling of the right-wing media as she tried to capitalise on Labour's demise and establish the Tories as the main unionist party in Scotland. But the development of Corbynism in England, with a new invigorated Labour Party putting forward a positive socialist message, had the potential to undermine the SNP from the left, particularly when Corbyn ally Richard Leonard was elected leader of the Labour Party in Scotland. However, in both the British and Scottish parliament elections, the SNP were able to see off the opposition. In Labour's case, Corbynism failed to ignite in Scotland because the right of the party retained effective control.

Perhaps the most important development in Scottish political life in this period was the arrival of a large number of pro-independence marches organised by All Under One Banner (AUOB). These started out with some small demonstrations in 2015 and grew until around 200,000 marched through the streets of Edinburgh in October 2019. Over the summer, a series of marches had taken place from Oban in the west to Galashiels in the borders, which mobilised a total figure of up to 800,000. Now, this does not mean that 800,000 different people took part; but with a population of 5 million in Scotland, the numbers are a remarkable indication of the active popular support for the cause.

Some on the left's approach to the AUOB has been coloured by the preponderance of Scottish flags covering the length of the protests, seeing this as evidence that the Scottish independence movement was dominated by nationalism. It would be wrong to dismiss this. There is an aspect of the movement that does see Scotland as a country exploited by English imperialism and Scottish history defined by its relation to England and English attempted dominance of Scotland. Nevertheless, it is important to point out that there are other characteristics of the movement. For many, the Scottish flag is seen as a symbol of resistance to Tory rule in Scotland. The demos were overwhelmingly working class and represented a real grassroots movement, separate from the SNP even though many were members. Indeed, the reaction of the SNP leadership initially was to oppose their members' involvement with marches, arguing that they were a distraction from campaigning. It was only when their members were obviously ignoring this, that the official SNP attitude changed; though it has to be pointed out that Sturgeon has refused to speak or take part in any of the AUOB demonstrations.

So, AUOB apart, what other factors have kept independence at the centre of Scottish, and to a certain extent, British politics?

Britain voted to leave the EU in 2016 by a margin of 52 percent to 48 percent. Scotland, on the other hand, voted 62 percent to 38 percent to remain. There are many valid reasons to oppose the EU from a left-wing socialist perspective. The

EU is a bosses' club with neoliberal economic policies at its heart. Its commitment to the free market and its opposition to state ownership where this involves public subsidy and state support and government restrictions on borrowing make it difficult for any member government to pursue a radical left-wing economic programme.

Nevertheless, the fact that the people of Scotland were told in 2014 that the only way they could remain in the EU was to vote to stay part of the United Kingdom created a huge democratic deficit for Scotland.

While the vote to remain part of Britain in 2012 seems decisive, this only tells part of the story. The enthusiasm generated by the campaign and the formation of Yes groups across Scotland committed to putting the case has ensured that independence will not go away, particularly because, since 2014, Britain has had Tory governments, contrary to the political voting attitude of the majority of Scots.

The role of the media in influencing the outcome of general elections and political attitudes in general is often given an exaggerated importance by many people on the left. The SNP and the independence movement in general face a hostile British press and the BBC, which is determined to oppose independence and exaggerate the possible dangers. Again, this feeds into the frustration of activists with the nature of the British state and the institutions and organisations that support it.

In certain respects, Scotland's political culture differs from England's, for example in the discourse around immigration, asylum seekers and refugees. The Scottish government, for instance, talks of 'welcoming refugees' while the British government seeks to create 'a hostile environment'. Statistics on racism are very similar and this needs emphasising. Yet, for some time, the public discourse in Scotland has been more positive and tolerant. Whatever the facts, the perceptions in this area strengthen the argument that Scotland is different from England and needs to go its own way.

Another element in keeping support for independence alive

has been the performance of the Labour Party. Traditionally, the Labour Party has been the main beneficiary of working class support in Scotland. All this changed after the 2014 referendum campaign. Labour failed to get to grips with the dynamic that led to working class communities supporting independence and the SNP. Continuing to characterise the movement as narrow, backward nationalism ensures they will be unable to win back support. The election of Corbyn to the leadership of the Labour Party and the development of Momentum initially offered some hope that a radical Labour Party could once again connect with its former supporters in Scotland. When Corbyn-supporting Richard Leonard took up the leadership of Scottish Labour, the possibility of a serious alternative to the SNP became a reality. Labour's failure to get to grips with the dynamics of politics in Scotland ensured that the main unionist vote consolidated behind the Tories, and potential working class support, particularly from young people looking for a radical break with the mainstream economic and political consensus, largely remained on the side of the SNP. There is, undoubtedly, plenty of room to criticise the SNP from a left-wing working class perspective. Unfortunately, the Labour Party's sectarian attitude towards the SNP, characterising them as almost worse than the Tories, along with their continuing opposition to independence and their confusion and splits over whether to even support the right of the Scottish people to have a second independence referendum has made sure that they continue to be a marginal force in Scotland. The failure of Labour at a British level has also cemented backing for independence.

SNP: reformist or nationalist?

Labour's problems in Scotland run deeper than their opposition to independence. Classic social democracy has been unable to offer an alternative for working class voters in a period of relentless economic stagnation. This has led to a collapse in support across Europe and beyond. Left alternatives such as Syriza in Greece, Podemos in Spain, Corbyn and Momentum in

Britain and the movement to support Bernie Sanders in the US raised hopes that a left alternative was possible. Unfortunately, some capitulated in government, like Syriza and Podemos, whereas Corbyn faced concerted and determined opposition from the right-wing establishment, including sections of the Labour Party, to ensure he would never become prime minister. In the case of Sanders, the Democrat establishment succeeded in denying him the presidential nomination.

Where does this leave the SNP? The party has skilfully maintained political support while running the Scottish government. In part this is because of the Tory governments. The election of the Johnson government and its disastrous handling of both Brexit and the coronavirus crisis has cemented the position of the SNP and increased support for independence.[32] While Nicola Sturgeon's government has made some dreadful decisions, giving Scotland along with the rest of Britain one of the worst death rates in the world, her choice not to follow Johnson's fatal decision taken on 'business' grounds to ease the lockdown has allowed the SNP government to disassociate itself from the worst aspects of British government policy.

Yet the SNP baulk at the same obstacle faced by all left of centre parties across the world; how to provide real reforms in a period of deepening economic crisis. Of course, the SNP claim they are prevented from doing this is because they have no real power in Scotland. In part, this is true. But their track record proves they will not use even the powers they do have unless they are forced into using them. Their record also shows they will not engage with the independence movement to campaign for a fundamental transformation of Scottish society and break with British and European capitalism

The left-wing advocates of independence need to face the facts about the SNP: it is a party that wants independence within the economic and social straitjacket of the capitalist economy. There are undoubtedly many committed left-wing activists who are SNP members, including former Labour Party members and former members of other far-left organisations.

The SNP has the electoral support of the majority of working class voters in Scotland and they have a large trade union section. At an All Under One Banner online talk in May 2020, former left-wing SNP MSP George Kerevan argued the SNP was a traditional social democratic party—the "mass party of the working class" in Scotland.[33]

This is wishful thinking on George's part. Unlike the Labour Party, the SNP have no formal links to the trade union movement. The connection between Labour and the unions is mediated through the trade union bureaucracy. This fact has maintained the Labour Party as a conservative force, primarily concerned with being "electable" at the expense of pursuing reforms that confront and challenge capitalism. Nevertheless, there exists the possibility within the relationship between Labour and organised workers for the latter to have some influence. The 2019 Labour Manifesto included renationalisation of the railways and the reversal of privatisation in the NHS, well to the left of the SNP programme. It is doubtful whether Corbyn and McDonnell could have included this without the support of the unions.

Also, there is no evidence the potential of the SNP Trade Union Group is used to influence SNP policy in favour of trade unionism. It does not actively campaign in support of workers on strike and neither does it campaign within the unions for independence. The TU Group did criticise the SNP's failure to support a Green Party motion in the Scottish parliament to lower rents for private tenants and to limit evictions during the coronavirus crisis, but what is important is that this is a departure from its past practice.

In relation to the European Union, the SNP are part of the European Free Alliance (EFA). On the surface, this seems to be a mainstream socially progressive group which "focuses its activity on the promotion of the right of self-determination of peoples" and "works for self-determination, for a Europe of the Peoples, for Peace and Linguistic justice, for a sustainable planet, for more gender equality and social justice".[34] A more rigorous look at some of their constituent organisation reveals something quite different and worrying.

The South Tyrolean Freedom Party calls itself a "national-conservative party that seeks to represent the German-speaking population in South Tyrol and advocates for the independence of South Tyrol". This means South Tyrol leaving Italy to become part of Austria—a situation that Austria's far-right Freedom Party is happy to exploit.[35]

The New Flemish Alliance (N-VA) believes "in the merits of a free-market economy" and thinks "the government must give individuals and companies all the opportunities possible to take initiatives". It describes itself as follows: "The N-VA is a Flemish nationalist party. Our nationalism is a healthy mixture of both civil and cultural elements". Their attitude to identity, immigration and integration—though they might deny it—is remarkably like the Islamophobia of the British Tory Party.[36]

A look at the organisations that make up the EFA reveals a mixture of ethnic nationalist groups, constitutional nationalists and organisations looking for autonomy and outright independence from established states. It includes diverse groups such as the Republican Left of Catalonia and the right-wing South Tyrolean Freedom Party.

Cuthbert and Cuthbert make it clear that "the SNP's economic strategy is a variant of the neoliberal 'Washington' consensus which has dominated the economic strategy of all major British parties, and more widely has landed the world economy in such deep trouble".[37]

How then should socialists categorise the SNP? Many Labour supporters ridicule them as "Tartan Tories". This is unfair to the vast majority of SNP members and certainly not true of the policy and attitudes the SNP has formed in government. They are a nationalist party which aims to deliver social and political reform and bring about Scottish independence. However, they are not a socialist organisation nor even social democratic in the traditional sense of the word. However, conventional social democratic organisations are themselves a mixture of nationalism and reformism. Perhaps the SNP can be characterised in the same way, with the emphasis on nationalism rather than reformism. Unfortunately, this is a source of weakness rather than a strength, and ultimately undermines both the battle for radical change and the struggle for independence itself.

Record support for independence

By October 2020, six months after Scotland had moved into a lockdown as a result of Covid-19, support for independence had reached record levels, with 58 percent of voters saying they would support a Yes vote.[38] According to John Curtice, it was the ninth poll since June 2020 showing Yes was ahead.[39] Perhaps the most startling part of the Ipsos/Mori poll was that 79 percent of people between 16 and 24 now backed independence. While support for independence remained solidly based in working class communities, there was plenty of evidence of shifting support in favour of a break from Britain across Scottish society. Even people who voted to leave the EU in 2016, some of whom, it might be assumed, had voted for the Johnson government, were moving in the direction of independence with support for the SNP and the Tories neck and neck among former leave voters.[40]

As well as Scotland, the rising level of support for independence in Wales and the growing support for Irish unity in Northern Ireland led the *Financial Times* to ask: "Will coronavirus break the UK?"[41] The article highlighted a number of important issues: the capacity of the devolved administrations to act independently and differently from the Johnson government; the "colonial mindset" in London which leads it to make decisions with little understanding of how devolved structures work and without agreement from Edinburgh or Cardiff; the lack of borrowing powers for the Welsh government and their limited nature in Scotland. All these were cited as issues driving Britain apart. The article also underscored the developing tension between the Tories and the English regions.

As far as Scotland is concerned, the actions of the Johnson government have led people, previously sceptical about independence, to change their minds. However, it would be wrong simply to see this as the only factor. The Tory failures only sharpen a rift that has been growing over a considerable period of time—perhaps from the election of the Thatcher government in 1979.

Brexit is also a major cause. The Johnson government's brinkmanship over a no deal break with the EU is also driving resentment. For example, the STUC has made it clear that they are firmly opposed to the Tories' Internal Market Bill, which, they insist, represents an attack on devolution: "Should the UK Government proceed with the bill, against the wishes of the Scottish parliament, it makes the case for a second independence referendum unanswerable".[42] The Internal Market Bill shifts the balance of power radically away from the Scottish parliament, giving Westminster much greater control over Scottish affairs.

The relationship between support for independence and the EU in Scotland is a complex one. One third of the vote for leaving the EU came from people who voted for Scottish independence in 2014. Nor should it be assumed that everyone in Scotland who voted leave did so for reactionary reasons. The nature of the EU, with its inhumane treatment of refugees, its commitment to neoliberal economics and its undemocratic centralism, hardly fits the model of independence most Scots espouse. The difference between Scotland and England is that people in Scotland were provided with an opportunity to register their dissent by expressing support for the break-up of the UK. Many English voters used the EU vote in a similar way, to register their alienation from government and the elite. It would be foolish to ignore the reactionary nature of the campaign to leave the EU, initiated by UKIP and the xenophobic Nigel Farage, subsequently commandeered by Gove and Johnson. Nevertheless, it is necessary to grasp the contradictions. People in Scotland voted to remain in the EU as a way of registering their disapproval at the nature of the campaign run by those arguing to leave. They did so for positive reasons with the vision of an independent Scotland that was open and inclusive. No one in Scotland voted for a Tory Brexit.

Another factor is the lack of serious opposition to the SNP. Ruth Davidson's elevation to the House of Lords and the advent of the Johnson government has wrecked any possibility of a serious Tory revival. Though, with Labour sitting third in the opinion polls at 13 percent in October 2020 behind the Tories on 19 percent, it is the latter that has been the main beneficiary of what is left of unionist support. How out of touch Labour is in Scotland is illustrated by the fact that 44 percent of their own voters support independence.

On the left of the party there is recognition that something has to change. Neil Findlay has called for greater local autonomy, stating that, "Democracy, devolution and subsidiarity should be the driving principles with powerful regional and national governments able to build strong, vibrant, regional and national sustainable communities within a democratised political system".[43] He accepts the right of Scotland to hold a second vote on independence, while at the same time counterposing the devolution of greater powers to the Scottish parliament as an alternative to full independence. Glasgow Councillor Mat Kerr genuinely believes Labour must return to its roots and fight alongside working people and, above all, listen. On independence he thinks "Ruling out another referendum in all circumstances leaves us looking intransigent, undemocratic, and tone-deaf".[44]

The problem for the Labour left is its influence on the Scottish party is diminishing. Neil Findlay retires as an MSP in 2021 and Matt Kerr lost the Scottish Labour Deputy Leadership to right-winger Jackie Baillie. The prominent Scottish writer Gerry Hassan's solution for the Labour Party in Scotland is for it to break with the national party and reform along the lines of the old ILP—and champion Scottish Home Rule, as did the Labour Party formally until the mid-1950s. So, Hassan argues, "A new ILP would stand unapologetically for self-government and for Scotland to decide its own future".[45] The problem is there seems little if any chance of this finding favour with the membership of the party in Scotland.

Tensions in the SNP

Since the formation of the Scottish Parliament in 1999, the SNP has been noted for its tight self-discipline. Unlike its opponents, it has largely presented a united face to voters focussing on its social democratic policies and its pursuit of the case for Scottish Independence, even though in practical terms it has done little to achieve this. By the beginning of 2021, the party was losing members and was divided over a number of issues. These are splits which can't be categorised on a simple left versus right basis and cut across traditional party loyalties. The most prominent public dispute revolves around former leader Alex Salmond. Salmond was charged with 14 offences against ten women, which included attempted rape against one, ten of sexual assault and two of indecent assault. The court case cleared him of all charges. Earlier, the Scottish Government admitted to acting unlawfully while investigating sexual harassment claims against Salmond and had to pay his £500,000 legal fees from the public purse.[46]

Salmond has claimed that Sturgeon broke the ministerial code and misled parliament, which she denies. He also claims there was a conspiracy by the SNP leadership to have him jailed. This has led to bitter divisions within the SNP. Some of Salmond's supporters have ignored the voices of the women involved, who said "they were devastated by the judgment" in the court case[47] and are among the most vocal opponents of reform to the Gender Recognition Act and transgender rights.

Both Salmond and Sturgeon appeared before the Scottish government's inquiry in February and March 2021. Salmond accused the Scottish Government and the SNP of a "malicious and concerted attempt to damage my reputation and remove me from public life in Scotland",[48] while Sturgeon responded by saying the complaints against Mr Salmond were "shocking" and his behaviour "was not always appropriate".[49]

In April 2021 Salmond announced the formation of a new party, Alba, which would contest seats on the regional lists across Scotland. The logic is that if the SNP win seats in the first past the post constituencies, because of the nature of the proportional voting system used in the election for the Scottish Parliament, they are expected to pick up a very few seats in the additional members part of the vote. So, vote SNP in the constituencies and vote Alba in the list. If this works then the Scottish Parliament would have a "supermajority in favour of independence". Prior to the formation of Alba, there were at least five other independence supporting parties formed with the intention of standing by using the same rationale. At least one of them, Action for Independence, which includes Tommy Sheridan, declared that they would stand down in favour of Salmond's new party.

Running parallel to this was the debate about how the SNP should respond if the UK Government failed to agree to grant a section 30 order. In answer to her critics on this, Sturgeon said that if the SNP were re-elected in May 2021 then they would bring forward a draft bill to the Scottish Parliament for an independence referendum. Many of the critics of the SNP leadership's handling of the Salmond case and the Gender Recognition Act are some of Sturgeon's fiercest critics of her failure to make a serious attempt to challenge the UK Government over a second independence referendum.

This complex situation creates a number of difficulties. As well as supporting a radical campaign to win independence, socialists are also committed to fighting all forms of oppression including women's oppression and trans oppression. These goals are not in opposition to each other.

A major part of the problem is the nature of the SNP itself and its conservative approach to independence, which seeks to assuage competing interest groups. An example of this is its failure to take up the case for trans rights. The Scottish Government launched a public consultation on reform of the

Gender Recognition Act in Scotland in December 2019, with a view to making it easier for individuals to have their chosen identity legally recognised.[50] Despite widespread support for this, the Scottish Government has put on hold moves to bring forward the necessary legislation after the public consultation ended in March 2020.[51] This failure has created a vacuum which has allowed a bitter and divisive debate to continue.

In April 2021 Salmond announced the formation of a new party—the Alba Party—which will contest seats on the regional lists across Scotland. The logic is that if the SNP win seats in the first past the post constituencies, because of the nature of the proportional voting system used in the election for the Scottish Parliament, they are expected to pick up a very few seats in the additional members part of the vote. So, Alba argues that people should vote SNP in the constituencies and vote Alba in the list. If this works then the Scottish Parliament would have a "supermajority in favour of independence". Prior to the formation of Alba, there were at least five other independence-supporting parties formed with the intention of standing by using the same rationale. One of them, Action for Independence, which includes Tommy Sheridan, quickly declared that they would stand down in favour of Salmond's new party and another the Independence for Scotland Party followed promptly thereafter.

Alba is unlikely to prove a serious or radical alternative to the SNP. It is attracting people who believe the case against Salmond was a manufactured conspiracy (including denigrating the women who complained about his behaviour) and some who are opposed to the Gender Recognition Act. However, there are contradictory pressures at play and Alba has won support from many genuine activists frustrated with the lack of a clear direction from the SNP leadership on how to win independence and who are concerned at the over-centralised control by SNP officials close to Sturgeon. A number of prominent SNP members have jumped ship including Kenny MacAskill, former SNP Justice Secretary and at least one SNP

Climate Justice Strike in
Glasgow 2019

Westminster MP. On the left, as well as Tommy Sheridan, former SNP MP George Kerevan has also joined.

Unfortunately, there are a number of strategic problems for socialists who have joined the Alba Party. As we have seen, Alex Salmond is no radical. Writing in *The National* in March 2021, right wing commentator Michael Fry explained why he was voting for Alba. For him, one of the major problems of the SNP is their pursuit of "equality and human rights", even though this is often more rhetorical than actual. Echoing Boris Johnson that "greed" and "capitalism" led to the UK's vaccine success, Fry believes that equality undermines entrepreneurship and holds Scotland back. For him "Alex Salmond understands this, and Nicola Sturgeon does not". Further issues emerged which should have made anyone on the left thinking of joining Salmond's Party think again. It was announced that one of the candidates was a former boxing champion Alex Arthur who will contest the list seat in Lothian. It transpired that he had made a number of highly offensive and racist tweets about Romani people and Romanians. Then it was announced that investment strategist Dr Jim Walker was to return from his job as chief economist at Aletheia Capital in Hong Kong to contest Central Scotland. This was hardly an indication that Alba was on the way to challenging the SNP from a left wing perspective.

There are fundamental issues in play which need to be confronted. Many on the left have gone down the route of believing that securing independence is about winning seats in the Scottish parliament. Even if Alba gain some seats this is likely to be at the expense of another independence supporting party, the Greens. And in terms of winning independence, it takes us no further forward. There remains the issue of how Scotland can force Britain to agree to a second referendum. Salmond like Sturgeon is a "constitutional nationalist". Unless the movement confronts the need to challenge the British State through mass action, including civil disobedience if necessary, then Scotland breaking from the British State will remain a pipe dream.

Then there is the issue of class. This book has argued

that the driving force behind independence is working class people looking for an end to years of neoliberal economic policies which have devastated communities across Scotland, with the impact of the pandemic only making matters worse. By bringing on board the likes of Jim Walker, Salmond is signalling that under him an independent Scotland will be the same as Andrew Wilson's Growth Commission, or worse. We should not be surprised. Alex Salmond extolled the virtues of Ireland's "Celtic Tiger" before its disastrous crash in 2008 and in the 2014 referendum insisted that Scotland should keep the pound, thus putting Scotland's economic future in the hands of the Bank of England.

The British state and its supporters have attempted to use the deep divisions within the SNP, to undermine the movement. Yet there was little evidence by early 2021 that the Sturgeon/Salmond divide had a major impact on support in Scotland for independence. This underlines the deep alienation felt by the majority of working class people in Scotland towards Britain and its main political parties.

For a radical response to the climate crisis

The rescheduled UN Climate Change Summit (COP26) in Glasgow in November 2021 can provide a platform to promote far more radical environmental policies. Renationalisation of the energy sector and taking it out of the hands of privately owned multinational corporations is a critical demand. Creating a well-planned and thoroughly-integrated energy strategy will be essential in an independent Scotland. Failure to move beyond the SNP vision will lead to lip service and hollow rhetoric on the environment. A recent example of the SNP's capitulation to giant corporations and European competition rules gets to the heart of the problem with their whole strategy.

In October 2020, Fife-based Canadian-owned company BiFab withdrew its bid to build the jackets (or sea-bed foundations) for a government licensed windfarm project on the Moray Firth. The Scottish Government had rescued

BiFab in 2017 with a loan of £37.4 million it converted into a 32.4 percent equity stake in the company.[53] The loan was to secure a contract to build jackets for turbines. French energy corporation EDF Energy was also commissioned by the Scottish Government to erect a large offshore windfarm at Neart na Gaoithe close to the BiFab yards. The idea was that a local supplier would produce the turbine sleeves for the wind farm. Except the Scottish Government did not impose any requirement on EDF to purchase the parts produced by BiFab in Scotland. EDF decided to look to the cheapest suppliers, who happened to be Indonesian. The STUC estimated that the carbon shipping impact of importing the parts from Indonesia would be the equivalent of 35,000 new cars on the road. A trade union campaign did force the company to agree to buy 8 out of 53 of the turbine sleeves from BiFab, saving 200 jobs, as opposed to 1,000 jobs if BiFab had won the whole contract. Meanwhile other contracts for the Seagreen wind farm off the coast of Fife went to China and the United Arab Emirates.

The SNP Government responded by claiming it was powerless in the face of state aid rules imposed by the European Union, which meant the Scottish Government could not force EDF Energy to buy the sleeves in Scotland. They also refused to spend extra money, again citing the same state aid rules, which meant that the Scottish Government could not legally pump extra cash into saving the project. Pat Rafferty, Scottish Regional Secretary of the Unite union, rightly claimed the Scottish Government were "walking away". This fiasco begs the question why the Scottish Government didn't nationalise the company in the first place and challenge a rotten regulatory system that is heavily weighted in favour of big multinational corporations that have no interest in transitioning to a zero carbon economy in Scotland.[54]

Another illustration of the SNP's limitations has been their reversal of opposition to the setting up of 'Free Ports' and their subsequent support for what they have called 'Green Ports'. Free Ports are the brainchild of Tory Chancellor Rishi Sunak, who first presented the idea in a policy paper to the right-wing Centre for Policy Studies in 2016.[55] These are ports that are permitted to operate as offshore tax havens and operate as low- or no-tax-based economies with a view to attracting jobs and investment. According to George Kerevan, "The Chinese Free Port model was a disaster for the environment, and we are all frying as a result. Chinese Free Ports are also the global centre for smuggling counterfeit goods".[56]

In February 2020, the Tory Government launched a bidding process for ten Free Ports across the UK, presenting it as one of the benefits of Brexit. By February 2021, around 30 cities were considering bids.[57]

Initially the Scottish Government opposed Free Ports labelling them "a shiny squirrel to draw attention away from all the other bad stuff that is going on in the trade arena". However, they later changed their mind, rebranding them as 'Green Ports'. In January 2021, SNP trade minister Ivan McKee said, "Instead, we propose to take the Free Port model and apply Scotland's priorities to it, so that it meets our ambition to deliver a net-zero, wellbeing economy that upholds the highest standards of environmental protections and fair work practices and supports our strategy of building clusters of high productivity businesses across Scotland's regions... We have listened to what businesses and communities have said and there is an appetite for new ways to support our economy through the recovery".[58]

There is no evidence that Free Ports create jobs or aid recovery. They simply switch investment and jobs from other parts of the world. The SNP's embrace of a neoliberal, low-tax economic future for Scotland is exposed as a race to the bottom, which will compound Scotland's structural problems of poverty and inequality.

Conclusion

Sturgeon's coronation as SNP leader after the 2014 referendum was seen by many as a move to the left by the SNP, further reinforcing the belief independence alone could lead Scotland to challenge the failed free-market orthodoxy. The reality has been quite different. Despite their bitter acrimonies, politically there is very little distinction between Sturgeon and Salmond in their vision for a future independent Scotland.

The SNP policies of retaining the monarchy, membership of NATO, membership of the EU, support for the North Sea oil industries and a moderate carbon reduction target expose the paucity of its radicalism. It also offers little in the way of resistance to Westminster's economic policies, despite the fact that it has considerable scope to do so. Nor does the SNP have a plan, other than its moral force argument, to force the British state to give the Scottish Parliament the power to hold a second referendum.

This stultifying conservatism was further underlined when Andrew Wilson, described in an interview in *The Herald* as the "brains of the Yes Movement", yet again presented the ultra-cautious approach of those who determine SNP policy: "If we're striving to be as good a society as somewhere like Denmark, it could take a generation—20 or 25 years".[59] Salmond and his new Alba Party offer little that is different and will take many good activists down a dead end. The challenge for the left in Scotland is how to break this impasse and build a radical alternative to the timid leadership of the SNP.

Chapter 8

Neoliberalism with a Heart? Life Under the SNP

Iain Ferguson & Gerry Mooney

Since 2007, the Scottish National Party (SNP) has established itself as the most popular and, in membership terms, the largest political party in Scotland and the third largest in Britain. Since 2007, it has won the most seats at Holyrood and Scottish seats at Westminster, the largest vote share in the 2009, 2014 and 2019 European elections, and the most local councillors of any party in the three council elections in 2007, 2012 and 2017.

The SNP's electoral success has been at the expense of the Labour Party, the dominant political force in Scotland for much of the post-war period. Its share of the vote at the December 2019 Westminster election was its lowest since 1910. By any measure, this is an impressive electoral record. As is argued in Chapter 1, an important reason for that success has been the SNP's ability to present itself to working class voters as a progressive centre left, social democratic party; occupying the 'Old Labour' ground abandoned in the 1990s with the emergence of New Labour.[1] That self-description suggests a willingness if not necessarily to challenge the fundamental causes of poverty and inequality then at least to address some of their main consequences.

There are *some* grounds for the SNP's claim to be a progressive party. The absence of tuition fees for students in higher education, for example, and the lack of an internal market in the NHS are amongst policies that contribute to the impression that Scotland under the SNP is different from the rest of the UK—if not exactly 'a land flowing with milk and honey', then at least a kinder, fairer and more equal society. On a range of social issues, welfare and social security, LGBT+ rights, racism and immigration, the rhetoric and tone of the SNP under the leadership of Nicola Sturgeon has been markedly different from that of Tory governments in Westminster. It is hard to imagine Boris Johnson calling for *more* immigration, as the SNP first minister has frequently done, or leading off a Pride march, as she did in Glasgow in 2019. More generally, Sturgeon's ability as a politician and communicator are also important factors in the SNP's success, which has been reflected in claims that during 2020-2021, Sturgeon has enjoyed a 'good pandemic' as her announcements have been regarded clear and coherent, at least in comparison with those from Prime Minister Boris Johnson.

However, given the dominant position the SNP has enjoyed for more than a decade—and above all since the 2014 referendum—it is an opportune time to assess to what extent it has used that position of dominance to bring about radical social and economic change in Scottish society. Here, the picture is much less impressive. A report published by the Scottish government in early 2020, for example, showed that those living in the most deprived parts of the country are now four times more likely to die early than they were 20 years ago.[2] The Crisis Scotland charity has described a 'homelessness death emergency' with fatalities of homeless people more than double the rate in England.[3] Scotland's drug-related death toll increased by almost a third in 2019 to reach a record high of 1,187, putting the country on a par with the United States. The death rate is now more than three times that of England and Wales and has more than doubled since 2008.[4] It is higher than any other EU country. And despite apparently progressive penal policies, after 14 years of SNP rule, Scotland continues to have the highest imprisonment rate in Western Europe. Any critical assessment of the party's record is open to the charge that while the SNP government might wish to do things differently, it lacks sufficient powers. Westminster determines the size of the annual budget it has available and, until 2018, retained control over what used to be called 'social security' spending. While aspects of this have been devolved to Scotland, Westminster still holds the key levers of the benefits system. This has imposed obvious constraints, but could the Scottish Government and SNP-led councils have responded differently in all of these areas? Could they have done more both to challenge austerity policies and, more generally, the poverty and inequality that blight the lives of so many people? And if so, what does that tell us about the politics of the SNP and about the kind of independent Scotland that its leadership envisages?

Arguably, in areas such as health and education, the SNP has pursued policies that are less market-driven than south of the border. Yet overall, there is little in the SNP's record that shows either a willingness or an ability to challenge the British state and the powerful financial, industrial, land-owning and political interests that dominate Scottish society. On the contrary, an unquestioning acceptance of neoliberal 'common sense', combined with a nod towards social democratic values—what some critics have called "neoliberalism with a heart"[5]—forms the dominant ideological framework of the SNP leadership.

Health

Margaret Thatcher's 1980s market-driven 'reforms' of the NHS were greeted with considerable scepticism in Scotland and, following the establishment of the Scottish Parliament in 1999 (when health was devolved), NHS Trusts north of the border were abolished, effectively ending the internal market in health care. That abolition took place under Labour/Liberal Democrat coalition Scottish governments (1999-2007), but, for the most part, SNP-led governments since 2007 have also rejected these 'anti-reforms' which have profoundly weakened the NHS south of the border. The Health and Social Care Act, which came into force in England in 2012, does not apply in Scotland (nor in Wales or Northern Ireland). This is important since that Act, by removing the duty on the Secretary of State to provide comprehensive health services across the country and by allowing NHS Foundation Trusts to receive up to 49 percent of their income from outside the NHS, both opened the NHS up to privatisation on an unprecedented scale and also effectively spelled the end of a truly *national* health service in England.

In 2011, the SNP abolished prescription charges in Scotland, a welcome reform but not especially radical as it followed precedents set by the devolved parliaments in Wales and Northern Ireland. Such limitations on the operation of the market in health are clearly welcome but their significance should not be overstated for several reasons. Firstly, the continuing dominance under the SNP of a managerialist ethos in public services, which prioritises meeting performance targets and 'efficiency savings' (or cuts), has meant that the day-to-day experience of workers in the health service in Scotland is not so different from that of their counterparts south of the border. A motion to the Scottish Trades Union Congress (STUC) conference in 2019, for example, highlighted that the number of days lost to stress in the NHS had risen by nearly 20 percent in the previous three years and demanded the Scottish government provide more support and resources to address the issue of work-related stress.

The experience of patients within the NHS in Scotland has worsened considerably since 2012. According to official figures published in 2019, the Scottish government's Treatment Time Guarantee, which promises inpatient or day care treatment within 12 weeks, was met for just over two-thirds of patients in the first three months of that year. The figures also show that overall performance had slumped to the lowest level since the legally binding guarantee was introduced in

October 2012. Meanwhile, the proportion of patients beginning treatment within 18 weeks of a referral, another key waiting time standard, has also dropped to the worst level ever. Finally, in 2020, the number of patients waiting more than 12 hours at accident and emergency in Scottish hospitals hit record levels. The SNP government's response, that "core A&E departments in Scotland continue to be the best-performing in the UK", may be true but it is unlikely to be of much comfort to those kept waiting for 12 hours or more.

While market forces may play less of a role in the NHS in Scotland, they nevertheless continue to shape health service provision in important ways, not least in the construction of new hospitals as well as other public sector projects. There have been ongoing problems with major new hospitals in Glasgow and Edinburgh, where, arguably, tight cost limits and design and appearance considerations took precedence over patient safety and healthcare needs. And while the SNP claims to have abolished the Private Finance Initiative (PFI) introduced by the Tories in the early-1990s (as the basis for funding the building of hospitals and other public sector projects), its alternative, the Scottish Futures Trust (SFT), is also based on the transfer of public money to the private sector.

The SFT was launched in 2008 by the then First Minister Alex Salmond to provide new hospitals, health centres, colleges, schools and roads. Mirroring the Private Finance Initiative (PFI), private companies are contracted to construct public buildings with debt finance paid off by the taxpayer over decades. Salmond insisted the SFT model would be cheaper than the previous system by capping debt interest payments and would include some level of public ownership. However, the model costs governments more over the long term than using cheaper public borrowing and the operations are less transparent than publicly run schemes. According to public health academic Professor Allyson Pollock, the main political advantage of the SFT is "its ability to give the SNP government the appearance of doing 'something different' to its more business-oriented southern neighbour, while in reality responding to the same budgetary incentives that gave rise to private finance in Scotland in the first place".[6]

Pollock's scepticism is well-founded. A 2018 report by Dexter Whitfield, an independent specialist in PFI schemes, analysed the ownership and investments of 47 Scottish projects overseen by the Scottish Futures Trust.[7] Whitfield found that nearly 30 percent of the investments in these schemes can be traced to companies based in tax havens such as the Channel Islands, Dubai, the Cayman Islands, the British Virgin Islands, Luxembourg and Cyprus. In all, those offshore companies stand to earn more than £1.7 billion from these contracts over the next 25-30 years, charging interest rates as high as 13 percent for their financing.

As in PFI schemes, private companies control maintenance of any new buildings for up to 30 years, charging commercial fees for their work. Data from the Scottish government also shows that the 47 schemes overseen by the SFT were built for a total cost of £2.7 billion but will cost taxpayers nearly £8 billion by the time the borrowing needed to finance their construction is paid off and their maintenance contracts finish.

Whitfield's analysis also shows offshore investments and shares in these projects are spread across 60 percent of these schemes. Only a small fraction of the shares and ownership of those 47 projects, equivalent to about 16 percent of their total lifetime costs, is from firms based in Scotland. As well as costing the taxpayer much more, such privately financed projects—whether those loved by the Tories, Labour or the SNP—are inherently flawed because they lack the higher levels of transparency and accountability used in the public sector. Finally, the main factors shaping the health and well-being of people in Scotland as elsewhere is not the state of services as such but fundamental issues such as poverty, inequality, disadvantage and oppression. And here the picture is grim indeed. A study published in 2019 found that life expectancy in many of Scotland's council areas is now falling. Statistics from

National Records of Scotland (NRS) shows that life expectancy is decreasing in 17 of Scotland's 32 council areas for men and in 12 for women. Inequality is also getting worse, with those living in wealthier areas living significantly longer and healthier lives than those in more deprived areas. And in the area of mental health, figures published in 2019 show that the number of people being prescribed anti-depressants in Scotland had risen to close to one million—a 48 percent increase over the previous decade.

Assessing the overall state of the nation's health in early 2019 after more than a decade of SNP government, the then Chief Medical Officer for Scotland Harry Burns observed:

> Although these themes of prevention and narrowing inequalities have consistently featured in policy statements throughout the life of the parliament, it is difficult to find consistent evidence that policy intentions have produced effective action. Judged by premature mortality rate—the number of people dying before the age of 75—the overall average health of Scotland has improved. However, the gap in mortality between rich and poor has increased. Between 1997 and 2017, the premature mortality rate in the least deprived areas of Scotland fell by 43 percent. Relatively, inequalities in mortality have widened. The most deprived areas experienced a fall of only 21 percent. The gap in mental wellbeing also remains significant, with 24 percent of adults in the most deprived areas experiencing low wellbeing while only seven percent of those in affluent areas experienced similar problems.[8]

Social Care

Social care is another area where policy and practice in Scotland is often portrayed as being more progressive than policy south of the border. During the 2019 UK General Election campaign, for example, Nicola Sturgeon was able to argue that the policy of free personal care for older people, flagged up as one of the most radical in the UK Labour Party Manifesto, had already been in operation in Scotland for many years (albeit that the policy was introduced not under an SNP administration but by the Labour/ Liberal Democrat coalition Scottish government in 2002).

There are, however, important limitations to this policy. So, for example, the award of free personal care is not automatic but is subject to assessment by social work departments. Here, as elsewhere, eligibility criteria (jargon for whether or not you meet the requirements for care) have been tightened as local authority budgets have been cut. In practice, this means that what is regarded as 'free personal care' in one authority may be seen differently in another and may be subject to charges. A large number of respondents to a 2019 Scottish government consultative paper on social care expressed concern that the tightening of criteria meant that people were no longer eligible for support that previously would have been available to them and also that the criteria were currently being set at levels such that only 'critical' need was being addressed.[9]

Westminster-imposed austerity policies and the failure of local councils, both Labour and SNP-led, to resist these has also shaped the implementation of another key Scottish social care policy, namely Self-Directed Support (SDS), similar to what is termed in England 'personalisation'. Against a background of paternalist and institutional provision, it is not hard to see how SDS, a policy which purported to give people with long-term impairments, mental health problems and older people control over their own care budgets and allow them a choice in the services they receive, could seem attractive to those affected. The reality, however, has often proved to be very different from early promotional case studies that show people choosing to spend their money on season tickets for their favourite football team or buying a caravan by the sea! In practice, the policy has been used by local authorities as a means of saving money, for example by closing day centres for adults with learning impairments in the name of 'promoting independence' and putting greater pressure on hard-pressed families and 'informal carers' to take on an even greater caring role.[10]

The limitations of social care in Scotland, however, are not simply the product of a decade of austerity-driven cuts, however devastating as these have been. They also reflect the way in which the market continues to shape all areas of social care, not least residential care of older people, as the coronavirus crisis vividly highlighted in 2020-2021. Between 2007 and 2017, under the SNP's watch, the number of residents in older people care homes run by the private sector in Scotland rose by 6 percent while those in local authority/NHS homes fell by 24 percent and those in homes run by the voluntary sector decreased by 21 percent.[11] Many of these private homes are owned by the same financial institutions and hedge funds that dominate the market elsewhere in the UK, with headquarters often located in offshore tax havens such as the Cayman Islands. The result is that:

> Private operators have extracted tens of millions of pounds of public money dedicated to care as private profit—and even more has been extracted by 'flipping' property which is effectively paid for by the public (the biggest profits in the care sector come from property and not from providing care). This is all exacerbated not only by the power of private providers and the way they have influenced the decision-making of successive Scottish Governments but also by prevailing management culture which, by emphasising 'partnership working', make criticism of the system almost impossible.[12]

Nor have voluntary and not-for-profit care providers in Scotland escaped the pressures of the market. Since 1993, voluntary organisations, including those defined as 'not-for-profit', have been forced to compete with other voluntary organisations and also private organisations to win contracts. That has usually involved cutting staff wages and conditions and operating like private companies, leading to a race to the bottom in wages and conditions and, in some cases, closures. So, for example, in 2017, Bield, one of Scotland's biggest voluntary sector providers of older people care, announced the closure of all 12 of its residential care homes, a move affecting 167 elderly residents in 12 local authority areas, citing "financial pressures" and the need to develop "a new business model". Despite a vigorous campaign involving UNISON, the Social Work Action Network and carers' organisations, the homes were closed and residents transferred with no intervention whatsoever by the SNP government. [13]

However, the real cost of the SNP government's promotion of the private sector in the residential care of older people was most vividly exposed during the coronavirus crisis in the early months of 2020. A report in May 2020 by the investigative BBC journalist Mark Daly[14] and research by public health academic Allyson Pollock,[15] highlighted in detail the catalogue of mistakes made by the Scottish government which, by July 2020, had contributed to the deaths of just under 2,412 people in care homes, 46 percent of the total number of coronavirus deaths in Scotland.[16] These included discharging almost 800 older people from hospitals into care homes in March 2020 without testing for the virus, failing to provide adequate PPE for staff, and abandoning the policy of testing and tracing. But the most damning account of the whole episode was that from the former Head of Older People's Services in Glasgow City Council Nick Kempe in a report produced for the Common Weal Think Tank. The roots of this 'unmitigated disaster', Kempe argued, lay not only in the poor performance of the private residential care sector but also in what he called 'the neoliberal mindset' of the SNP government. His conclusion is worth quoting at length:

In 1993 the Community Care Act transferred responsibility for providing nursing care for Older People from the NHS to the private sector and for the first eight weeks of the crisis the Scottish Government was adamant that the Providers (and not the Scottish Government) were responsible for protecting care home residents—until a mid-May U-turn. This effectively represented the privatisation of the responsibility for Older People in Care during the crisis and had the later U-turn been made at the beginning many lives would have been saved. This meant that medical treatments which could have been delivered in Care Homes (such as the provision of oxygen) were not supported by the Scottish Government who left treatment to the discretion of private companies geared around property finance. In addition the nature of the deaths of Care Home residents was not taken to be a government responsibility and so the use of palliative measures (to make deaths as comfortable as possible) was also left to Providers. This almost certainly means many old people faced an absolutely unnecessarily uncomfortable and painful death. Health staff were not instructed to take the clinical lead in Care Homes until 17 May.[17]

Education

As with health and social care, there are some clear differences between education policy in Scotland and the policies pursued in recent decades firstly by New Labour and subsequently by Tory governments south of the border. Almost 96 percent of school-age children in Scotland, for instance, continue to attend comprehensive schools funded by their local authority. While 4.1 percent of children attend 'independent' (i.e. fee-paying) schools, unlike in England there has been no development of 'academies' in the sense of schools funded directly by central government but operating outside local authority control. Nor has there been an increase in the number of 'faith' schools (though of course state education in Scotland has historically been segregated on religious lines).

However, a heavy price is being paid in terms of low pay and work-related stress by frontline teachers in Scotland by the SNP's failure at both national and local government level to resist Westminster's austerity policies. The impact of that failure on teachers' health and wellbeing was well summed up in 2019 by Nicola Fisher, the then President of the main teachers' union, the EIS:

We calculate that teachers' pay in Scotland has fallen by 16 percent in real terms. This means teachers are worse off by hundreds of pounds a month. Ordinary people did not cause the financial crisis, but we are certainly footing the bill... Workload is the iceberg of the education system. People think they understand the scale of the problem because they can see the tip of it, but unless you are experiencing it day in and day out, you cannot hope to grasp the full horror which lurks beneath the surface. Teachers are working far in excess of their contracted hours, with some reports saying teachers are regularly working 50 or 60 hour weeks. Even then all the work isn't done. The effect this is having on teacher health and wellbeing is disastrous.[18]

Fisher's comments are backed up by a 2019 EIS survey of 12,000 teachers which found that over 75 percent frequently feel stressed as a result of their workload and that 70 percent "would not recommend teaching as a career".[19]

As regards further and higher education, in contrast to the largely privatised system now in operation south of the border which is highly dependent on student fees and research income, the bulk of funding in Scotland continues to come from the Scottish government (via the Scottish Funding Council). Nevertheless, the college education sector in particular has seen some of the most bitter and protracted struggles under the SNP's watch. The background to these struggles is that, in the 1990s, the Conservative UK government, which resented Labour's control of Scottish local councils, took further education colleges in Scotland out of local authority control through a process of 'incorporation'. This involved creating new, and virtually unaccountable, fiefdoms under the control of college principals. Over time this led to a chaotic situation where these principals, who often ran colleges as private companies, were paying themselves huge salaries and indulging in numerous maverick or vanity projects. National bargaining for staff in colleges was replaced by individual college bargaining. Scottish New Labour did nothing to oppose any of this.

After 2007, the SNP adopted a different approach. They wanted to end the chaos in FE, but, in the process, to make major savings of around £50 million through rationalisation. This led to a college merger process (termed 'regionalisation' and which took place mainly in 2013) that reduced the number of colleges dramatically and put government appointed Board Chairs in control. Instead of around 49 colleges there are now 29 regional colleges.

As a sop to the trade unions and to ensure a smooth transition for the mergers, the SNP government brought back national bargaining to replace the individual bargaining units of incorporated colleges. A (definitely unintended) consequence, however, was that weak college branches were merged with strong ones and, in 2016, the leadership was able to mount three effective strikes to win a single national pay scale, harmonise national conditions, and a national pay rise. It should be emphasised, however, that the considerable progress lecturers had made was the result of their own efforts. The SNP government tried on every occasion to let the employers' side take on and defeat the EIS, but when faced with the political embarrassment of strikes under their watch, stepped in each time to force the employers to concede and thus end the disputes.

Despite these victories, spending on the grossly inflated salaries of senior managers has not gone down while the hoped-for rationalisation has been achieved mainly through the loss of lecturer and support staff jobs (again, making workload pressures a major issue).

Poverty and inequality

As noted earlier, more than a decade of SNP government has done little to address the obscene levels of poverty and inequality which blight Scottish society. According to Scottish government figures for 2015-2018, just over one million people in Scotland are defined as poor (based on receiving less than 60 percent of the average income], including 240,000 children, 640,000 working-age adults and 150,000 pensioners. Therefore, almost one in five people, around 20 percent of the entire population, and one in four children live in poverty.[20]

Child poverty is one of the most important dimensions of poverty. After a decline in child poverty during the first decade of the century, it has steadily increased, in particular since 2013. Projected trends for the immediate future point to a further deterioration in the Scottish child poverty rate, with estimates showing that it is likely to be higher in 2023-24 than in 2016-17, reaching a 20-year high of 29 percent, meaning that a further 100,000 Scottish children will be locked in poverty.[21]

Such figures mask significant differences in poverty rates in and across Scotland: the extent and geographical spread of poverty remains highly uneven and unequal. Research conducted for the campaigning group End Child Poverty in early 2019 found 37 percent of children in Glasgow live in families who struggle with poverty. However, in some parts of the city, such as the Glasgow Southside Scottish Parliamentary Constituency, this reaches 46 percent. In contrast, in neighbouring (and much more prosperous and affluent) East Renfrewshire, the figure is 11 percent. [22]

The response of the SNP government has been to seek to mitigate the worst effects of poverty and the brutal benefits system, but only to a very limited extent. Thus, under the 2016 Scotland Act that followed the 2014 independence referendum vote, Holyrood was given additional powers over 11 benefits worth £3 billion, roughly 15 percent of social security spending north of the border. On that basis, in 2018, the Scottish government established a new agency, Social Security Scotland, and promised some reforms to the current system. These include a commitment to no contracting with the private sector in the agency's assessment model; increases in carers' allowance payments; and a Best Start Grant offering financial support to new parents on low incomes. Even these very timid reforms need to be put in perspective, however. For example, while there is some tinkering with the worst aspects of Universal Credit (for example, rent payments can now be made directly to landlords and the payment can be made fortnightly, not monthly) there has been no commitment to abolish this hated benefit. And having initially promised that the process of transferring claimants from the Department of Work and Pensions to the new Scottish Agency would be completed by 2021, the minister responsible has since confirmed that this is unlikely to happen before 2024.

Housing policy

Neoliberalism is at the heart of the SNP government's housing policy. Beginning in the early 1980s with Thatcher's assault on council housing and a 'dependency culture', which she claimed it fostered, public sector housing has been slashed by successive governments. Ever since devolution in 1997, every successive Holyrood administration has been a culprit in this process. Reduced in size, status and significance, council housing in Scotland is now 'social housing', marginalised into a pale imitation of what had been a cornerstone of the post-war Welfare State.

Throughout the last 40 years—both north and south of the border—public sector housing has been starved of investment and the great majority of council stock either demolished, sold off under the right to buy or transferred to large, unelected companies or housing associations. In Scotland, many of these associations were once smaller, genuinely community-based and wholly publicly funded. Increasingly, they have been transformed into fewer, larger 'housing businesses', reliant on private finance, rising rents and market forces. Once tenant-led, they are now managed and controlled by professional directors, rather than tenant committees. Over the same period, public subsidies have been increasingly redirected to speculative private house builders and the private rented sector, with both profiting enormously at the expense of the poorest and the most vulnerable. Under the guise of 'tenure diversification', 'shared ownership' and 'housing for first-time buyers', government subsidy to public rented housing has diminished relative to the public subsidy directed towards 'home-ownership'.

Post-war Europe was full of 'social housing' experiments, but none went further than Scotland's. By the early 1970s, council housing had become so dominant that only 30 percent of Scotland's dwellings were in owner-occupation. In England, by contrast, private home ownership still accounted for over half its total housing stock.[23] Neal Ascherson captures the real significance of those years:

> A subsidised way of life is a steady way of life, and contemptuous hindsight—the view from the other side of the free-market counter-revolution—is too easy. The withering of Labour's housing empire into a patchwork of urban ghettos governed like penal colonies did not become patent until the 1980s. Until then, for something like thirty years, Scottish working people were able, for the first time, to live in security and some comfort, with baths, inside toilets and enough room to allow basic privacy. They deserved no less and knew how to appreciate it. They had come from a far more terrible dependency, whose agents were tuberculosis, hunger, rickets and the rent collector. To write off the council house years as a mirage, as a doomed bid to escape from 'the real world' of market forces is contemptible. These years happened and on balance they were good. The fact that they have come to an end, having lasted for more than a generation, does not discredit them.[24]

By the advent of the Scottish parliament and the end of 18 years of Tory rule in 1997, things had changed dramatically for the worse. Rents had been de-regulated, only 25.3 percent of Scots lived in council housing, 5.7 percent lived in Housing Associations, 6.7 percent were tenants of private landlords and 62.3 percent were owner-occupiers. Most Scots looked to their new Edinburgh parliament to reverse the onslaught on public sector housing but they looked in vain.

In 2010, the SNP government accepted David Cameron's savage Tory cut to the Scottish Block Grant and then slashed the already miniscule Scottish social housing budget by an unprecedented 35 percent. First Minister Alex Salmond responded to the public outcry claiming it was not as bad as what had happened in England and Wales, where Cameron had cut the housing budget by 65 percent. Despite SNP promises, the most recent Scottish breakdown by housing tenure (2018) shows that the downward trend begun by Thatcher has continued regardless of who governed us. By 2018, the ratio of Scottish council tenants had fallen by over half the 1997 figure to 12.1 percent, while the percentage of Housing Association tenants had risen to 10.8 percent. In the same period, the number of private rented tenancies almost trebled to 14.2 percent. The percentage of owner-occupiers fell slightly to 59.1 percent.

According to the Scottish government's own figures, housing demand and rent rises have continued to accelerate and while rises in the private rented sector have been the most dramatic, they are significant in the social rented sector too. "Over the last decade the average weekly rent for social housing has increased by 13 percent in real terms, which is over and above general inflation."[25]

In Britain, unlike the US, council housing was designed to meet a general need and was available to anyone regardless of income. Such universality was never part of US public housing policy; it was marginal and intended only as a safety net for the poorest, contributing hugely to its shortcomings. The dismantling of the welfare state by Tory and Labour governments saw the proportion of council tenancies fall from 30 percent of all households in Britian in 1979 to eight percent by 2015, moving public housing provision here sharply towards the marginal, transient status of its US equivalent. The housing policies of both Westminster and Holyrood governments have been heading in this direction for some time, though the rate of travel towards the US model is slower in Scotland.

At any rate, demolishing social housing and forcing working class communities out of expensive inner city land is being ruthlessly promoted both sides of the Atlantic. So we see the gentrification of high value areas of cities in the US and Britain, where over-heated housing markets are transforming entire neighbourhoods. In 2015 at a London convention of global property developers looking to close deals in Britain property market, a whole host of big US companies were represented. The key discussion topic at this event was *The American Way*—a US template for large-scale institutional investment in private renting, whereby big US companies could expand into Britain. One aspect of this is the rash of speculative, exploitative, overcrowded housing developments for student accommodation in our inner cities.

The same sort of chicanery with private finance and private developers is happening here in Scotland. Groups of local tenants working with the grassroots tenants' body *Living Rent* are campaigning against the prospect of private gated communities being built at the expense of badly needed public sector housing for rent in the working class districts of Maryhill and Possilpark in north Glasgow. These are communities where large swathes of inter-war and post-war council housing were cleared and demolished without adequate replacement. Recently, local campaigners wrote about the housing crisis in *Bella Caledonia*:

> The private rented sector has grown and we know it has the lowest standards and the highest costs. In 2017/18 local housing association rents averaged £82.28 per week, 16 percent higher than local authority housing rents of £70.73 per week. The large-scale transfer of tenants from publicly accountable council housing to housing associations and private organisations like the Wheatley Group—the largest landlord in Scotland— has come at a considerable cost to the tenants.

When we look at last year's completions for the Affordable Housing Programme, roughly a third of all affordable housing constructed was for some form of owner-occupied housing or 'mid-market rent'— expensive rental properties run by housing companies and housing associations, which generally bar tenants from claiming benefits and where landlords perform background checks to ensure prospective tenants are high earners. This, allied to the huge amount of public subsidy for 'first-time buyers', is actually fanning the flames of the housing crisis. The problem is that 'homes for first time buyers' have become homes for first time sellers. The seller can pocket the difference in the rise in equity and access the property market, while those not on the ladder get priced out.[26]

These problems are not unique to Glasgow. The SNP claim credit for mitigating the Bedroom Tax in Scotland, but, once again, the reality is rather different. As with the example of the further education lecturers highlighted earlier in this chapter where prolonged industrial action was necessary to bring about improvements in conditions, so, too, it took a lengthy struggle by a militant Scotland-wide grassroots campaign to force the Scottish government to soften the impact of the tax through increasing the discretionary housing payment fund to compensate any household impacted by cuts in housing benefit introduced by the Tory/LibDem British coalition government.

It is on the back of limited reforms such as these, even when achieved only as a result of grassroots struggle in workplaces and communities, that the SNP leadership have been able to portray themselves as a progressive party and win support from a wider section of Scottish society beyond those identifying as nationalists. However, the fact that the SNP government is prepared to act pragmatically when it suits— or when it is forced to by strikes or public pressure—is no substitute for a consistent political commitment to protecting some of the most vulnerable members of Scottish society. During the 2020-2021 Covid-19 pandemic, for instance, SNP and Tory MPs together voted down a proposal from the Scottish Green Party to introduce a two-year rent freeze for tenants and an end to evictions on the basis of arrears accrued during the coronavirus emergency period.

In relation to income and wealth inequalities, Scotland remains a massively divided and unequal society, a society in which wealth and high incomes bring prestige, authority and political power. The centralisation, ownership and control of land in the hands of a few wealthy families and individuals, which has long been and remains a scourge of Scotland, brings enormous power and influence over policy making in Scotland.[27] Together with the other sections of Scotland's ruling class, including large companies, banks and assorted corporate and private agencies, this power is exercised against the interests of the vast majority of people living in Scotland today. Such 'vested interests' are rarely questioned, let alone challenged by SNP governments.

One study has claimed that inequality in Scotland in 2018 was higher than it was in 2008. Importantly, this account highlights different aspects and consequences of inequality, not just income and wealth.[28] However, the authors argue that income inequality has increased in Scotland in recent years. These claims are in line with other research from Oxfam Scotland in 2018, which highlights that Scotland's wealth inequality is "out of control"[29] with the richest one percent having more wealth than the bottom half of the population combined.[30] A 2016 Oxfam report shows that the four richest Scottish families alone were wealthier than the most deprived 20 percent of the population combined.

The *Sunday Times Rich List* for 2019 claimed that Scotland's richest were worth £35 billion, highlighting that "Caledonia's gold coast turns out to be the east, with Moray's distillers, Dundee's gamers, Aberdeen's oil—and the capital's tycoons".[31] Not only are the wealthiest sections of Scotland's population already hugely wealthy and rich, their wealth is increasing. Scotland's top 11 billionaires were worth around £17.2 billion in 2019, an increase of over £1 billion on 2018 alone.[32]

The question of land ownership has been a major issue in Scotland for several hundred years, and it remains so. While there have been some policy interventions from SNP governments allowing community buyouts and an expansion of community ownership, we are still faced with a hugely unequal distribution of land ownership. A report in 2019 by the Scottish government agency the Scottish Land Commission found that around 1,200 owners, including public bodies such as the National Trust for Scotland, owned 70 percent of Scotland's rural land. Included here are the huge tracts of land owned by the Duke of Buccleuch and overseas owners such as the Danish billionaire Anders Povlsen. The Scottish Land Commission estimates that 57 percent of rural land is privately owned, with 1.25 percent owned by public agencies and a mere 3 percent under community ownership.[33]

Green MSP for the Lothians Andy Wightman has been to the fore in researching the pattern of land ownership in Scotland, both historically and today. His work has been instrumental in uncovering the extent of inequality in ownership, something that Scotland's powerful elite would rather was kept in the dark. His research has calculated that around 50 percent of all private land in Scotland is owned by only 432 families.[34]

While the huge inequities in land ownership are important in their own right, what is also significant, if not more so, is that land ownership brings more wealth and it allows vested interests a powerful say in many different aspects of Scottish society. It allows landowners to evade some of the rules and regulations by which many non-landowning folks in Scotland are expected to abide; to influence and shape planning and development policies and to resist demands for different patterns of ownership. Land ownership confers power well beyond that which should be acceptable in any so-called democracy. Scotland has the unenviable position as one of the world's most unequal societies when it comes to patterns of land ownership. This is socially corrosive, socially harmful and undermines policies which, the SNP claim, seek to make Scotland a fairer place. Despite their claims to be addressing such issues, the SNP is very reluctant to take on wealthy landowners. [35]

The SNP: what kind of party?

While electoral considerations, above all the need to make inroads into largely Labour-controlled West and Central Scotland, were the main factor behind the SNP's 'social democratic turn' under Alex Salmond's leadership in the early 2000s, the minor reforms and symbolic gestures discussed above have nonetheless contributed to a perception of the SNP as a progressive centre-left party. That process has been aided, of course, by the contrast with successive Conservative British governments, intent on imposing brutal austerity policies, and a pro-unionist Scottish Labour Party which has offered no strategy for opposing these policies. The SNP's commitment to social change, however, is a very limited one. For a start, the SNP is a *nationalist* party. Central to its ideology is the belief that all those who were born in or who live in Scotland—from the billionaire owner of Stagecoach Brian Souter to the lone parent in a council flat in Glasgow's Drumchapel housing estate—are members of a common Scottish national community and share an identity and interest which overrides divisions such as class.

While the SNP's brand of 'civic nationalism', even with all its limitations, is preferable to the racist and xenophobic nationalism of right-wing populists like Nigel Farage, Donald Trump in the US or Victor Orban in Hungary, it remains problematic. While nationalism can be a progressive force where it involves uniting an oppressed nation against an oppressor nation (with resistance to British oppression in Ireland being the nearest and most obvious example) as Chapter 1 in this book makes clear, Scotland is not and never has been an oppressed nation. The implications of that 'civic nationalism' for the SNP's willingness and capacity to

*Glasgow mass protest
at US President Donald
Trump's visit to Scotland
July 2018*

bring about real change in Scottish society, especially when combined with the Party's commitment to electoralism, were well-summed up by the Paisley & Renfrewshire South SNP MP Mhairi Black:

> I get the SNP has that wee string of neoliberalism through it and that kind of Edinburgh pandering to banks and to businesses, and stuff like that, and I get that I'm totally the opposite. I think it's almost like I'm a micro example of what the SNP is as a party in that you've got Karl Marx in one corner and then you've got somebody who's basically got a conservative point of view in the other and the two of us argue it out and by the time that's done, we reach something that's pretty digestible for most people and that is the SNP.[36]

As well as highlighting the ways in which the SNP's nationalism blunts and obscures the central division in Scottish society—class—Black's comments also point to a second core component of SNP ideology and politics which sets clear limits on its claim to be a progressive party—namely, 'the wee string of neoliberalism' or the Party's embrace, usually tacit but sometimes explicit, of market-driven capitalism. This should not come as a surprise and nor is it just 'a wee string'. Both Nicola Sturgeon and her predecessor, Alex Salmond, have always been at pains to emphasise that SNP governments pose no threat to 'business' and to powerful capitalist interests in Scotland. Salmond was, after all, a former Royal Bank of Scotland economist with many friends in the corporate world (including Rupert Murdoch) while Sturgeon, in an interview with the *Financial Times* shortly after her election as leader, reassured companies that they had "nothing to fear" from her government.[37] But perhaps the clearest evidence of the SNP's acceptance of capitalism and of neoliberal 'common sense' came in 2018 in the form of the Sustainable Growth Commission Report.

The Sustainable Growth Commission

*Scotland—the new case for optimism: a strategy for inter-generational economic renaissanc*e (also known as the Sustainable Growth Commission Report), was published in May 2018.[38] The Report was commissioned by Nicola Sturgeon in 2016 and its principal author, appointed by Sturgeon, was Andrew Wilson, another former Royal Bank of Scotland economist and former SNP MSP. Its recommendations, with some amendments, were accepted by the SNP's annual conference on 27 April 2019. The Report was commissioned as a response to the defeat of the Yes side in the 2014 independence referendum. As far as the SNP leadership was concerned, a major contributory factor to that defeat was then First Minister Alex Salmond's failure to give a clear account of what currency would be employed in an independent Scotland, especially if the UK Treasury were to reject SNP proposals for a currency union. More specifically, it was argued, the key audience whom Salmond had failed to convince was the Scottish business community. The Yes campaign may have won many of Scotland's working class housing schemes in 2014, one SNP insider is said to have quipped, but post-Brexit, it had to win the boardrooms.[39]

An alternative explanation for the defeat is that it was only in the final stages of the campaign when Salmond moved *away* from the currency issue and focused instead on the material issues affecting the lives of the majority of Scottish people—austerity, low pay, the NHS—most notably in his second television debate with ex New Labour Minister and leading light in the 'Better Together' campaign, Alastair Darling, that support for the Yes side increased significantly but by then it was too late to secure victory.[40]

Both the SNP leadership and Andrew Wilson saw things very differently, however, and the Report is best understood as a document intended to reassure the Scottish business establishment (as well as the international financial markets) of the fiscal moderation and economic competence of an

SNP-led government in an independent Scotland.

Thus, the Commission was composed entirely of what Wilson calls the 'experts'—mainly SNP politicians, academics and businesspeople. There was no representation whatsoever from Scottish civil society organisations, whether NGOs, community organisations or the biggest civil society organisation in Scotland, the trade union movement.

In terms of the content of the Report, any suggestion that there might be an alternative to the neoliberal capitalism which failed so dismally in the crash of 2008, resulting in the austerity policies which the SNP leadership so regularly denounce, is completely absent. Instead, in an example of what Mark Fisher called 'capitalist realism'[41] and Antonio Gramsci called 'common sense' (in the sense of the uncritical adoption of ruling-class ideas),[42] the Report's authors assume, with no apparent need for further explanation, that capitalism is the only show in town, to the extent that even the terms 'capitalism' and 'neoliberalism', let alone 'socialism' or 'social democracy', never appear in the report. Instead its authors' central argument is that:

Scotland should be seeking to emulate the performance of the best small countries in the world, rather than sticking to its current position as the best of the rest of the UK regions and nations outside of the south east of England.[43]

Economic growth is understood and represented as a technical economic issue rather than a political or ideological issue. And despite the fact that the gap between rich and poor has increased in Scotland, any notion of class division or class conflict is completely absent from the report. Instead the key concept is 'partnership':

Partnership is needed to ensure that our strategic approach is cross partisan, intergenerational and purposeful. This will mean government, business, trade unions and wider civic society working in concert.[44]

Two of the Report's recommendations in particular caused anger and concern among the party's left-wing. Firstly, the Report's answer to the currency issue, which caused so much grief in the 2014 independence campaign, was to recommend that "the currency of an independent Scotland should remain the pound sterling for a possibly extended transition period".[45] The rationale for that decision was "the necessity to maximise certainty and stability, and to minimise risks". At the same time, the Commission recognised that this would mean that "the Scottish Government would not secure monetary policy sovereignty in the initial period following an independence vote though the Scottish Government would not be in a formal monetary union". This would mean that for an extended period (some have suggested a period of up to ten years), the Scottish economy would be subject to monetary policy set by the Bank of England, as well as being subject to that Bank's regulatory framework. In other words, this would be independence in name only. The fact that an amendment to the Commission was unanimously passed by the 2019 SNP conference pledging to introduce an independent currency 'as soon as practicable' is hardly likely to alter that timescale.

A second key recommendation of the Commission—and one which sent shock waves through large swathes of the SNP membership—was its proposal to reduce the spending deficit by limiting public spending to a percentage of GDP, effectively keeping austerity in place for at least a decade. Again, this is hardly the 'independence' that hundreds of thousands have marched for before and since 2014. And, in fact, it could be even worse. According to the former left-wing SNP MP and journalist George Kerevan:

> Scottish productivity and growth rates would be tied
> to England's unless—and this is key—we were to try

to reduce wage costs directly through a combination of austerity and liberal market labour 'reforms'.

By way of reassurance, however, Kerevan adds:

The latter would be rejected by the SNP rank and file and—to give Andrew Wilson his due—the Growth Commission report explicitly rejects austerity.[46]

Kerevan's suggestion that resistance by the party membership would prevent the introduction by a future SNP government of austerity and labour market 'reforms' seems optimistic. In reality, as generations of British Labour Party supporters have found, as did supporters of Syriza in Greece in 2015, when the international markets turn the screw on would-be reformist governments to cut wages, pensions and benefits, then the views of the Party rank-and-file expressed in conferences, elections and referendums tend to count for little.[47] And there is nothing in the SNP's record to suggest that an SNP government would respond any differently to these pressures than did those governments which were at least initially committed to radical socialist change.

On the contrary, the Report's authors do not seem to see being dictated to by global markets and institutions as a problem, since they also argue that "The discipline of international competition can also help to drive innovation and new ways of working".[48]

While many on the left of the Party responded with anger to the Report's recommendations, others were more sanguine. As former SNP MP and Deputy Leader Jim Sillars acidly commented:

Would you condemn a duck because it produced a duckling? Of course not. Neither should we condemn the SNP Sustainable Growth Commission because it produced a middle-of-the-road, cautious, business-influenced report. The SNP is not a socialist party. It has some in its ranks, but Commission Chairman Andrew Wilson has never claimed to be one of them. To expect the party and he to appoint Commissioners equipped with left-wing ideology, and produce a left inclined report, was asking for what was not possible. The duck produced a duckling.[49]

Following the Nordic Model?

As discussed previously, the remit of the Commission was to explore ways in which Scotland could "emulate the performance of the best small countries in the world". Many SNP activists and other left-wing supporters of independence, including the Greens, have long held up 'the Nordic model'—the societies of Denmark, Norway, Sweden and Finland—as exemplars of what an independent Scotland could look like. The journalist and independence campaigner Lesley Riddoch, for instance, in her 2018 book *Blossom: What Scotland Needs to Flourish*, argues:

> Nordic society is a different world—and a successful one, as their top places in every international league table of productivity, well-being, health and GDP tend to demonstrate... So while we have had 'us versus them', a rampant market in every area of life and a disempowering centralised state as the only bulwark against cut-throat competition, the Nordics have been able to resist the hollow temptation of Get Rich Quick and have performed rather better.[50]

While the authors of the Growth Commission Report also flag up the achievements of the Nordic countries, their preference is for a 'hybrid' model based on Denmark, Finland and New Zealand.

The inclusion of New Zealand, in particular, is significant since it highlights the Commission's neoliberal leanings. Wilson and his co-authors lavish praise on New Zealand as an example of a country,

...that has implemented change [and] reformed its economy extensively in the 1980s and early 1990s, placing it on a stronger footing. It has performed well over the past 20 years, including in the post-crisis period, with growth rates frequently above 3 percent.[51]

A rather different take on the changes that took place during these earlier decades is offered in a 2017 article in *Jacobin* magazine:

Through the 1980s and 1990s—first under Labour, then under National Party rule—New Zealand ushered in neoliberal reform on an unprecedented scale. Controls on wages, prices, rents, interest rates, and more were scrapped. Finance markets were deregulated, and restrictions on foreign investment were removed or relaxed. Based on the belief that welfare helped create unemployment by encouraging dependency, the system was overhauled in ways that the government's own *official encyclopaedia* describes as "particularly swift and severe".[52]

Nor do the Nordic countries offer a model for a different kind of Scotland. Even putting to one side the very different circumstances and policies which made possible their economic growth in earlier decades (including in Norway's case the creation of a huge oil fund which acted as a buffer following the 2008 crash), the implementation of neoliberal policies in all these countries since the early 1990s, involving the usual mix of privatisation, deregulation, and cuts to welfare provision, has led to a situation where, for example, relative poverty and inequality has increased more in Sweden than in any other country in the OECD. According to Swedish academic Jessica Jonsson:

Following the neoliberal changes in the 1980s and the financial crises in the 1990s, comprehensive neoliberal reforms have been continued both by social democratic (1998-2006) and right-wing governments (1990-98, 2006-14). De-regulations and re-regulations of the welfare state have led to new forms of 'governance'... by introducing managerialism, privatisation and cuts in welfare provisions. Such changes have resulted in increasing socio-economic inequalities, discrimination and social problems in Sweden.[53]

A 2018 collection of papers by critical social work and social policy academics from across the four Nordic countries shows that the experience in Denmark, Finland and Norway is very similar.[54] And most concerningly, that similarity now extends to the growth of far-right movements, political parties and xenophobic policies in all of the Nordic countries.

The erosion of the welfare state and growing poverty and inequality has fuelled the growth of far-right parties such as the Progress Party in Norway (which has 26 MPs) and to the adoption in Denmark of some of the most draconian asylum legislation in Europe, including an Act in 2019, supported by the government, the far-right Danish People's Party and (disgracefully) the Social Democrats, which "shifts the focus" from integration of refugees to repatriation, a policy which neo-Nazi parties like the National Front and the British National Party in Britain have been seeking for decades and one which would be wholeheartedly rejected by most SNP and non-SNP members alike.

Conclusion

The SNP's commitment to neoliberal capitalism, as reflected in its support for the recommendations of the Sustainable Growth Commission Report, gives us an indication of what an independent Scotland under its leadership would look like. But if more proof were needed, then look no further than the Scottish government's response to the issue of rebuilding the Scottish economy in the wake of the 2020-2021 coronavirus crisis.

Once again, a committee of 'experts' was set up to advise

the government, with Sturgeon appointing as chair on this occasion one Benny Higgins. This is not a name with which most people will be familiar but, like Andrew Wilson and Alex Salmond before him, Higgins was previously a senior manager in the Royal Bank of Scotland (until 2005 part of the same team as the disgraced Fred Godwin and George Matthewson) and subsequently the CEO of Tesco Bank. In 2019, he became chairman of the Duke of Buccleuch's estates company, responsible for managing the extensive portfolio of property and land owned by the family. The current Duke of Buccleuch, Richard Scott, the 10th Duke, is the largest private landowner in Scotland, with some 280,000 acres (1,100 km²), as well as being chairman of the Buccleuch Group, a holding company with interests in commercial property, rural affairs, food and beverages. That the First Minister appointed as her most senior economic adviser the person in charge of the estates of the largest private landowner in Scotland, a country in which 0.008% of the population owns more than half the land, speaks volumes about the depth of the SNP's commitment to addressing the inequalities of Scottish society.

Coming from a committee chaired by such a prominent member of the Scottish—and British—ruling class, its central message, contained in the Scottish Government's report, *Towards a Robust, Resilient Wellbeing Economy for Scotland: Report of the Advisory Group on Economic Recovery* published in June 2020, should come as no surprise:

> We must seize the opportunity for a process of national renewal. Business in Scotland should be at the centre of this renewal. And since Scotland cannot thrive if it is not back to work, and since over 70 percent of Scots work in the private sector, Scottish businesses must lie at the heart of our recovery plan.

As others have done, the Higgins Committee calls for a 'new deal' but in this case a new deal of a particular type:

We must seize the opportunity for a process of national renewal, with economic recovery underpinned by a new deal with business.[55]

And the Committee's proposed mechanism for ensuring that process of national renewal? A "top-level Council of Business Advisers" to decide on economic priorities. It does not take a great deal of imagination to imagine whose interests would come first for such a Council.

The publication in February 2021 of the *Report of the Independent Review of Social Care in Scotland* highlighted a crisis in social care provision in Scotland and in the process further exposed the realities of care work that lies behind the SNP's rhetoric.[56] Set up by Sturgeon in September 2020 following 1,800 coronavirus-related deaths in Scottish care homes during the first wave of the pandemic that year, the review points to a reliance on private sector provision and an 'undervalued workforce'. But it also draws attention to the estimated 700,000 unpaid care workers, an overwhelmingly female workforce that is larger than paid health and social care support workforces combined. The value of unpaid care in Scotland is estimated at over £36 billion a year. For comparison, in 2019, the NHS Scotland budget was £13.4 billion.

The massive contribution that such unpaid labour provides for the reproduction of Scottish society should not be underestimated—there are few, if any, areas of life that are not supported by such work. However, the burden of this caring work has fallen more and more on unpaid and paid carers in recent years, not least on the back of austerity policies, cuts in benefits, in public services and amenities— accompanied by the reduction in the numbers of paid workers, and the intensification of work and poorer conditions for those remaining in paid employment.

SNP politicians have spoken warmly about the role of carers and their overall contribution to economic and social life in contemporary Scottish society. Yet for those in paid care employment, a sector dominated by private providers, pay levels are generally low and working conditions are unattractive. There has been no commitment on the part of the Scottish government to paying all care workers a living wage. Only through the nationalisation of social care will the standards of care for those in need of care greatly increase and the conditions of employment for all care workers improve.

Throughout this discussion, as well as in other chapters in this collection, the inability of the SNP to comprehend this, never mind enact policies that would pursue such goals, blows a very large hole in its rhetoric about inclusiveness, fairness and equality. It shares with the other main political parties a particular blind-spot when it comes to the conditions of hard-pressed public-sector workers—as is reflected in the numerous disputes across the sector in Scotland since 2007—as well as the huge burden shouldered by the army of unpaid workers. It is this which exposes the SNP as entirely within a neoliberal, pro-market tradition.

The break-up of the British state which Scottish independence would entail is something that would be welcomed by anti-imperialists everywhere. But for many of us who voted Yes in the 2014 referendum and who have marched for independence across Scotland in the period since, independence by itself is not the end goal. Rather, independence would provide the opportunity to reject Tory policies of austerity, privatisation and racism and to build a different kind of society, free from poverty, inequality and oppression. Without that vision, James Connolly's comments on Irish independence would apply no less to an independent Scotland:

> If you remove the English Army tomorrow and hoist the green flag over Dublin Castle, unless you set about the organisation of the Socialist Republic your efforts will be in vain. England will still rule you. She would rule you through her capitalists, through her landlords,

through her financiers, through the whole array of commercial and individualist institutions she has planted in this country and watered with the tears of our mothers and the blood of our martyrs.[57]

Both the SNP's record in office over more than a decade and their ideological reliance on advisers like Higgins suggests that, in any independent Scotland under their rule, these same Scottish and global capitalists, landlords and financiers would remain very much in charge.

Chapter 9

Scottish Independence: Beyond the Limitations of Nationalism

Bob Fotheringham

> Will we open up the borders
> Tear down the prison walls
> Declare that no one is illegal
> Watch the giant as it falls
> (From *No One is Illegal* by David Rovics)

The Scottish National Party is not known for its great intellectual tradition.[1] Travelling light ideologically has provided it with certain advantages. For a large part of its existence, the SNP presented itself as an alternative to the Tories and Labour, drawing support mainly from Protestant non-manual, salaried workers while being largely looked on with suspicion by Catholic voters in the West, who traditionally voted Labour. In the 1970s, they tried to form a coalition with the Liberals in Westminster in the hope of winning support away from the two big parties. Moving from the periphery to the centre of the political process after the establishment of the Scottish Parliament, the SNP then went out of its way to win Catholic votes by pledging support for Catholic education.[2]

In 1974, the SNP declared itself to be a social democratic

party.[3] With no attachment to the trade unions or organised workers, this was very much a watered-down version of social democracy. It could contain within its ranks committed socialists and anti-union businessman Brian Souter. It could declare that it was in favour of social justice while supporting a template for the economy based on the low-tax Irish model of the "Celtic Tiger".

An honourable exception to this was Stephen Maxwell, who, in a series of articles, pamphlets and books, eloquently put the case for what he described as "left-wing nationalism". Maxwell was a member of the 79 Group and was expelled from the party in 1982 along with other members of the group. He was later readmitted, but his thinking rarely fitted with mainstream SNP policy and philosophy and he remained essentially a party outsider until his death in 2012.

One of Maxwell's greatest strengths was to put class at the centre of the argument for Scottish independence.[4] For him, independence had to deal with the social and economic needs of the Scottish working class, and he looked to them for their support. He rejected the traditional idea of nationalism and the need to build a cross-class consensus.

For Maxwell, Scotland's weak middle class meant that it was only workers who had the interest and wherewithal to break apart the failing British state. At the time when the case for "left-wing nationalism" was formulated, around the late 1970s and early 1980s, the majority of male workers in Scotland were still employed in manual jobs. He later recognised that the 79 Group did not pay sufficient attention to other areas of working class "radical dissent" such as the women's movement and environmental issues. Nevertheless, given the developments around the 2014 Scottish independence referendum and the subsequent support for the SNP by working class communities across Scotland, it has to be acknowledged that in this regard Stephen Maxwell essentially got it right.

Another asset was his commitment to social justice and the need for independence to deal with Scotland's structural issues of poverty and inequality. It is more than a little ironic that in 2020, after 10 years of the SNP in government, with significant powers which now include full control of income tax, levels of poverty and inequality in Scotland have actually got worse.

Maxwell was never a great admirer of "social democracy" as practiced by the Labour Party. He opposed its strong centralising tendency and counterposed "community socialism" as an alternative political strategy. In one regard, he had a point. While the post-war Labour Government carried out important reforms such as the creation of the NHS and the Welfare State, this was done in a top down manner without working class communities having any real say in the processes and outcomes. One example of this is the post-war council housing boom across Britain. While the motivation was to move working class families from slum living conditions into modern accommodation at affordable rents, the outcome in some cases was disastrous, with communities split apart and the housing stock built less than adequate.

Maxwell, to his credit, was never a great believer in the myths that sustain much of the political aspirations of the nationalist movement in Scotland, whether it was the myth of English domination or that Scotland is intrinsically egalitarian and radical. For him the case for Scottish independence was based on the potential improvement it offered for the people of Scotland today and in the future, not the past.

However, ultimately, we have to reject Maxwell's nationalism. His book, *Arguing for Independence,* published in 2012, ends up putting the very compromise arguments which he rejected as part of the 79 Group. In the end, the lure of nationalism proved a greater pull than that of socialism and working class emancipation.[5]

A contemporary of Maxwell, who was, and remains, a major influence on the thinking of left-wing nationalism in Scotland is Tom Nairn. On the surface, they have much in common. Both came from the left and presented the case for nationalism and Scottish independence in a positive light. In other respects, they are radically different. Nairn started out as a "Marxist" and internationalist, which Maxwell never was. Nairn has spent most of his life as an academic working in England and presenting his case in the pages of publications such as *New Left Review* and the *London Review of Books*. Maxwell, on the other hand, was a political activist whose arguments flowed from the need to help develop a movement and programme which could lead directly to Scottish independence.

Nairn put forward two basic arguments which concern us here. The first is that Britain never had a fully-fledged bourgeois revolution and that as a consequence the decline of British capitalism in the 20th century stemmed not from its failure to compete effectively but rather that it was not capitalist enough.[6] Secondly, rejecting what he characterises as "hollowed out Marxism" and the "fossilised remains of internationalism", Nairn argued that the natural response of people to globalisation and the advance of capitalism across the world was to look to nationalism and the creation of their own state as the way forward.[7] The age of the "body builder" had ended and while smaller was not necessarily better it could, at least, do no worse, and freed from "the muscle and hidebound" could provide smaller states with the occasional advantage.[8] As a consequence, and because of books such as *The Break-Up of Britain*, Nairn's ideas were highly influential among those on the left who looked to Scottish independence as a way of dealing with the effects of Britain's industrial decline and its impact on Scotland.

Let's start by making a concession. There have been far too many compromises by the left historically to the claim that Britain must stay a unified country if working class interests are to be advanced. This can be presented as the need for unity, through for example a strong trade union movement. Or that in the world of international capitalism, effective reforms can only take place if workers are part of a larger entity such as the United Kingdom. The result of this for some on the left in Britain is to characterise those putting the case for Scottish independence as "backward nationalists" while failing to acknowledge their own compromise with British nationalism.

However, there remain a number of major problems with Nairn's work. While democracy and the British state certainly do not work for the vast majority of its people, that certainly cannot be said for capitalists, either in Britain or internationally. The UK remains, despite all its weaknesses, the world's fifth biggest economy. If tomorrow the monarchy was abolished, the House of Lords done away with and a federal structure established with considerable powers to regional governments, as Nairn argued, it is difficult to understand, without effective economic reforms, what would actually change. To put it crudely, how would a modernised British state, in and of itself, deal with zero hours contracts, offshore tax havens and structuralised inequality? Around the world various different political systems exist to manage and run countries with different forms of state structure. Are they any better than the UK? Are the American political system or French governmental structures, or Brazilian or Indian for that matter, any better than the British?

The Break-Up of Britain was first published in 1977. Since then, much has changed, including the collapse of the Soviet Union, the disintegration of the pro-Soviet eastern bloc, the Balkan wars, the emergence and retreat of the "Pink Tide" governments in Latin America, and the threat to the Spanish and British state by Catalan and Scottish nationalist movements respectively. There is now plenty of evidence against which to assess the validity of Nairn's argument.

The disintegration of Yugoslavia with Bosnia as its centrepiece, which led to the Balkan wars in 1991 to 1995 ,generated ethnic cleansing on a massive scale. While the main protagonists were the Bosnian Serbs, consisting mainly of former Yugoslavian army units and backed by Serb nationalists throughout the region, none of the different ethnic groups in the area came out of the conflict with a great deal of credit.[9] In the former eastern bloc, nationalist and right-wing governments are in power in Hungary and Poland, with far-right and even fascist parties making advances across Europe. Now, Nairn is quite well aware of the potential dangers of nationalism. As someone who was born in the 20th century, which witnessed two world wars and the horrors of the holocaust, it would be impossible for it to be otherwise. For him, however, nationalism was the modern version of the Roman God Janus, who "stood above gateways with one face looking forward and one backwards". Yet still, "there are two kinds of nationalism. The main, essentially healthy sort we applaud...".[10]

If we examine a type of nationalism that Nairn would applaud—the Scottish variety—how successful has it been in meeting its ultimate goal? The SNP's record is far from convincing. Let's leave aside its record in government and instead look at its capacity to win actual independence. It has been elected as the Scottish Government three times since 2007, when it first formed a minority administration. In 2014, an inspiring referendum campaign led to a close vote. The campaign itself gained momentum and found inspiration from the grassroots of the movement and the closeness of the vote happened almost despite the SNP, not because of it. Since then, support for independence in Scotland has remained high. Scotland continues to be politically hostile to Tory governments. Yet the country in many ways seems as far away as ever from gaining actual outright independence, despite the fact there is a huge popular movement in the country in support of it.

And if we look at what the SNP actually mean by independence—keep the monarchy, keep the pound, join another neoliberal club (the European Union), join NATO—then to what extent does the SNP's vision of sovereignty amount to actual independence? Nairn stated that "nationalism was Marxism's biggest failure". Perhaps we should turn this back on him; is it not the case that Scottish independence is nationalism's biggest failure?

Nairn counterposes class and nationality, with the latter seen as normal and the natural way of things. In one sense, this is incontestable. Marx understood "that the ideas in any society are the ideas of the ruling class". In a world in which capitalism operates through borders and national states, it is not surprising that the workers identify with their own nation and country. Globalisation in many ways has strengthened this.

For countless years, the working class in Scotland largely voted Labour. In doing so, they identified with a party which looked to provide reforms in the interest of its working class supporters. But the Labour Party also defended the interests of the British state. Labour's pitch has always been about the fact that a Labour government would govern in the best interests of the country. At times of crisis such as the Second World War, the Falklands war in the early 1980s and the financial crash of 2008/09, Labour came to the aid of the British state and British capitalism. By voting Labour in large numbers, workers in Scotland identified with British nationalism. The fact that they could also maintain a Scottish identity did not contradict this.

Support for independence grew in Scotland because of disillusionment with the neoliberal policies of austerity and cuts from successive British governments and what has become known as the "democratic deficit" of voting Labour and ending up with a Tory government in Westminster. This does not mean that Scottish nationalism is completely absent from support for independence in Scotland. But it does mean that its main driving force is class-based dissatisfaction with how Britain is governed. This paradox is no mystery to Marxists. The Italian revolutionary Antonio Gramsci identified that workers could have what he describes as a "contradictory consciousness"— one that is progressive and class conscious and another that is backward and reactionary.[11]

The active man-in-the-mass has a practical activity, but has no clear theoretical consciousness of his practical activity, which nonetheless involves understanding the world in so far as it transforms it. His theoretical consciousness can indeed be historically in opposition to his activity. One might almost say that he has two theoretical consciousnesses (or one contradictory consciousness): one which is implicit in his activity and which in reality unites him with all his fellow workers in the practical transformation of the real world; and one, superficially explicit or verbal, which he has inherited from the past and uncritically absorbed.

So, in the independence movement in Scotland, workers can identify with nationalism and a romanticised and inaccurate view of Scottish history as well as the need to defend the National Health Service and nationalise public services. Workers can be members and supporters of the SNP while at the same time being members of a trade union prepared to act, sometimes against the Scottish Government, as was the case with the Scottish teachers' dispute in 2019, to improve their pay and conditions.

Catalonia—the lessons for Scotland

The example of the Catalan Independence referendum of 2017 holds important lessons for the movement in Scotland.[12] This was a vote that took place in the face of massive opposition from the Spanish state and would not have happened without a vibrant popular movement pushing the Catalan nationalists into confrontation with the Spanish Government.

For many years, the question of independence for Catalonia was a marginal issue with the majority of people happy to go along with the limited autonomy provided by the Spanish state after the fall of the Franco regime. Two issues brought the question to the fore. The first was the judgment by the Spanish Constitutional Court to overturn a decision made with the support of the Spanish Socialist Party (PSOE) to extend self-government in Catalonia in 2006. This made basic democratic rights an issue and led to demonstrations of over one million in Barcelona. A series of non-binding local referendums across the region then developed support and passion for Catalan independence. The response of the right-wing Catalan nationalist leaders was to prevaricate and avoid confrontation with the Spanish state.

The second element in the development of the movement was the impact of austerity and cuts on working class communities in Spain after the crash of 2008/9. The reaction in Catalonia was particularly strong, with mass support for the 15 May movement to occupy the central squares of Spain. This meant increased support in Catalonia for left-wing organisations such as Podemos and the Republican Left and also found expression in support for Catalan independence.

The Catalan Nationalists did not win an outright majority during the 2015 election but formed a coalition with the Republican Left. They also looked to the Popular Unity Candidacy, known as the CUP, a Catalan left-wing anti-capitalist party, to help form a government. This, along with a series of massive demonstrations, led directly to a decision by the Catalan Government to hold the illegal 2017 referendum. The belief was that the Spanish Government would eventually acquiesce and agree to allow a vote. This did not happen, and it was only pressure from the grassroots movement, who effectively organised the actual ballot, that ensured a referendum materialised.

Unfortunately, the Catalan Government was completely unprepared for the response from the Spanish Government, who sent 10,000 Spanish troops and police to try to stop the vote taking place. The fact that the poll happened and that 92 percent voted in favour with a turnout of 43 percent was testament to the remarkable bravery and commitment of the Catalan people. In the aftermath of the vote, the Spanish Government refused to negotiate and arrested eight leading Catalan politicians, who were subsequently given long prison sentences. An arrest warrant was also issued for the President of the Catalan Parliament, Carles Puigdemont, who fled to Belgium.[13]

Despite the strength of the movement on the streets, there was little understanding by Catalan politicians regarding how to deal with the brutal reaction of the Spanish state. For some this has led to the belief that Spain has essentially remained unreformed from the days of Franco and that the fascist state remains. This is untrue. While aspects of Franco's regime remain, the state in Spain is one which has evolved to run capitalism and operates in a way that suits the class it represents.

Those who believed that the European Union would provide some form of support for the democratic rights of the Catalans have been sadly disappointed. At all times the EU have been fully supportive of the Spanish government. If Scotland as an independent country was to apply for membership, this could well be blocked by Spain because of the potential impact on the situation in Catalonia.[14]

There are also important lessons for the left. In Catalonia there was not sufficient attention paid to the need to develop support from organised workers. Positive examples of this were the refusal of dockers in Barcelona to allow food to be supplied to Spanish troops and police billeted in ships at the port, and firefighters defending demonstrators from being attacked by the police in 2017. Many workers in Catalonia are Spanish speaking and migrated to the region from other parts of Spain. While the Republican Left in Catalonia has been good at involving immigrants in their organisation, there has not been enough awareness of how the national struggle in Catalonia can build an alliance with Spanish workers to bring about social change. Class demands as well as national demands need to be central to the process. This is also true with regard to winning support from workers across the rest of Spain. During the 2017 referendum, huge demonstrations were taking place in the south of Spain against unemployment and poverty. No attempt was made by the Catalan left to make the obvious links that could have fused both struggles.

If there are criticisms that can be made of the left in Catalonia, then these pale in comparison with those that can be made of the Spanish left. The refusal of the PSOE to release the Catalan political prisoners when they came to power in 2019 and their insistence that they serve the full term in prison must be condemned and has only led to the strengthening of the far right and Spanish nationalists in Spain. The failure of Podemos to support the 2017 vote because it was "unconstitutional" and their decision to form a government with the PSOE in 2019 have effectively put them on the side of the Spanish state, despite formally expressing solidarity with the prisoners.

The parallels with Scotland are obvious. The role of the EU, the failure of much of the left across the UK to support Scottish independence, the lack of clarity by the official independence movement on how to bring together class demands over austerity, poverty, cuts and racism into the central core of the movement and a complete lack of understanding on how to confront a strong national state are there in both movements.

Scotland and independence

The nearest we have to an SNP vision for a future Scotland was a document produced and published in November 2013 called *Scotland's Future.*[15] The paper itself, true to form for the SNP, was a contradictory mix of social democracy and neoliberalism. It committed Scotland to abolish the bedroom tax, provide free childcare and end universal credit but also talked about a reduction in capital gains tax and a reduction in airport passenger duty and there was no promise to abolish the Tories' draconian anti-trade union laws. It says that an independent Scotland would get rid of Trident nuclear weapons yet will join NATO (a nuclear alliance). Scotland would be free to make its own economic decisions but retain the pound. The environment would be protected and renewable energy encouraged, but the North Sea oil industry would also be supported. A more humane approach to immigration and asylum was envisaged, but "This Government will take forward a points-based approach targeted at particular Scottish requirements".[16] The problem with this is that it places the needs of the economy above those of refugees and immigrants fleeing war, oppression and persecution. It also makes concessions to the very same racist arguments on migrants that the SNP, on the surface, seek to oppose.

Mhairi Black, who was elected SNP MP for Paisley and Renfrewshire South in 2015, later revealed that she hated the document so much that during the 2014 referendum campaign she told people to ignore it.[17]

In response to the defeat of 2014 for the Yes side, it would seem that the SNP felt the need to stress how little would change and how an independent Scotland would fit into the model of a mainstream European country. Their own vision is best summed up by the Growth Commission report published in 2018, which again indicates that Scotland will keep the pound (for a transitional period), will pay its share of the UK national debt and ensure sustainable finance after independence.[18]

However, perhaps the most important argument put forward by Nicola Sturgeon is that Scotland would immediately apply for membership of the EU after voting to leave the UK. Indeed, for a large part of 2019, keeping Britain part of the EU appeared, for the SNP, to take precedence over independence. Scotland's First Minister is entitled to her opinion on the EU. But "Scotland in Europe" became a mantra trotted out by the SNP during major political campaigns. Was this necessarily the best way forward? There are a number of grounds to believe otherwise.

One of the main arguments put forward to justify Scotland's automatic application for EU membership is the "democratic deficit" due to Scotland voting in favour of staying when England voted to leave. While it is correct that any decision regarding EU should be for the people of Scotland, surely this would be best done, for democratic reasons, once Scotland has actually become independent. It was not for the First Minister to decide the issue beforehand. The question of Scotland's independence and EU membership are two separate issues. This is important given the fact that around one third of independence supporters voted to leave the EU.[19] This is particularly crucial because EU membership will severely limit the possibility of Scotland departing from mainstream European economic orthodoxy.

EU regulations insist that member states limit the government deficit to 3 percent of GDP and debt to 60 percent of GDP. All EU member states are each year obliged to submit a Stability Growth Pact compliance report for the scrutiny and evaluation of the European Commission and the Council of Ministers. On public ownership, while the EU does not expressly forbid state ownership of companies, these must operate within the limits of EU fiscal and competition laws. This severely restricts the ability of publicly owned companies to operate as public services in the interest of the workers they employ and the society they represent. A good example is the operation of the ferry company Caledonian MacBrayne (CalMac), which is owned by the Scottish Government. CalMac operates as a private company and this has led to some important disputes with the RMT union over pay, conditions and pensions.

In other words, it is clear that EU membership will make it difficult, if not impossible, for an independent Scotland to pursue radical policies such as nationalisation and government investment in public services that the country needs. At the very least these are issues which need to be debated by the people of Scotland and should not be decided beforehand by the SNP.

One of the more constructive aspects of the SNP has been their attitude to immigrants and refugees, which stands in stark contrast to the attitude of Tory politicians in the UK. Attitudes to actual immigration in Scotland and England are remarkably similar, with a British and Scottish Social Attitudes survey conducted in the latter half of 2017 showing that both Scotland and England had a relatively positive attitude to the benefits of immigration.[20] This does not mean that Scotland is free from Islamophobia and racism, as an attack on two Asian shopkeepers by a gang of 20 thugs in January 2020 illustrates. It also has to be pointed out that, rhetoric apart, the Scottish Government have done very little in practical terms to oppose the British government's deportation policies.

One reason put forward for Scotland joining the EU is to preserve free movement of people to the rest of the European Union and vice versa. But those who think the EU is a pillar of progressive values need to confront the reality of the EU's Fortress Europe immigration policy that allows migrants to drown in the Mediterranean, Greek border guards to sink a boat full of refugees and Libyan coastguards, paid and trained by the EU, to shoot at migrants.

What about the Left?

In the run up to the 2014 referendum, a plethora of books were published mostly from a left-wing, or at least social democratic, perspective putting the case for independence. Former 79 Group member Kenny MacAskill, who was the Cabinet Secretary for Justice in the Scottish Government, put his case in a book titled *Building A Nation: Post Devolution Nationalism in Scotland.* [21] His arguments stem from what he saw as the uniqueness of the Scottish experience. He accepts the need for EU membership and looks to build on the Nordic model in a way that suits Scotland.

One of the most popular books produced at the time was *Blossom*, written by Scottish writer and journalist Lesley Riddoch.[22] In a book that is in many ways entertaining and informative, Riddoch takes us through some of the major problems in Scottish society—aristocratic land ownership, foreign ownership of the Scottish economy, poor housing, male-dominated society and much more—and using both anecdotal evidence and research puts forward an optimistic vision of a potential future Scottish society. Her version is outward looking and presents an alternative view of how communities with greater control over their destinies can change society for the better. Her model again rests on the experience of the Nordic countries and their achievements. She was later involved with a project called Nordic Horizons in which a number of Scottish professionals looked to "raise the standard of knowledge of debate about the life and policy of the Nordic Nations". This led to the development of the Nordic Policy Unit within the Scottish Government. One outcome was a book published in 2017 called *McSmorgasbord: What Post-Brexit Scotland Can Learn from the Nordics.* This is a collection of essays looking at how the experience of the Nordic countries can be applied to Scotland.[23]

While *Blossom* is a useful contribution to the debate, it says very little about how this is going to be achieved or about where power in society actually resides. Independence, in and of itself, will not solve all of the country's social and economic ills, particularly if the financial structures remain largely intact—even if they are controlled by Scots. Riddoch acknowledges that each of the Nordic countries has their own relationship with Europe and the EU, from being member states to complete detachment with others in between. Yet she has firmly hitched her own wagon to the EU, being one of the most consistent advocates of EU membership for a post-UK Scotland.

Scandinavian countries may have high levels of government spending, but they are far from unique in that respect, with France and Belgium's social spending higher as a percentage of GDP. Elsewhere in this book, Ferguson and Mooney have shown that the policies of neoliberalism in the Nordic countries have led to greater levels of inequality, which in turn has fuelled the growth of the far right. [24] Norway's economy depends on the oil industry to fund spending and Sweden is the world's tenth biggest exporter of arms, down from sixth only due to the fact that the world trade in arms has risen.[25] It is certainly true that Nordic countries have better welfare provision than most others. This developed in a period after the Second World War when the world economy was expanding and provided the opportunity for workers' organisations to force reforms. The Scandinavian embrace of the free market and neoliberalism stems from the global downturn and its impact. While it would be wrong to ignore some of the positive lessons that the Nordic states can provide for a country like Scotland, it would equally be a mistake to believe that they offer a way forward for those who are looking for a radical break from the crippling orthodoxy of the world economy.

A consistent critic of the SNP and Nicola Sturgeon from the left has been Robin McAlpine, former director of an organisation called the Common Weal. This was set up in 2013 as part of the Jimmy Reid Foundation and now operates as a "think tank" which supports and advocates for Scottish independence. This is done very much from the left and is in favour of a more socially just Scotland. After 2014, the Common Weal set about producing a range of policy papers confronting some of the major issues which arose during the referendum campaign.

These cover a variety of topics including a National Investment Bank, an independent Scottish currency and a Green New Deal, as well as suggestions on how Scotland could revitalise its democracy at all levels, and more. It has to be acknowledged that the work of the Common Weal has been helpful in keeping alive an alternative to the conservative approach adopted by the Scottish Government. Robin McAlpine in particular has been a fierce critic of Nicola Sturgeon and her lack of strategic thinking on how to force a second referendum and achieve sovereignty for Scotland.

However, the Common Weal also has its limitations. McAlpine in particular is very much in favour of the Nordic Model, which is an indication of a cross-class approach that puts bosses and workers in the same boat. After Ineos defeated the Unite union at Grangemouth in 2014, the Common Weal's response was to say, "The only way to 'vow never again' is to change industrial relations from a conflict model where employers and employees are pitted against another to a co-operative model".[26] This can also be illustrated by their approach to alternative energy. One of their policy documents is 'Carbon-Free, Poverty-Free: Heating Options for Rural Scotland', which looks at ways of addressing fuel poverty in rural properties not attached to the main gas grid.[27] Fuel poverty in rural areas is a big issue for those who are "income-poor". This was also a submission to the Scottish Government "for evidence in the future of low carbon heat for off-gas buildings", which was jointly presented as "A policy paper for Calor by Common Weal, Glasgow Caledonian University, and the Energy Poverty Research initiative".

Calor is one of the main suppliers in Britain of bottled gas. It is now providing BioLPG, which it sees as the way forward. This is a central part of the Common Weal report. Calor sources this from NESTE, a Finnish company with a major production unit in Rotterdam. But the Campaign Against Climate Change points out, "The impact of biofuel production on deforestation, and other detrimental land use change, makes them fantastically counter-productive as a climate change solution".[28] NESTE aims to be one of the world's major suppliers of aviation biofuels and is deeply enmeshed in crude palm oil sourcing linked to rainforest destruction. Greenpeace in 2011 identified NESTE as "one of six companies from which the public can choose the most socially irresponsible company in the world". [29]

None of this is to denigrate much of the good work done by the Common Weal in presenting an alternative to mainstream SNP thinking on the nature of Scottish independence and how this will be achieved. Nevertheless, the shortcomings of a cross-class nationalist approach to independence, even when this comes from a socially aware committed group, are more than effectively exposed by the Calor report.

One of the most interesting developments in recent years has been George Kerevan's growing criticism of the SNP leadership. George was a member of the International Marxist Group (IMG) until the early 1980s. He was part of the Scottish Labour Party, which was set up by Jim Sillars in 1975 due to the failure of the Labour government to bring forward an effective devolution scheme. He joined the SNP in 1996, was an associate editor of the *Scotsman* newspaper in 2000 and briefly an SNP MP from 2015 to 2017.

When writing for the *Scotsman*, he moved a considerable distance from his Marxist roots, arguing that "the SNP should cultivate an anti-paternalist politics that sought to enhance 'personal community choice' through lower taxes, a less expansive state, and a more dynamic market economy".[30] During his time as an MP, he wrote in the London financial paper *City AM* that fallout from Brexit meant that independence could be supported by "anti-Brexit groups who voted No to independence in 2014: Edinburgh's middle class, farmers and swathes of Scotland's business and financial community", that Scotland could emulate small countries like Ireland and Iceland, who quickly recovered from the financial crash of 2009, with a "separate Scottish currency tied to sterling". However, this would take "five years of painful budget cuts" which could turn

Scotland "into an economic powerhouse".[31]

When he was a member of the Labour party, Kerevan was a supporter of Tony Benn. Once he was no longer an MP, like Benn in his later years, he moved back to the left. He was one of the first, for example, to recognise the positive development of All Under One Banner.

The leadership of the SNP, particularly Nicola Sturgeon, did their best to distance themselves from the protests. Some MSPs finally agreed to speak at rallies after it became clear that thousands of their own members were enthusiastic participants. Writing in *The National*, he described AUOB in the following terms:

> As someone who has been active in left-wing politics for (hate to say it) half-a-century, I have never seen this level of working class political self-activity, except in rare moments such as the original Solidarnosc in Poland in 1980. It is testimony to the atrophy of the UK Labour Party that their leaders cannot appreciate this amazing proletarian movement north of the Border".[32]

During 2020, Kerevan, in a number of articles, developed an insightful and serious critique of the SNP's role in pursuing independence. These came to fruition with a couple of pieces in the online magazine *Conter*, headed 'SNP at the Crossroads'[33] and 'SNP at the Crossroads: What is to be done?'.[34]

He argued that after 2014, Nicola Sturgeon demobilised the movement in an attempt to win support from major capitalist groups and because of her uncritical support for the European Union. A growing conservative bureaucracy in the SNP around the leadership sought to stifle opposition and basically pursued policies in their own interest, rather than for the wider movement. His contention was that:

> Sturgeon and the present SNP leadership have adapted to the political and economic needs of the upper

echelons of the traditional Scottish middle class—
the conservative oligarchy of lawyers, accountants,
bankers, media consultants, kirk ministers and
university professors who have dominated Scottish
civil society since the Union of 1707.[35]

His solution to this is for the various constituent parts
of the movement to elect a new leadership "beholden to the
mass membership". This would be done through a National
Convention based on the model of the Catalan National
Assembly. He then goes on to argue that there is a need to
defend democracy inside the SNP and that a new workers'
party should be formed after independence "embracing the
trades unions, Labour supporters, and the left of the SNP, and
a broader left sentiment released from its old constitutional
commitments". Kerevan's appraisal of the SNP leadership was
a big step in the right direction.

The SNP's cautious and politically conservative approach
to independence means that both independence itself and the
goal of achieving a more socially just and equitable country
once Scotland is free from the shackles of the British state will
be a lot more difficult to achieve. It was also refreshing that
he was able to see the potential of a genuine mass movement,
which developed in 2014 around the referendum and has
continued to campaign and organise independent of the SNP
leadership.

Up till late March 2021 he failed to accept that the SNP
itself was a big barrier to achieving his aims, and then decided
to leave the SNP to join Alex Salmond's Alba Party believing it a
better option. The Alba Party's cross class approach to achieving
independence makes it little different from the SNP.

Leaving any socialist challenge to their dominance in the
movement until after independence means that the left will
continue to hand the initiative to the very people he seeks to
challenge.

A Scottish Road to Socialism?

The book *Is there a Scottish Road to Socialism?* published by *Scottish Left Review* in 2016 brought together a number of contributors from the left in Scotland who made the case both for supporting independence and the case against. Opposing independence, Neil Findlay and Tommy Kane argue that the vote in 2014 was "a fairly resounding result for remaining part of Britain".[36] Subsequent events have proven otherwise. They correctly attack the SNP for its attachment to neoliberalism and speculate that the advent of a Corbyn-led Labour Party opened up the possibility of building a British wide broad coalition in favour of redistribution and other radical policies to the left of the SNP, while the SNP's conservatism, not just on economic policies but also in its attitude to a second vote, would undermine its support. All this was to prove illusory. Far from Corbyn being able to change the Labour Party and challenge the political and economic orthodoxy of the British state, the opposite has happened. The SNP is riding high in the opinion polls and those supporting Scottish independence are now in the majority. The Labour Party in Scotland is polling in third place behind the Tories and with Labour leader Keir Starmer overtly presenting himself as a British nationalist set against agreeing to a second vote on Scottish independence, there is little, if any, prospect of Labour making a recovery in Scotland.

On behalf of the Scottish Communist Party, John Foster contends that "Radical Federalism" is the way ahead. After a piece of rather dubious research, based on the letters page of the independence supporting *National* newspaper, he foresees "the beginnings of an ideological realignment of Scottish voters who have currently moved within the SNP orbit—a realignment which, if continued, would substantially dilute the radical, class orientated content of Scottish national identity as inherited from the 20th century".[37] Foster again correctly takes the SNP to task for the limited nature of their project for independence and says the support it is given should be "weighed against what could be achieved by a more direct attack on capitalist state power at a British level that develops and maintains existing class organisations".[38] To this end he proposes a version of radical federalism that "seeks to deepen the existing distribution of income in terms of differential social need geographically at federal level at the same time as reinforcing class demand for an increase in the overall share of income going to labour. At Scottish, Welsh and regional level, it seeks to maximise economic democracy: ... to do so through the development of public and cooperative ownership".[39]

While Foster rightly points out the SNP's support for EU membership and its connection to big business, its commitment to NATO and allegiance to the crown, what guarantee is there that a federalist solution to the British state would be any different? Surely it would be more logical to argue the case within the context of the independence movement rather that stand aside.

Does support for Scottish independence necessarily lead to a weakening of working class organisation? As we have seen, support by working class voters in Scotland grew out of past defeats, the responsibility for which the traditional leadership of the working class movement in Britain—the Labour Party and the trade union leaders—must take a major share of the responsibility. In any case, for most of its history, working class support for reform and change has come through the prism of the British state and necessarily involved a compromise and identification with British nationalism. Why identification with Scottish nationalism as opposed to British nationalism should be seen as a threat by Foster is a mystery. Class consciousness and nationalism are contradictory, and it is the job of socialists to engage with the movement and to deepen and extend the ability of those involved to challenge the existing strongholds of economic and political power.

If we look at the issue simply in terms of votes, then it looks as if the SNP has succeeded both practically and ideologically in capturing the hearts and minds of working class voters. But the movement is also anti-racist, it supports the rights of immigrants and refugees, it is anti-nuclear weapons and anti-war and many of its activists are members of trade unions and supported, for example, the equal pay strikes by council workers in Glasgow who won a famous victory in 2020. The reason for much of this is because of the active involvement of socialists in the movement.

None of this means that we should be uncritical of the SNP and it is certainly the case that far too many on the left in Scotland have been only too willing to temper their criticism of them in the hope that this will ease the way to independence. However, criticism is best achieved within the context of the struggle, not from opposing it. Class consciousness and the ability of workers to fight is not confined by specific countries. Working class solidarity depends on organisation and the willingness to fight, not on borders.

For revolutionary Marxists, socialism in one country is unrealistic in a world dominated by capitalism. However, a common misunderstanding is that we believe revolutionary change must come about and begin in a number of countries simultaneously. Another common misunderstanding is that we are opposed to reform and change within the existing structures of capitalist society. Both of these are wrong. We exist in a world defined by nations, states and borders which are a product of the development of capitalism and the consequence of imperialism. It therefore follows that movements for change largely *begin* within the borders of a defined country. The interconnections of the world economy mean that similar movements are unlikely to be absent in other countries. Nevertheless, movements for change start with demands that flow from the particular circumstances in a specific location. These can be demands for greater democracy and freedom, for better wages or working conditions, for an end to austerity and cuts or from opposition by oppressed groups to repression. Socialists do not stand aside and preach from the side lines but should participate fully in the battle, particularly when workers face dogged opposition from the bosses and governments determined not to concede. Such struggles are the basis on which workers learn lessons about their own potential power and capacity to run society.

In Scotland, the terrain upon which working people have chosen to fight is around the question of Scottish independence. The reasons for this are complex and have been examined in earlier chapters of this book. Undoubtedly nationalism and the belief that Scotland is an oppressed nation is for some a reason they are involved. However, there are other reasons, and the class issues of poverty, poor working conditions, low wages, precarious employment, privatisation and cuts to the NHS as well as opposition to nuclear weapons, the British state's involvement in imperialist wars and the racism of large sections of the UK establishment, most notably the UK Tory party, have been essential elements in the drive for independence.

Scotland also has a strong tradition of identification with and solidarity with international movements. Scottish poet Robert Burns took inspiration from the French Revolution as did the leaders of the Calton Weavers' strike in Glasgow in 1787. Scots played an important role in the abolition of slavery and former American slave Frederick Douglass was given an enthusiastic welcome when he toured Scotland in 1846. Red Clydeside and the events in Glasgow in 1919 took place in parallel with working class struggle across Europe. During the 1930s and the rise in fascism, Scots went to fight in the International Brigades which battled against Franco and attempts by fascists to organise in Scotland were met by strong opposition from workers and anti-fascists. When Nelson Mandela was released from prison in South Africa and was then elected president, one of the first places he visited was Glasgow because of the support the people of the city had given to the struggle against apartheid. The city of Dundee twinned with the Palestinian city of Nablus in 1980 as an act of solidarity with Palestinians in their opposition to Israeli occupation. Scotland played a full role in the Campaign for Nuclear Disarmament (CND) in opposing nuclear weapons and in opposition to the invasion of Iraq in 2003. Scotland also has a strong tradition of welcoming refugees and immigrants as well as fighting racism and sectarianism. It would be wrong, of course, to pretend Scotland was a model of anti-racism, free from prejudice and petty nationalism. On the other hand, there is a strong international tradition which an outward looking and inclusive independence movement in Scotland can identify with and build upon.

Maclean and Connolly

There is also a revolutionary socialist tradition which comes from the working class movement in Scotland that we can learn from. John Maclean is a hero to many because of his bravery in opposing the First World War and his fight for revolutionary change and Scottish independence. James Connolly on the other hand is most strongly associated with the fight for Irish freedom and the 1916 Dublin Uprising. Connolly was born in Edinburgh and was a product of the socialist movement in Scotland.

In the aftermath of the First World War and the working class action around Red Clydeside, John Maclean believed that the way forward was through fighting for a Scottish workers' republic. Most of his comrades did not agree, with some joining the new British Communist Party and others joining the Labour Party. However, it is important to be clear on the political basis on which Maclean fought for Scottish independence.

> I mean to fight for a Scottish workers' republic in which all robbery shall cease. The break-up of every empire, including John Bull's, will make more easy the world revolution from capitalism to communism, and may help to avert a world war which otherwise might come before the workers were ready to take full possession of our planet.[40]

This is a million miles, politically, from those who believe that ensuring the election of the SNP into government or that establishing Scotland as an independent capitalist country is the way forward.

Ireland was a country, unlike Scotland, that was occupied and oppressed by British imperialism. The parallels with Scotland's battle for independence are therefore far from exact. Nevertheless, the writings and political actions of James Connolly are of immense value for those of us who support the breaking apart of the British state from a revolutionary socialist standpoint.

Two historical events led Connolly to support the Easter Rising in 1916. The first was the defeat of Irish workers in what was to become known as the Dublin Lockout in 1913. This involved an employer's attack on what was becoming an increasingly militant ITGWU membership led by Jim Larkin. At its height, 25,000 workers were locked out and Connolly was imprisoned. The Catholic Church condemned the unions and Sinn Féin leader Arthur Griffith denounced "Larkinism as an imported evil".[41]

Despite the fact that the Dublin workers received massive support from workers in Britain, the failure of the trade union leaders to organise effective solidarity meant the isolation and defeat of the strikes. The second event was the collapse of the socialist Second International and the support of respective national sections for their own governments' participation in the First World War.

Connolly believed it was necessary to find a way of fighting against the horror of war and to strike a blow against British imperialism. He supported an uprising because, as Kieran Allen in his book *1916: Ireland's Revolutionary Tradition* says,

> A revolt in Ireland, he thought, would be a hundred times more effective than elsewhere, because Ireland lay at the heart of the British Empire. He hoped that this would cause a chain reaction abroad, which would reawaken the socialist movement and lead to new revolts against a system which bred war.[42]

In the event the uprising came too early to catch the

revolutionary wave of working class action across Europe which ended the First World War. It was isolated and its leaders, including Connolly, were executed. But the huge revolt which began with the February Revolution in Russia in 1917 and included the October Russian Revolution, the German Revolution of 1918 and the two years of mass strikes and factory occupations in Italy from 1919 to 1921, fuelled a renewed war for Irish independence in the years afterwards.

Connolly's actions in 1916 are, from a socialist perspective, not above criticism. But again, we need to be clear that for him his support for Irish Independence had to end in a workers' republic because if it did not do so, then Irish independence would end up in the hands of the very same capitalists who attacked the Dublin workers and they "will guard the fraudulent gains of the capitalists and landlords 'from the thin hands of the poor' just as effectively as the scarlet-coated emissaries of England do so today".[43]

He also believed that fighting for a socialist Ireland was the only way to break down sectarian barriers between Protestant and Catholic workers. His prophesy that partition would lead to a carnival of reaction, north and south, proved to be all too true.

The lesson for socialists from the experience of Maclean and Connolly is that we cannot leave the argument for socialism and workers' self-emancipation out of the case for Scottish independence. To do so would condemn Scottish workers to the continued exploitation by the bosses, with all the consequences of poverty, exploitation and racism which we are subject to under the British state.

What kind of Scotland?

There is a growing frustration within the movement in Scotland at the lack of progress, under the leadership of Nicola Sturgeon, towards a second vote on independence. As we have seen this has led to the creation of the Alba Party under the leadership of Alex Salmond. Yet despite all the talk of a possible "plan B" or of a "supermajority" for independence in the Scottish Parliament,

Equal pay strikers,
Glasgow 2018

UCU Strikers St students
picket Glasgow University,
February 2018

that can simply declare independence because it has the mandate to do so, there is very little real discussion on how to confront a British state unwilling to concede a second vote or accept that Scotland has the right to determine its own future.

To do this the movement needs to build alliances with groups within society who have the potential power to challenge the political and economic representatives of Britain. Despite all their weaknesses, the organised working class and the trade unions in Scotland continue to be the best option. There are over half a million union members in Scotland. The impact of the coronavirus crisis is having a detrimental effect on the rate of unemployment in Scotland, as many companies use the situation to shed jobs and make people redundant. This can only partly be put down to the impact of the virus as struggling companies take the opportunity to cut costs. Nevertheless, there remain over 2.5 million workers employed in Scotland, with many of them in jobs and industries with huge potential economic power. The impact of the virus has highlighted what has become known as "key workers" in society. These include health workers, workers in social care, supermarket workers and transport workers. The reason the British and Scottish governments were desperate to get children back to school was not because they were concerned about their health and wellbeing, but because getting the teachers back to work would allow other sections of the economy to open up.

The Oil and Gas industry in Scotland generates a Gross Value Added (GVA) of £9.2 billion[44] and employs 168,750 people. Scotland's Financial Services has a GVA of £15.7 billion[45] and employs 247,000 people and the Food and Drink Industry has a GVA of £3.6 billon[46] while it employs 44,000. Jim Ratcliffe, the owner of the petrochemical plant at Grangemouth, is the UK's 5th richest person with a total wealth of £12.15 billion.[47] The plant at Grangemouth had an operating profit of £1.2 billion in 2019 and has 1,300 direct employees.[48] All the people involved in these industries are a potential source of support with the capacity to force real change.

Looking to workers in Scotland for backing is only partly about engaging with a group that can win independence— it is also about the nature of the society that arises after independence. If we want a future free from poverty, exploitation and oppression then we need to convince the workers in Scotland that the future will benefit them.

Unfortunately, a strategy based on persuading the bosses that independence will leave Scotland with business as usual will not achieve what people are looking for. The soft underbelly of the independence movement is its nationalism. It compromises the action we need and it undermines the future. We should not be limited by it.

The movement needs to continue to work with the anti-racist movement, climate change activists and the trade unions to win broad support. We should demand the Scottish Government ends the scandal of privatised care homes and all profit-making and private finance in schools and the NHS. The railways should be brought back fully into public ownership and companies such as CalMac, which are owned by the Scottish Government, should stop being run as if they were private companies and instead run for the benefit of the public and their employees. We should demand the Scottish Government does all it can to undermine the work of the UK Border Police and supports immigrants and refugees. The SNP-led Government could also do much more to undermine the working of the Trident nuclear base at Faslane.

Independence alone would be an immense victory. But for socialists this is not an end in itself. A movement with workers at its core and organised socialists at its heart, that is outward looking and international, can achieve so much more.

Conclusion

The thirst for Scottish independence seems to be growing day by day. Every new disaster, whether the economic crisis in 2008 or the worst economic contraction since the 18th century in the pandemic adds to that feeling. Every utterance from the mouth of Boris Johnson or additional death added to the over 125,000 does the same. The hope invested in the cause goes far beyond the limits of the SNP, and many in the independence movement are ready to march and campaign when the SNP holds back or tries to steer things towards the deadend of legal procedure or pleas for fair treatment by the Tories.

If the break up of the British state is achieved and nothing more, that would be a step forward. It would give heart to the victims of British imperialism the world over, weaken the foremost ally of US imperialism, create difficulties for the Trident fleet and so on. However, many of the supporters of independence want much more. The question at the heart of this book is whether independence on its own would bring a better, more just and more equal society. And the answer in this book is: that depends. There are two threads that run through the pages—class and nation.

The difference between them and their interaction is a central theme. This book is being published in the midst of a global pandemic and at a time in the rollout of vaccines when there is talk of 'vaccine nationalism'. We know that no one is safe from the virus until everyone is safe. We know the same applies to averting climate catastrophe. Our very survival depends on an understanding of the fundamental common interest of humanity encapsulated in the idea of solidarity and internationalism. This goal cannot be achieved within the capitalist economic system, or its state structures. These use every means possible to divide us, whether it is through racism, war, economic competition, jingoism or the phoney ideology of national interest. The working class is the majority on this planet and unless it asserts its needs and demands then disaster capitalism will triumph.

In the chapters dealing with working class history, we dealt with the ups and downs of class struggle. Since its birth in the late 18th century until the rise of the modern independence movement there was no distinct Scottish working class path. Inspiring working class struggles, from the Radical Rising in

1820 to Red Clydeside and beyond to the equal pay strike in Glasgow in 2018, may have won or lost, but they all contributed to the development of a widely-varied British labour movement that challenges bosses north and south. The same has applied to the struggle against racism. But the working class is not united by the British capitalist state which spends most of its time stirring divisions between people, stoking distrust of refugees, immigrants, other religions and so on. Unity of the British state is about the unity of British capitalism, which is why the left Labour position on independence is so mistaken.

At the same time the events described did take place in Scotland (and not elsewhere). A form of popular national consciousness of the Scottish kind was constructed alongside British national consciousness and has coexisted with it for a very long time. Scottish national consciousness could be used to suggest a common interest of workers and employers north of the border that undermines working class solidarity. The example of union leaders arguing 'it's Scotland's coal' weakened the united response of the NUM in the Great Miners' Strike of 1984-5. Today the same consciousness on the part of millions of ordinary people is leading to a demand for independence which is progressive and anti-Tory. The feeling that there is a 'democratic deficit'—the fact that for many years the wishes of many people in Scotland, which find partial expression in the ballot box, are at variance with the ruling party at Westminster is real and justified.

Several chapters are devoted to exploring the various manifestations of nation and nationalism. Nationalism cannot make sense of the real history of Scotland. The pretence of standing for all Scottish people is impossible. The rich and poor have opposite interests. But it is undeniable that the SNP, which is a nationalist party, has huge working class support. To understand this, the book gives over a considerable amount of space to discussing the failings of the Labour party and trade union bureaucracy—in both its Scottish and British forms. This leadership contributed to Labour's own decline while fuelling the electoral surge of the SNP (and the Tories to a lesser extent).

As a result of this background, the modern independence movement is neither simply nationalist nor reformist. Both elements are combined within it. Since independence is a political and constitutional issue, the SNP and its leadership plays the prominent role, while ideologically committed to the 'national interest' and the capitalist system. It walks a fine line between promoting that and projecting a social democratic commitment. But, ultimately, it will baulk at departing from the trajectory of neoliberal capitalism or leading a decisive battle against the British state. However, precisely because the independence movement is so much more than the SNP leadership, there is the potential to go further and mount a challenge to both the capitalist state and the capitalist system that the SNP champions.

The phrase 'socialism or barbarism' was coined over a hundred years ago during the First World War. In 2021 it is clearer than ever that this is the basic choice facing humanity. But ending capitalism is no easy thing. It needs to take into account the circumstances within which that fight takes place. The world as presently constituted is organised into states and competing units of capital. Any struggle to achieve a better society needs to take that into account. If that were not the case, by now we would have a single global organisation for all workers and oppressed people. And in terms of action, no one would strike to defend their jobs or pay until all workers were ready to do so. We would all demonstrate, or no one would. National politics, different economic sectors, and so on are real arenas of struggle which cannot be ignored and they influence how we organise to fight back.

The goal of Scottish independence is part of that fight. But there is a clear choice to be made within the movement itself. Though welcome, do we want the break-up of the British state to leave us with two nationalisms and two competing capitalist blocs on the island of Britain; or do we want it to be something more—a class challenge to nationalism and capitalism, becoming part of the battle against barbarism that is so sorely needed?

Notes

Preface

1   V I Lenin, 'The Right of Nations to Self-determination', *Selected Works Volume 1* (Moscow, 1975) pp 579-580.

Introduction

1   Robert Shrimsley, 'Scotland may be the price of Boris Johnson's place in history', *Financial Times*, 20 July 2020, https://www.ft.com/content/6929f1ca-69e7-419e-90b5-ca08a423004c

2   Allister Heath, 'Boris Johnson has six months left to save his premiership' *The Telegraph*, 16 September 2020. https://www.telegraph.co.uk/news/2020/09/16/boris-johnson-has-six-months-left-save-premiership/

3   Progress Scotland, 'Highest Ever Poll Total Predicting Scottish Independence', 11 October 2020. https://www.progressscotland.org/research/highest-ever-poll-total-predicting-scottish-independence

4   Although it is important to note that SNP membership has declined sharply from a high point of 125,000 to just over 80,000 members in late 2020. 'Membership of UK Political Parties', The House of Commons Library Research Briefing, 19 August 2019, https://commonslibrary.parliament.uk/research-briefings/sn05125/

5   Now Scotland, *Mission Statement*, February 2021, https://www.nowscotland.scot/about_us

6   'Brexit Vote: Nicola Sturgeon Statement in full', *BBC News*, 24 June 2016, https://www.bbc.co.uk/news/uk-scotland-36620375

7   Tom Gordon, 'Coronavirus in Scotland: Nicola Sturgeon formally drops plan for indyref2 this year', *The Herald*, 18 march 2020, https://www.heraldscotland.com/news/18315506.

coronavirus-scotland-nicola-sturgeon-formally-drops-plan-indyref2-year/

8   Libby Brooks, 'Sturgeon: SNP will hold Scottish Independence vote if it wins in May', *The Guardian*, 24 January, https://www.theguardian.com/politics/2021/jan/24/scotland-independence-referendum-nicola-sturgeon-snp-wins-may-

9   Elle Duffy, 'Senior independence campaigner Robin McAlpine slams Nicola Sturgeon in scathing 'f*** off' blog post', *The Herald*, 16 July 2020, https://bit.ly/3qHWATA

10   George Kerevan, 'SNP at the Crossroad: What is to be Done?', *Conter*, 29 September 2020 https://www.conter.co.uk/blog/2020/9/29/snp-at-the-crossroad-what-is-to-be-done

11   George Osborne, 'Unleashing nationalism has made the future of the UK the central issue', *Evening Standard*, 19 January 2021, https://www.standard.co.uk/comment/nationalism-union-brexit-b900299.html

12   Quoted in 'MSP's vote to reject UK internal market bill', *Holyrood* magazine, 8 October 2020, https://www.holyrood.com/news/view,msps-vote-to-reject-uk-internal-market-bill

13   Quoted in Kathleen Nutt, 'SNP back new independence referendum if Internal Market Bill proceeds', *The National*, 7 October 2020, https://www.thenational.scot/news/18776045.stuc-back-indyref2-power-grab-bill-proceeds/

14   Joseph Choonara, 'A Triple Crisis', *International Socialism*, 167, Summer 2020, http://isj.org.uk/a-triple-crisis/

15   Santi Amador, 'Occupations to ministries: where is Podemos going?', *Socialist Review* 458, 10 July 2020, http://socialistreview.org.uk/458/

occupations-ministries-where-podemos-going-0

16   Daniel Dombey, 'Spanish centre right licks wounds after drubbing in Catalan poll', *Financial Times,* 15 February 2021, https://www.ft.com/content/3931c7e5-dc12-42e3-aab8-b16539ce2317

17   Giorgos Pittas, 'Greece at a Crossroads', *Socialist Review* 370, June 2012, http://socialistreview.org.uk/370/greece-crossroads

18   Petros Constantinou, 'How we smashed Golden Dawn', *International Socialism* 169, Winter 2021, http://isj.org.uk/how-we-smashed-golden-dawn/

19   Campaign Against Climate Change, *One Million Climate Jobs* (London 2014), https://www.cacctu.org.uk/climatejobs

20   Jim Ratcliffe, 'Grangemouth: The battle with the union and why we trail behind Germany', *Inch Magazine*, Issue 5, December 2016, https://www.ineos.com/inch-magazine/articles/issue-5/the-battle-with-the-union/

21   Quoted in John Newsinger, *The Blood Never Dried: A People's History of the British Empire* (London, 2013) p17.

22   Mike Davis, *Late Victorian Holocausts: El Niño Famines and the Making of the Third World* (London, 2000), p139.

23   V I Lenin, *Draft Theses on the National and Colonial Questions for the Second Congress of the Communist International*, July 1920. https://www.marxists.org/archive/lenin/works/1920/jun/05.htm

24   John Maclean, *The Irish Tragedy: Scotland's Disgrace*, pamphlet 1920. Quoted in Keir McKechnie, *Yes to Independence: No to Nationalism*, (London, 2014). https://www.marxists.org/archive/maclean/works/1920-tit.htm

25   Tom Devine, *To the Ends of the Earth: Scotland's Global Diaspora* (Allen Lane, 2011) p249.

26   Laura Webster, 'Scottish Independence: Gove Sparks Anger with Voting Rights Comment', *The National*, 20 August 2020.

27   Tony Philips, 'Trotsky on the Labour Party', *International Socialism* 153 (Winter 2017) pp95-128.

Chapter 1 Scotland, the National Question and Marxism

1   Karl Marx & Friedrich Engels, *The Communist Manifesto* (1848) https://www.marxists.org/archive/marx/works/1848/communist-manifesto/ch01.htm

2   Marx & Engels, *The Communist Manifesto* (1848) https://www.marxists.org/archive/marx/works/1848/communist-manifesto/ch01.htm

3   Karl Marx, 'Letter to Ludwig Kugelman in Hanover' (29 November 1869), in Karl Marx & Friedrich Engels, *Selected Correspondence* (Moscow, 1975). https://www.marxists.org/archive/marx/works/1869/letters/69_11_29-abs.htm

4   Rosa Luxemburg, 'The National Question and Autonomy' (1907) in Horace B Davis (ed) *The National Question—Selected Writings by Rosa Luxemburg,* (New York, 1976). https://www.marxists.org/archive/luxemburg/1909/national-question/ch05.htm

5   V I Lenin, 'The Right of Nations to Self-determination' (1914), in *Collected Works* (Moscow, 1972) https://www.marxists.org/archive/lenin/works/1914/self-det/

6   V I Lenin, 'The Discussion On Self-Determination Summed Up' (July 1916) in *Collected Works* (Moscow, 1972) https://www.marxists.org/archive/lenin/works/1916/jul/x01.htm

7   V I Lenin, 'The Socialist Revolution and the Right of Nations to Self-determination' (1916) in *Collected Works* (Moscow, 1972) https://www.marxists.org/archive/lenin/works/1916/jan/x01.htm

8   V I Lenin, 'The Discussion On Self-Determination Summed Up' (July 1916) https://www.marxists.org/archive/lenin/works/1916/jul/x01.htm

9   Colm Bryce, 'Ireland and the Russian Revolution', *Irish Marxist Review*, Vol 6, No 17 (2017) http://www.irishmarxistreview.net/index.php/imr/article/view/231

10   Quoted in Neil Davidson, *The Origins of Scottish Nationhood,* (London,

2000), p56.

11 Rosalind Mitchison, *A History of Scotland*, (London 1970), p.345.

12 Tom Devine, *The Scottish Clearances* (London, 2018).

13 Tom Devine, *The Scottish Nation 1700 -2000* (London, 2000), p288.

14 David Fielding, 'The Social and Economic Determinants of Voting Behaviour: Evidence from the 1992 General Election in Scotland,' *Scottish Journal of Political Economy,* Vol. 45, No. 3, August 1998, p253.

15 Ian Dunt, 'Scottish Independence: The Class Issue', *Politics.co.uk* website, 22 August 2014, https://www.politics.co.uk/comment-analysis/2014/08/22/scottish-independence-the-class-issue/

16 Tim Bale, Paul Webb & Monica Poletti, *Grassroots: Britain's party members: who they are, what they think and what they do, Queen Mary University* (Mile End Institute, 2018) https://esrcpartymembersprojectorg.files.wordpress.com/2018/01/grassroots-pmp_final.pdf, pp. 11-13.

17 'Social Background of Members of Parliament 1979-2019', House of Commons Library Research Briefing (2020), https://commonslibrary.parliament.uk/research-briefings/cbp-7483/

18 Karl Marx, *Preface to A Contribution to the Critique of Political Economy*, (Moscow, 1977) https://www.marxists.org/archive/marx/works/1859/critique-pol-economy/preface.htm

19 Karl Marx & Friedrich Engels, *The German Ideology* (1846) in *Collected Works*, Volume 5 (Moscow, 1932) https://www.marxists.org/archive/marx/works/1845/german-ideology/ch01b.htm

20 Though the reformist impulse is a universal tendency for the working class under capitalism it should be noted that it does not inevitably find expression. Dictatorships may crush all opposition; and the USA, a country with a parliamentary-style system, lacks a mass reformist party (despite the efforts of people like Bernie Sanders to convert the Democratic Party). Whatever criticisms are made of the reformist project for failing to end capitalism, it is important to note that it is far better not to live under a dictatorship and to have organisations which, however imperfectly, can express working class aspirations. They can also provide a springboard to go further because, as experience has shown, reformists can be won to taking a further step—revolution.

21 Tony Cliff, Donny Gluckstein & Charlie Kimber, *The Labour Party: A Marxist History*, (London, 2018). p415.

22 George Osborne, 'Unleashing nationalism has made the future of the UK the central issue', *Evening Standard*, 19 January 2021, https://www.standard.co.uk/comment/nationalism-union-brexit-b900299.html

23 Philip Sim, 'Could indyref2 be held without UK's consent', *BBC News,* 21 January 2021, https://www.bbc.co.uk/news/uk-scotland-scotland-politics-55751064

24 Tony Blair, 'Leaders' Speech', Labour Party Conference, Brighton, 30 September 1997, http://www.britishpoliticalspeech.org/speech-archive.htm?speech=203

25 Jeremy Corbyn, 'Speech to Labour Party Conference', Brighton, 24 September 2019, https://www.youtube.com/watch?v=svCXfetnTWs

26 *It's Time for Real Change: The Labour Party Manifesto 2019* (London, 2019) https://labour.org.uk/wp-content/uploads/2019/11/Real-Change-Labour-Manifesto-2019.pdf

27 *Strong for Scotland: The SNP Manifesto 2019* (Edinburgh, 2019) https://www.snp.org/general-election-2019/

28 Ernest Bevin quoted in Cliff, Gluckstein & Kimber, 2018, p36.

29 Rosa Luxemburg, *Reform or Revolution* (1908) https://www.marxists.org/archive/luxemburg/1900/reform-revolution/ch07.htm

30 V I Lenin, 'Lecture on the 1905 Revolution', (1917) in *Collected Works, Volume 23* (Moscow, 1964) https://www.marxists.org/archive/lenin/works/1917/jan/09.htm

31 'The Bloody Sunday Petition to the

Tsar' (1905) https://alphahistory.com/russianrevolution/bloody-sunday-petition-1905/

32 Quoted in Richard Day & Daniel Gaido (eds), *Witnesses to Permanent Revolution. The Documentary Record* (Chicago 2011), p6.

33 Quoted in Day & Gaido, p8.

34 Quoted in Day & Gaido, p10.

35 Leon Trotsky, 'Up to the Ninth January' (1905) in Day & Gaido, p283.

36 Leon Trotsky, 'Up to the Ninth January' (1905) in Day & Gaido, p285.

37 Leon Trotsky, *The Permanent Revolution & Results and Prospects* (1906) https://www.marxists.org/archive/trotsky/1931/tpr.

38 Leon Trotsky, *Problems of the Chinese Revolution* (1931), https://www.marxists.org/archive/trotsky/1932/pcr.

39 Tony Cliff, *Deflected Permanent Revolution* (London, 1963) https://www.marxists.org/archive/cliff/works/1963/xx/permrev.htm..

Chapter 2: The Formation of Scotland

1 Keith Webb, *The Growth of Nationalism in Scotland* (London, 1978) p9.

2 Robin McKie, 'Neolithic discovery: why Orkney is the centre of ancient Britain', *Guardian*, 6 October 2012, https://www.theguardian.com/science/2012/oct/06/orkney-temple-centre-ancient-britain.

3 Maev Kennedy, 'Arrival of Beaker folk changed Britain for ever, ancient DNA study shows', *Guardian*, 22 February 2018, https://www.theguardian.com/science/2018/feb/21/arrival-of-beaker-folk-changed-britain-forever-ancient-dna-study-shows

4 Quoted in T C Smout, *A History of the Scottish People, 1560-1830* (London, 1985) p31.

5 Stuart McHardy, *Scotland's Future History* (Edinburgh, 2015) p44.

6 Benedict Anderson, *Imagined Communities,* (London, 2006) https://is.muni.cz/el/1423/jaro2016/SOC757/um/61816961/Benedict_Anderson_Imagined_Communities.pdf

7 McHardy, p82.

8 Jenny Wormald, *Scotland: A History* (Oxford, 2011) p220.

9 Wormald p39.

10 McHardy, p101.

11 Thomas Johnston, *History of the Working Classes in Scotland* (Glasgow, 1929) p11.

12 Chronicle of Walter of Guisborough quoted in Colm McNamee, *The Wars of the Bruces: England and Ireland 1306–1328* (Edinburgh 2006) p63.

13 Sir James Fergusson, *The Declaration of Arbroath*, 6 April 1320 (1970) https://www.nrscotland.gov.uk/files//research/NRS_DoA_English_booklet_700_Spreads_WEB.pdf.

14 Michael Brown & Steve Boardman, 'Survival and Revival: Late Medieval Scotland', in Wormald, p80.

15 GWS Barrow, *Robert Bruce and the community of the Realm of Scotland*, 2nd edition, (Edinburgh, 1976), p.430 quoted in Neil Davidson, *The Origins of Scottish Nationhood* (London, 2000) p48.

16 Sir James Fergusson, *The Declaration of Arbroath*, 6 April 1320 (1970)

17 Johnston p17.

18 John Ball, *Cast off the yoke of bondage*, Speech given at Blackheath, London, June 1381 in https://en.wikisource.org/wiki/Cast_off_the_Yoke_of_Bondage

19 Smout, p38.

20 Robert Burns, *Such a Parcel of Rogues in a Nation* (1791), http://www.robertburns.org/works/344.shtml

21 James D Young, *The Rousing of the Scottish Working Class* (London, 1979) p11.

22 Leanda de Lisle, *Tudor: The Family Story* (London, 2014) p381.

23 Smout, p224.

24 Sir James Steuart, quoted in Neil Davidson, 'Scotland's Bourgeois Revolution' in Chris Bambery (ed), *Scotland, Class and Nation* (London, 1999) p57.

25 Smout, p225.

26 Smout, p262.

27 Johnston, p86.

28 R Mitchison, *A History of Scotland* (London, 1982) p36.

29 Johnston, p86.

30 Smout, p85.

31 Mitchison, p109.

32 Mitchison, p46.

33 On this see Neil Davidson, *Discovering*

the Scottish Revolution, 1692-1746
(London, 2003) pp145-6, 218 & 292.

34   Quoted in Mitchison, p65.

35   Robert Baillie in 1656, quoted in
Mitchison, p65.

36   William Paterson quoted in Neil
Davidson, *Discovering the Scottish
Revolution 1692–1746* (London, 2003)
p94.

37   Quoted in Davidson, 2003, p97.

38   Melville to Carstares, 4 June 1700,
*State Papers and Letters Addressed to
William Carstares* (Edinburgh, 1774),
quoted in Davidson, 2003, p98.

39   Davidson, 2003, p98.

40   Davidson, 2003 and Christopher
Harvie, *Scotland and Nationalism*
(Abingdon, 1994) p109.

41   Quoted in Davidson, 2003, p168.

42   Thomas Kirke, quoted in Mitchison,
p92.

43   Davidson, 2003, p158.

44   Davidson, in Bambery, 1999, p100.

45   Quoted in Davidson, 2003, p136.

46   Quoted in Davidson, 2003, p146.

47   Earl of Mar, quoted in Davidson, 2003,
p141.

48   Sidney Pollard, 'A New Estimate
of British Coal Production, 1750-
1850', *The Economic History Review*,
New Series, 33, No. 2 (1980):
212-35 https://www.jstor.org/
stable/2595840

49   Quoted in Smout, p404.

50   Wormald, p210.

51   Wormald, p212.

52   Wormald, p211.

53   Wormald, p211.

54   Wormald, p213.

55   W H Fraser and C H Lee (eds),
History of Everyday Life in Scotland
(Manchester 1996) p.46.

56   Adrian Gallop, *Scottish mortality:
past, present and future, PAMS
conference*, Office of National
Statistics, 30 October 2009 https://
www.nrscotland.gov.uk/files//
statistics/seminars/30-oct-2009/
uiphs09-scottish-mortality.pdf.

57   Wormald, p. 219.

58   Karl Marx, *Capital, Volume 1*, Ch 27
(Moscow, 1977) p527. https://www.
marxists.org/archive/marx/works/
download/pdf/Capital-Volume-I.pdf,

59   Davidson, 2000, p.146.

60   Quoted in Davidson, 2000, pp148-9.

61   Davidson, 2000, p147.

62   Quoted in Davidson, 2000, p148.

63   Davidson, 2000, p113-4.

64   Quoted in Wormald, p293.

65   Quoted in Davidson, 2000, p117.

66   Davidson, 2000, p118.

67   James Kerr, *Scotland and the Impact
of the Great War, 1914-1928* (Paisley,
2010), p28.

68   Kerr, p18.

69   Wormald, p293.

70   Davidson, 2000, p108.

71   Wormald, p297.

72   Bruce Lenman, quoted in Davidson,
2000, p111

**Chapter 3: The Making of the Scottish
Working Class 1787 to 1850**

1   Tom Devine, *The Scottish Clearances,
A History of the Dispossessed* (Milton
Keynes, 2018), p139.

2   Friedrich Engels, *The Condition of the
Working Class in England in 1844*, (first
published 1845) (Newton Stewart,
2019) p81.

3   *Glasgow Mercury*, 1787 (4 July—11
July).

4   *Glasgow Mercury*, 1787.

5   *Glasgow Mercury*, 1787 (4 July—11
July).

6   Glasgow Trades Council, *The Calton
Weavers Memorial 1787* (Glasgow 1957)

7   Glasgow Trades Council, 1957.

8   The stones were preserved largely
through the efforts of the great Red
Clydesider and leader of the National
Unemployed Workers Movement,
Harry McShane. He wrote the first
history of the strike in 1931 for
Glasgow Trades Council. When the
People's Palace commissioned a
portrait of McShane to be painted by
the writer Alistair Gray, he chose to be
painted standing next to the memorial
stones. Elspeth King, *The Strike of the
Glasgow Weavers 1787* (Glasgow, 1987).

9   Glasgow Trades Council, 1957.

10   Karl Marx, *The International
Workingmen's Association, General
Rules* (1864) https://www.marxists.
org/history/international/iwma/
documents/1864/rules.htm

11   Smith was the most celebrated figure
of the Scottish Enlightenment, often
regarded as the founder of modern
economics.

12 See Karl Marx, *Economic and Philosophical Manuscripts of 1844, Profit of Capital, Section 1— Capital.* https://www.marxists.org/archive/marx/works/1844/manuscripts/capital.htm

13 Adam Smith, *An Inquiry into the Nature and Causes of the Wealth of Nations 1786* (Edinburgh and New York), pp28-31.

14 Elspeth King, *The Strike of the Glasgow Weavers 1787* (Glasgow, 1987).

15 Tom Devine, *The Scottish Nation, A Modern History* (London, 2012), p218.

16 Henry William Meikle, *Scotland and the French Revolution* (Leopold Classic Library, 1912) p71.

17 Meikle, p76.

18 Devine, *The Scottish Nation*, pp196-197.

19 Meikle, p90.

20 Meikle, p81.

21 Chris Bambery, *A People's History of Scotland* (London, 2018) p85.

22 Meikle, pp96-97.

23 Tom Johnston, *The History of the Working Classes in Scotland*, (Wakefield, 1974) p218.

24 Meikle, p90.

25 By far the best account of Muir's life is Murray Armstrong's excellent book *The Liberty Tree* (Edinburgh, 2014).

26 'The Minutes of the Proceedings of the First General Convention of the delegates for the Societies of the Friends of the People throughout Scotland', 1793, in Meikle, Appendix A.

27 McIlvaney, *Burns the Radical: Poetry and Politics in late 18th Century Scotland,*(East Lothian, 2002) p202.

28 Quoted in Robert Crawford, *The Bard* (London, 2010), p393.

29 Quoted in Janet Todd, *Mary Wollstonecraft: A Revolutionary Life* (New York, 2000) p168.

30 Meikle, p103.

31 Quoted in Armstrong, p185.

32 Quoted in Armstrong, p189.

33 Meikle, p145.

34 Meikle, p145.

35 Bambery, 2018, p91.

36 Meikle, p158.

37 Paul Foot, *The Vote: How it Was Won and How it Was Undermined* (London, 2012) p56.

38 Johnston, 1974.

39 William M Roach, *Radical Reform Movements in Scotland 1815—1822*, PhD Thesis (Glasgow, 1970) p73, theses.gla.ac.uk/1212.

40 Roach, p163.

41 Roach, p168.

42 The Free Library, *Remembering the 'Radical Laird': George Kinloch as Local Hero in Nineteenth Century Scottish Reform Poetry* https://www.thefreelibrary.com/Remembering+the+Radical+Laird'.

43 Peter Berresford Ellis & Seumas Mac a'Ghobhainn, *The Radical Rising: The Scottish Insurrection of 1820 2001* (Edinburgh, 2016) pp15-16.

44 Quoted in Devine, *The Scottish Nation,* p226.

45 Berresford Ellis and Mac a'Ghobhainn, p200.

46 Quoted in Roache, 1970, p231.

47 Berresford Ellis and Mac a'Ghobhainn, p279.

48 Berresford Ellis and Mac a'Ghobhainn, p306.

49 Alexander Somerville, *The Autobiography of a Working Man (*London, 1848) pp16-20

50 For a brilliantly researched and evocative account of the Radical Rising which convincingly refutes the nationalist interpretation of the rising see Murray Armstrong, *The Fight for Scottish Democracy, Rebellion and Reform in 1820* (London, 2020).

51 Berresford Ellis and Maca'Ghobhainn, p327.

52 James D Young, *The Rousing of the Scottish Working Class* (London, 1979) p61.

53 Quoted in Berresford Ellis and Mac a'Ghobhainn, pp146-147.

54 Johnston, p239.

55 Berresford Ellis and Mac a'Ghobhainn, p18.

56 Neil Davidson, *The Origins of Scottish Nationhood* (London, 2000), p192.

57 Berresford Ellis and Mac a'Ghobhainn, p323.

58 Berresford Ellis and Mac a'Ghobhainn, p330.

59 Johnston, p238.

60 Tom Devine, James D Young and Neil Davidson all hold this view.

61 Berresford Ellis and Mac a'Ghobhainn, pp326-327.

62   Young, p45.
63   Davidson, *The Origins of Scottish Nationhood,* p167.
64   Friedrich Engels, *The Condition of the Working Class in England in 1844* (Dumfries and Galloway, 2019), p81.
65   For an excellent analysis of the consequences of combined and uneven development for Scotland at this time see Neil Davidson, *The Origins of Scottish Nationhood* (London, 2000) pp167-182 and Henry Heller, *The Birth of Capitalism, A Twenty First Century Perspective* (London, 2011), pp145-149. See also Neil Davidson & Jamie Allinson, 'De-Provincializing 1820: The West of Scotland General Strike in the Mirror of Uneven and Combined Development' (Part 1), *Scottish Labour History*, Volume 55 (Glasgow, 2020). This is an excellent analysis of the Radical Rising set in the context of uneven and combined development. which argues that the rising was the first general strike in the history of capitalism and that working class militancy spread globally as capitalism developed. Part 2 will be published later in 2021.
66   Somerville, pp93-94.
67   Johnston, p245.
68   Johnston, p243.
69   Leon Trotsky, *Writings on Britain, Volume 2, Where is Britain Going,* (London, 1974), p97.
70   Young, pp86-87.
71   *Northern Star*, 1838, (17th March 1838, Edition 2 of 2) p3.
72   Quoted in Bambery, 2018, p101.
73   W Hamish Fraser, *Chartism in Scotland* (Brecon, 2010), p33.
74   Fraser, p106.
75   Ray Challinor, 'Peter Murray McDouall and "Physical Force Chartism"', *International Socialism* 2:12 (Spring 1981). https://www.marxists.org/history/etol/writers/challinor/1981/xx/mcdouall.html
76   Tom Leonard, *Radical Renfrew: Poetry in the West of Scotland from the French Revolution to the First World War* (Edinburgh, 1990), pp162-165.
77   *Northern Star*, 19 January 1838, p8.
78   *Northern Star*, 18 August 1838, p6.
79   Johnston, p249.
80   Foot, p99.

81   Fraser, p61.
82   Quoted in Fraser, p117.
83   Fraser, p121.
84   Young, p97.
85   Fraser, p155.
86   Fraser, p159
87   Chartist Ancestors Databank, www.chartistancestors.co.uk
88   *Northern Star*, 7 November 1840.
89   *Northern Star*, 5 November 1840.
90   *Northern Star*, 7 November 1840.
91   Fraser, p198.
92   *Northern Star*, 16 November 1839.
93   *Glasgow Constitutional*, 20 November 1839.
94   *Scottish Patriot*, 30 November 1839.
95   David Black, *Helen MacFarlane: Red Republican: Essays, articles and her translation of the Communist Manifesto* (London, 2014), pvi.
96   'Manifesto of the German Communist Party', *Red Republican*, 9, 16, 23 & 30 November 1850, in Black pp119-149.
97   See 'The Red Flag in 1850', *Red Republican*, 13 July 1850, quoted in Black.
98   See 'The Democratic and Social Republic', *Red Republican*, 12 October 1950 in Black.
99   Quoted in Black, pxxviii
100   See 'Signs of the Times. Red Stockings versus Lawn-Sleeves', *Friend of the People*, 21 and 26 December 1850, quoted in Black, pp103-110.
101   *Scottish Patriot*, 14 September 1839.
102   Karl Marx, 'The Chartists', *New York Tribune*, 25 August 1852. https://wikirouge.net/texts/en/The_Chartists_(August_10,_1852)
103   Foot, p119.
104   Trotsky, p94.
105   'Protestors rally to attack Sutherland statue', *Press & Journal*, 23 June 2020, https://www.pressandjournal.co.uk/fp/news/highlands/2278892/protestors
106   One of the best accounts of the lowland clearances is in Peter Aitchison & Andrew Cassel, *The Lowland Clearances, Scotland's Silent Revolution* (Edinburgh 2019).
107   Devine, 2018, p83.
108   Johnston, p200.
109   Karl Marx, 'Chapter 27: Expropriation of the Agricultural Population from the Land', *Capital, Volume 1* (Moscow, 1977)

https://www.marxists.org/archive/
marx/works/1867-c1/ch27.htm

110   Eric Richards, *The Highland
Clearances* (Edinburgh 2016) p170.

111   Devine, p320.

112   For an excellent account of the
Levellers Revolt see Devine, 2018,
Chapter 5, pp102-106 and Aitchison
and Cassell, 2019, chapter 3 pp30-50.
A very good analysis of the Ross-shire
Insurrection can be found in Richards,
2016, Chapter 6, pp112-129.

113   Johnston, p185.

114   Richards, 2016. p115.

115   Richards, 2016, p121.

116   For a detailed discussion of the Ross-
shire Insurrection see Richards, 2016,
chapter 6.

117   Donald Baillie, 'Satire on Patrick
Sellar', in Donald S Meek, *Tuath is
Tighearna: Tenants and Landlords*
(Edinburgh 1995), quoted in Eric
Richards, *Debating the Highland
Clearances*, (Edinburgh, 2007) pp205-
208.

118   'The Duchess of Sutherland and
Slavery', *The People's Paper*, No 45, 12
March 1853, https://www.marxists.
org/archive/marx/works/1853/03/12.
htm

119   The Duchess found support in none
other than Harriet Beecher Stowe, the
anti-slavery campaigner and author
of *Uncle Tom's Cabin*. She defended
the actions of the duchess and the
Sutherland family in a dreadful
sycophantic letter. See Harriet
Beecher Stowe, 'Letter XVII', *Sunny
Memories of Foreign Lands* (London,
1854), in Richards, 2007, p198-199.

120   Devine, 2018, p294-295.

121   James Hunter, *Insurrection: Scotland's
Famine Winter* (Edinburgh, 2019)

122   Hunter, p217-218.

123   Hunter, p171.

124   Hunter, p218.

125   Hunter, p205.

126   Hunter, 2019, p141-144.

127   Hunter, p144.

128   D W Cowley, 'The Crofters Party—
1885 to 1892', *Scottish Historical
Review*, Volume 35, (1956) www.
caledonia.org.uk/land/documents/
CroftersParty.pdf.PDFfile

129   Johnston, p207-208.

130   Cowley, 1956.

131   Cowley, 1956.

132   See Donald Ross, Letter to the Lord
Advocate, reprinted in *Northern
Ensign*, 4 May 1854, in Richards 2007,
p195, p197 and Hugh Miller in *Eig*,
1845, p197, p198.

133   Hunter, p224-225.

134   The Crofters Party was the
parliamentary group of the HLLRA.
Cowley argues that the Crofters Party
can be regarded as the first British
independent common people's party.
See Cowley, 1956.

135   Devine, 2018, p343.

136   Devine, 2018, p343.

137   Andrew Picken & Stuart Nicolson,
'Who Owns Scotland? The Changing
Face of Scotland's Landowners',
BBC Scotland News, 21 May 2019,
https//: www.bbc.com/news/
uk-scotland-47963208

138   Davidson, 2003, p298-299.

139   Young, 1979, p94.

140   Richards, 2016, p12.

141   Richards, 2016, p12.

142   Neil Davidson, *Discovering the
Scottish Revolution 1692-1746* (London
2003) p296.

143   See Michael Fry, *Wild Scots: Four
Hundred Years of Highland History*,
(John Murray, 2005)

144   Richards, 2011, p24-25.

145   One of Glasgow's best-known
landmarks is the "Heilanman's
Umbrella", a Victorian railway bridge
in Argyle Street. It became a meeting
place for Highland workers during
the Highland Clearances and offered
shelter for those who were homeless
in bad weather.

146   Engels, 2019, p100.

147   Engels, 2019, p106.

148   International Labour Organisation,
*Wage and salaried workers, total (%
of total employment)*, https://data.
worldbank.org/indicator/SL.EMP.
WORK.ZS

Chapter 4: Red Clydeside

1   For example, even Tom Devine's
otherwise rewarding account of the
last 300 years, devotes very little
space to the period and claims: "The
emergence of Red Clydeside and the
labour breakthrough was only part of
the re-alignment of Scottish politics

after the war". Tom Devine, *The Scottish Nation: 1700-2000*(London, 1999) p313-314.

2   Rosalind Mitchison, *A History of Scotland,* (London, 1970), p345.

3   See Neil Davidson, *The Origins of Scottish Nationhood,* (London, 2000), p168.

4   Leon Trotsky,*Where is Britain Going?* Cited in Nan Milton, *John Maclean,* (London, 1973), p10.

5   Tom Devine, *The Scottish Nation: 1700-2000*, Penguin Press, 1999, p300.

6   Joan Smith, 'Taking Leadership of the Movement: the ILP in Glasgow 1906-14', in McKinlay & Morris (eds), *The ILP on Clydeside 1893-1932*, (Manchester, 1991), p74.

7   John Maclean, *In the Rapids of Revolution: Essays, Articles and Letters 1902-23* (London, 1978), p76.

8   Harry McShane & Joan Smith, *Harry Shane: No Mean Fighter* (London, 1978), p63-64.

9   T C Smout, *A History of the Scottish People, 1560-1830* (London, 1985) p63.

10   *Socialist Labour Press*, 1918, p15 cited in William Kenefick, *Red Scotland! The Rise and Fall of Radical Left 1872-1932*, (Edinburgh, 2007), p134.

11   See socialist suffragette Jenny Stephens's account in Megan McEachern, 'Suffra-jiu-jitsu: New exhibition sheds light on little known facts about Scotland's suffragettes', *Sunday Post*, 28 February 2019, https://www.sundaypost.com/fp/ suffra-jiu-jitsu-new-exhibition-sheds-light-on-little-known-facts-about-scotlands-suffragettes/

12   Leaflet signed by Willie Gallacher (president) and J M Messer (secretary), 'Clyde Workers Committee: To All Clyde Workers' (1915) https://www.marxists.org/ archive/gallacher/1915/clyde-committee.htm

13   Willie Gallacher, *Revolt on the Clyde* (London, 1978) p 51.

14   Ray Challinor, *The Origins of British Bolshevism* (London, 1977) p33. https://www.marxists.org/history/ etol/writers/challinor/1977/british-bolshevism/index.htm

15   Lesley Orr, 'In Praise of Dangerous Women', *Scottish Sunday Herald*, 23 April 2017, p31.

16   William Knox, *Scottish Labour Leaders 1918-39* (Edinburgh, 1984), p185.

17   See McShane & Smith, p77.

18   McShane & Smith, p77.

19   Brian Ripley & John McHugh, *John Maclean: Lives of the Left* (Manchester, 1989) p88.

20   Cabinet Papers quoted in James Hinton, *The First Shop Stewards' Movement* (London, 1973) p140.

21   Hinton, p135.

22   *Forward*, 1 January 1915, cited in Kenny MacAskill, *Glasgow 1919–The Rise of Red Clydeside*, (London 2019), p82.

23   Hinton, p135.

24   Gallacher, p116.

25   Hinton, p141.

26   *Glasgow Herald*, 21 May 1915.

27   *Forward*, 5 February 1916, cited in MacAskill, p101 and Hinton, p121.

28   Hinton, p131. Petroff was deported to Russia but not until the Tsar had been toppled. Its Provisional Government exchanged him for British spies they were holding. For a time, he became a Diplomat for the Bolshevik government and worked alongside Trotsky at the Brest–Litovsk negotiations which enabled Russia to pull out of the war.

29   Sir Christopher Addison, appointed Munitions Minister after Lloyd George became Secretary for War later in 1916, quoted in Hinton, p156.

30   Hinton, p161.

31   Challinor, p187.

32   Hinton, p250.

33   Chris Fuller, 'Fighting the War on the Home Front', *Socialist Review*, 388, (February 2014), p24.

34   *Solidarity*, paper of the National Shop Stewards & Workers Committee Movement, February 1918 issue, cited in Dave Sherry, *Empire and Revolution: a Socialist History of the First World War*, (London, 2014), p148.

35   *The Scotsman*, 30 January 1918.

36   John Foster, 'Strike Action and Working Class Politics on Clydeside 1914-19' paper presented at a conference on Working Class Movements and their Revolutionary Potential at the end of WW1, Graz,

Austria, June 1989. Published in *International Review of Social History*, Volume 35, (Amsterdam, 1990-91) p53.

37 Maclean, p101.

38 Ripley & McHugh, p108.

39 E H Carr, *The Bolshevik Revolution: Volume 3*, (London, 1983), p135.

40 *The Times*, 30 January 1919.

41 Andrew Rothstein, *The Soldiers' Strikes of 1919* (London, 1980), p94

42 Challinor, p196.

43 Basil Thomson, *The Scene Changes*, (London, 1939), p410.

44 Lord Shinwell, *I've Lived Through It All* (London, 1973), p17.

45 John Leopold, 'The Forty Hours Strike', in Laurie Flynn (ed) *We Shall be All: Recent Chapters on the History of Working Class Struggle in Scotland* (London, 1978), p38.

46 *The Scottish Coalminer*, quoted in, Nan Milton, *John Maclean,* (London, 1973), p199-200.

47 Leopold, p39-40.

48 Rothstein, p94.

49 *The Evening Times,* 30 January 1919.

50 Maggie Craig, *When the Clyde Ran Red,* (Edinburgh, 2011), p162.

51 Cited in Chris Bambery, *A Peoples History of Scotland* (London, 2014), p156.

52 Iain S McLean, *The Legend of Red Clydeside* (London, 1983) p133.

53 McShane & Smith, p106.

54 McShane & Smith, p107.

55 D S Morton, *The 40 Hours Strike,* SLP pamphlet (Glasgow, 1919), p6.

56 John Leopold, p40.

57 Kieran Allen, *1916; Ireland's Revolutionary Tradition* (London, 2016) p93.

58 J T Murphy, *Preparing for Power* (London, 1972), p176-7.

59 John Maclean, p153.

60 *ILP Conference Report 1919*, p72.

61 *British Government Cabinet Papers*, CAB 23/9, WC 514/9, http://filestore.nationalarchives.gov.uk/pdfs/large/cab-23-9.pdf

62 Andrew Rothstein, p94.

63 *British Government Cabinet Papers*, CAB23/9, WC 525/1, http://filestore.nationalarchives.gov.uk/pdfs/large/cab-23-9.pdf

64 Gallacher, p234.

65 McShane & Smith, p109.

66 Lloyd George, *War Memoirs*, 1938, p

67 John Maclean, p148.

68 Quoted in Nye Bevan, *In Place of Fear,* (London, 1961), pp 20-21

69 Quoted in Nye Bevan, *In Place of Fear,* (London, 1961), p21.

70 *British Government Cabinet Papers*, CAB 23/9, WC 525/1, http://filestore.nationalarchives.gov.uk/pdfs/large/cab-23-9.pdf

71 Ripley and McHugh, p164.

72 J Maclean, p220.

73 See for example, Gordon Barclay, *The Deployment of the Army to Glasgow, 31 January to 17 February 1919*, Edinburgh University Press blog, 3 October 2018, https://euppublishingblog.com/2018/10/03/georgesquarebattle/

74 C A Oakley, *The Second City* (Glasgow, 1975).

75 J Wheatley, quoted in the November 1922 issue of *Forward*, the ILP newspaper.

76 J Wheatley, quoted in the November 1922 issue of *Forward*, the ILP newspaper.

77 It is now available from the Marx Memorial Library and the Glasgow Women's Library. https://www.marx-memorial-library.org.uk/project/socialist-opposition-ww1/autobiography-helen-crawfurd

78 Philip Snowden, *Autobiography* (London, 1934) Vol. 1, p127.

79 David Kirkwood, *My Life of Revolt* (London, 1935) p201/2

80 Ian S McLean, *The Legend of Red Clydeside* (London, 1983) p133.

81 Kirkwood, p116-8.

82 Quoted in Hinton, p17.

Chapter 5: The Decline of the Labour Party in Scotland

1 Gerry Hassan & Eric Shaw, *Strange Death of Labour in Scotland* (2012) and Tom Devine, 'The Strange Death of Labour Scotland', *New Statesman*, 2 March 2016.

2 Chris Harman, *The Fire Last Time: 1968 and After* (London, 1988), p229.

3 Quoted in Hazel Croft, 'How Labour Tried to Outlaw Strikes', *Socialist Worker*, 6 January 2000, https://bit.ly/3fclE2f

4 *Glasgow Evening Times*, 12 November 1969.

5   R A Leeson, *Strike: A Live History 1887-1971* (London, 1973), p233.

6   Chris Harman, *The Fire Last Time* (London, 1988) p242.

7   Figures from Chris Harman, 'Communist Party in Decline', *International Socialism* 63, first series, (October 1973), p21.

8   BBC TV 6 O'Clock News, 2 August 1971 quoted in John Foster & Charles Woolfson, *The Politics of the UCS Work-In* (London, 1986)..

9   Roger Rosewall, 'Work-ins, Sit-ins and Redundancy', *International Socialism*, 1:50,(January 1972), p18.

10 *Socialist Worker*, 11 September 1971, p1.

11 *Morning Star*, 1 February 1973.

12 Chris Harman, 'Notes of the Month', *International Socialism* 64, 1st series, (November 1973), p3.

13 Quoted in Duncan Hallas, *The Labour Party: Myth and Reality* (London, 1985), https://www.marxists.org/archive/hallas/works/1981/02/labour.html

14 Quoted in Hallas, 1985.

15 'The workers who sabotaged Pinochet's murder machine', *Socialist Worker*, 31 October 2018, p13, https://bit.ly/2P4aK3Q

16 Neil Davidson, 'In Perspective: Tom Nairn', *International Socialism* 82, (London, March 1999), p123.

17 Hallas, 1985.

18 Tony Cliff, 'The Balance of Class Forces', *International Socialism* 2:6 (Autumn, 1979), p4.

19 Pat Clark, 'The 1981 Lee Jeans occupation: women showed how to win', *Socialist Worker*, 26 Mar 2005, https://bit.ly/3kgaUAE

20 Alex Callinicos & Mike Simons, *The Great Strike; the Miners' Strike of 1984-5 and its Lessons* (London, 1985) p91.

21 Callinicos & Simons, p88.

22 James Naughtie, 'Labour, 1979–1988' in I Donachie, C Harvie & I Wood, *Forward! Labour Politics in Scotland, 1888-1988* (Edinburgh, 1989) p167.

23 David Butler & Dennis Kavanagh, *The British General Election of 1992* (Basingstoke, 1992) p 269.

24 Ewan Cameron, *Impaled upon a Thistle: Scotland since 1880,* (Edinburgh, 2010), p 322.

25 Chris Bambery, *A Peoples History of Scotland* (London, 2014) p276.

26 *New Statesman and Society*, 11 June 1993.

27 Francis Fukuyama,*The End of History?* (New York, 1989), p3.

28 Fukuyama, p3.

29 Quoted in 'Notes of the Month', *Socialist Worker Review*, 162 (March 1993), p4.

30 Quoted in Charlie Kimber, *Jeremy Corbyn, Labour and the fight for Socialism* (London, 2017) p 29.

31 Quoted in Tony Cliff, Donny Gluckstein & Charlie Kimber, *The Labour Party: A Marxist History*, (London, 2018), p417.

32 Quoted in Cliff, Gluckstein & Kimber, 2018, p 414.

33 Cliff, Gluckstein and Kimber, p415.

34 Jim Main & Gerry Mooney, *Resisting Austerity Urbanism: The Case of Public Sector Workers in Glasgow* (Glasgow, 2019) p6-8.

35 Cited in Gerry Hassan, *The Scottish Labour Party* (Edinburgh, 2004) p47.

36 Gill Hubbard & David Miller (eds), *Arguments Against the G8,* (London, 2005).

37 Tom Devine, 'The Strange Death of Labour Scotland', *New Statesman*, 2 March 2016.

38 'Vote2001: Results & Constituencies UK Breakdown', *BBC News,* https://bbc.in/2OAx4l6

39 'Election 2015: Results, Scotland', *BBC News,* https://bbc.in/2LUcnj5

40 Phillip Sim, 'Election 2017: Scotland's Results in Numbers', *BBC News*, 12 June 2017, https://bbc.in/3bdlRi2

41 'Election 2019: Results, Scotland', *BBC News*, https://bbc.in/3puxbvb

42 Brian Deer, 'Glasgow politics: Labour's wild west of Scotland– Hang 'Em High', *The Sunday Times Magazine*, 25 January 1998, https://briandeer.com/glasgow-labour.htm

43 Rosa Luxemburg, *The Mass Strike,* chapter IV. *The Interaction of the Political and the Economic Struggle*, (1906) https://bit.ly/2LZAe10

44 'Prestwick protest stops flights carrying Israeli bombs', *Socialist Worker,* 5 August 2006, https://bit.ly/3qqRlYh

45   'Election 2010: Scotland Results', *BBC News*, https://bbc.in/2Nrav1L

46   Charlie Kimber, 'In the balance: the class struggle in Britain', *International Socialism*, issue 122 (Spring edition), http://isj.org.uk/in-the-balance-the-class-struggle-in-britain/

47   'Diageo strike ballot to go ahead', *BBC News*, 30 October 2009, https://bbc.in/37m2LVR

48   Simon Johnson, 'More than 20,000 take to streets to protest Johnnie Walker plant closure', *The Telegraph*, 26 July 2009, https://bit.ly/3beR6JJ

49   Danny McGregor, 'Wave of revolt at job losses sweeps Kilmarnock', *Socialist Worker*, 28 July 2009, https://bit.ly/3quKJse

50   'Diageo chief executive sees salary package hit £3.5m as 900 lose jobs', *The Herald*, 14 September 2009, https://bit.ly/3dhRauG

51   'Diageo branding overcomes temporary setbacks', *Beverage Daily*, 19 July 2008, https://bit.ly/3djBG9O

52   'Diageo unions end closure protest', *BBC News*, 9 December 2009, https://bbc.in/2Nfbp1s

53   Mark Aitkin, 'MP calls for Diageo jobs to be saved with public money', *Daily Record*, 5 July 2009, https://bit.ly/3bfuske

54   'Des Browne MP on Johnnie Walker', *Youtube,* 27 August 2009, https://www.youtube.com/watch?v=opvD7sUDplk

55   Charlene Sweeney, 'Strikes and sweeteners to forstall Diageo closure', *The Times*, 6 July 2009, https://bit.ly/3d2hibq

56   'Unite's Derek Simpson plays down strikes threat', *BBC News*, 8 August 2010, https://www.bbc.co.uk/news/business-10906288

57   'March for the alternative–Saturday 26 March', *Guardian*, 27 March 2011, https://bit.ly/3slNBso

58   'N30 strikes: picket line, march and rally reports from across the country', *Socialist Worker*, 30 November 2011, https://bit.ly/3tIkdfS

59   'Massive Support from EIS members: Strike Day 30 Nov 2011', *Educational Institute Scotland (EIS)*, 30 November 2011, https://www.eis.org.uk/Pension-Archive/Supportfrommembers

60   Charlie Kimber, 'The rebirth of our power? After the 30 November mass strike', *International Socialism*, 2:133 (Winter 2012), https://bit.ly/2NLtpRB

61   Annette Mackin, 'CWU union's damaging deal with Royal Mail is a blow that strikes could have stopped', *Socialist Worker*, 11 February 2014, https://bit.ly/3rjg2pk

62   'Unison conference recalled in revolt over local government pay', *Socialist Worker*, 9 December 2014, https://bit.ly/3lIIiR2

63   'Recall Conference: FBU political engagement strategy', *Fire Brigade Union (FBU), Circular: 2015HOC0596MW*, 10 November 2014.

64   Dave Sewell, 'Jerry Hicks gets an 'amazing' 80,000 votes in Unite election', *Socialist Worker*, 13 April 2013, shorturl.at/pxBHP

65   Simon Basketter, Ian Bradley & Alan Kenny, *Sparks Revolt: How Rank and File Electricians Beat Besna (victory edition) (*2012).

66   'Grangemouth: a betrayal foretold', *Socialist Worker*, 3 December 2013, https://bit.ly/3tSVjKR

67   Jim Ratcliffe, 'Grangemouth – The battle with the union and why we trail behind Germany', *The Sunday Telegraph*, 3 November 2013, https://bit.ly/31co6xu

68   Dave Sewell et al, *Grangemouth: where now for the unions?, Socialist Worker* pamphlet (London, 2013), p9.

69   'Ed Miliband attacks Unite leader Len McCluskey's comments', *BBC News*, 25 April 2013, https://bbc.in/2QsEhVf

70   Julie Sherry, 'Can Len McCluskey reclaim Labour?', *International Socialism*, 2:140 (Autumn 2013), https://bit.ly/3slQysY

71   'Ed Miliband naive on pay, says Unison boss Dave Prentis', *BBC News*, 18 January 2012, https://bbc.in/3sbEeey

72   Jon Stone, 'Labour loses control of Glasgow City Council for the first time in 40 years', *Independent*, 5 May 2017, https://bit.ly/3vTAZL1

73   Raymie Kiernan, 'Kamikaze council declares war on Glasgow's workers', *Socialist Worker*, 16 November 2016, https://bit.ly/3vVKglG

74   Patrick Sawer & Robert Mendick,

'Tiny band of left-wing radicals bring jobs policy to its knees', *The Telegraph*, 25 February 2012, https://bit.ly/3cg2dDQ

75 Gary MacLachlan, 'Bedroom tax campaign celebrates in Scotland - and prepares for new battles', *Socialist Worker*, 11 February 2014, https://bit.ly/3vSoX4D

76 'Johann Lamont insists taxes will have to rise as she calls for an end to 'something for nothing' culture', *Daily Record*, 25 September 2012, https://bit.ly/3sjOwcO

77 Julie Sherry, 'Anger as Scottish Labour confirms Lamont's lurch right', *Socialist Worker*, 3 October 2012, https://bit.ly/3vVwobp

78 'UK: Empire strikes back as 'imperial masters' gather in Glasgow', *Youtube*, 11 September 2014, https://bit.ly/2PgWncm

79 'Has Scottish Labour learned any lessons from the referendum?', *Socialist Worker*, 28 October 2014, https://bit.ly/3d1MeZ7

80 Raymie Kiernan, 'Ruling class panics after Yes campaign takes lead in Scottish independence poll', *Socialist Worker*, 9 September 2014, https://bit.ly/3vVUpie

81 Andrew Learmonth, 'Scottish Labour councillor gets top job at Orange Order', *The National*, 29 July 2019, https://bit.ly/310FTSt

82 'North Lanarkshire Council–Member and Committee Information', *North Lanarkshire Council*, https://bit.ly/3w1cDiK

83 Alan Whitaker, 'Orange Order elected to councils as Labour and Tory members', *The Herald*, 7 May 2017, https://bit.ly/3rgx1Zi

84 Freya McClements, 'Scottish and Orange: 'In Scotland there's a hatred of anything unionist', *Irish Times*, 7 December 2020, https://bit.ly/3aK5bzV

85 Raymie Kiernan, 'Ruling class panics after Yes campaign takes lead in Scottish independence poll', *Socialist Worker*, 9 September 2014, https://bit.ly/3vVUpie

86 Charlie Kimber, 'Labour's betrayals let Tories back in', *Socialist Worker*, 8 May 2015, https://bit.ly/3ceE9kX

87 'Scottish Labour holding Corbyn back – Change is needed', *Campaign For Socialism*, 21 July 2017, https://bit.ly/2QBWoZf

88 'Scottish Labour holding Corbyn back – Change is needed', *Campaign For Socialism*, 21 July 2017, https://bit.ly/2QBWoZf

89 Chris Campbell, 'Scottish Labour leader faces backlash after urging Scots to vote Tory to keep Sturgeon out', *The Express*, 22 May 2017, https://bit.ly/399rk9m

90 Nicola Slawson, 'Jeremy Corbyn 'absolutely fine' with second Scottish vote', *Guardian*, 11 May 2017, https://bit.ly/3cg5KlA

91 'Labour to block new Scottish independence vote', *BBC* News, 23 September 2018, https://bbc.in/3reREp0

92 Nicola Sturgeon, on *Twitter*, @NicolaSturgeon, 23 September 2018, https://bit.ly/3sf4W6d

93 Adam Withnall & Charlie Cooper, 'Jeremy Corbyn accuses head of UK military of 'breaching' constitutional principle of neutrality on Trident', *Independent*, 8 November 2015, https://tinyurl.com/yalnj9k9

Chapter 6: Racism and anti-racism in Scotland

1 Karl Marx and Friedrich Engels, *The German Ideology* (1846), https://www.marxists.org/archive/marx/works/1845/german-ideology/

2 "One might almost say that he has two theoretical consciousnesses (or one contradictory consciousness): one which is implicit in his activity and which in reality unites him with all his fellow workers in the practical transformation of the real world; and one, superficially explicit or verbal, which he has inherited from the past and uncritically absorbed." Antonio Gramsci, *Selections from the Prison Notebooks* (London, 1971) p641.

3 Heinrich Himmler, Posen Speech, 4 October 1943, https://www.jewishvirtuallibrary.org/himmler-s-posen-speech-quot-extermination-quot

4 University of Glasgow Senate

minutes, Vol 19, 23 June 1938, p104; A. Sherman, *Island Refuge: GB and Refugees from the Third Reich*, (London, 1973), p48.

5   Angus Calder, *Revolutionary Empire*, (London, 1998 edition) p.x.

6   Neal Ascherson, *London Review of Books*, Vol 33, Number 19, 6 October 2011, https://www.lrb.co.uk/the-paper/v33/n19/neal-ascherson/the-money-s-still-out-there

7   Ascherson, 2011

8   Ascherson

9   Ascherson, 2011.

10   Devine, p227.

11   Alistair Durie, *The Scottish Linen Industry in the Eighteenth Century* (Edinburgh, 1979), pp158-60.

12   Tom Devine, 'Scotland and Transatlantic Slavery' in Devine, 2015, p11.

13   Tom Devine, *Scotland's Empire* (London, 2003) p 224.

14   Hilary Beckles, 'The 200 Years' War: slave resistance in the British West Indies, an overview of the historiography', *Jamaican Historical Review*, 13 (1982), pp1–10.

15   Adam Smith, *Wealth of Nations* (London, 1937), p366.

16   Iain Whyte, 'The Upas Tree' in Devine (ed) (2015) p189.

17   David Hume *Essays, Moral and Political* (1741–42).

18   Felix Wadham, 'David Hume was a brilliant philosopher but also a racist involved in slavery', *The Scotsman*, 17 July 2020, https://bit.ly/3qMErUX

19   E.W. Andrews (ed.) *Janet Schaw, Journal of a Lady of quality, being the Narrative of a journey from Scotland to the West Indies, North Carolina and Portugal in the years 1774-1776* (Newhaven: Yale University Press (1939) p127

20   *Glasgow Courier* 18 April, 15, 17, 22 June 1826

21   Iain MacKinnon & Andrew Mackillop *Plantation slavery and landownership in the west Highlands and Islands – legacies and lessons*) (Community Land Scotland), November 2020

22   Frederick Douglass Letter to William Lloyd Garrison 16 April 1846 https://docsouth.unc.edu/neh/douglass/support11.html

23   Henry C Wright, *The Free Church of Scotland and American Slavery: Speeches from Music Hall in Edinburgh, Scotland* (1846) https://docsouth.unc.edu/neh/douglass/support11.html

24   George McGilvary, The Scottish Connection with India 1725–1833, *Etudes Ecossaises* 14 (2010) p13.

25   Tom Devine *Scotland's Empire* (London, 2003) Ch 11.

26   Tom Devine, *The Scottish Nation 1700-2000* (London, 2000), p60.

27   John Newsinger, 'Declassified History: James Matheson', in *Socialist Review* 460 (September 2000) p36.

28   Newsinger, 2000.

29   Chris Harman, *A People's History of the World* (London, 1999) p358.

30   Harman, 1999, p 296

31   Martin Hannan, 'Spotlight on re-naming of David Hume Tower amid racism row', *The National*, 13 January 2021, https://bit.ly/3skftwi

32   V I Lenin, 'National Culture' in *Critical Remarks on the National Question* (1913), https://www.marxists.org/archive/lenin/works/1913/crnq/2.htm#v20pp72-023

33   *Daily Record*, 27 July 2014.

34   Friedrich Engels, *The Condition of the Working Class in England in 1844*, (1845) (Stanford, 1968).

35   Tom Gallagher: *Glasgow The Uneasy Peace; Religious Tension in Modern Scotland* (Manchester, 1987) p12.

36   Ronnie Booker, *Orange Alba: The Civil Religion of Loyalism in the Southwestern Lowlands of Scotland since 1798,* PhD thesis, (University of Tennessee, 2010) p33 and pp57-72 https://trace.tennessee.edu/utk_graddiss/777

37   Karl Marx 'Letter to Sigfrid Meyer and August Vogt' (1870) in Karl Marx & Friedrich Engels *Selected Correspondence* (Moscow, 1975) https://www.marxists.org/archive/marx/works/1870/letters/70_04_09.htm

38   Dave Sherry, 'Ireland and Scotland in the First World War: From the Dublin Rising to Red Clydeside', *Irish Marxist Review* Vol. 4, No. 14 (2015) pp50-53.

39   Scottish Government, *An Examination of the Evidence on Sectarianism in Scotland: 2015 Update*, 29 May 2015,

https://bit.ly/3soH8wl

40   'Protesters kettled after converging on George Square despite police warnings', *Herald Scotland*, 20 June 2020, https://bit.ly/3pEkXjW

41   Ben Tillet, quoted in John Garrard, *The English and Immigration* (Oxford, 1971) p157.

42   Glasgow Trades Council, *Yearly Report*, 1887-8. Mitchell Library, Glasgow

43   TUC Annual Report, 1892, British Library, London, p53.

44   *House of Commons Select Committee on Emigration and Immigration* (HCSCEI) 1889, Vol.10, lines 1410-18 British Library, London.

45   HCSCEI British Library.

46   HCSCEI, lines 1490-1.

47   Satnam Virdee, 'Socialist antisemitism and its discontents in England, 1884–98' in *Patterns of Prejudice*, Vol. 51, 3-4, (2017) pp 356-373.

48   Virdee, 2017, p360.

49   HCSCEI, line 1550.

50   *Glasgow Herald*, 10 February 1905, p8.

51   Glasgow Trades Council, *Yearly Report*, 1889-90, p12.

52   Yvonne Kapp, *Eleanor Marx: The Crowded Years, 1884–1898* (London, 1979).

53   Kapp, p525.

54   Hyndman's SDF would later become the British Socialist Party (BSP)

55   James Connolly. *The Socialist Labour Party of America and the London SDF*, (1903) https://www.marxists.org/archive/connolly/1903/06/slpsdf.htm

56   For a full discussion on this, see Jacqueline Jenkinson, 'Black Sailors on Red Clydeside: Rioting, Reactionary Trade Unionism and Conflicting Notions of 'Britishness' Following the First World War', *Twentieth Century British History*, Vol. 19, 1, 2008, pp 29–60.

57   Henry Bell, *John Maclean: Hero of Red Clydeside* (London, 2018) p230.

58   John Leopold, 'The Forty Hours Strike', in Laurie Flynn (ed), *We Shall Be All* (London, 1978), p44.

59   *Glasgow Herald*, 20 September 1937, p13; 15 October 1937, p13; 16 October 1937, p9.

60   Monty Berkley, interviewed by author (hereafter Berkley).

61   Morris Smith, interviewed by author (hereafter Smith).

62   G C Webber, 'Patterns of Membership and Support for the BUF', *Journal of Contemporary History*, 19, 4 (1984), p606.

63   Liz Kibblewhite and Andy Rigby, *Fascism in Aberdeen* (Aberdeen, 1978) p23.

64   *Motherwell Times*, 4 May 1934.

65   *Wishaw Press*, 17 March 1933; 14 April 1933; 31 August 1934.

66   *Motherwell Times*, 5 October 1934.

67   Kibblewhite and Rigby, p23.

68   *Glasgow Herald*, 26 July 1937, p11; *Aberdeen Press and Journal*, 26 July 1937.

69   *Glasgow Herald*, 4 October 1937, pp10-11; *Aberdeen Evening Express*, 24 July 1937; *Aberdeen Press and Journal*, 7 October 1937.

70   *Glasgow Herald*, 12 September, 12; *Aberdeen Press and Journal*, 6 July 1938.

71   Finlay Hart, interviewed by author, 1988.

72   For more on the issues of the formation and development of both the Scottish Protestant League and Protestant Action and their relationship to Catholics and Irish immigration, see Tom Gallagher, *The Uneasy Peace* (Manchester, 1987); Henry Maitles, 'Blackshirts Across the Border: The BUF in Scotland', *The Scottish Historical Review*, Vol. LXXII, No. 213, pp92-99.

73   *Scotland's Census 2011,* National Records of Scotland, https://www.scotlandscensus.gov.uk/labour-market

74   'Everyday Racism in Scotland; A case study of East Pollokshields', *Scottish Affairs* 49 (Autumn 2004); Peter Hopkins (ed) *Scotland's Muslims: Society, Politics and Identity.* (Edinburgh, 2017).

75   Libby Brooks, 'Man found guilty of murdering Surjit Singh Chhokar after retrail', Guardian, 5 October 2016, https://bit.ly/3cN2oXt

76   E Kelly, 'Racism, Police and Courts in Scotland', *Scottish Affairs,* No.30, (2000) pp141-159

77   'Racism and sexism rife in macho police culture', *Herald*, 12 November

2020, p1 and p7.

78 UNHCR, *Sharp decline in refugees, others of concern in 2003,* 17 June 2004, https://bit.ly/2ZDPvYy

79 UNHCR, *Refugee Data Finder,* https://bit.ly/37FVctf

80 National Records of Scotland, *Migration Statistics,* 30 April 2020, https://bit.ly/2NzW2AV

81 *Scotland's Census 2011,* National Records of Scotland, https://bit.ly/3qMULoH

82 Stefan Iulian Harda, 2006, *Policies on Roma's social Inclusion in Europe: Towards succeeding in social intervention – ROMAin: a quantitative analysis of 85 projects,* (2006) www.anr.ro/docs/programme/Roma percent 20in/Romain_final_supervised_analysis.pdf

83 *Scotsman,* 8 November 2012.

84 'Scottish Gypsies still face 'acceptable racism'', *BBC News,* 7 December 2017 https://www.bbc.co.uk/news/uk-scotland-42193431

85 Nicholas Keyden, 'Vandals 'violently destroy' Roma Holocaust memorial plaque in Glasgow', *Daily Record,* 7 November 2019, https:/bitly/3bu2dys

86 Paul Kelbie, 'Sighthill killing leads to big fall in racist attacks', *Independent,* 14 November 2013, https://bit.ly/3dHOXJh

87 Sighthill residents stage 'unity' march, *BBC News,* 25 August, 2001 http://news.bbc.co.uk/1/hi/scotland/1507511.stm

88 Amelia Hill, 'Racism has turned the good people here bad', *Guardian,* 12 August 2001 https://www.theguardian.com/uk/2001/aug/12/race.immigration

89 Peter Cassidy, 'The Glasgow Girls 15 years on', *Glasgow Live,* 8 August 2016, https://bit.ly/2ZHG2zy

90 'Serco to restart asylum seeker lock-change evictions', *BBC News,* 12 June 2019 https://www.bbc.co.uk/news/uk-scotland-glasgow-west-48608323

91 Tony Cliff, *Marxism at the Millennium* (London, 2000)

92 V I Lenin, *What is to be done?* (1902) https://www.marxists.org/archive/lenin/works/download/what-itd.pdf.

93 Angela Davis, 'We can't eradicate racism without eradicating racial capitalism', *Democracy Now,* 14 June 2020, https://www.youtube.com/watch?v=qhh3CMkngkY

Chapter 7: A History of the Independence Movement

1 Tom Devine, *The Scottish Nation 1700–2000,* (New York, 1999) p95.

2 Tom Steel, *Scotland's Story: A New Perspective* (London, 1984) p296-297.

3 Tom Devine, 1999, p287–289.

4 Tom Devine, 1999, p305.

5 David Howell, *British Workers and the Independent Labour Party 1888-1906* (Manchester, 1983) p134-136.

6 Nicola Sturgeon's Address to SNP Conference #SNP19, 15 October 2019, https://www.snp.org/nicola-sturgeons-address-to-snp19/

7 Graham Walker, 'Scotland in the 20th Century', in Devine and Findlay (ed), *Scotland in the Twentieth Century* (London, 1996), p259.

8 Richard Finlay, 'The Early Years: From the Inter-War Period to the Mid-1960's', in Gerry Hassan (ed), *The Modern SNP from Protest to Power* (London, 2009) p19-24.

9 Dave Sherry, *John MacLean* (London, 1998).

10 James Mitchell, 'From Breakthrough to Mainstream: The Politics of Potential and Blackmail', in Hassan, 2009, p31-41.

11 William Walker, 'Dundee's Disenchantment with Churchill: A Comment upon the Downfall of the Liberal Party', in *The Scottish Historical Review,* 1970.

12 Tony Cliff & Donny Gluckstein, *The Labour Party: A Marxist History* (London, 1988) p279-319.

13 Mitchell, in Hassan, 2009, p33.

14 Gerry Hassan, 'The Auld Enemies: Scottish Nationalism and Scottish Labour', in Hassan, 2009, p152-154.

15 Neal Ascherson, *Stone Voices: The Search for Scotland* (London, 2002) p95.

16 Ascherson, p109.

17 Ascherson, p109.

18 David Torrance, 'The Journey from 79 Group to the Modern SNP', in Hassan (2009), p162-164.

19 Torrance, p163.

20 Torrance, p169-172.

21   Tom Devine, 1999, p616-617.

22   Chris Bambery, *A People's History of Scotland* (London, 2014) p270-274.

23   For more on the Timex dispute see Chapter 5.

24   James Mitchel, 'From Breakthrough to Mainstream: The Politics of Potential and Blackmail', in Hassan (2009) p36.

25   Russell Leadbetter, 'Those were the days: Referendum rally in George Square, 1992', *The Herald*, 21 January 2020, https://bit.ly/3pN3rtV

26   'Scotland Demands Democracy March, 1992' *Scottish Political Archive*, 23 June 2011, http://www.scottishpoliticalarchive.org.uk/2011/06/23/scotland-demands-democracy-march-1992/

27   Jean-Philippe Fons, 'Poverty and inequality: has New Labour delivered?' *Observatoire de la Société Britannique*, 10 (2011), pp153-166, https://journals.openedition.org/osb/1174

28   The Scottish Parliament, *Effects of the Electoral System*, http://www.parliament.scot/visitandlearn/Education/18663.aspx

29   'SNP did not oppose action in Afghanistan', *The Herald*, 21 December 2004, https://www.heraldscotland.com/news/12409039.snp-did-not-oppose-action-in-afghanistan/

30   Iain MacWhirter, *Disunited Kingdom: How Westminster Won a Referendum but Lost Scotland* (Glasgow, 2014) p14

31   Scottish Government, *Scotland's Future Your Guide to an Independent Scotland*, November 2013, https://www2.gov.scot/resource/0043/00439021.pdf

32   Kathleen Nutt, 'John Curtice: 'Poll shows support for Union has never been weaker'', *The National*, 6 July 2020. https://www.thenational.scot/news/18562858.john-curtice-support-union-never-weaker/

33   AUOB, *A Talk with George Kerevan*, 29 May 2020, https://www.facebook.com/649195548512568/videos/687308188758017

34   European Free Alliance, https://www.e-f-a.org/

35   Bethany Bell, 'Austria-Italy passport row tests Europe's populist allies', *BBC News,* 21 October 2018 https://www.bbc.co.uk/news/world-europe-45888287

36   'The N-VA's Ideology and Purpose', *N-VA website*, https://english.n-va.be/frequently-asked-questions#ideology

37   Jim and Margaret Cuthbert, 'SNP Economic Policy: Neo-liberalism with a Heart' in Hassan, 2009, p106.

38   'Record Support for Scottish Independence', *Ipsos MORI,* 14 October 2020, https://www.ipsos.com/ipsos-mori/en-uk/record-public-support-scottish-independence

39   John Curtice, 'Why are more Scots supporting independence?', *BBC News*, 14 October 2020, https://www.bbc.co.uk/news/uk-scotland-scotland-politics-54542712

40   John Curtice, 'A Coronavirus swing in favour of Independence?' *Scottish Centre for Social Research*, 5 July 2020, https://whatscotlandthinks.org/2020/07/a-coronavirus-swing-in-favour-of-independence/

41   'Will Coronavirus Break the UK', *Financial Times*, 21 October 2020, https://on.ft.com/3dFo4G6

42   Kathleen Nutt, 'STUC back new independence referendum if Internal Market Bill proceeds', *The National*, 7 October 2020, https://bit.ly/3sjwCGr

43   Neil Findlay, 'Scottish Labour must take its head out of the sand', *Scottish Left Review*, Issue 119, https://www.scottishleftreview.scot/neil-findlay-proposes-a-way-forward-for-scottish-labour-on-its-constitutional-crisis/

44   Matt Kerr, 'Why Scottish Labour Declined and How it Can Rebuild', *Tribune*, 16 June 2020, https://tribunemag.co.uk/2020/06/why-scottish-labour-declined-and-how-it-can-rebuild

45   Gerry Hassan, 'Labour Trouble: The Independence Question and the Future of Britain', https://www.gerryhassan.com/blog/labour-troubles-the-independent-question-and-the-future-of-britain/

46   'Salmond and Sturgeon: What is the controversy all about', *BBC News*, 23 March 2021, https://www.bbc.co.uk/news/uk-scotland-scotland-politics-55996021

47   Charlie Kimber, 'Salmond and Sturgeon—what's behind the SNP

crisis?', *Socialist Worker,* 25 February 2021, https://bit.ly/38Ytmcq

48   'Alex Salmond alleges 'malicious' attempt to damage him', *BBC News,* 22 February 2021, https://www.bbc.co.uk/news/uk-scotland-scotland-politics-56163460

49   'Sturgeon faces questioning at Salmond Inquiry amid calls to resign', *ITV News*, 3 March 2021, https://www.itv.com/news/2021-03-03/sturgeon-faces-questioning-at-salmond-inquiry-amid-calls-to-resign

50   'Gender Recognition Act: What Is It?', *Stonewall Scotland* https://www.stonewallscotland.org.uk/get-involved/get-involved-campaign-us/gender-recognition-act

51   Vic Parsons, 'Scotland's plans to reform gender-recognition laws could be 'kicked into the long grass' because of coronavirus', *Pink News*, 20 March 2020, https://bit.ly/30YyMzN

52   Mark Brown, 'Salmond's new party is no alternative to weak SNP strategy', *Socialist Worker*, 27 March 2021, https://socialistworker.co.uk/art/51535/

Chapter 8: Neoliberalism with a Heart? Life Under the SNP

1   Callum Ross, 'Sturgeon: The SNP is a social democracy model which is under threat across the world', *The Press and Journal*, 9 June 2018, https://www.pressandjournal.co.uk/fp/news/politics/scottish-politics/1494100/sturgeon/

2   Scottish Government, *Scotland and the sustainable development goals: a national review to drive action,* 30 July 2020, https://bit.ly/2ZESK1X

3   Karin Goodwin, 'Scotland has Highest Rate of Homeless Deaths in the UK, new figures reveal', *The Ferret*, 5 February 2020, https://theferret.scot/scotland-homeless-deaths-uk-figures/

4   National Records of Scotland, *Drug Related Deaths*, 2019, https://bit.ly/3soVnRR

5   Jim & Margaret Cuthbert, 'SNP Economic Policy: Neo-liberalism with a Heart' in Gerry Hassan (ed), *The Modern SNP From Protest to Power*, (London, 2009), p106.

6   Mark Hellowell & Allyson M Pollock,

7   Dexter Whitfield *Ownership and Offshoring of NPD and Hub Projects: Scottish Futures Trust*, European Services Strategy Unit (May 2018), https://bit.ly/3qMRuWo

8   'Sir Harry Burns: devolution has been good for Scotland's health, but approaches still need to improve',*Holyrood magazine*, 5 March 2019, https://bit.ly/3bALcCI

9   Scottish Government/COSLA Discussion Paper, *Social Care Support: An investment in Scotland's people, society, and economy*, 12 June 2019, https://bit.ly/3kg7ZYn

10   Jim Main, 'Up close and personal: the harmful carer, service user and workforce effects of personalisation' in Peter Beresford (ed.) *Personalisation* (Bristol, 2014) pp 33-46.

11   ISD Scotland, *Care Home Census for Adults in Scotland Figures for 2007-2017*, 11 September 2018, https://bit.ly/2NWIMGE

12   Nick Kempe, 'The Predicable Crisis: Why Coiv-19 Has Hit Scottish Care Homes So Hard', *Common Weal*, 20 May 2020, https://commonweal.scot/policy-library/predictable-crisis

13   'Government urged to act over Bield Care Home Closures', *BBC News,* 13 January 2018, https://www.bbc.co.uk/news/uk-scotland-42667329.

14   Mark Daly, 'Scotland's Lockdown', *BBC News,* 11 May 2020, https://www.bbc.co.uk/programmes/m000j6ry

15   Allyson Pollock & Louisa Harding-Edgar, 'Coronavirus crisis: underfunding, restructuring, privatisation and fragmentation at the heart of the crisis in Holyrood and Westminster', *Scottish Centre on European* Relations. 23 Apr 2020, https://www.scer.scot/database/ident-12745

16   National Records of Scotland, *Deaths involving coronavirus (COVID-19) in Scotland, Week 27 (29 June to 05 July 2020)*, 8 July 2020, https://bit.ly/3aHmBwR

17   Nick Kempe, 'The Predicable Crisis: Why Coiv-19 Has Hit Scottish Care Homes So Hard', *Common Weal*, 20 May 2020, https://commonweal.scot/policy-library/predictable-crisis

18   'EIS President says that workload and pay having disastrous effect on teacher health and wellbeing', EIS websitehttps://www.eis.org.uk/AGM-2018/PresidentSpeech

19   Gemma Fraser, 'Stressed teachers would not recommend teaching as a career' *Holyrood*, 11 January 2019, https://bit.ly/2NSG4St

20   Scottish Government, *Poverty and income inequality in Scotland: 2015-2018, (*Edinburgh, 2018) https://www.gov.scot/publications/poverty-income-inequality-scotland-2015-18/. See also the Joseph Rowntree Foundation report, *Poverty in Scotland 2020*, https://www.jrf.org.uk/report/poverty-scotland-2020

21   Adam Corlett, 'Wrong direction: can Scotland hit its child poverty targets?', *Resolution Foundation*, 22 March 2019. https://bit.ly/3ukDxBj

22   Catrine Bussey, 'Child Poverty Levels are Up in Glasgow, new figures show', *Glasgow Live*, 15 May 2019, https://bit.ly/2NPOSID.

23   Figures in this paragraph taken from Neal Ascherson, *Stone Voices: The Search for Scotland*, (London, 2014), p146.

24   Neal Ascherson, p147.

25   Scottish Government, *Housing Statistics: Stock By Tenure 2018,* https://www.gov.scot/publications/housing-statistics-stock-by-tenure/

26   Joey Simons, Norman Cunningham & Angela McCormick, 'Housing Crisis: The Burning Issue', *Bella Calendonia,* 1 December 2020, https://bellacaledonia.org.uk/202012/01/housing-crisis-the-burning-issue

27   Kevin Keane, 'Abuse of power' over Scottish land ownership', *BBC News*, 20 March 2019.https://www.bbc.co.uk/news/uk-scotland-47627863

28   Gwilym Pryce & Meng Le Zhang, 'Inequality in Scotland: Despite Nordic aspirations, things are not improving', *The Conversation*, 7 November 2018, https://bit.ly/3sdSO4O; 'Fact check: claim wealth inequality in Scotland',

The Ferret, 29 January 2018, https://theferret.scot/wealth-inequality-scotland-oxfam/; 'Inequality worse In Scotland since devolution, says study', *The Ferret*, 7 November 2018, https://theferret.scot/inequality-scotland-devolution/,

29   Sandra Dick, 'The gap between the have and the have nots in Scotland widens', *The Herald*, 22 January 2018, https://bit.ly/3aKwMAQ

30   'Wealth of super-rich Scots reveals scale of national inequality', *Commonspace*, 26 April 2016, https://bit.ly/37FaVJe

31   Macaskill, Mark, 'The Sunday Times Rich List 2019: Scotland's richest worth £35bn', *The Sunday Times*, 12 May 2019, https://bit.ly/3pLaXpc

32   'Scotland's richest 1 percent have more wealth than bottom 50 percent put together', *Commonspace*, 22 January 2018. https://bit.ly/3dMgLMu

33   Steven Carrell, 'Report calls for reform of 'unhealthy' land ownership in Scotland', *Guardian*, 20 March 2019; Scottish Land Commission, https://landcommission.gov.scot/

34   Andrew Picken and Stuart Nicolson, 'Who owns Scotland? The changing face of Scotland's landowners', *BBC News Online*, 21 May 2019, https://bbc.in/3shGiRS

35   Andy Wightman, 'Land Matters: Who owns Scotland?' , http://www.andywightman.com/archives/category/who-owns-scotland

36   Mandy Rhodes, 'Exclusive Interview with Mhairi Black', *Holyrood*, 18 December 2017, https://bit.ly/3pOW2do

37   Mure Dickie, 'Nicola Sturgeon: 'Business has nothing to fear'', *Financial Times*, 30 November 2014, https://www.ft.com/content/45fab178-78a5-11e4-b518-00144feabdc0

38   *Scotland: The New Case for Optimism,* Sustainable Growth Commission Report (2018) (hereafter SGCR) https://www.sustainablegrowthcommission.scot/report

39   Cat Boyd, 'Not even 1 step forward, 2 steps back', *Scottish Left Review,* 3 July 2018, https://www.scottishleftreview.

scot/not-even-one-step-forward-two-steps-back/

40   Keir McKechnie, 'Scotland: the genie is out of the bottle', *International Socialism* 2:144 (Autumn 2014) https://isj.org.uk/scotland-the-genie-is-out-of-the-bottle

41   Mark Fisher, *Capitalist Realism: Is There No Alternative?* (London, 2009).

42   Forgacs, David (ed.) *The Antonio Gramsci Reader* (London, 1999), p333.

43   SGCR, p12.

44   SGCR, p10.

45   SGCR, p50

46   'Kerevan criticises SNP-commissioned Growth Commission Report', *Morning Star*, 1 August 2018 https://morningstaronline.co.uk/article/kerevan-criticises-snp-commissioned-growth-commission-report.

47   Tony Cliff, Donny Gluckstein & Charlie Kimber, *The Labour Party: A Marxist History*, 3rd ed. (London, 2019); see also Panos Garganas, 'Why did Syriza fail?', *International Socialism* 149 (Autumn 2015) https://isj.org.uk/why-did-syriza-fail/

48   SGCR, p22.

49   Jim Sillars, 'Of Wars of Position and Wars of Manoeuvre', *Scottish Left Review*, Issue 106 (July/August 2018), p10, https://bit.ly/2Po82Mt

50   Lesley Riddoch, *Blossom: What Scotland Needs to Flourish* (Luath Press, 2018), p332.

51   SGCR, p60.

52   Branco Marcetic, 'New Zealand's Neoliberal Drift', *Jacobin*, 15 March 2017, https://bit.ly/3shJLjm

53   Jessica Jonsson, 'The contested field of social work in a retreating welfare state: the case of Sweden', *Critical and Radical Social Work*, 3 (3), (Bristol, 2017) pp358.

54   Masoud Kamali & Jessica H Jonsson (eds.), *Neoliberalism, Nordic Welfare States and Social Work: Current and Future Challenges*, (Routledge, 2018).

55   Scottish Government, *Towards a Robust, Resilient Wellbeing Economy for Scotland: Report of the Advisory Group on Economic Recovery*, 22 June 2020, https://bit.ly/2ZVaIxn

56   Scottish Government, *Adult social care: independent review*, 3 February

2021, https://bit.ly/3dF7Xby

57   James Connolly, Socialism and Nationalism, *Shan Van Vocht*, January 1897, https://www.marxists.org/archive/connolly/1897/01/socnat.htm

Chapter 9: Beyond the Limitations of Nationalism

1   Stephen Maxwell, *The Case for Left-wing Nationalism* (Edinburgh, 2013) p35.

2   'Salmond: let's celebrate Catholic schools rather than grudgingly accept them', *Herald Scotland*, 2 February 2008, https://bit.ly/37hH0GA

3   Gerry Hassan, 'The Making of the Modern SNP: From Protest to Power', in Gerry Hassan (ed), *The Modern SNP from Protest to Power* (Edinburgh, 2009), p4.

4   Stephen Maxwell, *The Case for Left-wing Nationalism* (Edinburgh, 2013) p76-9.

5   Stephen Maxwell, *Arguing for Independence* (Edinburgh, 2012), p169-181.

6   Tom Nairn, *The Break-Up of Britain: Crisis and Neo-Nationalism*, (Verso, 1981) p56.

7   See Nairn's introduction to Stephen Maxwell's, *The Case for Left-wing Nationalism*, (Edinbrugh, 2013) p9-12.

8   Tom Nairn, 'Union on the Rocks', *New Left Review*, 43 (January-February 2007) https://newleftreview.org/issues/II43/articles/tom-nairn-union-on-the-rocks

9   Lindsey German, 'The Balkan war: can there be peace?', *International Socialism*, 2:69 (Winter 1995) http://pubs.socialistreviewindex.org.uk/isj69/german.htm

10   Tom Nairn, *The Break-Up of Britain,* (London, 1981), p348-349.

11   Antonio Gramsci, *Selection from the Prison Notebooks*, (London, 1978) p333.

12   Héctor Sierra 'Catalonia, Class and Independence', *Socialist Review*, 429, (November 2017), http://socialistreview.org.uk/429/catalonia-class-and-independence

13   'Catalonia: The prison sentences are an attack on democracy', *Marx21*, 16 October 2019, https://marx21.net/2019/10/16/

catalonia-the-prison-sentences-are-an-attack-on-democracy/

14   Eddy Wax, 'Spain fires diplomat in Scotland over EU membership letter', *Politico*, 8 June 2019, https://www.politico.eu/article/spain-fires-diplomat-in-scotland-over-eu-membership-letter/

15   Scottish Government, *Scotland's Future: Your Guide to an Independent Scotland,* (November 2013), https://www2.gov.scot/resource/0043/00439021.pdf

16   Scottish Government, *Scotland's Future: Your Guide to an Independent Scotland,* (November 2013), https://www2.gov.scot/resource/0043/00439021.pdf, p16

17   'SNP's Mhairi Black 'Hated' Independence White Paper', *The Scotsman*, 7 April 2018, https://bit.ly/2Zlq25V

18   'Scotland: The New Case for Optimism', *Sustainable Growth Commission Report,* (2018), https://www.sustainablegrowthcommission.scot/report

19   Michael Settle, '36% of SNP and Labour supporters backed Brexit, finds survey', *Herald Scotland*, 7 December 2016, https://bit.ly/3po4ssc

20   John Curtice & Ian Montagu, 'Do Scotland England and Wales Have Different Views About Immigration?' *National Centre for Social Research*, (December 2018) https://bit.ly/3praPuA.

21   Kenny MacAskill, *Building a Nation Post Devolution Nationalism in Scotland* (Edinburgh, 2008).

22   Lesley Riddoch, *Blossom: What Scotland Needs to Flourish* (Edinburgh, 2015).

23   Lesley Riddoch, and Eberhard Bort, *McSmorgasbord: What Post Brexit Scotland Can Learn From The Nordics* (Edinburgh, 2017).

24   See Iain Ferguson & Gerry Mooney, 'Neo-liberalism with a Heart? The Reality of Life Under the SNP', Ch 8 in this book.

25   'Sweden Still in Top 10 of Weapons Exporters', *Radio Sweden* (14 March 2011) https://sverigesradio.se/sida/artikel.

26   Chris Newlove, 'Common Weal:

Nothing in Common', *Socialist Review* 389 (March 2014). http://socialistreview.org.uk/389/common-weal-nothing-common.

27   Common Weal, *The Future of Low Carbon Heat for Off-Gas Buildings*, https://commonweal.scot/policy-library/future-low-carbon-heat-gas-buildings.

28   Campaign Against Climate Change, *Climate Emergency* (London, 2011) p35. https://www.campaigncc.org/sites/data/files/Docs/climateemergencypamphlet.pdf

29   'Neste Oil and Anglo Gold in the Public Eye Pillory in Davos' *Public Eye,* 13 April 2011, https://bit.ly/3apilCc.

30   Ben Jackson, *The Case for Scottish Independence—A History of Nationalist Political Thought in Modern Scotland* (Cambridge, 2020) p120.

31   Tom Freeman, 'SNP MP claims independence would lead to five years of austerity', *Holyrood magazine*, 20 July 2016, https://bit.ly/3dg9pAH.

32   George Kerevan, 'AUOB Provide Real Food for Thought on Way Ahead for Yes', *The National*, 17 February 2020, https://bit.ly/3aqy6bX.

33   George Kerevan, 'SNP at the Crossroads', *Conter*, 7 July 2020, https://www.conter.co.uk/blog/2020/7/7/snp-at-the-crossroads

34   George Kerevan, 'SNP at the Crossroad: What is to be Done?' *Conter*, 29 September 2020, https://www.conter.co.uk/blog/2020/9/29/snp-at-the-crossroad-what-is-to-be-done

35   George Kerevan, 'SNP at the Crossroad: What is to be Done?' *Conter*, 29 September 2020, https://www.conter.co.uk/blog/2020/9/29/snp-at-the-crossroad-what-is-to-be-done

36   Neil Findlay & Tommy Kane, 'The British road has now re-emerged', in Gregor Gall (ed.), *Is there a Scottish Road to Socialism?* (Glasgow, 2016), p86-87.

37   John Foster, 'Beware the downgrading of class by nation', in Gregor Gall (ed.), *Is there a Scottish road to Socialism?* (Glasgow, 2016), p100.

38   Foster, 2016, p103.

39   Foster, 2016, p104.

40   John Maclean, 'Red Flag Flutters' (1922) https://www.marxists.org/archive/maclean/works/1922-redflag.htm

41   Kieran Allen, *The Politics of James Connolly* (London, 1990) p118.

42   Kieran Allen, *1916—Ireland's Revolutionary Tradition* (London, 2016) p58.

43   James Connolly, *Socialism and Nationalism*, (1897) https://www.marxists.org/archive/connolly/1897/01/socnat.htm

44   Scotland Is Now, 'Business: Key Sectors' (2020) https://www.scotland.org/business/key-sectors

45   Scottish Enterprise, 'Financial and Business Services in Scotland' (February 2020), https://bit.ly/3apF94x.

46   Food and Drink Federation Scotland, 'Facts and Stats' (2020) https://www.fdfscotland.org.uk/fdf/business-insights-and-economics/facts-and-stats/

47   'The Sunday Times Rich List 2020', *Sunday Times,* 17 May 2020, https://www.thetimes.co.uk/sunday-times-rich-list.

48   Ineos, 'Facts and Figures' (2020) https://www.ineos.com/sites/grangemouth/about/

Index

Index